Can you find the missing number?

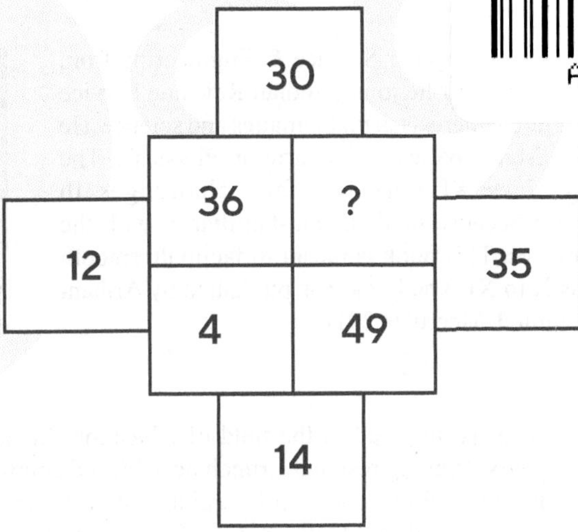

Today's world is full of digital devices like computer, laptop, mobile etc. Information flowing over internet to and from these digital devices need security just as our homes or almirahs need security. We put a lock at the doors of our homes or in our almirahs to secure them. But how do we secure the information flowing over internet? Number Theory helps in putting *lock* over the information flowing through internet. This technique of securing information is called cryptography.

This book **"Number Theory for Olympiads"** is an attempt to present the interesting world of numbers in a playful manner. This book is intended to be used by the students of class 7 to 12. The book will be useful for various examinations such as Mathematics Olympiads etc. Certain concepts discussed in this book will be useful for examinations like JEE Mains & JEE Advanced (Entrance Examinations for Admission to 'Indian Institute of Technology' [IITs] in India) as well. These days there is emphasis on creative or fun mathematics in school curriculum. This book can very well serve as part of creative or fun mathematics. Number theory is an essential part of mathematics courses at undergraduate level. This book can also serve as an introductory course of Number Theory at undergraduate level.

KNOW THE AUTHORS

This book is a result of combined efforts of a group of people from different fields. Their brief profile is as under.

Abhishek Kumar

Abhishek did B. Tech. in Computer Science & Engineering from IIT Kanpur in 2005. Thereafter he joined Indian Revenue Service (IRS) in 2006. He has deep interests in mathematics and science. He authored the book "Mathematics for Learning Physics". The students entering class XI normally face challenges in understanding Physics because of their non-familiarity with the concepts of Mathematics. This book is meant to facilitate smooth transition from class X to XI. The book was published by Arihant Publications India Limited, Meerut in 2011.

Amit Kumar

Amit is involved in the field of education for last more than 25 years. Braving resource crunch he achieved commendable success in the field of education by guiding students in Mathematics for school studies, Mathematics Olympiad, various scholarship examinations like NTSE, KVPY etc, various entrance examinations like JEE Mains, JEE Advanced etc. He has been mentoring students of Sainik School, Karnal, Haryana for last more than 8 years.

Karmveer Kumar

Karmveer is a graduate from IIT Kanpur (class of 2005). He is known for his unique teaching style. His great passion for Mathematics led him to impart guidance to the IIT-JEE aspirants. He has nearly 18 years of teaching experience. He has a great interest in developing the subject from basics to the advanced level. Presenting the magical world of numbers in a playful manner fascinates him the most.

Sanjay Kumar Bharati

Sh. Sanjay Kumar Bharati did B.Tech. from IIT Kanpur. Currently he is serving as a member of the prestigious Indian Revenue Service (IRS), in the capacity of Commissioner of Income Tax. He has a keen interest in pursuing mathematics as a hobby and mentoring students for Mathematics Olympiad which involves application of concepts in creative and innovative ways. His areas of interest are Number Theory, Combinatorics and Geometry. He has successfully mentored one of his students to represent India in APMO 2020 and IMO 2021.

Number Theory for OLYMPIADS

ABHISHEK KUMAR
IRS, IIT KANPUR

KARMVEER KUMAR
IIT KANPUR

SANJAY KUMAR BHARATI
IRS, IIT KANPUR

AMIT KUMAR
MATHS TRAINER

arihant
SUCCESS AND NOTHING LESS

ARIHANT PRAKASHAN (Series), MEERUT

卐 **Administrative & Production Offices**

Regd. Office

'Ramchhaya' 4577/15, Agarwal Road, Darya Ganj, New Delhi -110002
Tele: 011- 47630600, 43518550

Head Office

Kalindi, TP Nagar, Meerut (UP) - 250002
Tel: 0121-7156203, 7156204

卐 **Sales & Support Offices**

Agra, Ahmedabad, Bengaluru, Bareilly, Chennai, Delhi, Guwahati, Hyderabad, Jaipur, Jhansi, Kolkata, Lucknow, Nagpur & Pune.

卐 **PRICE** ₹ 450.00

卐 **PO No :** TXT-XX-XXXXXXX-X-XX

Published by Arihant Publications (India) Ltd.

For further information about the books published by Arihant, log on to www.arihantbooks.com or e-mail at info@arihantbooks.com

Follow us on

"Views expressed in this book are personal views of the authors, and not those of the Government of India."

TABLE OF CONTENTS

ABOUT THE BOOK

1. Do you notice anything peculiar about this square?

4	9	2
3	5	7
8	1	6

No?

Add all numbers in the 1st row. You get 15.

4	9	2
3	5	7
8	1	6

→ 15

Add all numbers in the 2nd row. You get 15.
Add all numbers in the 3rd row. You get 15.

Add all numbers in the 1st column. You get 15.

4	9	2
3	5	7
8	1	6

↓ 15

Add all numbers in the 2nd column. You get 15.
Add all numbers in the 3rd column. You get 15.

Now, add all numbers along a diagonal. You again get 15

4	9	2
3	5	7
8	1	6

↘ 15

Isn't this very interesting property?

15 ⇖			⇗ 15
4	9	2	⇒ 15
3	5	7	⇒ 15
8	1	6	⇒ 15
⇓ 15	⇓ 15	⇓ 15	
15 ⇙			⇘ 15

Such a square is called **magic square.**

This is a 3×3 square.

Now suppose you have to construct a 5×5 square with this property.
Can you do it?
Playing with numbers is fun. Isn't it?

2. **Suppose you are given the task of adding all natural numbers from 1 to 100. How much time will it take to complete this task?**

Quite a lot. Isn't it?
Now, see the following approach to complete this task.
Write all numbers from 1 to 100 in a row in ascending order.
Write all numbers from 100 to 1 in the next row in descending order.

1	2	3	4	....	97	98	66	100
100	99	98	97	....	4	3	2	1
⇓	⇓	⇓	⇓		⇓	⇓	⇓	⇓
101	101	101	101		101	101	101	101

You can see that the sum of numbers in each column is 101. Hence, we get 101 hundred times, one time for exactly one column and there are total 100 columns.
Please note that we have added each number twice (each number appears exactly once in each row and there are two rows).

Hence, $2 \times (1+2+3+....+100) = 101 \times 100 = 10100$

Thus, $(1+2+3+....+100) = 10100/2 = 5050$

How much time did it take to add numbers from 1 to 100? Very little. Isn't it?

This is an interesting way to solve this problem. Playing with numbers is such a fun.

3. **Suppose you are constructing your own house. The picture below is floor of a room in your house.**

The length of the floor is 20 feet whereas its width is 15 feet. You want to put square-shaped tiles of fixed size on this floor. What is the maximum possible length of the side of the tiles?

Can it be 7 feet or 10 feet?

The answer to this question lies in the concept of greatest common divisor (gcd).

More than 2000 years ago a Greek mathematician named **Euclid** provided the method for finding the greatest common divisor.
In this case, maximum possible length of the side of the tiles
= gcd of 15 and 20
= 5 feet

4. **Now see the following pattern:**

$4^2 = 16 = 1 + 3 + 5 + 7$
$5^2 = 25 = 1 + 3 + 5 + 7 + 9$
$6^2 = 36 = 1 + 3 + 5 + 7 + 9 + 11$
$7^2 = 49 = 1 + 3 + 5 + 7 + 9 + 11 + 13$

You can see that the square of any integer n is equal to the sum of first n odd integers.
The world of numbers is full of such interesting patterns.

5. $3^2+4^2 = 5^2$ $(9+16=25)$

$5^2+12^2 = 13^2$ $(25+144=169)$

You can see that the sum of squares of two positive integers can be equal to the square of another positive integer.

Now, suppose we replace power 2 by 3 (or higher power). Can we get two positive integers then such that the sum of cubes (or higher power) of those two integers is equal to the cube (or higher power) of another positive integer?

How can you answer this question?

The numbers are infinitely many. So you cannot verify it.

You will need to prove it in an intelligent manner. British mathematician **Andrew Wiles**[1, 2] proved in 1994 that no such integers exist.

The paper consisting of proof is just 129 pages long!!!

And its solution came almost 357 years after the problem was formulated for the first time. The problem is known as the Fermat's last theorem.

6. **Are you familiar with prime numbers? A prime number has only two divisors- 1 and the number itself.**

For example, 2, 3, 5, 7, 11, 13, 17 and 19 are prime numbers smaller than 20. All other numbers upto 20 are not prime numbers.

3 and 5 are prime numbers.

5 and 7 are prime numbers.

11 and 13 are prime numbers.

Such primes are called twin primes.

Thus, primes p and $p+2$ are called twin primes.

Are there infinitely many twin primes?

The answer to this question is not known yet.

There are many such unsolved problems related to numbers.

[1]. https://en.wikipedia.org/wiki/Fermat%27s_Last_Theorem

[2]. https://en.wikipedia.org/wiki/Wiles%27s_proof_of_Fermat%27s_Last_Theorem

7. Study of numbers, called Number Theory, is a dedicated branch in mathematics. What are the applications of Number Theory in day-to-day life?

Today's world is full of digital devices like computer, laptop, mobile etc. Information flowing over internet to and from these digital devices need security just as our homes or almirahs need security. We put a lock at the doors of our homes or in our almirahs to secure them.

But how do we secure the information flowing over internet?

Numbers come to our rescue here.

Suppose your friend sends a secret code to you over internet. This secret code is a 2-digit number. You are worried that the information may get corrupted during transmission. So, you decide to share a key with your friend. The key stored is, if ab is the secret code then $2a+3b$ is divisible by 10.

Now, suppose you receive 22 as secret code.

$$2a+3b = 2\times 2+3\times 2=10$$

Hence, this secret code is likely to be correct.

Now, suppose you receive 34 as secret code.

$$2a+3b = 2\times 3+3\times 4=18$$

18 is not divisible by 10. Hence, this secret code is incorrect. The information definitely got corrupted while moving from your friend to you.

In this manner Number Theory helps in securing the information flowing over internet.

This technique of securing information is called cryptography.

AUTHORS' NOTE

This book "Number Theory for Olympiads" is an attempt to present the interesting world of numbers in a playful manner. Sufficient number of examples and illustrations have been given to explain the concepts. The chapter "Key Concepts & Results of Number Theory" summarizes all the key concepts & results discussed in the book. The same will be handy for quick revision of concepts. Further the chapter "Olympiad Problems" consists of a wide range of problems compiled from the question papers of previous years of various regional, national & international mathematics Olympiad and other problems involving complexities.

This book is intended to be used by the students of class 7 to 12. The book will be useful for various examinations such as Mathematics Olympiad etc. Certain concepts discussed in this book will be useful for examinations like JEE Mains & JEE Advanced (Entrance Examinations for Admission to 'Indian Institute of Technology' [IITs] in India) as well. These days there is emphasis on creative or fun mathematics in school curriculum. This book can very well serve as part of creative or fun mathematics. Number theory is an essential part of mathematics courses at undergraduate level. This book can also serve as an introductory course of Number Theory at undergraduate level.

Please do write to us for any feedback / comments at numbertheory24@gmail.com.

Suggestions for further improvements are welcome.

Abhishek Kumar, IRS
B. Tech. (Computer Science & Engineering)
IIT Kanpur

Amit Kumar
Mathematics Trainer

Karmveer Kumar
B. Tech.
IIT Kanpur

Sanjay Kumar Bharati, IRS
B. Tech.
IIT Kanpur

01

Interesting World of Science and Mathematics

"God created the natural numbers, and all the rest is the work of man"

—*Leopold Kronecker*

1. Introduction

Your school examination is scheduled tomorrow. Your school teacher designs question paper for the examination and keeps it on the table. Suppose somehow you get this question paper before examination. Hurray! You score 100 out of 100 in the examination. To take care of such scenarios, your teacher keeps the question paper under lock in her room.

Now suppose the examination is to be conducted online. You know that the teacher has kept the question paper in her computer and the computer is connected to internet. Do you know that it may still be possible to steal the question paper from the computer of your teacher? And for doing it one need not physically touch the computer. ''Hacking'' is the term used for this kind of stealing. Just like the question paper in physical form, data flowing on the internet needs to be protected. Prime numbers play an important role in protecting the data flowing over internet.

2. Prime Number

A prime number is a number which has only two divisors, 1 and the number itself. For example, 2 has only two divisors, 1 and 2. Hence, 2 is a prime number. 3 has only two divisors, 1 and 3. Hence, 3 is also a prime number. 4 has three divisors, 1, 2 and 4. Hence 4 is not a prime number. 5, 7, 11, 13, 17, 19, 23 etc are another few examples of prime numbers. 2 is an even prime number. Can you think of any other even prime number?

3. Goldbach Conjecture

$$6 = 3 + 3$$
$$8 = 3 + 5$$
$$10 = 3 + 7 \qquad \text{(3, 5, 7, 11 are all prime numbers)}$$
$$12 = 5 + 7$$
$$14 = 3 + 11$$

Even numbers 6, 8, 10, 12 and 14 can be expressed as the sum of two odd prime numbers. Can we write every even integer greater than 4 as the sum of two odd prime numbers?

Let us try to do it for few more numbers.

$$16 = 3 + 13 \quad \text{or} \quad 5 + 11$$
$$18 = 5 + 13 \quad \text{or} \quad 7 + 11$$
$$20 = 3 + 17 \quad \text{or} \quad 7 + 13$$
$$22 = 3 + 19 \quad \text{or} \quad 5 + 17 \quad \text{or} \quad 11 + 11$$
$$24 = 5 + 19 \quad \text{or} \quad 7 + 17 \quad \text{or} \quad 11 + 13$$
$$26 = 3 + 23 \quad \text{or} \quad 7 + 19 \quad \text{or} \quad 13 + 13$$
$$28 = 5 + 23 \quad \text{or} \quad 11 + 17$$
$$30 = 7 + 23 \quad \text{or} \quad 11 + 19 \quad \text{or} \quad 13 + 17$$

Thus, we can write every even integer (other than 2 and 4) upto 30 as the sum of two odd prime numbers.

The challenge and beauty of numbers is that they are infinite. So, it is not possible to verify these properties for each and every number. In fact, this property has been found to be true for each even integer verified so far. In 1742, Christian Goldbach [1] wrote a letter to another mathematician Leonard Euler. In the letter he made a guess that every even integer greater than 4 can be written as the sum of two odd prime numbers. Till date no even integer (greater than 4) has been found for which this guess is not true. However, we can't verify this guess for each and every even integer (greater than 4). So, we need a mathematical proof to ascertain the correctness of this guess. Nobody has been able to prove it till date and hence, it remains a guess only. Therefore, this unsolved problem is known as Goldbach Conjecture.

Goldbach Conjecture : Every even integer greater than 4 can be written as the sum of two odd prime numbers.

In the year 2000, publisher Faber [2] announced a prize of $1 million (INR 8.2 crore at a conversion rate of 82) to anyone who can prove Goldbach Conjecture. Nobody could claim the prize.

---

[1] https://en.wikipedia.org/wiki/Goldbach%27s_conjecture

[2] https://www.math.tugraz.at/~elsholtz/WWW/papers/papers14faber.html

4. Largest Prime

We know that 2, 3, 5, 7, 11, 13, 17, 19, 23, 29 . . . are all prime numbers. So what is the largest prime number? Answer of this question was known to Euclid, a mathematician around 2400 years ago. Euclid proved that the number of primes is infinite. In other words, for every prime number p we can find a prime number q greater than p. How do we find such prime number q? Is it possible to generate prime numbers through some formula?

5. $n^2 + n + 41$

Years ago, it was believed that the formula $n^2 + n + 41$ yields only prime numbers.

For $n = 0$, $n^2 + n + 41 = 41$

For $n = 1$, $n^2 + n + 41 = 43$

For $n = 2$, $n^2 + n + 41 = 47$

For $n = 3$, $n^2 + n + 41 = 53$

For $n = 4$, $n^2 + n + 41 = 61$

For $n = 5$, $n^2 + n + 41 = 71$

Thus, we can see that the formula produces prime numbers only for $n = 0, 1, 2, 3, 4, 5$.

In fact, the formula produces prime numbers only for $n = 0, 1, 2, 3, \ldots, 39$.

For $n = 40$, $n^2 + n + 41 = 40^2 + 40 + 41 = 40(40 + 1) + 41 = 41(40 + 1) = 41^2$

For $n = 41$, $n^2 + n + 41 = 41^2 + 41 + 41 = 41(41 + 2) = 41 \times 43$.

Thus, $n^2 + n + 41$ does not produce prime numbers for $n = 40$ and 41. It was mathematician Euler who showed in 1772 that the formula $n^2 + n + 41$ does not produce prime numbers for all n.

6. Fermat's Last Theorem

Consider following sums:

$$3^2 + 4^2 = 5^2 \qquad (\because 9 + 16 = 25)$$

$$6^2 + 8^2 = 10^2 \qquad (\because 36 + 64 = 100)$$

Obviously, the equation $x^2 + y^2 = z^2$ has a solution. (x, y, z are positive integers).

Can you find out any positive integers x, y and z such that,

$$x^3 + y^3 = z^3$$

or, $$x^4 + y^4 = z^4 \,?$$

Consider the equation $x^n + y^n = z^n$

where x, y, z and n are positive integers.

Statement : This equation has no solution for $n > 2$.

This statement is called Fermat's last theorem. Fermat[1, 2] wrote this statement in his book "Artihmetica" in the year around 1637.

He also stated "I have discovered a truly marvelous proof of this, which this margin is too narrow to contain". That narrow margin proved too costly for humanity and mathematicians. After a very long gap of 357 years, British mathematician Andrew Wiles proved Fermat's Last Theorem in 1994. Wiles devoted seven years of his life to prove this theorem. The paper consisting of proof is 129 pages long.

We can see that the Fermat's Last Theorem couldn't be proved for a very long time. During 1980s and early 1990s it was generally believed that it was impossible to prove Fermat's Last Theorem. Even then Andrew Wiles took up the challenge and proved it after seven years of hard work.

We also discussed earlier that Goldbach Conjecture remains an unsolved problem since 1742. So, the struggle of humanity to solve old and new problems continues. There are successes as well as failures. But the only thing that really matters is the zeal and the passion to solve unsolved problems.

7. Lagrange's Four-square Theorem

Numbers have very interesting properties. You can play with numbers just as kids play with toys.

Consider following problem :

Write every natural number as the sum of squares of four integers.

$$1 = 1^2 + 0^2 + 0^2 + 0^2$$

$$2 = 1^2 + 1^2 + 0^2 + 0^2$$

$$3 = 1^2 + 1^2 + 1^2 + 0^2$$

$$4 = 1^2 + 1^2 + 1^2 + 1^2 = 2^2 + 0^2 + 0^2 + 0^2$$

$$10 = 3^2 + 1^2 + 0^2 + 0^2 = 2^2 + 2^2 + 1^2 + 1^2$$

$$100 = 10^2 + 0^2 + 0^2 + 0^2 = 6^2 + 8^2 + 0^2 + 0^2$$

$$999 = 30^2 + 9^2 + 3^2 + 3^2$$

$$1000 = 30^2 + 10^2 + 0^2 + 0^2$$

You can verify for as many natural numbers as you want. You will find that every natural number can be expressed as the sum of squares of four integers. But the tricky

[1] https://en.wikipedia.org/wiki/Fermat%27s_Last_Theorem

[2] https://en.wikipedia.org/wiki/Wiles%27s_proof_of_Fermat%27s_Last_Theorem

point is that you can't verify it for every natural number. So how do you know that it is true for all natural numbers?

"Every natural number can be expressed as the sum of squares of four integers." This statement is called Lagrange's four-square theorem. The theorem was proved by the French mathematician Joseph Louis Lagrange.

8. Carl Friedrich Gauss

When can you prove theorems like the ones discussed above? Are you too young for attempting those problems? German mathematician Carl Friedrich Gauss (1777 - 1855) was asked in his primary school to add all the numbers from 1 to 100. Purpose of asking this problem was probably to keep a naughty kid busy for a long time. But Gauss solved it instantly. How? Write all numbers from 1 to 100 in a row in the increasing order.

Write all numbers from 100 to 1 in the next row in the decreasing order.

1	2	3	4	.....	97	98	99	100
100	99	98	97	.....	4	3	2	1
⇓	⇓	⇓	⇓		⇓	⇓	⇓	⇓
101	**101**	**101**	**101**		**101**	**101**	**101**	**101**

You can see that the sum of numbers in each column is 101. Hence, we get 101 hundred times (one time for exactly one column and there are total 100 columns).

Please note that by adding in this manner we have added each number twice *(each number appears exactly once in each row and there are two rows).*

Hence, $2\times(1+2+3+\ldots+100)$

$$=101\times 100$$

$$=10100$$

Thus, $1+2+3+\ldots+100$

$$=\frac{10100}{2}$$

$$=5050$$

Gauss was able to recognize this pattern at a very early age.

Now consider following problem :

What will be the remainder when 2^{981} is divided by 3?

How much time will it take to solve this problem?

It will take hours, if not days if you start multiplying to obtain the value of 2^{981} and then divide by 3. Further the number will become so large that you will have to write the number on the roof or the floor of your house instead of your notebook.

But do you know that you can solve this problem in a few seconds if you know the "Theory of Congruences"? It is a very important concept in number theory. This concept of "Theory of Congruences" was introduced for the first time by Gauss.

Do you know that Gauss invented this theory just at the age of 24? So Gauss invented an entire branch of Number theory just at the age of 24!!! You too are not too young for discovery and inventions. Isn't it?

9. Ramanujan's Number

Can you find anything special about the number 1729? Why is 1729 known as Ramanujan's number? This is a taxicab number and is variously known as Ramanujan's number and the Rmanujan-Hardy number.

British mathematician G.H. Hardy once visited Indian mathematician Srinivasa Ramanujan at a hospital. As Hardy called his taxi number (1729) "dull", Ramanujan exclaimed it was "the smallest number expressible as the sum of two different cubes in two different ways."

$$\begin{aligned} 1729 &= 1^3 + 12^3 \\ &= 9^3 + 10^3 \end{aligned}$$

The world of numbers is full of such interesting properties. These properties may not be very obvious most of the times.

10. Want to Win One Million Dollar ?

The world of mathematics and science is full of interesting and challenging problems. There are so many problems which are lying unsolved for hundreds of years. Do you know that there are so many problems for which you will get a prize of 1 million dollar (₹ 8.2 crore, at a conversion rate of 82) if you solve them?

The Clay Mathematics Institute (a US based organization), announced seven problems in the year 2000. There is a prize of 1 million dollar on the solution of each problem. The seven problems pertain to various fields of science and mathematics.

How many of these seven problems have been solved till 2023?

Only one[1].

Russian mathematician Grigori Perelman solved one problem, namely, Poincare conjecture in the year 2003. It took three years to verify correctness of his solution. In the year 2006 he was offered 1 million dollar prize. However, he refused to take the prize!!!

The world of mathematics and science is full of challenging problems and tempting rewards for their solution. You can also solve few such problems and remember, you need not refuse the prize!!!.

---

[1] https://brilliant.org/wiki/millennium-prize-problems/#:~:text=The%20only%20Millennium%20Problem%20that,topology%20of%20objects%20called%20manifolds.

02

Magic of Numbers

"Integral numbers are the fountainhead of all mathematics." —*H. Minkowski*

1. Some Interesting Patterns

Playing with numbers is fun. Let us see some examples.

(a) Square of a number is obtained by multiplying the number with itself.

For example, square of 1(denoted by 1^2) $=1\times1=1$

$$2^2=2\times2=4$$

$$3^2=3\times3=9$$

$$4^2=4\times4=16$$

$$5^2=5\times5=25$$

Now see the following interesting property of squares.

$$1^2=1=1$$

$$2^2=4=1+3$$

$$3^2=9=1+3+5$$

1^2 is equal to the first positive odd integer.

2^2 is equal to the sum of the first two positive odd integers.

3^2 is equal to the sum of the first three positive odd integers.

This pattern continues.

$$4^2=16=1+3+5+7$$

$$5^2=25=1+3+5+7+9$$

$$6^2=36=1+3+5+7+9+11$$

$$7^2 = 49 = 1+3+5+7+9+11+13$$

$$8^2 = 64 = 1+3+5+7+9+11+13+15$$

$$9^2 = 81 = 1+3+5+7+9+11+13+15+17$$

You can verify it for higher integers.

(b) How do we obtain cube of a number?

Cube of 1(denoted by 1^3) $= 1\times1\times1 = 1$

$$2^3 = 2\times2\times2 = 8$$

$$3^3 = 3\times3\times3 = 27$$

$$4^3 = 4\times4\times4 = 64$$

$$5^3 = 5\times5\times5 = 125$$

You can see the following interesting property of cubes.

$$1^3 = 1 = 1$$

$$2^3 = 8 = 3+5$$

$$3^3 = 27 = 7+9+11$$

1^3 is equal to the first positive odd integer.

2^3 is equal to the sum of the next two positive odd integers.

3^3 is equal to the sum of the next three positive odd integers.

This pattern continues.

$$4^3 = 64 = 13+15+17+19$$

$$5^3 = 125 = 21+23+25+27+29$$

$$6^3 = 216 = 31+33+35+37+39+41$$

$$7^3 = 343 = 43+45+47+49+51+53+55$$

$$8^3 = 512 = 57+59+61+63+65+67+69+71$$

$$9^3 = 729 = 73+75+77+79+81+83+85+87+89$$

You can verify it for higher integers.

(c) What is the relationship between the square of an integer (n) and that of the next integer $(n+1)$?

$$2^2 = 4$$

$$3^2 = 9 = 4+5 = 4+(2+3) = 4+(2+2+1)$$

or, $$3^2 = 2^2 + (2+2+1)$$

$$4^2 = 16 = 9+7 = 3^2 + (3+3+1)$$

This pattern continues.

$$5^2 = 4^2 + (4+4+1)$$
$$6^2 = 5^2 + (5+5+1)$$
$$7^2 = 6^2 + (6+6+1)$$
$$8^2 = 7^2 + (7+7+1)$$
$$9^2 = 8^2 + (8+8+1)$$
$$10^2 = 9^2 + (9+9+1)$$

You can verify it for higher integers.

When basic operations like sum, multiplication, squares etc are applied on certain numbers, it results into interesting patterns.

Let us see some examples.

(d)

$$4^2 = 16$$
$$34^2 = 1156$$
$$334^2 = 111556$$
$$3334^2 = 11115556$$
$$33334^2 = 1111155556$$

Can you find 3333334^2 without actually doing the multiplication?

(e)

$$7^2 = 49$$
$$67^2 = 4489$$
$$667^2 = 444889$$
$$6667^2 = 44448889$$
$$66667^2 = 4444488889$$

Can you find 666667^2 without actually doing the multiplication?

(f)

$$9^2 = 81$$
$$99^2 = 9801$$
$$999^2 = 998001$$
$$9999^2 = 99980001$$
$$99999^2 = 9999800001$$

Can you find 9999999999^2 without actually doing the multiplication?

(g)

$$6 \times 7 = 42$$
$$66 \times 67 = 4422$$
$$666 \times 667 = 444222$$
$$6666 \times 6667 = 44442222$$
$$66666 \times 66667 = 4444422222$$

Can you now find the value of 666666×666667?

Let us now see few patterns which involve both addition and multiplication.

(h)

$$1 \times 8 + 1 = 9$$
$$12 \times 8 + 2 = 98$$
$$123 \times 8 + 3 = 987$$
$$1234 \times 8 + 4 = 9876$$
$$12345 \times 8 + 5 = 98765$$

Now find the value of $123456789 \times 8 + 9$.

(i)

$$1 \times 9 + 2 = 11$$
$$12 \times 9 + 3 = 111$$
$$123 \times 9 + 4 = 1111$$
$$1234 \times 9 + 5 = 11111$$
$$12345 \times 9 + 6 = 111111$$

Now find the value of $123456 \times 9 + 7$.

(j)

$$7 \times 9 = 63$$
$$77 \times 99 = 7623$$
$$777 \times 999 = 776223$$
$$7777 \times 9999 = 77762223$$
$$77777 \times 99999 = 7777622223$$

Now find the value of $7777777777 \times 9999999999$.

(k)

$$9 \times 9 + 7 = 88$$
$$98 \times 9 + 6 = 888$$
$$987 \times 9 + 5 = 8888$$
$$9876 \times 9 + 4 = 88888$$
$$98765 \times 9 + 3 = 888888$$
$$987654 \times 9 + 2 = 8888888$$
$$9876543 \times 9 + 1 = ? \quad \text{(Find it)}$$

(l)

$$1 \times 8 = 8$$
$$11 \times 88 = 968$$
$$111 \times 888 = 98568$$
$$1111 \times 8888 = 9874568$$
$$11111 \times 88888 = ?\ \text{(Find it)}$$

(m) Power of 11 has interesting properties.

$$11^1 = 11$$
$$11^2 = 11 \times 11 = 121$$
$$11^3 = 11 \times 11 \times 11 = 1331$$
$$11^4 = 11 \times 11 \times 11 \times 11 = 14641$$

Thus, $11^1 =$ 1 1

$11^2 =$ 1 2 1

$11^3 =$ 1 3 3 1

$11^4 =$ 1 4 6 4 1

Can you see the pattern?

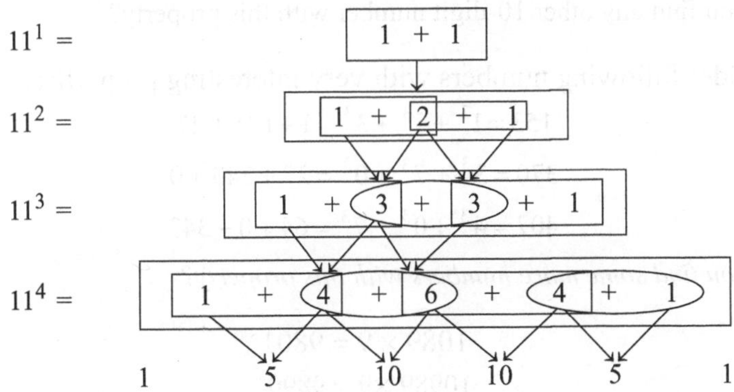

The sum of any two consecutive numbers in a row is the number lying between these two numbers in the next row.

Does this pattern hold true for power 5?

(n) Consider the number 3816547290.

This is a 10-digit number.

Each of the ten digits- 0, 1, 2, 3, 4, 5, 6, 7, 8, 9 appears exactly once in this number.

Consider leftmost digit 3 which is obviously divisible by 1. ($\because 3 = 3 \times 1 + 0$)

Now, consider the number formed by leftmost two digits *i.e.*, 38.

38 is divisible by 2. ($\because 38 = 2 \times 19 + 0$)

Now, consider the number formed by leftmost three digits *i.e.*, 381.

381 is divisible by 3. ($\because 381 = 3 \times 127 + 0$)

Now, consider the number formed by leftmost four digits *i.e.*, 3816.
3816 is divisible by 4. ($\because 3816 = 4 \times 954 + 0$)

Now, consider the number formed by leftmost five digits *i.e.*, 38165.
38165 is divisible by 5. ($\because 38165 = 5 \times 7633 + 0$)

Now, consider the number formed by leftmost six digits *i.e.*, 381654.
381654 is divisible by 6. ($\because 381654 = 6 \times 63609 + 0$)

Now, consider the number formed by leftmost seven digits *i.e.*, 3816547.
3816547 is divisible by 7. ($\because 3816547 = 7 \times 545221 + 0$)

Now, consider the number formed by leftmost eight digits *i.e.*, 38165472.
38165472 is divisible by 8. ($\because 38165472 = 8 \times 4770684 + 0$)

Now, consider the number formed by leftmost nine digits *i.e.*, 381654729.
381654729 is divisible by 9. ($\because 381654729 = 9 \times 42406081 + 0$)

Now, consider the number formed by leftmost ten digits *i.e.*, 3816547290.
3816547290 is divisible by 10. ($\because 3816547290 = 10 \times 381654729 + 0$)

Isn't it a number with very interesting property?
Can you find any other 10-digit number with this property?

(o) Consider following numbers with very interesting properties.

$$153 = 1^3 + 5^3 + 3^3 = 1 + 125 + 27$$

$$370 = 3^3 + 7^3 + 0^3 = 27 + 343 + 0$$

$$407 = 4^3 + 0^3 + 7^3 = 64 + 0 + 343$$

Can you find some more numbers with this property?

(p)

$$1089 \times 9 = 9801$$

$$10989 \times 9 = 98901$$

$$109989 \times 9 = 989901$$

$$1099989 \times 9 = 9899901$$

Multiplying by 9 results in reversal of digits. Reversal of digits of 1089 gives 9801. Similarly, reversal of digits of 10989 gives 98901 and so on.
Can you find any other number with this property?

(q) Power of 9 has very interesting properties.

$9^1 = 9$ (Sum of digits of $9 = 9$)

$9^2 = 81$ (Sum of digits of $81 = 8 + 1 = 9$)

$9^3 = 729$ (Sum of digits of $729 = 7 + 2 + 9 = 18$. Sum of digits of $18 = 1 + 8 = 9$)

$9^4 = 6561$ (Sum of digits of 6561 $= 6+5+6+1 = 18$. Sum of digits of 18 $= 1+8 = 9$)

$9^5 = 59049$ (Sum of digits of 59049 $= 5+9+0+4+9 = 27$. Sum of digits of 27 $= 2+7 = 9$)

Does this pattern hold good for all powers?

(r)

$$3^2 + 4^2 = 5^2$$

$$6^2 + 8^2 = 10^2$$

$$5^2 + 12^2 = 13^2$$

Such triples- (3, 4, 5), (6, 8, 10), (5, 12, 13) — are called Pythagorean triples.

Can you generate more such triplets?

There is an easy way to generate such triplets.

$$(2m)^2 + (m^2 - 1)^2 = 4m^2 + m^4 - 2m^2 + 1 = m^4 + 2m^2 + 1 = (m^2 + 1)^2$$

Thus, $(2m, m^2 - 1, m^2 + 1)$ is a Pythagorean Triplet for all $m > 1$.

For $m = 2$, it gives (4, 3, 5)

For $m = 3$, it gives (6, 8, 10)

For $m = 4$, it gives (8, 15, 17)

It is easy to verify that $8^2 + 15^2 = 64 + 225 = 289 = 17^2$.

(s) Prime numbers

A prime number is a number which has only two divisors, 1 and the number itself. For example, 2 has only two divisors, 1 and 2. Hence, 2 is a prime number. 3 has only two divisors, 1 and 3. Hence, 3 is also a prime number. 4 has three divisors, 1, 2 and 4. Hence 4 is not a prime number. 5, 7, 11, 13, 17, 19, 23 etc are another few examples of prime numbers.

Sum of two or more consecutive primes may be a prime number.

For example :

Sum of two consecutive primes : $2 + 3 = 5$ (a prime number)

Sum of three consecutive primes : $5 + 7 + 11 = 23$ (a prime number)

Sum of four consecutive primes : $2 + 3 + 5 + 7 = 17$ (a prime number)

Sum of five consecutive primes : $5 + 7 + 11 + 13 + 17 = 53$ (a prime number)

Sum of six consecutive primes : $2 + 3 + 5 + 7 + 11 + 13 = 41$ (a prime number)

Sum of seven consecutive primes : $17 + 19 + 23 + 29 + 31 + 37 + 41 = 197$ (a prime number)

Can you find eight consecutive primes whose sum is a prime number?

(t) Consider prime number 5.

Sum of all prime numbers less than 5

$= 2 + 3$

$= 5$

So, sum of primes is divisible by 5.

Consider another prime number 71.

Sum of all prime numbers less than 71

$= 2 + 3 + 5 + 7 + 11 + 13 + 17 + 19 + 23 + 29 + 31 + 37 + 41 + 43 + 47 + 53 + 59$

$+ 61 + 67 = 568$

Thus, 568 is divisible by 71.

$568 = 71 \times 8.$

Can you find any other prime with this property?

(u) Consider prime number 113.

What are the other 3-digit numbers which can be formed using digits of 113?

131 and 311.

113, 131, 311 are all prime numbers.

Can you find any other 3-digit number with this property?

Verify it for 199 and 337.

(v) Consider following numbers

$$1 = 1$$
$$3 = 1 + 2$$
$$6 = 1 + 2 + 3$$
$$10 = 1 + 2 + 3 + 4$$
$$\ldots\ldots$$

All these numbers represent the number of dots that can be arranged evenly in an equilateral triangle.

1

3

6

10

These numbers are called triangular numbers.
Triangular numbers have many interesting properties.
For example,

$$1+3=4=2^2$$
$$3+6=9=3^2$$
$$6+10=16=4^2$$
$$\ldots\ldots$$

Do you notice any pattern here?
The sum of any two consecutive triangular numbers is a perfect square.
How do you know that this statement is true for any two consecutive triangular numbers? Since you can't verify it for all consecutive triangular numbers, you will need a "proof" to establish it.
In subsequent chapters you will learn what a proof is and how to prove any such statement.

(w) Find the sum $\frac{1}{1\times 2}+\frac{1}{2\times 3}+\frac{1}{3\times 4}+\ldots+\frac{1}{99\times 100}$.

Please note that $\frac{1}{1\times 2}=\frac{1}{1}-\frac{1}{2}$

$$\frac{1}{2\times 3}=\frac{1}{2}-\frac{1}{3}$$
$$\frac{1}{3\times 4}=\frac{1}{3}-\frac{1}{4}$$

Hence, $\frac{1}{1\times 2}+\frac{1}{2\times 3}+\frac{1}{3\times 4}+\ldots+\frac{1}{99\times 100}$

$$=\left(\frac{1}{1}-\frac{1}{2}\right)+\left(\frac{1}{2}-\frac{1}{3}\right)+\left(\frac{1}{3}-\frac{1}{4}\right)+\ldots\left(\frac{1}{99}-\frac{1}{100}\right)$$
$$=\frac{1}{1}-\frac{1}{2}+\frac{1}{2}-\frac{1}{3}+\frac{1}{3}-\frac{1}{4}+\ldots+\frac{1}{90}-\frac{1}{100}$$
$$=1-\frac{1}{100}$$

Such a series is called telescoping series.

2. Pascal's Triangle

Consider following expressions

$$(a+b)^2=(a+b)\,(a+b)$$
$$=a(a+b)+b(a+b)$$
$$=a^2+ab+ba+b^2$$
$$=a^2+2ab+b^2$$

Similarly, by direct multiplication,

$$\begin{aligned}(a+b)^3 &= (a+b)(a+b)^2\\ &= a(a+b)^2 + b(a+b)^2\\ &= a(a^2+2ab+b^2)+b(a^2+2ab+b^2)\\ &= a^3+2a^2b+ab^2+ba^2+2ab^2+b^3\\ &= a^3+3a^2b+3ab^2+b^3\end{aligned}$$

Similarly, you can establish that

$$(a+b)^4 = a^4+4a^3b+6a^2b^2+4ab^3+b^4$$

$$(a+b)^5 = a^5+5a^4b+10a^3b^2+10a^2b^3+5ab^4+b^5$$

Let us arrange in order coefficients of various terms in the expansion of powers of $a + b$.

Coefficients of terms in $(a + b)$ are 1, 1.

Coefficients of terms in $(a+b)^2 = a^2+2ab+b^2$ are 1, 2, 1.

Coefficients of terms in $(a+b)^3 = a^3+3a^2b+3ab^2+b^3$ are 1, 3, 3, 1.

Coefficients of terms in $(a+b)^4 = a^4+4a^3b+6a^2b^2+4ab^3+b^4$ are 1, 4, 6, 4, 1.

Coefficients of terms in $(a+b)^5 = a^5+5a^4b+10a^3b^2+10a^2b^3+5ab^4+b^5$ are 1, 5, 10, 10, 5, 1.

Let us arrange these coefficients in the form of a triangle.

Coefficients in $(a + b)$ ____ 1 1

Coefficients in $(a+b)^2$ ____ 1 2 1

Coefficients in $(a+b)^3$ ____ 1 3 3 1

Coefficients in $(a+b)^4$ ____ 1 4 6 4 1

Coefficients in $(a+b)^5$ ____ 1 5 10 10 5 1

Can you see any pattern in this triangle?

Let us rewrite it in following manner

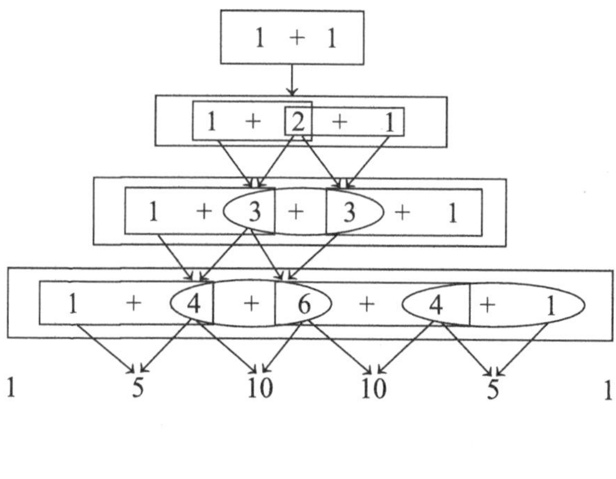

The sum of any two consecutive numbers in a row is the number lying between these two numbers in the next row. This triangle is known as Pascal's triangle.

Can you now write expanded form of $(a + b)^6$ *using this pattern?*

3. Magic Squares

8	1	6
3	5	7
4	9	2

Sum of numbers in 1st row $= 8 + 1 + 6 = 15$

Sum of numbers in 2nd row $= 3 + 5 + 7 = 15$

Sum of numbers in 3rd row $= 4 + 9 + 2 = 15$

Sum of numbers in 1st column $= 8 + 3 + 4 = 15$

Sum of numbers in 2nd column $= 1 + 5 + 9 = 15$

Sum of numbers in 3rd column $= 6 + 7 + 2 = 15$

Sum of numbers along diagonals $= 8 + 5 + 2 = 4 + 5 + 6 = 15.$

Thus, Sum of numbers in any row = Sum of numbers in any column
= Sum of numbers along any diagonal
= 15.

This square of numbers has very interesting property. Such squares are known as magic squares.

But how do we construct such magic squares?

It is very easy to construct a 3×3 magic square.

A 3×3 magic square has three elements along rows as well as columns.

3.1. Let us start constructing a 3×3 magic square.

Step 1 Write 1 in the middle of 1st row :

	1	

Step 2 Move 1 step right and 1 step up :

	1 ↗	

We can move right from 1 but not up. So, we come to the bottom row and place 2 there.

	1 ↗	
		2

Step 3 Repeat this exercise of moving 1 step right and one step up. If you can't move up, come to the bottom row. If you can't move right, come to the leftmost column.

	1	
3		
		2 ↗

Step 4 Repeat same exercise of moving one step right and one step up:

	1	
3 ↗		
		2

But now 1 step right and 1 step up leads to a cell which is already full (Cell already has 1). So we write next number below 3.

	1	
3		
4		2

Step 5 Repeat same exercise of moving one step right and one step up :

	1	
3	↗ **5**	
4		2

Step 6 Repeat same exercise of moving one step right and one step up :

	1	↗ **6**
3	5	
4		2

Step 7 Repeat same exercise of moving one step right and one step up :

	1	6 ↗
3	5	**7**
4		2

This leads to the cell containing 4. So we write 7 in the cell below the cell containing 6.

Step 8 Repeat same exercise of moving one step right and one step up

8	1	6
3	5	7 ↗
4		2

Step 9 Repeat same exercise of moving one step right and one step up :

8 ↗	1	6
3	5	7
4	**9**	2

Congratulations!!!

You have got your magic square.

You can easily verify for this square that

- Sum of numbers in each row = 15
- Sum of numbers in each column = 15
- Sum of numbers along each diagonal = 15

3.2. Using this method you can construct a 5×5 or 7×7 magic square.

17	24	1	8	15
23	5	7	14	16
4	6	13	20	22
10	12	19	21	3
11	18	25	2	9

This is a 5×5 magic square. You can construct it using the same method as described above.

Can you construct a 7×7 magic square now?

In general, using this method you can construct a magic square with an odd number of cells.

Can you come up with your own strategy to construct a magic square with an even number of cells?

Exercise

1. Can you find the missing number?

7	1	48
4	2	12
9	4	?

2. Can you find the missing number?

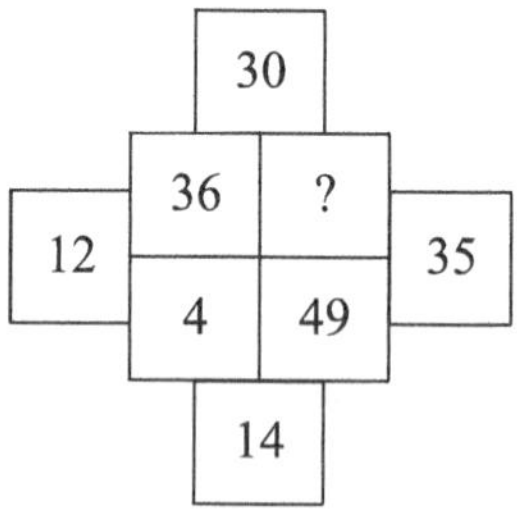

3. Can you find the missing numbers?

```
      8 2 3
        * *
  ---------
    * * * 5
  * * * 4
  ---------
  * * * * *
```

4. Can you find the missing number?

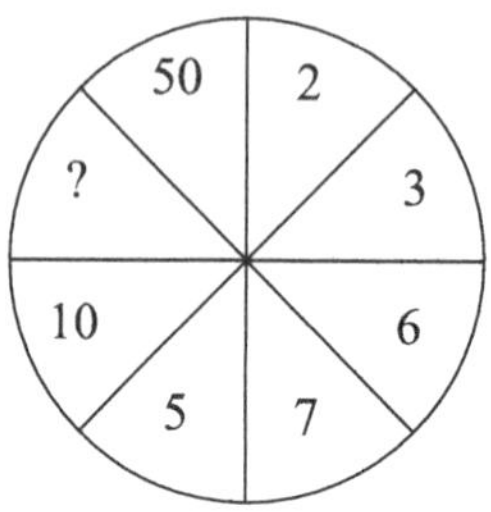

5. Can you find the missing number?

2	1	3
4	2	14
5	3	?

Answers

1. 65

2. 25

3.

$$\begin{array}{r} 823 \\ \times\ 85 \\ \hline 4115 \\ 6584\times \\ \hline 69955 \end{array}$$

4. 37

5. 22

03

Elementary Concepts

"Mathematics is the queen of the sciences and number-theory the queen of mathematics."

—*Gauss*

1. Numbers

Consider following numbers

$$1, 2, 3, 4, 5, 6, \ldots\ldots$$

These numbers are called **natural numbers**.

If we add 0 to these numbers, we get **whole numbers**

$$0, 1, 2, 3, 4, 5, 6, \ldots..$$

If we further add negative numbers, we get **integers**

$$\ldots.., -6, -5, -4, -3, -2, -1, 0, 1, 2, 3, 4, 5, 6, \ldots..$$

Numbers 1, 2, 3, 4, 5, 6, ... are positive integers whereas ...., – 6, – 5, – 4, – 3, – 2, – 1 are negative integers.

Now consider following numbers

$$\frac{1}{2}, \frac{3}{4}, \frac{-5}{7}, \frac{11}{13}, 67, \frac{-31}{5} \text{ etc.}$$

These are numbers of the form $\frac{p}{q}$ where p and q are integers and $q \neq 0$.

Please note that 67 can be written as $\frac{67}{1}$.

These are called **rational numbers**.

Now consider the number π (read as pi). The ratio of circumference of a circle to its diameter is constant. This ratio is known as π. π cannot be expressed as $\frac{p}{q}$ where p and q are integers. The value of π is approximately 3.14. Such numbers are called **irrational numbers**.

Rational and irrational numbers together are called **real numbers**.

Real numbers can be represented on a line.

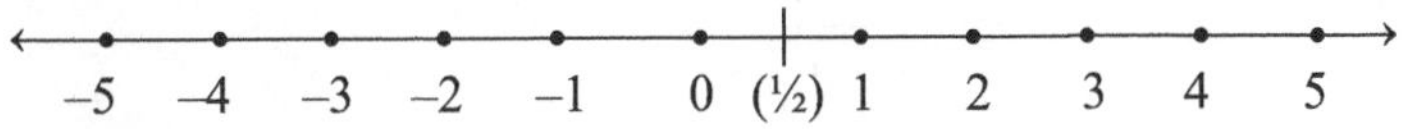

This line is called number line.

2. Decimal Form of Numbers

Numbers can be represented in decimal form.

Let's obtain decimal representation of $\frac{1}{2}$.

$$\begin{array}{r} 0.5 \\ 2\overline{)\,1.0} \\ -10 \\ \hline 0 \\ \hline \end{array}$$

$\therefore \qquad \frac{1}{2} = 0.5$

Let's obtain decimal representation of $\frac{3}{5}$.

$$\begin{array}{r} 0.6 \\ 5\overline{)\,3.0} \\ -30 \\ \hline 0 \\ \hline \end{array}$$

$\therefore \qquad \frac{3}{5} = 0.6$

These are all examples of **terminating decimals** as the process of division terminates after a finite number of steps.

Let's obtain decimal representation of $\frac{1}{3}$.

$$\begin{array}{r|l} & 0.333 \\ 3 & 1.0 \\ & -9 \\ \hline & 10 \\ & -9 \\ \hline & 10 \\ & -9 \\ \hline & 1 \end{array}$$

$$\therefore \quad \frac{1}{3} = 0.333...$$

$$= 0.\overline{3} \text{ (0.333... is denoted as } 0.\overline{3})$$

This is an example of **non-terminating recurring** decimal.

Now consider following number

$$0.1010010001...$$

This is an example of **non-terminating non-recurring decimal**. Such numbers are irrational numbers.

3. Squares and Cubes

$$2 \times 2 = 4$$

2×2 is denoted as 2^2 (read as '2 square') and 4 is called square of 2.

Square of 3 (denoted as 3^2) $= 3 \times 3 = 9$

$$4^2 = 4 \times 4 = 16$$

Now consider following number

$$2 \times 2 \times 2 = 8$$

$2 \times 2 \times 2$ is denoted as 2^3 (read as '2 cube') and 8 is called cube of 2.

Cube of 3 (denoted as 3^3) $= 3 \times 3 \times 3 = 27$

$$4^3 = 4 \times 4 \times 4 = 64$$

4. Power

In general, for any integers p and n $(n > 0)$, p^n (read as "p to the power n") is defined as $p^n = p \times p \times \ldots \times p$ (n times).

Thus, $\quad 3^5 = 3 \times 3 \times 3 \times 3 \times 3$ (5 times)

$$= 243$$

$$2^7 = 2\times2\times2\times2\times2\times2\times2 \text{ (7 times)}$$
$$= 128$$
$$5^4 = 5\times5\times5\times5 \text{ (4 times)}$$
$$= 625$$

5. Square Root and Cube Root

$$2^2 = 2\times2 = 4$$

4 is square of 2 and 2 is called square root of 4 (denoted by $\sqrt{4}$).

$$\sqrt{4} = 2$$

In other words, if $2^2 = 4$, then $\sqrt{4} = 2$

Similarly, $3^2 = 9$

$\therefore$ $\sqrt{9} = 3$ (Square root of 9 = 3)

$4^2 = 16$

$\therefore$ $\sqrt{16} = 4$

$5^2 = 25$

$\therefore$ $\sqrt{25} = 5$

$$2^3 = 2\times2\times2 = 8$$

2 is called cube root of 8 (denoted by $\sqrt[3]{8}$).

Similarly, $3^3 = 27$

$\therefore$ $\sqrt[3]{27} = 3$

$4^3 = 64$

$\therefore$ $\sqrt[3]{64} = 4$

$5^3 = 125$

$\therefore$ $\sqrt[3]{125} = 5$

In general, if $p^n = q$ (p, q and n are integers, $n > 0$), then p is called n^{th} root of q and it is denoted by $\sqrt[n]{q}$.

6. Modulus

For any real number x, modulus x or mod x, denoted as $|x|$, is defined as

$$|x| = \begin{cases} x, & \text{if } x \ge 0 \\ -x, & \text{if } x < 0 \end{cases}$$

Thus, $|2| = 2$

$$|-2| = -(-2) = 2$$

$$|5| = 5$$
$$|-2.5| = -(-2.5) = 2.5$$

$|x|$ represents the distance of x from the origin (0) on number line.

7. Factorial

$$1 \times 2 = 2$$

1×2 is called factorial 2 and denoted by 2!.

$$1 \times 2 \times 3 = 6$$

$1 \times 2 \times 3$ is called factorial 3 and denoted by 3!.

$$4! = 1 \times 2 \times 3 \times 4 = 24$$
$$5! = 1 \times 2 \times 3 \times 4 \times 5 = 120$$

In general, $n!$ (for a positive integer n, $n > 0$) is defined as $n! = 1 \times 2 \times 3 \times \ldots \times n$.
0! is defined to be equal to 1.

8. Counting

There are 2 students- *A* and *B*. There are 2 chairs in a row.

In how many ways can the students be seated in the row?

A	B
B	A

Thus, number of ways = 2 = 2!

Now, suppose there are 3 students- A, B and C. There are three chairs in a row.
In how many ways can the students be seated in the row?

A	B	C
A	C	B
B	A	C
B	C	A
C	A	B
C	B	A

Thus, number of ways = 6 = 3!

In general, n students can be seated in a row with n chairs in $n!$ ways. This is one example of problem of counting.

9. Permutations and Combinations

Now let's consider another problem of counting.

Suppose you have to select 2 students out of 3 students- A, B and C. In how many ways can you select 2 students out of 3 given students A, B and C?

Possible selections are :

A	B
A	C
B	C

Unlike preceding problem at para 8, here the order is not important.

Hence, total number of ways of selecting 2 students out of given 3 students

$$= 3$$

$$= \frac{1 \times 2 \times 3}{(1 \times 2) \times 1} = \frac{3!}{2!1!}$$

$$= \frac{3!}{2! \cdot (3-2)!}$$

Now suppose there are 4 students A, B, C and D. You have to select 2 students out of given 4 students.

In how many ways can these selections be done?

A	B
A	C
A	D
B	C
B	D
C	D

Again, order of selection is not important here.

Total number of ways of selection :

$$= 6$$

$$= 1 \times 2 \times 3$$

$$= \frac{1 \times 2 \times 3 \times 4}{(1 \times 2) \times (1 \times 2)} = \frac{4!}{2!2!}$$

$$= \frac{4!}{2!\,(4-2)!}$$

In general, if we have to select r objects from given n distinct objects $(r \leq n)$, the number of ways in which selection can be made

$$= \frac{n!}{r!\,(n-r)!}$$

$\frac{n!}{r!\,(n-r)!}$ is denoted by ${}^nC_r$ or $\binom{n}{r}$.

$\binom{n}{r}$ is also called **binomial coefficient.**

Now, suppose that order of selection is important. Then, in how many ways can r objects be selected from the given n objects?

If order is not important, number of ways of selection

$$= \binom{n}{r} \left(\text{or } {}^nC_r\right)$$

$$= \frac{n!}{r!\,(n-r)!}$$

Now given r objects can be arranged in $r!$ ways (refer to para 8 above) as arranging r objects is similar to seating arrangements of r students in a row.

Hence if order is important, number of ways in which r objects can be selected from given n distinct objects

$$= \binom{n}{r} r! = \frac{n!}{r!\,(n-r)!}\, r!$$

($\because$ For every selection of r objects, there are $r!$ posible arrangements.)

$$= \frac{n!}{(n-r)!}$$

$\frac{n!}{(n-r)!}$ is denoted by ${}^nP_r$. The symbols C and P in ${}^nC_r$ and ${}^nP_r$ respectively have special meanings.

"C" denotes **"combinations"** whereas **"P"** denotes **"permutations"**.

If order is important in a given selection, it is called permutation. If order is not important in a given selection, it is called combination.

10. Arithmetic Progression

Consider the following sequence of numbers :

$$1, 3, 5, 7, 9, 11, \ldots$$

There is difference of 2 between any two consecutive numbers of this sequence.

Similarly, there is difference of 5 between any two consecutive numbers of the following sequence,

$$3, 8, 13, 18, 23, \ldots$$

Such a sequence or progression of numbers is called an arithmetic progression.

In general, an arithmetic progression can be represented as a, $a+d$, $a+2d$, $a+3d$, $a+4d$, ... where a is the first term and d is the difference between any two consecutive terms.

d is called common difference.

Thus, n^{th} term of the arithmetic progression a_n (denoted as a_n)

$$= a + (n-1)d$$

Sum of first n terms of the arithmetic progression S_n (denoted by S_n)

$$= a + (a+d) + (a+2d) + \ldots + \{a + (n-1)d\}$$

Thus, $S_n = a + (a+d) + (a+2d) + \ldots + \{a+(n-1)d\}$

$S_n = \{a+(n-1)d\} + \{a+(n-2)d\} + \{a+(n-3)d\} + \ldots + a$

(Written in reverse order)

$\therefore \quad 2S_n = \{2a+(n-1)d\} + \{2a+(n-1)d\} + \{2a+(n-1)d\} + \ldots + \{2a+(n-1)d\}$

(n times)

$$= \{2a+(n-1)d\}n$$

$$= 2an + n(n-1)d$$

$$\therefore \quad S_n = an + \frac{n(n-1)d}{2}$$

This formula is very useful.

Let's find out $1+2+3+\ldots+n$.

For $1+2+3+\ldots+n$, $a=1$, $d=1$

$$\therefore \quad S_n = 1 \times n + \frac{n(n-1)1}{2}$$

$$= n + \frac{n^2-n}{2} = \frac{2n+n^2-n}{2}$$

$$= \frac{n^2+n}{2} = \frac{n(n+1)}{2}$$

11. Geometric Progression

Now, consider the following sequence of numbers :

$$1, 2, 2^2, 2^3, 2^4, 2^5, \ldots$$

If we multiply any term of this sequence by 2, we get the next term.

Similarly, if we multiply any term of the following sequence by 5, we get the next term.

$$4, 4\times 5, 4\times 5^2, 4\times 5^3, 4\times 5^4, \ldots$$

Such a sequence or progression of numbers is called geometric progression.

In general, a geometric progression can be represented as a, ar, ar^2, ar^3... where a is the first term and r is the ratio of any term to its preceding term. r is called common ratio.

n^{th} term of the geometric progression a_n (denoted by a_n)

$$= ar^{n-1}$$

Sum of first *n* terms of the geometric progression S_n (denoted by S_n)

$$= a + ar + ar^2 + \ldots + ar^{n-1}$$

$$rS_n = ar + ar^2 + \ldots + ar^{n-1} + ar^n$$

$$\therefore \quad rS_n - S_n = (ar + ar^2 + ar^3 + \ldots + ar^{n-1} + ar^n) - (a + ar + ar^2 + \ldots + ar^{n-1})$$

$$= a \times r^n - a$$

or, $(r-1)S_n = a(r^n - 1)$

$$\therefore \quad S_n = \frac{a(r^n - 1)}{(r-1)}$$

This is a very useful formula.

Let's find out $1 + 2 + 2^2 + \ldots + 2^n$.

For $1 + 2 + 2^2 + \ldots + 2^n$, $a = 1$, $r = 2$

$\therefore \quad 1 + 2 + 2^2 + \ldots + 2^n$

$$= \frac{1(2^n - 1)}{2-1}$$

$$= 2^n - 1$$

Let's consider one more special case.

$$S_n = \frac{a(r^n - 1)}{r-1} = \frac{a(1 - r^n)}{1-r}$$

Now, suppose that $-1 < r < 1$.

r^n gets smaller and smaller as n gets bigger.

For example, $\left(\frac{1}{2}\right)^5 = \frac{1}{32} < \left(\frac{1}{2}\right)^4 = \frac{1}{16} < \left(\frac{1}{2}\right)^3 = \frac{1}{8}$

Thus, r^n approaches 0 as n becomes very large.

Thus, for $-1 < r < 1$, S_n approaches $\frac{a\,(1-0)}{(1-r)} = \frac{a}{1-r}$ as n becomes very large.

Thus,
$$1 + \frac{1}{2} + \frac{1}{2^2} + \frac{1}{2^3} + \frac{1}{2^4} + \ldots \quad \text{(infinitely many terms)}$$
$$= \frac{1}{1 - \frac{1}{2}} \quad \left(\because\ a = 1, r = \frac{1}{2}\right)$$
$$= \frac{1}{\left(\frac{1}{2}\right)} = 2$$

12. Commonly Used Identities/Formulas

Some identities are very commonly used in mathematics:

For example, **1.** $(a + b)^2 = (a + b)\,(a + b)$
$$= a(a + b) + b(a + b)$$
$$= a^2 + ab + ba + b^2$$
$$= a^2 + 2ab + b^2$$

Similarly, **2.** $(a + b)^3 = a^3 + 3a^2b + 3ab^2 + b^3$

3. $(a + b)^4 = a^4 + 4a^3b + 6a^2b^2 + 4ab^3 + b^4$

Now, refer to the pattern at para 2 of chapter 2 of this book.

Coefficients in $(a + b)$ ___ 1 1

Coefficients in $(a + b)^2$ ___ 1 2 1

Coefficients in $(a + b)^3$ ___ 1 3 3 1

Coefficients in $(a + b)^4$ ___ 1 4 6 4 1

Coefficients in $(a + b)^5$ ___ 1 5 10 10 5 1

Thus, we can find $(a + b)^n$ for any positive integral value of n.

Now, let's consider few more identities.

$$(a + b)^2 = a^2 + 2ab + b^2$$

5. $(a-b)^2 = a^2 - 2ab + b^2$

$\therefore$ 6. $(a+b)^2 + (a-b)^2 = 2(a^2 + b^2)$

7. $(a+b)^2 - (a-b)^2 = 4ab$

8. $(a+b)(a-b) = a^2 - b^2$

9. $(a+b)^3 = a^3 + 3a^2b + 3ab^2 + b^3$

10. $(a-b)^3 = a^3 - 3a^2b + 3ab^2 - b^3$

$\therefore$ 11. $(a+b)^3 + (a-b)^3 = 2a^3 + 6ab^2$

$= 2a(a^2 + 3b^2)$

12. $(a+b)^3 - (a-b)^3 = 6a^2b + 2b^3$

$= 2b(3a^2 + b^2)$

13. $a^3 + b^3 = (a+b)(a^2 - ab + b^2)$

14. $a^3 - b^3 = (a-b)(a^2 + ab + b^2)$

15. $a^4 + 4b^4 = (a^2 + 2b^2)^2 - 4a^2b^2$

$= (a^2 + 2b^2 + 2ab)(a^2 + 2b^2 - 2ab)$

16. $(a+b+c)^2 = a^2 + b^2 + c^2 + 2ab + 2bc + 2ca$

17. $a^3 + b^3 + c^3 - 3abc = (a+b+c)(a^2 + b^2 + c^2 - ab - bc - ca)$

13. Inequality

We know that $1 < 2$

$5 < 7$

Also, $1 + 5 < 2 + 7$

or, $6 < 9$

In general, for real numbers a, b, c and d,

if $a < b$ and $c < d$,

then $a + c < b + d$

What about multiplying an inequality by a number?

$1 < 2$

Multiplying by 2 yields

$2 < 4$

This is perfectly fine.

But what about multiplication by -1?

$$-1<-2$$

Is this inequality correct?

No

In fact, $$-1>-2$$

Thus, multiplication by a negative number reverses the inequality.

In general, for real numbers a, b and $c(c \neq 0)$,

if $a<b$ then

$ac<bc$ (if $c>0$) and

$ac>bc$ (if $c<0$)

14. Set Theory

Any collection of objects is called a set.

For example, 1, 2, 3 represents a set consisting of 1, 2 and 3.

Normally a set is denoted by a capital letter.

Let's call this set S.

Then, $$S=\{1,2,3\}$$

1, 2 and 3 are called elements of S.

Thus, S has 3 elements, 1, 2 and 3.

Let $$A=\{a, b, c, d, \dots z\}$$

and $$B=\{1, 2, 3, 4, \dots, 100\}$$

A is the set of all English alphabets from a to z and it has 26 elements.

B is the set of all natural numbers from 1 to 100 and it has 100 elements.

15. Function

For given sets A and B, a function f from A to B (denoted by $f: A \to B$) is a relationship which relates every elements of A to a unique elements of B.

Let $$A=\{1, 2, 3\}$$
$$B=\{P, Q\}$$

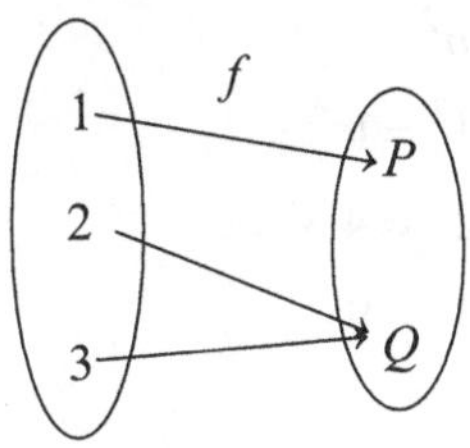

f relates 1 to P, 2 to Q and 3 also to Q. This is an example of a function because every element of A is related to a unique elements of B.

Symbolically, it is denoted as

$$f(1)=P$$
$$f(2)=Q$$

$$f(3) = Q$$

This relationship is also expressed by saying that f maps 1 to P and both 2 and 3 to Q. A is called domain of f and B is called co- domain of f.

Now let's consider following relationship among elements of A and B.

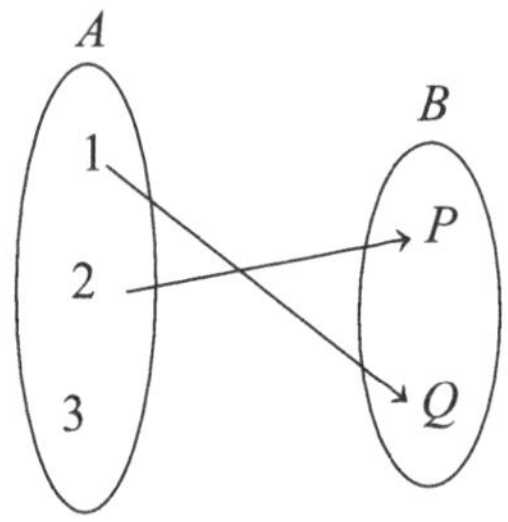

This relationship is not a function because element 3 of A is not mapped to any element of B.

What about following relationship?

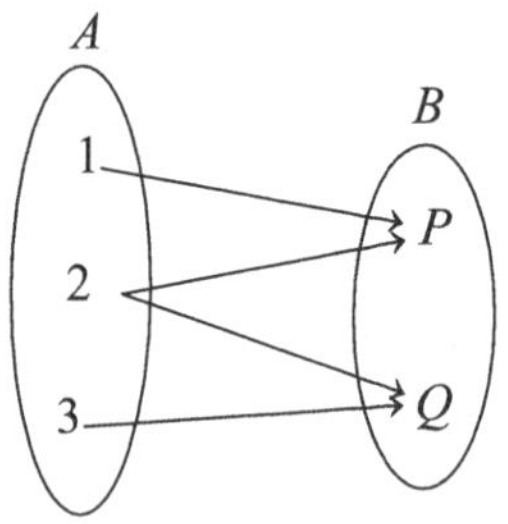

Again, this relationship is not a function because 2 is not mapped to a unique element of B. 2 is mapped to both P and Q.

Let's consider another type of function.

$$f : N \to N \qquad (N \text{ denotes the set of natural numbers}).$$

$$f(n) = n^2$$

$\therefore$

$$f(1) = 1^2 = 1$$

$$f(2) = 2^2 = 4$$

$$f(3) = 3^2 = 9$$

And so on.

16. Symbols and Notations

Certain symbols and notations are very commonly used.

(a) N denotes the set of natural numbers.

W – Set of whole numbers

I – Set of integers
Q – Set of rational numbers
R – Set of real numbers

(b) There is an interesting way to represent the sum $1+2+3+\ldots+n$.

$1+2+3+\ldots+n$ is denoted as $\sum_{r=1}^{n} r$

Thus,

$$\sum_{r=1}^{5} r = 1+2+3+4+5$$

$$\sum_{r=0}^{3} r = 0+1+2+3$$

$$\sum_{r=3}^{7} r = 3+4+5+6+7$$

$$\sum_{r=1}^{5} r^2 = 1^2+2^2+3^2+4^2+5^2$$

Similarly for multiplication,

$$\prod_{r=1}^{5} r = 1\times2\times3\times\ldots\times5$$

$$\prod_{r=2}^{5} r = 2\times3\times4\times5$$

17. Pythagoras Theorem

You must have heard about this theorem.

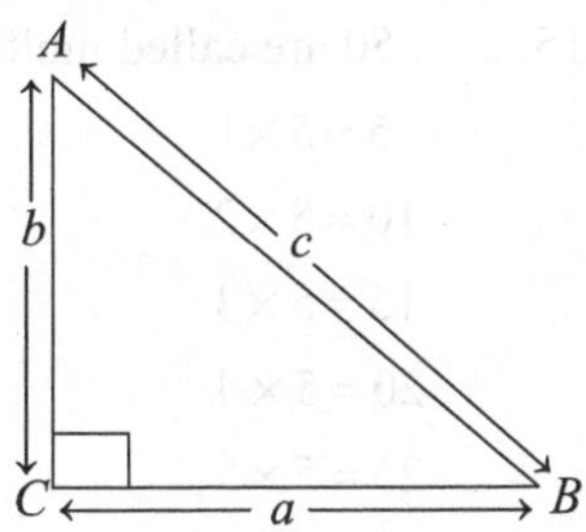

For right angled triangle ABC, $a^2+b^2=c^2$

The elementary concepts of this chapter will be very useful in subsequent chapters.

04
Divisibility

1. Do you remember the table of 5?

5

10

15

20

25

30

35

40

45

50

All these numbers 5, 10, 15, ..., 50 are called multiples of 5. Why?

$$5 = 5 \times 1$$
$$10 = 5 \times 2$$
$$15 = 5 \times 3$$
$$20 = 5 \times 4$$
$$25 = 5 \times 5$$
$$30 = 5 \times 6$$
$$35 = 5 \times 7$$
$$40 = 5 \times 8$$
$$45 = 5 \times 9$$
$$50 = 5 \times 10$$

All these numbers 5, 10, 15, ..., 50 can be obtained by multiplying 5 to some integer. That is why these numbers 5, 10, 15, ..., 50 are called multiples of 5. 5 is called factor or divisor of these numbers. All these numbers 5,10, 15, ..., 50 are divisible by 5.

2. Find all the factors or divisors of 12.

$$12 = 1 \times 12$$
$$12 = 2 \times 6$$
$$12 = 3 \times 4$$

Therefore, 1, 2, 3, 4, 6 and 12 are divisors of 12. You can verify that 12 has no other divisor or factor.

3. An integer a is said to be divisible by another integer b if there exists an integer c such that $a = bc$

Please note that $b \neq 0$ as division by 0 is not defined.

If a is divisible by b, it is denoted as $b \mid a$. Similarly, $b \nmid a$ denotes that a is not divisible by b.

4. $3|12$ because $12 = 3 \times 4$

$5|25$ because $25 = 5 \times 5$

$6|24$ because $24 = 6 \times 4$

$7|(-21)$ because $-21 = 7 \times (-3)$

$3 \nmid 11$ because $11 = 3 \times 3 + 2$

5. An integer greater than 1 is called a prime number if its only positive divisors are 1 and the number itself.

For example,

2 has only two positive divisors 1 and 2.
3 has only two positive divisors 1 and 3.
5 has only two positive divisors 1 and 5.

All these numbers 2, 3, 5 are prime numbers.

What about 6? Is it a prime number?

No $6 = 2 \times 3$

$\therefore$ 2 and 3 are divisors of 6.

Thus, 6 has a divisor other than 1 and 6. 6 is called a composite number.

An integer greater than 1 that is not a prime is called a composite number.

10, 15, 18 etc. are few other examples of composite numbers.

6. Suppose you have to verify divisibility of 14 by 3.

How do you do it?

$$14 = 1 \times 3 + 11$$
$$14 = 2 \times 3 + 8$$
$$14 = 3 \times 3 + 5$$
$$14 = 4 \times 3 + 2 *$$

You can see that 14 cannot be written as a multiple of 3.

Please note the 4th expression above (with *mark):

$$14 = 4 \times 3 + 2$$

Here, $2 > 0$ and $2 < 3$.

2 is called remainder and 4 is called quotient in the division of 14 by 3.

Similarly, you can verify the following.

(i) Division of 18 by 5

$$18 = 3 \times 5 + 3, \quad 0 < 3 < 5$$

(ii) Division of 23 by 4

$$23 = 5 \times 4 + 3, \quad 0 < 3 < 4$$

(iii) Division of 35 by 7

$$35 = 5 \times 7 + 0$$

(iv) Division of 39 by 11

$$39 = 3 \times 11 + 6, \quad 0 < 6 < 11$$

(v) Division of 45 by 6

$$45 = 7 \times 6 + 3, \quad 0 < 3 < 6$$

7. The Division Algorithm

a and b are integers, with $b > 0$.

Then there exist unique integers d and r satisfying,

$$a = db + r \qquad 0 \le r < b$$

d is called **quotient** and ***r*** is called **remainder** in the division of a by b.

Let's verify this claim with few examples.

(i) Division of 32 by 5

$$32 = 6 \times 5 + 2 \qquad 0 < 2 < 5$$

Thus, there exist integers 6 (quotient) and 2 (remainder) as per the division algorithm.

(ii) Division of 47 by 7

$$47 = 6 \times 7 + 5 \qquad 0 < 5 < 7$$

Thus, there exist integers 6 (quotient) and 5 (remainder) as per the division algorithm.

(iii) Division of -32 by 3

$$-32 = (-11) \times 3 + 1 \qquad 0 < 1 < 3$$

Thus, there exist integers -11 (quotient) and 1 (remainder) as per the division algorithm.

Please also note that the quotients and the remainders are unique in the given examples.

Can you find a quotient d other than 6 and remainder r other than 2 when 32 is divided by 5? Try.

8. Any claim or statement in mathematics requires a proof. So does the division algorithm. The proof of division algorithm involves use of well-ordering principle.

9. Well-ordering Principle

Every non-empty set S of non-negative integers contains a least element.

Do we need to prove this principle? Think.

10. Proof of the Division Algorithm

For given integers a and b, with $b > 0$, consider following numbers:

$$\ldots\ldots, a-2b, a-b, a+b, a+2b, \ldots \qquad \ldots \text{(i)}$$

The given numbers are nothing but the numbers obtained by adding and subtracting all multiples of b to (from) a.

As $b > 0$ all terms to the right of a certain number will be positive.

(Can you prove it?) Even though it appears intuitively correct, your intuitions many times may be wrong. Remember, intuitively the Sun appears to be revolving around the Earth!

Now form a set S of all non-negative integers from the numbers given above.

By well-ordering principle, S has a least element.

Let's call it r.

Then, $r = a - qb$ for some integer q.

or, $\qquad a = qb + r$

Since r is the least element, $r < b$.

Otherwise $r - b = a - (q+1)b \geq 0$. Hence $r - b$ is also a member of S and smaller than r. This is a contradiction.

Hence, $\qquad r < b$

Obviously $r \geq 0$ as $r \in S$.

Thus, $\qquad 0 \leq r < b$

Now we have to prove uniqueness of q and r.

Suppose there is another pair q' and r' satisfying the given conditions.

So, $\qquad a = qb + r$

and $\qquad a = q'b + r'$

Suppose $\qquad r' > r$

So, $\qquad 0 < r' - r < b \qquad [\text{As } 0 \leq r < b, 0 \leq r' < b]$

$$r' - r = (a - q'b) - (a - qb)$$

$$= b(q - q')$$

Thus, $r' - r \geq b$ $[\because r' - r > 0]$

This is a contradiction.

Thus, our assumption of multiple possible remainders is incorrect.

With this, the proof is complete.

Please note that we have proved the following

For given integers a and b, with $b > 0$,

(i) there exist integers q and r such that $a = qb + r$

(ii) $0 \leq r < b$

(iii) q and r are unique for given integers a and b.

11. Representation of Integers

Consider a 2-digit number, say, 37.

37 can be written as $3 \times 10 + 7$.

Any 2-digit number can be represented in this manner.

$$42 = 4 \times 10 + 2$$

$$56 = 5 \times 10 + 6$$

$$83 = 8 \times 10 + 3$$

$$99 = 9 \times 10 + 9$$

Now consider few 3-digit numbers.

$$112 = 1 \times 100 + 1 \times 10 + 2$$

or, $$= 1 \times 10^2 + 1 \times 10^1 + 2 \times 10^0$$

$$322 = 3 \times 10^2 + 2 \times 10 + 2$$

$$685 = 6 \times 10^2 + 8 \times 10 + 5$$

$$882 = 8 \times 10^2 + 8 \times 10 + 2$$

Now consider few 4-digit numbers.

$$1230 = 1 \times 10^3 + 2 \times 10^2 + 3 \times 10 + 0$$

$$7235 = 7 \times 10^3 + 2 \times 10^2 + 3 \times 10 + 5$$

$$8341 = 8 \times 10^3 + 3 \times 10^2 + 4 \times 10 + 1$$

In general, let N be an n-digit number.

$N = a_{n-1} \ldots a_1 a_0$ where $a_{n-1}, \ldots, a_1, a_0$ are digits of N

N can be written as

$$N = a_{n-1} 10^{n-1} + \ldots + a_1 10^1 + a_0$$

Here 10 is called the base and this representation of integers is called decimal representation.

This representation can be generalised by taking a base other then 10.

For example, let's take 2 as base. The representation of integers with base 2 is called binary representation of integers.

How do we write 11(in decimal system) in binary system (with base 2)?

$$11 = 8 + 2 + 1 = 2^3 + 2^1 + 2^0$$

$$= 1\times 2^3 + 0\times 2^2 + 1\times 2^1 + 1\times 2^0 = (1011)_2$$

Thus, 11 (in decimal system) is written as 1011 in binary system.

Let us write $(110101)_2$ in decimal system.

$$(110101)_2 = 1\times 2^5 + 1\times 2^4 + 0\times 2^3 + 1\times 2^2 + 0\times 2^1 + 1\times 2^0$$

$$= 32 + 16 + 0 + 4 + 0 + 1 = 53$$

Similarly, you can verify that $27 = (11011)_2$

$$32 = (100000)_2$$

$$42 = (101010)_2$$

Please note that all integers in LHS (Left Hand Side) are in decimal representation (base 10) whereas the same on RHS are in binary representation (base 2).

12. Theorem : For any integer $a \neq 0$, $a \mid 0$

Proof : For any integer $a \neq 0$, we can write $0 = a \times 0$

Hence, by definition of divisibility, it follows that $a \mid 0$.

13. Theorem : For any integer a, $1 \mid a$

Proof : For any integer a, $a = 1 \times a$

Hence, $1 \mid a$

14. Theorem : For any integer $a \neq 1$, $a \mid a$

Proof : For any integer a, $a = a \times 1$

Hence, $a \mid a$

15. Theorem : For any integer a, $a \mid 1$ if and only if $a = \pm 1$

Proof : Suppose $a = \pm 1$

Then, $1 = 1 \times 1$

and $1 = (-1) \times (-1)$

Hence, $a \mid 1$ [in each case $a = 1$ or $a = -1$]

Now suppose $a \mid 1$.

Suppose $a \neq \pm 1$

Obviously a cannot be 0 because division by 0 is not defined.

Hence, $|a| > 1$

As $a \mid 1$, there exists integer $(b \neq 0)$ such that

$$1 = a \times b \quad \text{.... (i)}$$

Now, $|a| > 1$

$|b| \geq 1$

Hence, $|a \times b| = |a| \times |b| > 1$

But $|a \times b| = 1$ [From (i) above]

This is a contradiction.

Hence, our assumption is incorrect.

Thus, $a = \pm 1$

This completes the proof.

16. $2 \times 3 = 6$

$3 \times 3 = 9$

Thus, $2 \mid 6$ and $3 \mid 9$

$6 \times 9 = 54$

Thus, $6 \mid 54$

You can see that $2 \mid 6$, $3 \mid 9$ and (2×3) divides (6×9).

$3 \mid 6$, $5 \mid 10$

$3 \times 5 = 15$

$6 \times 10 = 60$

$60 = 15 \times 4$

$15 \mid 60$

You can see that $3 \mid 6$, $5 \mid 10$ and (3×5) divides (6×10).

Theorem : If $a \mid b$ and $c \mid d$, then $ac \mid bd$. (a, b, c, d are integers and $a \neq 0$, $c \neq 0$.)

Proof : $a \mid b$

Hence, there exists integer m such that

$$b = am$$

Similarly, $d = cn$ for some integer n.

Thus, $bd = (am) \times (cn)$

or, $bd = (ac) \times (mn)$

Hence, $ac \mid bd$

17. $2 \mid 8$ and $8 \mid 24$

Please note that $2 \mid 24$.

$3 \mid 6$ and $6 \mid 36$

Again, $3 \mid 36$

$5 \mid 35$ and $35 \mid 70$

Again, $5 \mid 70$

Theorem : If $a \mid b$ and $b \mid c$, then $a \mid c$ (a, b, c are integers and $a \neq 0, b \neq 0$.).

Proof : $a \mid b$ and $b \mid c$

Hence, there exist integers m and n such that $b = am$ and $c = bn$

Hence, $c = bn = (am)n$

$= a(mn)$

Thus, $a \mid c$

18. Theorem : $a \mid b$ and $b \mid a$ if and only if $a = \pm b$.

Proof : Suppose $a = \pm b$

Then $a = (\pm 1) \times b$

and $b = (\pm 1) \times a$

Thus, $b \mid a$ and $a \mid b$

Now, suppose $a \mid b$ and $b \mid a$

Thus, there exist integers m and n such that

$b = am$ and $a = bn$

Please note that $m \neq 0, n \neq 0$ as a and b cannot be 0.

Hence, $|b| = |a||m|$ and $|a| = |b||n|$

$\therefore$ $|b| \geq |a|$ and $|a| \geq |b|$

Thus, $|a| = |b|$

Hence, $a = \pm b$

19. $3 \mid 6$

Please note that $3 \leq 6$

$6 \mid 60$

Please note that $6 \leq 60$

$7 \mid 21$

Please note that $7 \leq 21$

Theorem : If $a \mid b$ and $b \neq 0$, then $|a| \leq |b|$

Proof : $a \mid b$

Hence, there exists integer m such that

$$b = am \qquad (m \neq 0 \text{ as } b \neq 0)$$

Taking modulus on both sides, we get

$$|b| = |am| = |a||m|$$

$$|m| \geq 1 \qquad [\because m \neq 0]$$

Hence $$|b| \geq |a|$$

20. $3 \mid 6, 3 \mid 15$

Please note that $3 \mid 57\ (6 \times 2 + 15 \times 3)$

$3 \mid 111\ (6 \times 1 + 15 \times 7)$

$3 \mid 48\ (6 \times 3 + 15 \times 2)$

Theorem : If $a \mid b$ and $a \mid c$, then $a \mid (bx + cy)$ for arbitrary integers x and y

Proof : $a \mid b$ and $a \mid c$

Hence, there exist integers m and n such that

$$b = am \text{ and } c = an$$

Thus, $bx + cy$ [for arbitrary integers x and y]

$$= (am)x + (an)y = a(mx + ny)$$

Hence, $a \mid bx + cy$

21. Divisibility Criterion

(i) Divisibility by 2

Which of the following numbers is divisible by 2?

7, 16, 57, 395, 10320, 5231791

16 and 10320 are divisible by 2.

7, 57, 395 and 5231791 are not divisible by 2.

How do you know whether some number is divisible by 2 or not?

In case of small numbers, you can simply divide by 2 and see if you obtain 0 as remainder or not.

However, this process of division becomes very time-consuming in case of large numbers (like dividing 5231791 by 2).

Is there an easy way to find out whether some number is divisible by 2 or not?

Refer to section 11 of this chapter, representation of integers.

Any integer $N(a_n a_{n-1} \dots a_1 a_0)$ can be written as

$$N = a_n 10^n + a_{n-1}10^{n-1} + \dots + a_1 10^1 + a_0$$

where $a_n, a_{n-1}, \dots, a_1, a_0$ are digits of N.

Obviously, $2 | 10$

In fact 2 divides 10^n for $n \geq 1$.

Hence,
$$2 | a_n 10^n$$
$$2 | a_{n-1}10^{n-1}$$
$$\dots\dots$$
$$\dots\dots$$
$$2 | a_1 10^1$$

Thus, $$a | (a_n 10^n + a_{n-1} 10^{n-1} + \dots + a_1 10^1) \quad \dots\text{(i)}$$

Refer to Theorem in section 20 of this chapter. If $a | b$ and $a | c$, then $a | (bx + cy)$ for arbitrary integers x and y. This theorem can be generalised as under :

$$a | b_1$$
$$a | b_2$$
$$\dots\dots$$
$$\dots\dots$$
$$a | b_n$$

Then, $a | (b_1 x_1 + b_2 x_2 + \dots + b_n x_n)$ for arbitrary integers $x_1, x_2, \dots, x_n$

Now, $$N = a_n 10^n + a_{n-1}10^{n-1} + \dots + a_1 10^1 + a_0$$

Let $$X = a_n 10^n + a_{n-1}10^{n-1} + \dots + a_1 10^1$$

So, $$N = X + a_0$$

By (i), $2 | X$

Thus, if $2 | a_0$, then $2 | (X + a_0)$ or $2 | N$.

If $2 \nmid a_0$, then $2 \nmid (X + a_0)$ or $2 \nmid N$

Please note that a_0 is unit digit of integer N.

Thus, an integer is divisible by 2 if and only if its unit digit is divisible by 2.

An integer divisible by 2 is called an even integer. An integer not divisible by 2 is called an odd integer.

Hence, an integer with unit digit 0, 2, 4, 6 or 8 is divisible by 2 whereas the integer with unit digit 1, 3, 5, 7 or 9 is not divisible by 2.

WOW!!!

So, you have arrived at the criterion for divisibility by 2. You don't need to divide any number by 2 to verify its divisibility by 2.

Whatever be the size of the number, you simply need to look at the unit digit. If the unit digit is 0, 2, 4, 6 or 8, the number is divisible by 2. Otherwise, the number is not divisible by 2.

(ii) Divisibility by 4

Any integer $N(a_n a_{n-1} \dots a_1 a_0)$ can be written as

$$N = a_n 10^n + a_{n-1}10^{n-1} + \dots + a_2 10^2 + a_1 10^1 + a_0$$

where $a_n, a_{n-1}, \dots, a_1, a_0$ are digits of N.

$$4 \mid 10^2$$

In fact $4 \mid 10^n$ for $n \geq 2$

Hence,

$$4 \mid a_n 10^n$$

$$4 \mid a_{n-1}10^{n-1}$$

$$\dots\dots$$

$$\dots\dots$$

$$4 \mid a_2 10^2$$

Thus, $4 \mid \left(a_n 10^n + a_{n-1}10^{n-1} + \dots + a_2 10^2\right)$

Let $X = a_n 10^n + a_{n-1}10^{n-1} + \dots + a_2 10^2$

So $N = X + (a_1 10 + a_0)$

As $4 \mid X$, $4 \mid N$ if and only if $4 \mid (a_1 10 + a_0)$

Thus, an integer is divisible by 4 if and only if the number formed by last two digits of the integer is divisible by 4.

23548 is divisible by 4 as 48 is divisible by 4. (48 is the number formed by last two digits of 23548.)

3298 is not divisible by 4 as 98 is not divisible by 4.

2004 is divisible by 4 as 04 is divisible by 4.

(iii) Divisibility by 8

You can deduce in the same manner that an integer is divisible by 8 if and only if the number formed by last three digits of the integer is divisible by 8.

(iv) Divisibility by 16

Similarly, you can deduce that an integer is divisible by 16 if and only if the number formed by last four digits of the integer is divisible by 16.

What about divisibility by 32? Can you deduce the criterion for divisibility by 32?

(v) Divisibility by 5

Any integer $N(a_n a_{n-1} \ldots a_1 a_0)$ can be written as

$$N = a_n 10^n + a_{n-1}10^{n-1} + \ldots + a_2 10^2 + a_1 10^1 + a_0$$

where $a_n, a_{n-1}, \ldots, a_1, a_0$ are digits of N.

$$5 \mid 10$$

In fact $5 \mid 10^n$ for $n \geq 1$

Hence, $5 \mid a_n 10^n$

$5 \mid a_{n-1}10^{n-1}$

......

......

$5 \mid a_1 10$

Thus, $5 \mid (a_n 10^n + \ldots + a_1 10)$

Let $X = (a_n 10^n + \ldots + a_1 10)$

So $N = X + a_0$

$5 \mid X$

Hence, $5 \mid (X + a_0)$ or $5 \mid N$ if and only if $5 \mid a_0$.

Thus, an integer is divisible by 5 if and only if its unit digit is divisible by 5.

It implies that an integer is divisible 5 if its unit digit is 0 or 5.

For example,

35 is divisible by 5.

93 is not divisible by 5.

430 is divisible by 5.

9327 is not divisible by 5.

(vi) Divisibility by 3

For deducing rule of divisibility by 3, we shall need to use the following result.

$$(a+1)^n = xa + 1 \qquad \text{(where } a, n \text{ and } x \text{ are integers and } n > 0\text{)}$$

Let's see some examples to understand it.

$$(2+1)^2 = 3^2 = 9 = 4 \times 2 + 1$$

Here, $a = 2$

$n = 2$

$x = 4$

$$(6+1)^3 = 7^3 = 343$$
$$= 57 \times 6 + 1$$

Here,
$$a = 6$$
$$n = 3$$
$$x = 57$$

Now, let us get back to the task of deducing criterion for divisibility by 3.

Any integer $N(a_n a_{n-1} \ldots a_1 a_0)$ can be written as

$$N = a_n 10^n + a_{n-1}10^{n-1} + \ldots + a_2 10^2 + a_1 10^1 + a_0$$

where $a_n, a_{n-1}, \ldots, a_1, a_0$ are digits of N.

$$10^n = (9+1)^n = x_n 9 + 1 \text{ for some integer } x_n$$

$$10^{n-1} = (9+1)^{n-1} = x_{n-1}9 + 1 \text{ for some integer } x_{n-1}$$

......

......

$$10^1 = 9 + 1$$

Hence,
$$N = a_n 10^n + a_{n-1}10^{n-1} + \ldots + a_1 10^1 + a_0$$
$$= a_n(x_n 9 + 1) + a_{n-1}(x_{n-1}9 + 1) + \ldots + a_1(9+1) + a_0$$
$$= (a_n x_n 9 + a_n) + (a_{n-1}x_{n-1}9 + a_{n-1}) + \ldots + (a_1 9 + a_1) + a_0$$
$$= (a_n x_n 9 + a_{n-1}x_{n-1}9 + \ldots + a_1 9) + (a_n + a_{n-1} + \ldots + a_1 + a_0)$$
$$= 9(a_n x_n + a_{n-1}x_{n-1} + \ldots + a_1) + (a_n + a_{n-1} + \ldots + a_1 + a_0)$$
$$= 9X + \text{sum of digits of } N$$

where $X = a_n x_n + a_{n-1}x_{n-1} + \ldots + a_1$

Obviously, $9X$ is divisible by 3.

Hence, N is divisible by 3 if and only if the sum of digits of N is divisible by 3.

For example,

111 is divisible by 3. (Sum of digits of $111 = 1+1+1 = 3$, divisible by 3)

529 is not divisible by 3. (Sum of digits of $529 = 5+2+9 = 16$, not divisible by 3)

1026 is divisible by 3. (Sum of digits of $1026 = 1+0+2+6 = 9$, divisible by 3)

(vii) Divisibility by 9

In the manner similar to derivation of criterion for divisibility by 3, we can deduce that an integer is divisible by 9, if and only if the sum of digits of the integer is divisible by 9. Can you deduce it?

For example,

89 is not divisible by 9. (Sum of digits of 89 $= 8 + 9 = 17$, not divisible by 9)
729 is divisible by 9. (Sum of digits of 729 $= 7 + 2 + 9 = 18$, divisible by 9)

(viii) Divisibility by 11

For deducing criterion for divisibility by 11, we need to use the following result.

$$(a-1)^n = xa + (-1)^n$$

where a, n and x are integers and $n > 0$.

Now we can deduce divisibility criterion in the same way as we deduced it for divisibility by 3. We leave this deduction as an exercise for you.

An integer is divisible by 11 if and only if the difference of sums of alternate digits of the integer is divisible by 11.

For example,

101

Sum of digits at even places $= 1 + 1 = 2$

Sum of digits at odd places $= 0$

Difference $= 2 - 0 = 2$

2 is not divisible by 11.

Hence, 101 is not divisible by 11.

121

Sum of digits at even places $= 1 + 1 = 2$

Sum of digits at odd places $= 2$

Difference $= 2 - 2 = 0$

$11 | 0$

Hence, 121 is divisible by 11.

What about divisibility by 7? Can you deduce the criterion for divisibility by 7?

22. Some Interesting Results

You may find following results interesting.

(a) $4 \nmid (n^2 + 2)$ for any integer n.

(b) If n is an odd integer, $n^2 - 1$ is divisible by 8.

(c) The product of any three consecutive integers is divisible by 6.

(d) The product of any four consecutive integers is divisible by 24.

Aren't these results interesting?

But how do you arrive at these results?

As we shall see in the succeeding paragraphs, we can arrive at these results in a very simple manner.

23. Any integer can be written in the form of $2k$ or $2k+1$.

Is this claim obvious to you?

Refer Division Algorithm in para 7 of this chapter.

Suppose an integer n is divided by 2. Then, these exist integers k and r satisfying

$$n = 2k + r$$

where $$0 \le r < 2$$

Therefore, $r = 0$ or 1

Hence, n is of one of the forms $2k$ or $2k+1$.

All integers of the form $2k$ are even integers whereas all integers of the form $2k+1$ are odd integers.

You can verify it for few integers.

$16 = 2 \times 8$ ($2k$ form)

$33 = 2 \times 16 + 1$ ($2k+1$ form)

$51 = 2 \times 25 + 1$ ($2k+1$ form)

$96 = 2 \times 48$ ($2k$ form)

Similarly, any integer is of one of the forms $3k$, $3k+1$ or $3k+2$.

For example,

$10 = 3 \times 3 + 1$ ($3k+1$ form)

$12 = 3 \times 4$ ($3k$ form)

$17 = 3 \times 5 + 2$ ($3k+2$ form)

$39 = 3 \times 13$ ($3k$ form)

$56 = 3 \times 18 + 2$ ($3k+2$ form)

Similarly, any integer is of one of the forms $4k$, $4k+1$, $4k+2$ or $4k+3$. And so on.

In general, for any positive integer p, any integer is of one of the forms pk, $pk+1$, $pk+2$, ..., or $pk+(p-1)$.

24. As we discussed in the preceding paragraph, any integer n is of one of the forms $3k$, $3k+1$ or $3k+2$.

What about the forms of squares?

$$(3k)^2 = 9k^2 = 3(3k^2)$$

$$(3k+1)^2 = 9k^2 + 6k + 1 = 3(3k^2 + 2k) + 1$$

$$(3k+2)^2 = 9k^2 + 12k + 4 = 3(3k^2 + 4k + 1) + 1$$

Thus, we can see that the squares can be of the forms $3k$ or $3k+1$ only.

Similarly, any integer is of one of the forms $4k$, $4k+1$, $4k+2$ or $4k+3$.

What about the forms of squares?

$$(4k)^2 = 16k^2 = 4(4k^2)$$

$$(4k+1)^2 = 16k^2 + 8k + 1 = 4(4k^2 + 2k) + 1$$

$$(4k+2)^2 = 16k^2 + 16k + 4 = 4(4k^2 + 4k + 1)$$

$$(4k+3)^2 = 16k^2 + 24k + 9 = 4(4k^2 + 6k + 2) + 1$$

Thus, we can see that the squares can be of the forms $4k$ or $4k+1$ only.

You can verify these results for few integers.

$4^2 = 16 = 3 \times 5 + 1$ ($3k+1$ form)

$= 4 \times 4$ ($4k$ form)

$7^2 = 49 = 3 \times 16 + 1$ ($3k+1$ form)

$= 4 \times 12 + 1$ ($4k+1$ form)

Now we are in a position to prove few interesting results stated in paragraph 22.

25. $4 \nmid n^2 + 2$ for any integer n.

Proof : Any integer n is of one of the forms $4k$, $4k+1$, $4k+2$ or $4k+3$.

Hence, square of the integer n^2 is of one of the forms $4k$ or $4k+1$.

Hence, n^2+2 is of one of the forms $4k+2$ or $4k+3$.

An integer of the form $4k+2$ or $4k+3$ obviously cannot be divisible by 4.

Hence, $4 \nmid n^2 + 2.$

26. If n is an odd integer, $n^2 - 1$ is divisible by 8.

Proof : Any integer n is of one of the forms $8k$, $8k+1$, $8k+2$, $8k+3$, $8k+4$, $8k+5$, $8k+6$ or $8k+7$.

As n is odd, it can only be of the forms $8k+1$, $8k+3$, $8k+5$ or $8k+7$.

$$(8k+1)^2 = 64k^2 + 16k + 1 = 8(8k^2 + 2k) + 1$$

$$(8k+3)^2 = 64k^2 + 48k + 9 = 8(8k^2 + 6k + 1) + 1$$

$$(8k+5)^2 = 64k^2 + 80k + 25 = 8(8k^2 + 10k + 3) + 1$$

$$(8k+7)^2 = 64k^2 + 112k + 49 = 8(8k^2 + 14k + 6) + 1$$

Thus, n^2 has only one possible form $8k+1$.

Hence, n^2-1 is of the form $8k$.

Thus, n^2-1 is divisible by 8.

27. The product of any three consecutive integers is divisible by 6.

Proof : Let n, $n+1$ and $n+2$ be three consecutive integers.

Let $N = n(n+1)(n+2)$

n is of one of the forms $2k$ or $2k+1$.

Hence, either n or $n+1$ is always divisible by 2.

Thus, N is divisible by 2.

Also, n is of one of the forms $3k$, $3k+1$ or $3k+2$.

If n is of the form $3k$, n is divisible by 3.

If n is of the form $3k+1$, $n+2$ is divisible by 3.

If n is of the form $3k+2$, $n+1$ is divisible by 3

Hence, one of the terms n, $n+1$ or $n+2$ is always divisible by 3.

Thus, N divisible by 3.

Therefore, N is divisible by both 2 and 3. Hence, N is divisible by 6 $(6 = 2 \times 3)$.

2 and 3 do not have any common factors other than 1. Hence, they are called relatively prime.

In case of relatively prime numbers p and q, if $p \mid N$ and $q \mid N$ then $pq \mid N$ for any integer N.

We shall discus the proof of this result in succeeding paras.

28. The product of any four consecutive integers is divisible by 24.

Proof : Let n, $n+1$, $n+2$ and $n+3$ be four consecutive integers.

Let
$$N = n(n+1)(n+2)(n+3)$$
$$24 = 3 \times 8$$

It is evident from para 27 that N is divisible by 3.

n is of one of the forms $4k$, $4k+1$, $4k+2$ or $4k+3$.

If n is of the form $4k$, n is divisible by 4 and $n+2$ is divisible by 2.

Hence, N is divisible by 8.

If n is of the form $4k+1$, $n+1$ is divisible by 2 and $n+3$ is divisible by 4.

Hence, N is divisible by 8.

If n is of the form $4k+2$, n is divisible by 2 and $n+2$ is divisible by 4.

Hence, N is divisible by 8.

If n is of the form $4k+3$, $n+1$ is divisible by 4 and $n+3$ is divisible by 2.

Hence, N is divisible by 8.

Thus, N is always divisible by 8.

Now, as N is divisible by both 3 and 8, N is divisible by 24.

Please not that $24 = 3 \times 8$ and 3 and 8 are relatively prime.

29. If integers p and q are odd, then $p^2 + q^2$ is even but not divisible by 4.

Proof : As p and q are odd, they are of one of the forms $4k+1$ or $4k+3$.

Hence, their squares is of the form $4k+1$ only. (Refer to para 24)

Let
$$p^2 = 4k_1 + 1$$
$$q^2 = 4k_2 + 1$$

$\therefore$
$$p^2 + q^2 = (4k_1 + 1) + (4k_2 + 1) = 4(k_1 + k_2) + 2$$

Thus, $p^2 + q^2$ is of the form $4k+2$.

Hence, $p^2 + q^2$ is divisible by 2 but not by 4.

30. For any integer a, one of the integers $a, a+2, a+4$ is divisible by 3.

Proof : a is of one of the forms $3k$, $3k+1$ or $3k+2$.

If a is of the form $3k$, a is divisible by 3.

If a is of the form $3k+1$, $a+2$ is divisible by 3.

If a is of the form $3k+2$, $a+4$ is divisible by 3.

Hence, one of the integers a, $a+2$ or $a+4$ is always divisible by 3.

31. The sum of the squares of two odd integers cannot be a perfect square.

Proof : Let p and q be the given odd integers.

An odd integer is of one of the forms $4k+1$ or $4k+3$.

Hence, p^2 and q^2 are of the form $4k+1$.

Let
$$p^2 = 4k_1 + 1$$
$$q^2 = 4k_2 + 1$$
$$p^2 + q^2 = (4k_1 + 1) + (4k_2 + 1)$$
$$= 4(k_1 + k_2) + 2$$

Thus, $p^2 + q^2$ is of the form $4k+2$.

We know that the square of any integer is of one of the forms $4k$ or $4k+1$.

Hence, $p^2 + q^2$ cannot be a perfect square.

32. The sum of squares of three consecutive integers cannot be a perfect square.

Proof : An integer is of one of the forms $3k$, $3k+1$ or $3k+2$. Square of an integer is of one of the forms $3k$ or $3k+1$.

Let n, $n+1$ and $n+2$ be three consecutive integers.

It is obvious that the three consecutive integers are of the forms $3k$, $3k+1$ and $3k+2$, one number of each form in some order.

You can verify it by taking n to be of one of the forms $3k$, $3k+1$ or $3k+2$ and then verifying the forms of $n+1$ and $n+2$.

Square of an integer of the form $3k$ is of the form $3k$.

Square of an integer of the form $3k+1$ is of the form $3k+1$.

Square of an integer of the form $3k+2$ is of the form $3k+1$.

Hence, sum of squares of n, $n+1$ and $n+2$

$$= 3k_1 + (3k_2 + 1) + (3k_3 + 1) \text{ for some integers } k_1, k_2, k_3$$
$$= 3(k_1 + k_2 + k_3) + 2$$

Thus, the sum of squares of three consecutive integers is of the form $3k+2$.

But we know that the square of an integer is of one of the forms $3k$ or $3k+1$ only.

Hence, the sum of squares of three consecutive integers cannot be a perfect square.

33. For integer $n > 3$, n, $n+2$ and $n+4$ cannot be all prime.

Proof : Any integer n is of one of the forms $6k$, $6k+1$, $6k+2$, $6k+3$, $6k+4$ or $6k+5$.

Suppose n is prime. Then its only divisors are 1 and n itself.

$6k$ is divisible by 2.

$6k+2$ is divisible by 2.

$6k+3$ is divisible by 3.

$6k+4$ is divisible by 2.

Hence, n can only be of the forms $6k+1$ or $6k+5$.

In all other cases, n is divisible by either 2 or 3, a number other than 1 and n. ($\because$ Please not that $n > 3$.)

If n is of the form $6k+1$, $n+2$ (of the form $6k+3$) is divisible by 3. Hence, $n+2$ is not a prime.

If n is of the form $6k+5$, $n+4$ (of the form $6k+9$) is divisible by 3. Hence, $n+4$ is not a prime.

Thus, n, $n+2$ and $n+4$ cannot be all prime.

34. If $p \geq 5$ is a prime number then $p^2 + 2$ is always a composite number.

Proof : As p is a prime number, it is of one of the forms $6k + 1$ or $6k + 5$ (refer to para 33).

In either case, p^2 is of the form $6k + 1$.

Hence, $p^2 + 2$ is of the form $6k + 3$.

Thus, $p^2 + 2$ is divisible by 3.

It is obvious that $p^2 + 2 > 3$ $(\because p \geq 5)$

Hence, $p^2 + 2$ is a composite number.

Please note that $p^2 + 2$ is not composite for $p = 3$. Where does our reasoning fail in case of $p = 3$? Think.

35. If a and b are both odd integers then $a^4 + b^4 - 2$ is divisible by 16.

Proof : a and b are odd integers.

Hence, they are of one of the forms $8k + 1$, $8k + 3$, $8k + 5$ or $8k + 7$. Therefore, their squares is of the form $8k + 1$ only.

$$(8k + 1)^2 = 64k^2 + 16k + 1$$
$$= 16(4k^2 + k) + 1$$

Thus, a^4 and b^4 are of the form $16k + 1$.

Let $a^4 = 16k_1 + 1$ and $b^4 = 16k_2 + 1$

$$\therefore \quad a^4 + b^4 - 2 = (16k_1 + 1) + (16k_2 + 1) - 2$$
$$= 16(k_1 + k_2)$$

Hence, $a^4 + b^4 - 2$ is divisible by 16.

36. The sum of squares of five consecutive integers is not a square.

Proof : Let $n - 2$, $n - 1$, n, $n + 1$ and $n + 2$ be five consecutive integers.

Now, $(n-2)^2 + (n-1)^2 + n^2 + (n+1)^2 + (n+2)^2$

$$= [(n-2)^2 + (n+2)^2] + [(n-1)^2 + (n+1)^2] + n^2$$
$$= 2(n^2 + 2^2) + 2(n^2 + 1^2) + n^2$$
$$= 2n^2 + 8 + 2n^2 + 2 + n^2 = 5n^2 + 10$$

Let $N = 5n^2 + 10$

$$= 5(n^2 + 2)$$

Suppose N is a square.

Then $N = p^2$ for some integer p.

p is of one of the forms $5k$, $5k+1$, $5k+2$, $5k+3$ or $5k+4$.

As $5 \mid N$, only possible form of p is $5k$. In all other cases, p^2 is not divisible by 5.

Thus, $N = p^2$ is of the form $25k^2$.

Thus, $$25 \mid N$$

Hence, $N = 25s$ for some integer s.

or, $$5(n^2+2) = 25s$$

or, $$n^2+2 = 5s$$

or, $$n^2 = 5s-2 = 5(s-1)+3$$

Thus, n^2 is of the form $5k+3$.

But only possible forms of a square are $5k$, $5k+1$ and $5k+4$.

This is a contradiction.

Hence, our original assumption that N is a square is incorrect.

Thus, it is established that the sum of squares of five consecutive integers is not a square.

37. We know that if $a \mid b$ $(a \neq 0)$, then there exists an integer c such that $b = ac$.

For example, $3 \mid 12$

$$12 = 3 \times 4$$

Thus, divisors occur in pairs. For every divisor a of b, there exists another divisor c such that $b = ac$.

Given the fact that divisors occur in pairs, can we conclude that any integer has even numbers of divisors (or factors)?

Let us see few examples.

$$12 = 1 \times 12 = 2 \times 6 = 3 \times 4$$

Thus, 12 has total six factors 1, 2, 3, 4, 6 and 12.

Hence, 12 has an even number of factors.

$$28 = 1 \times 28 = 2 \times 14 = 4 \times 7$$

Thus, 28 has total six factors which is again an even number.

What about 16?

$$16 = 1 \times 16 = 2 \times 8 = 4 \times 4$$

16 has total five factors 1, 2, 4, 8 and 16.

Thus, 16 has an odd number of factors.

So, what changed in case of 16?

You can see that the factor 4 is repeated in this case.

$$16 = 4 \times 4$$

That is why we got an odd number of factors.

16 is a perfect square ($16 = 4^2$).

In general, $b = ac$

Suppose $a = c$

Then $b = a^2$ *i.e.* b is a perfect square.

In case of a perfect square, a factor is repeated twice.

Therefore, a perfect square has an odd number of factors.

Thus, any integer has an even number of factors except when it is a perfect square.

38. Consider integers 12 and 16.

1, 2, 3, 4, 6 and 12 are divisors of 12.

1, 2, 4, 8 and 16 are divisors of 16.

Thus, 1, 2 and 4 divide both 12 and 16.

1, 2 and 4 are common divisors of 12 and 16.

{1, 2, 4} is the set of common divisors of 12 and 16. 4 is the largest integer in this set. Thus, 4 is the greatest common divisor (gcd) of 12 and 16.

Let a and b be given integers with at least one of a and b not being zero.

The greatest common divisor of a and b, denoted by gcd (a, b), is the positive integer d satisfying following conditions:

(i) $d \mid a$ and $d \mid b$, and

(ii) If $c \mid a$ and $c \mid b$, then $c \leq d$

39. Find gcd (16, 51).

1, 2, 4, 8 and 16 are divisors of 16.

1, 3, 17 and 51 are divisors of 51.

Thus, 16 and 51 have only one common divisor *i.e.* 1.

Hence, gcd (16, 51) = 1

16 and 51 are called relatively prime or co-primes.

Two integers a and b (at least one of them being non-zero) are said to be relatively prime or co-primes if gcd(a, b) = 1.

40. Consider integers 4 and 6.

4, 8, 12, 16, 20, 24 ..... are multiples of 4.

6, 12, 18, 24, 30, 36 .... are multiples of 6.

Integers 12, 24 etc. appear in the list of multiples of both numbers 4 and 6. 12 and 24 are common multiples of 4 and 6. 12 is the least among common multiples. Therefore, 12 is called the least common multiple (lcm) of 4 and 6.

The least common multiple of two non-zero integers a and b, denoted by lcm(a , b), is the positive integer m satisfying following conditions:

(i) $a \mid m$ and $b \mid m$, and

(ii) If $a \mid c$ and $b \mid c$, with $c > 0$, then $m \leq c$

41. Theorem :

Given integers a and b (both a and b are not zero), there exist integers x and y such that gcd $(a, b) = ax + by$.

Before getting into formal proof of this theorem, let us see some examples.

$$\gcd(12, 16) = 4 \qquad (a = 12, b = 16)$$
$$4 = 12 \times (-1) + 16 \times (1) \qquad (x = -1, y = 1)$$

$$\gcd(8, 18) = 2 \qquad (a = 8, b = 18)$$
$$2 = 8 \times (-2) + 18 \times (1) \qquad (x = -2, y = 1)$$

$$\gcd(6, 15) = 3 \qquad (a = 6, b = 15)$$
$$3 = 6 \times (-2) + 15 \times (1) \qquad (x = -2, y = 1)$$

Now let us formally prove this theorem.

Considers the set $S = \{au + bv \mid au + bv > 0 ; u, v \text{ are integers}\}$.

If $a > 0$, take $u = 1$ and $v = 0$.

Then, $au + bv = a > 0$

Thus, $a \in S$

If $a < 0$, take $u = -1$ and $v = 0$.

Then, $au + bv = -a > 0$

Thus, $-a \in S$

If $a = 0$, we can take u and v in the similar manner and we get b (or $-b$) which belongs to S. ($\because b \neq 0$ in this case as both a and b are not zero.)

Since a and b both are not zero, S is obviously non- empty set.

From the well - ordering principle, it follows that S has a least element (Refer paragraph 9 of this chapter). Let d be the least element.

Thus, there exist integers x and y for which

$$d = ax + by \quad \dots \text{(i)}$$

Now let us examine properties of d, the least element of S.

If a is divided by d we obtain integers q and r such that $a = dq + r, 0 \le r < d$

Hence, $r = a - dq = a - (ax + by)q$

$= a(1 - qx) + b(-qy)$

From this form of r, you can see that $r \in S$ if $r > 0$.

Further $r < d$. But d is the smallest element of S. Hence, we arrive at a contradiction.

Thus, r cannot be greater than zero and only possibility is $r = 0$.

Therefore, $a = dq$ or $d \mid a$

Similarly, $d \mid b$

Hence, $d \mid a$ and $d \mid b$

Let c be a common divisor of a and b.

Then, $c \mid d$ $[\because d = ax + by]$

(Refer to paragraph 20 of this chapter)

Thus, $|c| \le |d|$ (Refer paragraph 19 of this chapter)

or, $|c| \le d$ $[\because d > 0]$

Thus, d is the greatest of common divisor of a and b. .... (ii)

From (i) and (ii), it follows that $\gcd(a, b) = ax + by$ for some integers x and y.

42. Theorem :

If a and b are given integers (a and b are not both zero), then the set $T = \{ax + by \mid x, y \text{ are integers}\}$ is precisely the set of all multiples of $d = \gcd(a, b)$.

Before getting into formal proof of the theorem let us see few examples.

$\gcd(6, 15) = 3$ $a = 6, b = 15$

Now, $ax + by = 21$ (for $x = 1, y = 1$)

$= -6$ (for $x = -1, y = 0$)

$= 15$ (for $x = 0, y = 1$)

$= 24$ (for $x = -1, y = 2$)

$= 42$ (for $x = -3, y = 4$)

You can clearly see that all these numbers, 21, – 6, 15, 24 and 42, are multiples of 3.

Now let us formally prove the theorem.

By definition of gcd, $d \mid a$ and $d \mid b$.

Hence, for any member $ax + by$ of T, $d \mid ax + by$.

Thus, each member of T is a multiple of d. .... (i)

By preceding theorem,

$$d = ax_0 + by_0 \qquad \text{(for some integers } x_0 \text{ and } y_0\text{)}$$

Any multiple of d can be written as nd where n is an integer.

$$nd = n(ax_0 + by_0) = a(nx_0) + b(ny_0)$$

Thus, nd lies in T. ....(ii)

Now, as each member of T is a multiple of d (By (i)) and each multiple of d lies in T (By (ii)), it is established that T is precisely the set of all multiples of d.

43. Theorem :

a and b are integers (a and b are not both zero). Then a and b are relatively prime if and only if there exist integers x and y such that $ax + by = 1$.

Proof : Suppose a and b are relatively prime.

Then, by definition $\gcd(a, b) = 1$.

Hence from theorem at paragraph 41, it follows that there exist integer x and y such that $ax + by = 1$.

Conversely, suppose that there exist integers x and y such that $ax + by = 1$.

Let $\quad d = \gcd(a, b)$

As $d \mid a$ and $d \mid b$ (by definition of gcd), it implies that $d \mid ax + by$.

or, $\quad d \mid 1 \qquad [\because ax + by = 1]$

Hence, $\quad d = 1 \qquad$ (Refer para 15. By definition, d is a positive integer.)

Thus, a and b are relatively prime.

44. Theorem :

If $\gcd(a, b) = d$, then $\gcd\left(\frac{a}{d}, \frac{b}{d}\right) = 1$

Proof : $\gcd(a, b) = d$

Hence, $d \mid a$ and $d \mid b$.

Thus, both $\frac{a}{d}$ and $\frac{b}{d}$ are integers.

As $\gcd(a, b) = d$, it follows from theorem at paragraph 41 that there exist integers x and y such that $ax + by = d$

or, $$\left(\frac{a}{d}\right)x + \left(\frac{b}{d}\right)y = 1$$

As $\frac{a}{d}$ and $\frac{b}{d}$ are integers, it follows from preceding theorem at paragraph 43 that $\frac{a}{d}$ and $\frac{b}{d}$ are relatively prime.

Hence, $\gcd\left(\frac{a}{d}, \frac{b}{d}\right) = 1$.

45. Suppose integers *a* and *b* divide integer *c*.

Does *ab* divide *c*?

Let us take some examples to understood it.

$$4 \mid 12$$

$$6 \mid 12$$

$$4 \times 6 = 24$$

But $24 \nmid 12$

Please note that 4 and 6 are not relatively prime.

$$10 \mid 20$$

$$5 \mid 20$$

$$10 \times 5 = 50,\ 50 \nmid 20$$

Please note that 10 and 5 are not relatively prime.

$$3 \mid 45$$

$$5 \mid 45$$

and $3 \times 5 = 15, 15 \mid 45$

Please note that 3 and 5 are relatively prime.

46. Theorem :

If $a \mid c$ and $b \mid c$ with $\gcd(a, b) = 1$, then $ab \mid c$.

Proof : $a \mid c$ and $b \mid c$

Therefore, there exist integers *m* and *n* such that

$$c = am$$

$$c = bn$$

$$\gcd(a, b) = 1.$$

Hence, there exist integers *x* and *y* such that $ax + by = 1$

Now, $c = c \times 1 = c(ax + by) = cax + cby$

$= (bn)\,ax + (am)by = ab(nx + my)$

Thus, $ab \mid c$

47. Euclid's lemma :

If $a \mid bc$ with $\gcd(a, b) = 1$, then $a \mid c$.

Proof : $\gcd(a, b) = 1$

Hence, there exist integers x and y such that $ax + by = 1$.

$$c = c \times 1 = c(ax + by)$$
$$= cax + cby$$
$$a \mid ca \text{ and } a \mid cb$$

Hence, $a \mid c$.

48. Please note that the preceding theorem at paragraph 47 is not a trivial statement.

Let's see few examples.

$$5 \mid 40$$
$$40 = 10 \times 4$$

But $5 \nmid 4$

Please note that $\gcd(5, 10) \neq 1$.

$$6 \mid 60$$
$$60 = 3 \times 20$$

But $6 \nmid 20$

Please note that $\gcd(6, 3) \neq 1$.

$$4 \mid 36$$
$$36 = 2 \times 18$$

But $4 \nmid 18$

Please note that $\gcd(4, 2) \neq 1$.

$$6 \mid 84$$
$$84 = 7 \times 12$$

Here $6 \mid 12$

Please note that $\gcd(6, 7) = 1$.

49. Theorem :

a and b are integers, not both zero. For a positive integer d, $d = \gcd(a, b)$ if and only if

(a) $d \mid a$ and $d \mid b$

(b) whenever $c \mid a$ and $c \mid b$, then $c \mid d$

Proof : Let $d = \gcd(a, b)$

Then, $d \mid a$ and $d \mid b$

Obviously there exist integers x and y such that $d = ax + by$.

If $c \mid a$ and $c \mid b$, then $c \mid (ax + by)$ or $c \mid d$.

Conversely, if $d \mid a$ and $d \mid b$, then d is a common divisor of a and b.

Also, it is given that for any common divisor c of a and b, $c \mid d$.

From result at para 19, it follows that

$$|c| \leq |d|$$

or, $$|c| \leq d \qquad [\because d \text{ is a positive integers}]$$

Hence, $$d = \gcd(a, b).$$

50. Find $\gcd(4, 6)$.

1, 2 and 4 are divisors of 4.

1, 2, 3 and 6 are divisors of 6.

Hence, 1 and 2 are common divisors of 4 and 6.

Thus, 2 is the greatest common divisor of 4 and 6.

$$\gcd(4, 6) = 2$$

You can see that finding gcd(4, 6) is quite straightforward.

Now, find $\gcd(12, 16)$.

1, 2, 3, 4, 6 and 12 are divisors of 12.

1, 2, 4, 8 and 16 are divisors of 16.

Hence, 1, 2 and 4 are common divisors of 12 and 16.

Thus, 4 is the greatest common divisor of 12 and 16.

Now, find $\gcd(24, 54)$.

1, 2, 3, 4, 6, 8, 12 and 24 are divisors of 24.

1, 2, 3, 6, 9, 18, 27 and 54 are divisors of 54.

Hence, 1, 2, 3 and 6 are common divisors of 24 and 54.

Thus, 6 is the greatest common divisor of 24 and 54.

You can clearly see that finding greatest common divisor becomes cumbersome for larger numbers.

Is there an alternate way to find greatest common divisor?

The next theorem provides the alternate method.

51. If $a = qb + r$, then $\gcd(a, b) = \gcd(b, r)$.

Proof : Let $d = \gcd(a, b)$

Then, $d \mid a$ and $d \mid b$

Hence, $d \mid r$ $[\because r = a - qb]$

Thus, d is a common divisor of b and r.

Suppose, c is a common divisor of b and r.

Then, $c \mid a$ $[\because a = qb + r]$

Thus, $c \mid a$ and $c \mid b$

c is a common divisor of a and b.

As $d = \gcd(a, b)$, $c \le d$

Thus, d is the greatest of common divisor of b and r.

Hence,
$$\gcd(b, r) = d$$
$$= \gcd(a, b)$$

52. Find $\gcd(24, 54)$.

$$54 = 24 \times 2 + 6$$

Hence, $\gcd(24, 54)$ (By preceding theorem at para 51)

$$= \gcd(24, 6)$$

$$6 \mid 24$$

$$\gcd(24, 6) = 6$$

Thus, $\gcd(24, 54) = 6$

You can clearly see that finding gcd by this method is quite simple.

Let's take another example.

Find $\gcd(36, 96)$

$$96 = 36 \times 2 + 24$$

Hence, $\gcd(96, 36) = \gcd(36, 24)$

$$36 = 24 \times 1 + 12$$

Hence, $\gcd(36, 24) = \gcd(24, 12)$

$$12 \mid 24$$

Hence, $\gcd(24, 12) = 12$

Thus, $\gcd(96, 36) = 12$

By doing this process iteratively, we can find the greatest common divisor of any two integers.

53. Let's rewrite the theorem at para 41.

Theorem : Given integers a and b (a and b are both not zero), there exist integers x and y such that $\gcd(a, b) = ax + by$

Please note that this is an existence theorem. It does not tell us how to find x and y. However, using the method given in the preceding paragraph we can find x and y.

Let's find gcd(96, 36).

$$96 = 36 \times 2 + 24 \quad \text{.... (i)}$$

$$36 = 24 \times 1 + 12 \quad \text{.... (ii)}$$

$$\gcd(96, 36) = \gcd(36, 24)$$
$$= \gcd(24, 12) = 12$$

Now,
$$12 = 36 - 24 \times 1 \quad \text{[By (ii)]}$$
$$= 36 - (96 - 36 \times 2) \quad \text{[By (i)]}$$
$$= 96 \times (-1) + 36 \times 3$$

Thus, $x = -1$ and $y = 3$

54. For any given integers a and b, we can apply the method given in para 52 and find $\gcd(a, b)$. This method of finding the greatest common divisor is called the Euclidean Algorithm.

55. Theorem :

If $n > 0$, then $\gcd(na, nb) = n\ \gcd(a, b)$

Proof : $\gcd(na, nb)$ is the smallest positive integer of the form $(na)x + (nb)y$ (Refer to theorem at para 41).

But then it is n times the smallest positive integer of the form $ax + by$.

Hence, $\gcd(na, nb) = n\ \gcd(a, b)$.

56. We discussed least common multiple (lcm) in para 40 of this chapter. Is there any **correlation** between gcd and lcm?

Consider integers $a = 12$ and $b = 20$.

$$\gcd(a, b) = 4$$

What's lcm (a, b)?

It is obvious that $\text{lcm}(a, b) \le |ab|$.

12, 24, 36, 48, 60, 72, ... are multiples of 12.

20, 40, 60, 80, 100, ... are of 20.

It follows from the definition of lcm that 60 is the lcm of 12 and 20.

So,
$$\gcd(a, b) = 4 \text{ and } \text{lcm}(a, b) = 60$$
$$\gcd(a, b) \times \text{lcm}(a, b) = 4 \times 60 = 240$$

$$ab = 12 \times 20 = 240$$

Thus, $$\gcd(a, b) \times \text{lcm}(a, b) = ab$$

Is this result true in general?

It turns out that the result is indeed true in general.

57. Theorem :

For positive integers a and b,

$$\gcd(a, b) \times \text{lcm}(a, b) = ab$$

Proof : Let $\gcd(a, b) = d$

So, $$a = dr$$

$$b = ds \qquad \text{(for some integers } r \text{ and } s\text{)}$$

Let, $$m = \frac{ab}{d} = \frac{(dr)b}{d} = rb$$

Also, $$m = \frac{ab}{d} = \frac{a(ds)}{d} = as$$

Thus, m is a multiple of both a and b.

Let c be a positive common multiple of a and b.

Thus $a \mid c$ and $b \mid c$

Now, $$\frac{c}{m} = \frac{cd}{md} = \frac{cd}{ab}$$

$$d = \gcd(a, b)$$

Hence, $d = ax + by$ for some integers x and y

Now, $$\frac{c}{m} = \frac{cd}{md} = \frac{cd}{ab} = \frac{c}{ab}(ax + by)$$

$$= \frac{cax}{ab} + \frac{cby}{ab} = \left(\frac{c}{b}\right)x + \left(\frac{c}{a}\right)y$$

$$= ux + vy \qquad (\because a \mid c \text{ and } b \mid c)$$

for some integers u and v.

Thus, $$m \mid c$$

Hence, $$m \leq c$$

Thus, m is the least among all common multiples of a and b.

Hence, by definition,

$$\text{lcm}(a, b) = m = \frac{ab}{d}$$

or, $$\gcd(a, b) \times \text{lcm}(a, b) = ab$$

58. Corollary : For positive integers a and b, $\text{lcm}(a, b) = ab$ if and only if $\gcd(a, b) = 1$

Proof : By preceding theorem at para 57,

$$\gcd(a, b) \times \text{lcm}(a, b) = ab$$

Hence, if $\gcd(a, b) = 1$, $\text{lcm}(a, b) = ab$

Also if $\text{lcm}(a, b) = ab$, it implies that $\gcd(a, b) = 1$.

59. How do you compute lcm of any two integers?

Compute their gcd by Euclidem Algorithm and then use theorem at para 57 to compute their lcm.

Solved Examples

1. Which of the following numbers is divisible by 2?

(i) 36 (ii) 59 (iii) 26 (iv) 12945

Sol. Unit digits of 36 and 26 are even.

Hence, 36 and 26 are divisible by 2

59 and 12945 are not divisible by 2 as their unit digits are not divisible by 2.

2. Which of the following numbers is divisible by 3?

(i) 108 (ii) 9531

(iii) 10254 (iv) 111007

Sol. (i) Sum of digits of 108 = 9

9 is divisible by 3.

Hence, 108 is divisible by 3.

(ii) Sum of digits of 9531 = 18

18 is divisible by 3.

Hence, 9531 is divisible by 3.

(iii) Sum of digits of 10254 = 12

12 is divisible by 3.

Hence, 10254 is divisible by 3.

(iv) Sum of digits of 111007 = 10

10 is not divisible by 3.

Hence, 111007 is not divisible by 3.

3. Which of the following numbers is divisible by 4 but not by 8?

(i) 116 (ii) 12004 (iii) 10284 (iv) 1675208

Sol. (i) Number formed by last two digits is 16.

16 is divisible by 4.

Hence, 116 is divisible by 4.

Number formed by last 3 digits is 116.

116 is not divisible by 8.

Hence, 116 is divisible by 4 but not by 8.

(ii) Number formed by last two digits is 04.

4 is divisible by 4.

Hence, 12004 is divisible by 4.

Number formed by last 3 digits is 004.

4 is not divisible by 8.

Hence, 12004 is divisible by 4 but not by 8.

(iii) Number formed by last two digits is 84.

84 is divisible by 4.

Hence, 10284 is divisible by 4.

Number formed by last 3 digits is 284.

284 is not divisible by 8.

Hence, 10284 is divisible by 4 but not by 8.

(iv) Number formed by last two digits is 08.

8 is divisible by 4.

Hence, 1675208 is divisible by 4.

Number formed by last 3 digits is 208.

208 is divisible by 8.

Hence, 1675208 is divisible by both 4 and 8.

4. Which of the following numbers is divisible by 3 but not by 9?

(i) 312 (ii) 50213 (iii) 39015 (iv) 120741

Sol. (i) Sum of digits of 312 = 6

6 is divisible by 3 but not by 9.

Hence, 312 is divisible by 3 but not by 9.

(ii) Sum of digits of 50213 = 11

11 is neither divisible by 3 nor by 9.

Hence, 50213 is not divisible by either 3 or 9.

(iii) Sum of digits of 39015 = 18

18 is divisible by both 3 and 9.

Hence, 39015 is divisible by both 3 and 9.

(iv) Sum of digits of 120741 = 15

15 is divisible by 3 but not by 9.

Hence, 120741 is divisible by 3 but not by 9.

5. Which of the following numbers is divisible by 11?

(i) 2157 (ii) 591250

(iii) 9120357 (iv) 111111

Sol. (i) For the number 2157,

Sum of digits at odd places $= 7 + 1 = 8$

Sum of digits at even places $= 5 + 2 = 7$

Difference $= 8 - 7 = 1$

1 is not divisible by 11.

Hence, 2157 is not divisible by 11.

(ii) For the number 591250,

Sum of digits at odd places $= 0 + 2 + 9 = 11$

Sum of digits at even places $= 5 + 1 + 5 = 11$

Difference $= 11 - 11 = 0$

0 is divisible by 11

Hence, 591250 is divisible by 11.

(iii) For 9120357,

Sum of digits at odd places $= 7 + 3 + 2 + 9 = 21$

Sum of digits at even places $= 5 + 0 + 1 = 6$

Difference $= 21 - 6 = 15$

15 is not divisible by 11.

Hence, 9120357 is not divisible by 11.

(iv) For 111111,

Sum of digits at odd places $= 1 + 1 + 1 = 3$

Sum of digits at even places $= 1 + 1 + 1 = 3$

Difference $= 0$

0 is divisible by 11.

Hence, 111111 is divisible by 11.

6. Which of the following numbers is divisible by 15?

(i) 515 (ii) 645 (iii) 1200 (iv) 1710

Sol. $15 = 3 \times 5$

3 and 5 are relatively prime.

Hence, for a number to be divisible by 15, the number should be divisible by both 3 and 5.

(i) 515

Sum of digits = 11

11 is not divisible by 3.

Hence, 515 is not divisible by 3.

Accordingly, 515 is not divisible by 15.

(ii) 645

Sum of digits = 15

15 is divisible by 3.

Hence, 645 is divisible by 3.

Also, unit digit of 645 is 5.

Hence, 645 is divisible by 5.

Thus, 645 is divisible by both 3 and 5.

Hence, 645 is divisible by 15.

(iii) 1200

Sum of digits = 3

3 is divisible by 3.

Hence, 1200 is divisible by 3.

Also, 1200 is divisible by 5 because its unit digit is 0.

Hence, 1200 is divisible by 15.

(iv) 1710

Sum of digits = 9

9 is divisible by 3.

Hence, 1710 is divisible by 3.

Also, 1710 is divisible by 5 because its unit digit is 0.

Hence, 1710 is divisible by 15.

7. For any integer $N = 10X + Y$, N is divisible by 7 if and only if $X + 5Y$ is divisible by 7. Prove.

Sol. $N = 10X + Y = 10(X + 5Y) - 49Y$

$$7 \mid 49Y$$

Hence, $7 \mid N$ if and only if $7 \mid (X + 5Y)$.

This result can be used for verifying divisibility by 7.

(i) $741 = 74 \times 10 + 1$, $X = 74$, $Y = 1$

$$X + 5Y = 74 + 5 = 79$$

79 is not divisible by 7. Hence, 741 is not divisible by 7.

(ii) $1197 = 119 \times 10 + 7$, $X = 119$, $Y = 7$

$$X + 5Y = 119 + 5 \times 7 = 154$$

154 is divisible by 7. Hence, 1197 is divisible by 7.

8. Prove that if $a \mid b$ then $a \mid bc$ for any integers a, b, c.

Sol. As $a \mid b$ there exists integer q such that

$$b = aq$$

Hence, $bc = aqc$

or, $bc = a(qc)$

Thus, $a \mid bc$

9. Prove that if $a \mid b$ and $a \mid c$ then $a^2 \mid bc$ for any integers a, b, c.

Sol. As $a \mid b$ and $a \mid c$ there exist integers q and r such that

$$b = aq$$

and $c = ar$

Hence, $bc = a^2qr = a^2(qr)$

Hence $a^2 \mid bc$

10. Which of the following numbers has an odd number of factors?

(i) 98 (ii) 626 (iii) 919 (iv) 1600

Sol. Among the given numbers, only 1600 is a perfect square.

Hence, 1600 has an odd number of factors.

All the other numbers have an even number of factors.

11. Prove that the cube of any integer has one of the forms $9n$, $9n + 1$ or $9n + 8$.

Sol. We know that any integer is of one of the forms:

$9n, 9n + 1, 9n + 2, 9n + 3, 9n + 4, 9n + 5, 9n + 6, 9n + 7$ or $9n + 8$

Now, $(9n)^3 = 729n^3 = 9(81n^3)$

$$(9n + 1)^3 = (9n)^3 + (1)^3 + 3(9n)^2 1 + 3(9n)(1^2)$$

$$= (9n)^3 + 3(9n)^2 + 3(9n) + 1$$

$$= 9m + 1 \text{ for some integer } m$$

Similarly,

$$(9n+2)^3 = 9m+8, \quad \text{for some integer } m$$
$$(9n+3)^3 = 9m, \quad \text{for some integer } m$$
$$(9n+4)^3 = 9m+1, \quad \text{for some integer } m$$
$$(9n+5)^3 = 9m+8, \quad \text{for some integer } m$$
$$(9n+6)^3 = 9m, \quad \text{for some integer } m$$
$$(9n+7)^3 = 9m+1, \quad \text{for some integer } m$$
$$(9n+8)^3 = 9m+8, \quad \text{for some integer } m$$

Thus, we can see that the cube always has one of the forms $9m, 9m+1$ or $9m+8$.

12. Prove that $\dfrac{a(a^2+2)}{3}$ is an integer for all integers a, $a>1$.

Sol. a has one of the forms $3n$, $3n+1$ or $3n+2$.

If $a=3n$,

$$\frac{a(a^2+2)}{3} = \frac{3n[(3n)^2+2]}{3} = n(9n^2+2), \text{ an integer}$$

If $a=3n+1$,

$$\frac{a(a^2+2)}{3} = \frac{(3n+1)\,[(3n+1)^2+2]}{3}$$
$$= \frac{(3n+1)\,(9n^2+6n+3)}{3}$$
$$= (3n+1)\,(3n^2+2n+1), \text{ an integer}$$

If $a=3n+2$,

$$\frac{a(a^2+2)}{3} = \frac{(3n+2)\,[(3n+2)^2+2]}{3}$$
$$= \frac{(3n+2)\,[9n^2+12n+4+2]}{3}$$
$$= \frac{(3n+2)\,(9n^2+12n+6)}{3}$$
$$= (3n+2)\,(3n^2+4n+2), \text{ an integer}$$

Hence, $\dfrac{a(a^2+2)}{3}$ is always an integer.

13. Prove that $\dfrac{n(n+1)\,(2n+1)}{6}$ is an integer for all integers $n>1$.

Sol. We know that n is of one of the forms $6k$, $6k+1, 6k+2, 6k+3, 6k+4$ or $6k+5$.

Now, let's consider all possible forms of n.

(i) $n = 6k$

$$\frac{n(n+1)(2n+1)}{6} = \frac{6k(6k+1)(12k+1)}{6}$$

$$= k(6k+1)(12k+1), \text{ an integer}$$

(ii) $n = 6k+1$

$$\frac{n(n+1)(2n+1)}{6} = \frac{(6k+1)(6k+2)(12k+3)}{6}$$

$$= (6k+1)(3k+1)(4k+1), \text{ an integer}$$

(iii) $n = 6k+2$

$$\frac{n(n+1)(2n+1)}{6} = \frac{(6k+2)(6k+3)(12k+5)}{6}$$

$$= (3k+1)(2k+1)(12k+5), \text{ an integer}$$

(iv) $n = 6k+3$

$$\frac{n(n+1)(2n+1)}{6} = \frac{(6k+3)(6k+4)(12k+7)}{6}$$

$$= (2k+1)(3k+2)(12k+7), \text{ an integer}$$

(v) $n = 6k+4$

$$\frac{n(n+1)(2n+1)}{6} = \frac{(6k+4)(6k+5)(12k+9)}{6}$$

$$= (3k+2)(6k+5)(4k+3), \text{ an integer}$$

(vi) $n = 6k+5$

$$\frac{n(n+1)(2n+1)}{6} = \frac{(6k+5)(6k+6)(12k+11)}{6}$$

$$= (6k+5)(k+1)(12k+11), \text{ an integer}$$

Hence, $\frac{n(n+1)(2n+1)}{6}$ is always an integer.

14. Prove that no integer in the following sequence is a perfect square.

11, 111, 1111, …

Sol.

$$11 = 8 + 3$$

$$111 = 108 + 3$$

$$1111 = 1108 + 3$$

$$111....111 = 111....108 + 3$$

Thus, all integers in this sequence are of the form $4n + 3$.

But we know that the square of an integer can only be of the form $4n$ or $4n + 1$.

Hence, no integer in the given sequence is a perfect square.

15. Prove that $n^4 + 4n^2 + 11$ is of the form $16m$ for any odd integer *n*.

Sol. As *n* is an odd integer, it has one of the forms $8m+1$, $8m+3$, $8m+5$ or $8m+7$.

$$(8m+1)^2 = 64m^2 + 16m + 1$$

$$(8m+3)^2 = 64m^2 + 48m + 9$$

$$(8m+5)^2 = 64m^2 + 80m + 25$$

$$(8m+7)^2 = 64m^2 + 112m + 49$$

All these squares are of the form $8k+1$.

Let $n^2 = 8k+1$

Hence, $n^4 + 4n^2 + 11 = (8k+1)^2 + 4(8k+1) + 11$

$$= 64k^2 + 16k + 1 + 32k + 4 + 11$$

$$= (64k^2 + 48k + 16)$$

$$= 16(4k^2 + 3k + 1)$$

Hence, $n^4 + 4n^2 + 11$ is of the form $16m$.

16. Prove that $a^2 + (a+2)^2 + (a+4)^2 + 1$ is divisible by 12, for any odd integer *a*.

Sol. As *a* is an odd integer, it has one of the forms $6k+1$, $6k+3$ or $6k+5$.

Now let's consider all possible forms

(i) $a = 6k+1$

$$a^2 + (a+2)^2 + (a+4)^2 + 1 = (6k+1)^2 + (6k+3)^2 + (6k+5)^2 + 1$$

$$= (36k^2 + 12k + 1) + (36k^2 + 36k + 9) + (36k^2 + 60k + 25) + 1$$

$$= 108k^2 + 108k + 36 = 12(9k^2 + 9k + 3)$$

Thus, in this case, the given expression is divisible by 12.

(ii) $a = 6k+3$

$$a^2 + (a+2)^2 + (a+4)^2 + 1 = (6k+3)^2 + (6k+5)^2 + (6k+7)^2 + 1$$

$$= (36k^2 + 36k + 9) + (36k^2 + 60k + 25) + (36k^2 + 84k + 49) + 1$$

$$= 108k^2 + 180k + 84$$

$$= 12(9k^2 + 15k + 7)$$

Thus, in this case, the given expression is divisible by 12.

(iii) $a = 6k+5$

$$a^2 + (a+2)^2 + (a+4)^2 + 1 = (6k+5)^2 + (6k+7)^2 + (6k+9)^2 + 1$$

$$= (36k^2 + 60k + 25) + (36k^2 + 84k + 49) + (36k^2 + 108k + 81) + 1$$

$$= 108k^2 + 252k + 156$$

$$=12(9k^2+21k+13)$$

Thus, in this case, the given expression is divisible by 12.

Hence, the given expression is divisible by 12 for any odd integer a.

17. Prove that n^5-n is divisible by 30, for any integer n.

Sol. Let
$$N=n^5-n=n(n^4-1)$$
$$=n(n^2-1)(n^2+1)$$

n is of one of the forms $5k$, $5k+1$, $5k+2$, $5k+3$ or $5k+4$.

Hence, n^2 is of one of the forms $5k$, $5k+1$, $5k+4$.

If n is of the form $5k$, N is obviously divisible by 5.

If n is not of the form $5k$, n^2 obviously is of one of the forms $5k+1$ or $5k+4$.

In either case ($5k+1$ or $5k+4$ forms), $(n^2-1)(n^2+1)$ is always divisible by 5.

($\because 5 \mid n^2-1$ if n^2 is of the form $5k+1$ and $5 \mid n^2+1$ if n^2 is of the form $5k+4$)

Thus, N is always divisible by 5.

Also, n is of one of the forms $6k$, $6k+1$, $6k+2$, $6k+3$, $6k+4$ or $6k+5$.

If n is of the form $6k$, N is divisible by 6.

If n is not of the form $6k$, n^2 is of one of the forms $6k+1$, $6k+3$, $6k+4$.

(i) If $n^2=6k+1$,
$$(n^2-1)(n^2+1)=(6k+1-1)(6k+1+1)=6k(6k+2)$$

Thus, N is divisible by 6.

(ii) If $n^2=6k+3$ (Only possible form of n in this case is $6m+3$)
$$N=n(n^2-1)(n^2+1)$$
$$=(6m+3)(6k+3-1)(6k+3+1)$$
$$=(6m+3)(6k+2)(6k+4)$$
$$=12(2m+1)(3k+1)(3k+2)$$

Thus, N is divisible by 6.

(iii) If $n^2=6k+4$ (Only possible form of n in this case is $6m+2$ or $6m+4$)
$$(n^2-1)(n^2+1)=(6k+4-1)(6k+4+1)$$
$$=(6k+3)(6k+5)=3(2k+1)(6k+5)$$

Also n is of the form $6m+2$ or $6m+4$.

Thus, N is divisible by 6.

From the above, it is evident that N is divisible by both 5 and 6.

As 5 and 6 are relatively prime, N is divisible by their product *i.e.*, 30.

18. Find the smallest natural number such that its first digit is 4 and the number obtained by moving this 4 to the last place is 1/4 of the given number.

Sol. Let N be the given number.

Suppose N has $n+1$ digits.

So $N = 4a_{n-1}a_{n-2}\ldots a_1a_0$ $\quad$ ($\because 4, a_{n-1}, a_{n-2}, \ldots, a_1, a_0$ are digits of N.)

$= 4\times 10^n + (a_{n-1}a_{n-2}\ldots a_1a_0)$

$= 4\times 10^n + x$ $\quad$ ...(i) $\quad$ (Let $x = a_{n-1}a_{n-2}\ldots a_1a_0$)

Number obtained by moving 4 to the last place

$$= a_{n-1}a_{n-2}\ldots a_1a_0 4$$
$$= (a_{n-1}10^n + a_{n-2}10^{n-1} + \ldots + a_1 10^2 + a_0 10^1) + 4$$
$$= 10(a_{n-1}10^{n-1} + a_{n-2}10^{n-2} + \ldots + a_1 10 + a_0) + 4$$
$$= 10x + 4 \quad \text{...(ii)}$$

It is given that the number obtained by moving 4 to the last place $= \dfrac{N}{4}$

or, $\quad 10x + 4 = \dfrac{(4\times 10^n + x)}{4}$ $\quad$ [by (i) and (ii)]

or, $\quad 40x + 16 = 4\times 10^n + x$

or, $\quad 39x = 4\times (10^n - 4)$

or, $\quad 39x = 4\times 99\ldots 96$ $\quad$ (9 appears $n-1$ times)

or, $\quad 13x = 4\times 33\ldots 32$ $\quad$ (3 appears $n-1$ times)

By verifying the cases for $n = 1, 2, 3, \ldots.$, we see that the minimum possible value of n is 5.

$$33332 \div 13 = 2564$$

Hence, $\quad x = 4\times 2564 = 10256$

Thus, $\quad N = 410256$

410256 is the desired number.

19. Let *abcdef* be a 6-digit integer such that *defabc* is 6-times the value of *abcdef*. What is the value of $a+b+c+d+e+f$?

Sol. $abcdef = a\times 10^5 + b\times 10^4 + c\times 10^3 + d\times 10^2 + e\times 10^1 + f$

$= 10^3(a\times 10^2 + b\times 10^1 + c) + (d\times 10^2 + e\times 10^1 + f)$

$= 1000(abc) + def$

Similarly, $\quad defabc = 1000(def) + abc$

It is given that $\quad defabc = 6\times abcdef$

or, $1000(def)+abc=6[1000(abc)+def]$

or, $(994)(def)=(5999)(abc)$

or, $(142)(def)=(857)(abc)$

Thus, $857\,|\,(142)(def)$

142 and 857 are relatively prime.

Thus, $857\,|\,def$

$2\times 857>1000$ and it is not a 3-digit number.

Hence, $def=857$

Thus, $abc=142$

Therefore, $a+b+c+d+e+f=1+4+2+8+5+7=27$

20. $x=(1101)_2$

$y=(110)_2$

What is the value of x^2-y^2?

Sol. Please note that x and y are in binary representation of integers (base 2).

$$x=(1101)_2$$
$$=1\times 2^3+1\times 2^2+0\times 2^1+1\times 2^0$$
$$=8+4+0+1=13$$
$$y=(110)_2=1\times 2^2+1\times 2^1+0\times 2^0$$
$$=4+2+0=6$$
$$x^2-y^2=13^2-6^2=169-36=133$$

133 can be represented in binary form as under.

$$133=128+4+1=2^7+2^2+1$$
$$=1\times 2^7+0\times 2^6+0\times 2^5+0\times 2^4+0\times 2^3+1\times 2^2+0\times 2^1+1$$
$$=(10000101)_2$$

21. $(10x010)_2-(11y1)_2=(10z)_2$

What are the possible values of x, y and z respectively?

Sol.

$$(10x010)_2=1\times 2^5+0\times 2^4+x\times 2^3+0\times 2^2+1\times 2^1+0$$
$$=32+0+8x+0+2+0=8x+34$$
$$(11y1)_2=1\times 2^3+1\times 2^2+y\times 2^1+1$$
$$=8+4+2y+1=2y+13$$
$$(10z)_2=1\times 2^2+0\times 2^1+z$$
$$=4+0+z=z+4$$
$$(8x+34)-(2y+13)=z+4$$

or, $8x-2y+21=z+4$

or, $8x-2y-z=-17$

or, $2y+z-8x=17$

As x, y, z are binary digits, they can take only 0 and 1 as their values.

There are no possible solutions for this equation consisting of binary digits x, y and z.

Hence, there are no possible values of x, y and z.

22. Prove that $\gcd(a, a+1)=1$ for any integer a.

Sol. Let $d=\gcd(a, a+1)$

Hence, $d \mid a$

and $d \mid a+1$

Hence, $d \mid [(a+1)-a]$

or, $d \mid 1$

$\therefore$ $d=\pm 1$

By definition gcd is a positive integer.

Hence, $d=1$.

23. For any integer a, $\gcd(5a+2, 7a+3)=1$. Prove.

Sol. Let $d=\gcd(5a+2, 7a+3)$

Hence, $d \mid 5a+2$

and $d \mid 7a+3$

Hence, $d \mid [5(7a+3)-7(5a+2)]$

or, $d \mid [(35a+15)-(35a+14)]$

or, $d \mid 1$

Hence, $d=1$.

24. $\gcd(a, b)=1$ and $\gcd(a, c)=1$ for integers a, b, c. Prove that $\gcd(a, bc)=1$.

Sol. $\gcd(a, b)=1$ and $\gcd(a, c)=1$

Hence, there exist integers x, y, u, v such that

$$ax+by=1$$

$$au+cv=1$$

or, $(ax+by)(au+cv)=1$

or, $a(aux+cvx+byu)+bc(yv)=1$

Thus, there exist integers $m=(aux+cvx+byu)$ and $n=(yv)$ such that

$$am+bcn=1$$

This is possible if and only if $\gcd(a, bc)=1$.

25. Find gcd(32, 144). Also find $lcm(32, 144)$.

Sol. We use Euclidean Algorithm to find gcd(32, 144).

$$144 = 32 \times 4 + 16$$

$$32 = 16 \times 2 + 0$$

Hence, $\gcd(32, 144) = \gcd(32, 16) = 16$

Also, $16 = 144 - 32 \times 4$

$$= (144) \times 1 + 32 \times (-4)$$

Thus, 16 can be written as $ax + by = 32 \times (-4) + 144 \times 1$

where $x = -4$, $y = 1$ $(a = 32, b = 144)$

We know that $\gcd(a, b) \times lcm(a, b) = a \times b$

Hence, $lcm(32, 144) = \dfrac{32 \times 144}{16} = 2 \times 144 = 288$

26. Let $S(M)$ denote the sum of the digits of a positive integer M written in base 10. Let N be the smallest positive integer such that $S(N) = 2013$. What is the value of N?

Sol. In order to find the smallest positive integer, N should have the least number of digits.

Therefore, N should have as many '9' as possible.

We have, $223 \times 9 = 2007$, and $6 + 2007 = 2013$

$\therefore$ N is $6\underbrace{99......9}_{223 \text{ times } '9'}$

There is no number lesser than this number, with sum of digits as 2013.

27. Let $S_n = n^2 + 20n + 12$. n is positive integer. What is the sum of all possible values of n for which S_n is a perfect square?

Sol. $S_n = n^2 + 20n + 12 = (n + 10)^2 - 88$

Let $S_n = x^2$

Or, $n^2 + 20n + 12 = x^2$

Or, $(n + 10)^2 - 88 = x^2$

Or, $(n + 10)^2 - x^2 = 88$

Or, $88 = (n + 10 + x)(n + 10 - x)$

$\therefore$ $(n + 10 + x)$ and $(n + 10 - x)$ are factors of 88.

Both the factors of 88 should be even as both $n+10+x$ and $n+10-x$ are either both even or odd. As 88 is even, both $(n+10+x)$ and $(n+10-x)$ are even.

Thus, only two possibilities are

$$88 = 2 \times 44 = 4 \times 22$$

(i) $$n+10+x = 44$$

$$n+10-x = 2$$

$\therefore$ $$2(n+10) = 46 \text{ or } n = 13$$

(ii) $$n+10+x = 22$$

$$n+10-x = 4$$

$\therefore$ $$2(n+10) = 26 \text{ or } n = 3$$

So, the two solutions are $n = 13$ and $n = 3$.

Thus, required sum = 16

28. What is the sum (in base 10) of all the natural numbers less than 64 which have exactly three 1's in their base 2 representation?

Sol. 64 in base 2 is 1000000.

$\therefore$ All the numbers satisfying the given conditions are binary numbers, with six or lesser number of digits and exactly three 1's.

The highest number here will be 111000.

Now, number of unique ways of arranging these six digits, 1, 1, 1, 0, 0, 0 is

$$\frac{6!}{3! \times 3!} = 20$$

$\therefore$ We have a total of 20 numbers satisfying the given conditions.

Now, total numbers with 1 in their unit place can be found out by calculating the number of possible arrangements of remaining five digits 1, 1, 0, 0, 0 which is $\frac{5!}{2! \times 3!} = 10.$

Similarly, total numbers with 1 in their second place will be 10. It will again be the same for 1 in the third, fourth, fifth and sixth place.

$\therefore$ The Binary Addition of all these numbers is the binary addition of all the place values of all these 1's (in unit place, second place, ..., sixth place), which is 1 + 10 + 100 + 1000 + 10000 + 100000 (all in base 2)

$$= 111111 \text{ (base 2)}$$

$$= 63 \text{ (base 10)}$$

$\therefore$ $$\text{Required sum} = 10 \times 63 = 630$$

($\because$ 1 appears at each place in 10 of the 20 numbers satisfying given conditions)

29. For natural numbers x and y, let (x, y) denote the greatest common divisor of x and y. How many pairs of natural numbers x and y with $x \le y$ satisfy the equation $xy = x + y + (x, y)$?

Sol. Let's consider the case when $x = y$.

So, $$x \times x = x + x + (x, x)$$

or, $$x^2 = x + x + x$$

$\Rightarrow$ $$x^2 - 3x = 0$$

$\Rightarrow$ $$x = 3 \quad (\because x \text{ is a natural number})$$

Now let's consider the case when $x < y$

Let us take the case, $3 \le x$

$\Rightarrow$ $$3y \le xy = x + y + (x, y)$$

But, $x + y + (x, y) < y + y + y = 3y$

Therefore, both the inequalities contradict each other.

Hence, $x < 3$ and it can be only 1 or 2.

For $x = 1$, the equation becomes

$$1 \times y = 1 + y + (1, y)$$

or, $$y = 1 + y + 1$$

This equation has no solution.

For $x = 2$, the equation becomes

$$2y = 2 + y + (2, y)$$

or, $$y = 2 + (2, y)$$

If y is odd, $(2, y) = 1$

$\therefore$ $$y = 2 + 1 = 3$$

If y is even, $(2, y) = 2$

$\therefore$ $$y = 2 + 2 = 4$$

Hence, we have three solutions as (3, 3), (2, 3) and (2, 4).

30. N is a 10-digit number.

$$N = a_1 a_2 a_3 \ldots a_{10}$$

$a_1, a_2, a_3, \ldots\ldots$ are digits of N.

All the digits of N are distinct.

The number formed by leftmost n digits of N is divisible by n [for $(1 \le n \le 10)$].

For example, $a_1 a_2$ is divisible by 2; $a_1 a_2 a_3 a_4 a_5$ is divisible by 5 etc.

Find N.

Sol. $N = a_1 a_2 a_3 a_4 a_5 a_6 a_7 a_8 a_9 a_{10}$

$N = a_1 a_2 a_3 \ldots a_{10}$ is divisible by 10.

Hence, $\boldsymbol{a_{10} = 0}$

$a_1 a_2 a_3 a_4 a_5$ is divisible by 5.

Hence, $a_5 = 0$ or 5.

Thus, $\boldsymbol{a_5 = 5}$ ($\because$ $a_{10} = 0$ and the digits of N are distinct.)

$a_1 a_2$ is divisible by 2.

$a_1 a_2 a_3 a_4$ is divisible by 4.

$a_1 a_2 a_3 a_4 a_5 a_6$ is divisible by 6.

$a_1 a_2 a_3 a_4 a_5 a_6 a_7 a_8$ is divisible by 8.

Hence, $\boldsymbol{a_2, a_4, a_6}$ and $\boldsymbol{a_8}$ are even digits other than 0, *i.e.*, one of 2, 4, 6 and 8.

Now, $a_1 a_2 a_3$ is divisible by 3.

$a_1 a_2 a_3 a_4 a_5 a_6$ is divisible by 6.

Hence, $a_1 + a_2 + a_3$ and $a_1 + a_2 + a_3 + a_4 + a_5 + a_6$ are divisible by 3.

Thus, $\boldsymbol{a_4 + a_5 + a_6}$ is divisible by 3.

a_4 and a_6 are both even digits *i.e.*, one of 2, 4, 6 or 8 and $a_5 = 5$.

Thus, only choices possible for a_4 and a_6 are (2, 8) and (4, 6). In all other cases $a_4 + a_5 + a_6$ is not divisible by 3.

So, following four possibilities are there:

(i) $a_4 = 2$ $a_6 = 8$

(ii) $a_4 = 8$ $a_6 = 2$

(iii) $a_4 = 4$ $a_6 = 6$

(iv) $a_4 = 6$ $a_6 = 4$

Let's consider these possibilities one-by-one,

(i) $a_4 = 2$, $a_6 = 8$

$N = a_1 a_2 a_3 258 a_7 a_8 a_9 0$

$a_1 a_2 \ldots . a_8$ is divisible by 8.

Hence, $8 a_7 a_8$ is divisible by 8.

Only possible choices for a_8 are 4 or 6 ($\because$ 0, 2, 8 values are already taken)

If $a_8 = 4$, none of 814, 834, 874 and 894 are divisible by 8. (Please note that a_7 can only take values 1, 3, 7 or 9 because all even digits appear at a_2, a_4, a_6, a_8 and a_{10} and value 5 is already taken by a_5)

Thus, $a_8 = 4$ is not possible.

If $a_8 = 6$, 816 and 896 are divisible by 8.

(ii) $a_4 = 8, a_6 = 2$

$2a_7a_8$ is divisible by 8.

Possible values of a_8 are 4 and 6.

If $a_8 = 4$, none of 214, 234, 274 or 294 are divisible by 8.

Hence, $a_8 = 4$ is not possible.

If $a_8 = 6$, 216 and 296 are divisible by 8.

(iii) $a_4 = 4, a_6 = 6$

$6a_7a_8$ is divisible by 8.

Possible values of a_8 are 2 and 8.

If $a_8 = 2$, 632 and 672 are divisible by 8.

If $a_8 = 8$, none of 618, 638, 678 or 698 are divisible by 8.

(iv) $a_4 = 6, a_6 = 4$

$4a_7a_8$ is divisible by 8.

Possible values of a_8 are 2 and 8.

If $a_8 = 2$, 432 and 472 are divisible by 8.

If $a_8 = 8$, none of 418, 438, 478 and 498 are divisible by 8.

Hence following choices are possible for $a_6a_7a_8$:

(i) 816, $a_4 = 2$ (ii) 896, $a_4 = 2$

(iii) 216, $a_4 = 8$ (iv) 296, $a_4 = 8$

(v) 632, $a_4 = 4$ (vi) 672, $a_4 = 4$

(vii) 432, $a_4 = 6$ (viii) 472, $a_4 = 6$

Now, let's consider each possibility.

(i) $a_6a_7a_8 = 816, a_4 = 2$

$$N = a_1a_2a_3 25816 a_9 0$$

Hence, $a_2 = 4$ ($\because$ 4 is the only remaining even digit.)

$\therefore$ $N = a_1 4 a_3 25816 a_9 0$

Out of odd digits, 1 and 5 are already taken.

Hence, a_1, a_3 and a_9 can take values 3, 7 and 9.

Now, $a_1 4 a_3$ is divisible by 3.

For any choice of a_1 and a_3 (out of 3, 7 and 9), $a_1 + 4 + a_3$ is not divisible by 3.

Hence, we need to discard this possibility.

(ii) $a_6a_7a_8 = 896$, $a_4 = 2$

$N = a_1a_2a_3 25896a_9 0$

$N = a_1 4a_3 25896a_9 0$ ($\because$ 4 is the only remaining even digit.)

Out of odd digits, 5 and 9 are already taken.

Hence, a_1, a_3 and a_9 can take values 1, 3 and 7.

Now, $a_1 4a_3$ is divisible by 3.

Hence, $a_1 = 1$, $a_3 = 7$ or $a_1 = 7$, $a_3 = 1$ are only two possibilities.

Let's consider these two possibilities.

(a) $N = 14725896a_9 0$
(for $a_1 = 1$, $a_3 = 7$)
$= 1472589630$ (3 is the only digit left. $\therefore$ $a_9 = 3$)

1472589 is not divisible by 7.

Hence, this is not the desired number.

(b) $N = 7412589630$ (for $a_1 = 7$, $a_3 = 1$)

Again 7412589 is not divisible by 7.

Hence, we need to discard this possibility.

(iii) $a_6a_7a_8 = 216$, $a_4 = 8$

$N = a_1a_2a_3 85216a_9 0$

$N = a_1 4a_3 85216a_9 0$ ($\because$ 4 is the only remaining even digit.)

Only possible values for a_1, a_3 and a_9 are 3, 7 and 9.

$a_1 4a_3$ is divisible by 3.

But $a_1 + 4 + a_3$ is not divisible by 3 for any given choices for a_1 and a_3.

Hence, we need to discard this possibility.

(iv) $a_6a_7a_8 = 296$, $a_4 = 8$

$N = a_1 4a_3 85296a_9 0$ ($\because$ 4 is the only remaining even digit.)

Only possible values for a_1, a_3 and a_9 are 1, 3 and 7.

$a_1 4a_3$ is divisible by 3.

Hence, $a_1 + 4 + a_3$ is divisible by 3.

Thus, $a_1 = 7$, $a_3 = 1$ or $a_1 = 1$, $a_3 = 7$ are only possibilties.

Let's consider these two possibilities.

(a) $N = 7418529630$ ($a_1 = 7$, $a_3 = 1$)

7418529 is not divisible by 7.

Hence, this is not the desired number.

(b) $N = 1478529630$ ($a_1 = 1$, $a_3 = 7$)

1478529 is not divisible by 7.

Hence, this is not the desired number.

(v) $a_6a_7a_8 = 632$, $a_4 = 4$

$$N = a_1 8 a_3 45632 a_9 0$$

Only possible values for a_1, a_3 and a_9 are 1, 7 and 9.

$a_1 8 a_3$ is divisible by 3.

Hence, $a_1 + 8 + a_3$ is divisible by 3.

Thus, (1, 9), (9, 1), (7, 9) and (9, 7) are possible values of a_1, a_3.

Hence, 1894563270, 9814563270, 7894563210 and 9874563210 are possible numbers.

None of these numbers is the desired number as the number formed by left most seven digits is not divisible by 7.

Hence, we need to discard this possibility as well.

(vi) $a_6a_7a_8 = 672$, $a_4 = 4$

$$N = a_1 8 a_3 45672 a_9 0$$

Only possible values for a_1, a_3 and a_9 are 1, 3 and 9.

$a_1 8 a_3$ is divisible by 3.

Hence, $a_1 + 8 + a_3$ is divisible by 3.

Thus, (1, 3), (3, 1), (1, 9) and (9, 1) are possible values of a_1, a_3.

Hence, 1834567290, 3814567290, 1894567230 and 9814567230 are possible numbers.

None of these numbers is the desired number as the number formed by left-most four digits is not divisible by 4.

Hence, we need to discard this possibility as well.

(vii) $a_6a_7a_8 = 432$, $a_4 = 6$

$$N = a_1 8 a_3 65432 a_9 0$$

Only possible values for a_1, a_3 and a_9 are 1, 7 and 9.

$a_1 8 a_3$ is divisible by 3.

Hence, $a_1 + 8 + a_3$ is divisible by 3.

Thus, (1, 9), (9, 1), (7, 9) and (9, 7) are possible values of a_1, a_3.

Hence, 1896543270, 9816543270, 7896543210 and 9876543210 are possible numbers.

None of these numbers is the desired number as the number formed by left most seven digits is not divisible by 7.

Hence, we need to discard this possibility as well.

(viii) $a_6a_7a_8 = 472$, $a_4 = 6$

$$N = a_1 8 a_3 65472 a_9 0$$

Only possible values for a_1, a_3 and a_9 are 1, 3 and 9.

$a_1 8 a_3$ is divisible by 3.

Hence, $a_1 + 8 + a_3$ is divisible by 3.

Hence, (1, 3), (3, 1), (1, 9) and (9, 1) are possible values of a_1, a_3.

Thus, 1836547290, 3816547290 ,1896547230 and 9816547230 are possible value of N.

Out of these numbers, 3816547290 is the only number for which the number formed by left-most seven digits is divisible by 7.

So, 3816547290 appears to be the desired number.

Let's verify the divisibility of this number 3816547290 once again.

3 is divisible by 1.

38 is divisible by 2.

381 is divisible by 3.

3816 is divisible by 4.

38165 is divisible by 5.

381654 is divisible by 6.

3816547 is divisible by 7.

38165472 is divisible by 8.

381654729 is divisible by 9.

3816547290 is divisible by 10.

Thus, 3816547290 is the desired number.

31. Find the number of pairs of positive integers (m, n), with $m \le n$, such that the 'Least Common Multiple' (LCM) of m and n equals 600.

Sol. We have $600 = 2^3 \times 3 \times 5^2$

For two numbers to have this LCM, they have to be of the form $2^a 3^b 5^c$.

Let one number be $2^r 3^s 5^t$ and another number be $2^m 3^n 5^p$.

$$0 \le r \le 3, 0 \le m \le 3$$

So, we have 7 choices for (r, m).

If $r = 3$, $m = 0$ to 3 (4 choices)

If $m = 3$, $r = 0$ to 2 (3 choices, $m = 3$, $r = 3$ is already taken care of)

$$0 \le s \le 1, 0 \le n \le 1$$

Following 3 choices are possible :

$$s = 0, n = 1$$

$$s = 1, n = 1$$

$$s = 1, n = 0$$

$$0 \le t \le 2, 0 \le p \le 2$$

So, we have 5 choices.

$t = 2$, $p = 0$ to 2 (3 choices)

$p = 2$, $t = 0$ to 1 (2 choices)

So, number of pairs $(m, n) = 7 \times 3 \times 5 = 105$

Out of possible number of pairs, there is one case in which both m and n are 600. (m, n) pair is same as (n, m).

Therefore, total number of pairs (m, n), with $m \le n$

$$= 1 + \frac{105 - 1}{2} = 53$$

32. Consider all 6-digit numbers of the form *abccba* where b is odd. Determine the number of all such 6-digit numbers that are divisible by 7.

Sol. $abccba = a(10^5 + 1) + b(10^4 + 10) + c(10^3 + 10^2)$

$$= a(100002 - 1) + b \times 10010 + c(1099 + 1)$$

$$= a(7 \times 14286) + b(7 \times 1430) + c(7 \times 157) + (c - a)$$

$$= 7(X) + (c - a) \text{ where } X \text{ is an integer}$$

Also, a will be non-zero as *abccba* is a 6-digit number.

Now, for *abccba* to be a multiple of 7, $(c - a)$ needs to be a multiple of 7.

Difference of two digits can only take values between -9 to 9.

Hence, $c - a = -7, 0, 7$

$c - a = -7$ when (a, c) is (7, 0), (8, 1), (9, 2)

$c - a = 0$ when (a, c) is (1, 1), (2, 2), (3, 3), (4, 4), (5, 5), (6, 6), (7, 7), (8, 8), (9, 9)

$c - a = 7$ when (a, c) is (1, 8), (2, 9)

Thus, we have a total of 14 combinations for (a, c) and there will be 5 choices for b *i.e.* 1, 3, 5, 7, 9 as b is odd.

Thus, we get a total of $14 \times 5 = 70$ numbers.

33. The equation $166 \times 56 = 8590$ is valid in some base b (that is, 1, 6, 5, 8, 9, 0 are digits in base b in this equation). Find the sum of all possible value of $b \ge 10$ satisfying the equation.

Sol. $(166)_b = b^2 + 6b + 6$

$$(56)_b = 5b + 6$$

$$(8590)_b = 8b^3 + 5b^2 + 9b$$

Now, $(166)_b \times (56)_b = (8590)_b$

$\Rightarrow \quad (b^2 + 6b + 6)(5b + 6) = 8b^3 + 5b^2 + 9b$

$\Rightarrow \quad 3b^3 - 31b^2 - 57b - 36 = 0$

$\Rightarrow \quad (b - 12)(3b^2 + 5b + 3) = 0$

$\therefore$ $b = 12$ is the only possible value here as $b \ge 10$.

So, sum of possible values of $b = 12$

Exercise

1. Which of the following numbers is divisible by 16?

(a) 1264 (b) 1028

(c) 509126 (d) 100324716

2. Which of the following numbers is divisible by 6?

(a) 1924 (b) 201810

(c) 120176 (d) 986100

3. Which of the following numbers is divisible by 3 but not by 9?

(a) 3900 (b) 12078

(c) 2541972 (d) 192078

4. Which of the following numbers is divisible by 24?

(a) 13824 (b) 12018

(c) 9234 (d) 2100768

5. n is a positive integer with following properties

(a) n is a 3-digit number. (b) n is divisible by 9

(c) n is divisible by 11 (d) n is odd

(e) $\gcd(n, 125) = 5$

What is the value of n?

6. Which of the following integers has an even number of factors?

(a) 625 (b) 784

(c) 990 (d) 14400

7. Value of $(1111)_2 + (1001)_2 - (1010)_2$ equals

(a) $(111)_2$ (b) $(1100)_2$

(c) $(1110)_2$ (d) $(1010)_2$

8. Write following numbers in binary representation.

(a) 524 (b) 3915 (c) 112 (d) 991

9. N is a perfect square.

Let n = Number of factors of N

What are the possible values of n?

(a) 4 (b) 8

(c) 16 (d) None of these

10. Prove that the square of an integer always has one of the forms $8k$, $8k+1$ or $8k+4$.

11. An integer is simultaneously a square and a cube. Prove that the integer must be of the form $7k$ or $7k+1$.

12. Prove that the integer $16n^2+12m+2$ cannot be a perfect square for any integers m and n.

13. What is the smallest positive integer k such that $k(3^2+4^3+5^3)=a^n$ for some positive integers a and n, with $n>1$?

14. Prove that $6 \mid a(a^2+11)$ for an arbitrary integer a.

15. Prove that $24 \mid a(a^2-1)$ for an odd integer a.

16. Prove that if a is an integer not divisible by 2 or 3, then $24 \mid (a^2+23)$.

17. If $a \mid (b+c)$, then either $a \mid b$ or $a \mid c$. Prove or disprove.

18. If $a \mid bc$ and $a \nmid c$, then $a \mid b$. Prove or disprove.

19. If $a \mid (b-c)$ and $a \nmid b$, then $a \nmid c$. Prove.

20. For integers a and n, $\gcd(a, a+n)$ divides n. Prove.

21. Prove that $\gcd(a,\ a+2)=1$ or 2 for every integer a.

22. Prove that $\gcd((n!+1),(n+1)!+1)=1$ for any integer n.

23. Prove that for integers a, b, if $\gcd(a,b)=1$, then $\gcd(ac,b)=\gcd(c,b)$.

24. Prove that for integers a, b, c, if $\gcd(a,b)=1$, $d \mid ac$ and $d \mid bc$, then $d \mid c$.

25. Prove that for integers a, b, if $\gcd(a,b)=1$, then $\gcd(a^2,b^2)=1$.

26. Integers a, b, c are relatively prime. [In other words, $\gcd(a,b,c)=1$. In case of three integers a, b, c, not all zero, $\gcd(a,b,c)$ is defined as d where $d \mid a$, $d \mid b$, $d \mid c$ and d is the greatest of all such common divisors.]

    Then (a, b), (a, c) are (b, c) all are relatively prime in pairs. Prove or disprove.

27. Find $\gcd(324, 624)$. Use Euclidean Algorithm to obtain integers x and y such that $\gcd(324, 624) = 324x + 624y$.

28. Let d be a common divisor of a and b. Then $d = \gcd(a, b)$ if and only if $\gcd(a \mid d, b \mid d) = 1$. Prove.

29. If $\gcd(a, b) = 1$, prove that $\gcd(a + b, a - b) = 1$ or 2.

30. If $\gcd(a, b) = 1$, prove that $\gcd(a + b, ab) = 1$.

31. Find $lcm\,(120, 650)$.

32. Given non-zero integers a and b, $\gcd(a, b) = lcm(a, b)$ if and only if $a = \pm\, b$. Prove.

33. Given integers $a, b, k, k > 0$, $lcm(ka, kb) = k \times lcm(a, b)$. Prove.

34. $\gcd(a, 4) = \gcd(b, 4) = 2$ for integers a and b. Prove that $\gcd(a + b, 4) = 4$.

35. For integers a and b, if $b \mid (a^2 + 1)$, then $b \mid (a^4 + 1)$. Prove or disprove.

36. Prove that for a prime number p and integer a, if $p \mid a^2$, then $p^2 \mid a^2$.

37. For a prime number p and integer m, if $p \mid m$ and $p^2 \nmid m$ then prove that m cannot be a perfect square.

38. Prove that $n^3 + 2n$ is divisible by $3n$ for any integer n not divisible by 3.

39. Find all positive integers with initial digit 6 such that the integer formed by deleting this 6 is 1/25 of the original integer.

40. Find the least natural number n, such that its value will become $5n$ when its last digit is moved to the first place.

41. Let n be a 3-digit integer with following properties:

(a) Sum of digits of n is 21.

(b) If the digits of n are reversed, the number thus formed exceeds n by 495.

What is the value of n?

42. Find all 2-digit numbers such that the number is divisible by the product of its two digits.

43. Prove that each number in the sequence 12, 1122, 111222, ... is a product of two consecutive integers.

44. Find all 3-digit numbers such that the number is equal to the sum of the factorials of its own digits.

45. How many two-digit positive integers N have the property that the sum of N and the number obtained by reversing the order of the digits of N is perfect square?

46. If 3-digit number abc is a multiple of 37, then so is the number bca (a, b, c are digits of the integer). Prove.

47. Given integers x and y, let $m = ax + by$ and $n = cx + dy$. a, b, c, d are integers such that $ad - bc = \pm 1$. Prove that $\gcd(m, n) = \gcd(x, y)$.

48. The 4-digit number $aabb$ is a perfect square. Find $aabb$.

49. Prove that the product of four consecutive natural numbers cannot be a perfect cube.

50. Let $N = 6 + 66 + 666 + \ldots + 666\ldots66$, where there are hundred 6's in the last term in the sum. How many times does the digit 7 occur in the number N?

51. How many positive integers less than 1000 have the property that the sum of the digits of each such number is divisible by 7 and the number itself is divisible by 3?

Answers

1. (a) **2.** (b, d) **3.** (a, c) **4.** (a, d) **5.** 495

6. (c) **7.** (c)

8. (a) 1000001100 (b) 111101001011 (c) 1110000 (d) 1111011111

9. (d) **13.** 22 **27.** gcd (324, 624) = 12, $x = -25$, $y = 13$ **31.** 7800

39. $N = 625 \times 10^{n-2}$, $n \geq 2$, n is an integer **40.** 142857 **41.** 489

42. 11, 12, 15, 24, 36 **44.** 145 **45.** 8 **48.** 7744

50. 33 **51.** 28

05
Diophantine Equation

1. Write 100 as a sum of two integers such that one is divisible by 7 and the other by 11.

How do you solve this problem?

Let $$100 = m + n$$

m is divisible by 7 and n is divisible by 11.

Hence, $m = 7x$ and $n = 11y$ for some integers x and y.

Thus, $$100 = 7x + 11y$$

Now, we need to solve this equation for integral values of x and y.

2. Find four integers such that the product of any two, increased by 1, is a square.

Let a, b, c and d be the required integers.

Then $ab+1$, $ac+1$, $ad+1$, $bc+1$, $bd+1$ and $cd+1$ are squares. One solution of the given problem is 1, 3, 8, 120.

$$1 \times 3 + 1 = 4 = 2^2$$

$$1 \times 8 + 1 = 9 = 3^2$$

$$1 \times 120 + 1 = 121 = 11^2$$

$$3 \times 8 + 1 = 25 = 5^2$$

$$3 \times 120 + 1 = 361 = 19^2$$

$$8 \times 120 + 1 = 961 = 31^2$$

3. The preceding two problems are examples of equation in one or more unknowns that is to be solved in the integers. Such equation in one or more unknowns that is to be solved in the integers is called Diophantine equation. The name 'Diophantine equation' honours the Greek mathematician ***Diophantus*** who studied this topic in third century A.D.

4. Let's discus the simplest type of Diophantine equation.

The linear Diophantine equation in two unknowns :

$$ax + by = c$$

where a, b, c are given integers and a, b are not both zero.

If pair of integers x_0, y_0 is a solution to this problem, then

$$ax_0 + by_0 = c$$

5. Consider one example of a linear Diophantine equation.

$$2x + 3y = 5$$

$$2 \times 1 + 3 \times 1 = 5$$

Hence, $x = 1$, $y = 1$ is a solution of this equation.

$$2 \times 7 + 3 \times (-3) = 5$$

Hence, $x = 7$, $y = -3$ is another solution of this equation.

Thus, you can see that a linear Diophantine equation may have multiple (non-unique) solutions.

6. Let's consider another example.

$$4x + 12y = 14$$

Can you find any integral solution to this equation?

$4x + 12y$ is always divisible by 4 for any values of integers x and y.

But 14 is not divisible by 4.

Hence, this equation cannot have any integral solution.

Thus, you can see that a linear Diophantine equation may not have any solution.

7. Theorem :

$ax + by = c$ is a linear Diophantine equation in unknowns x and y.

a, b, c are given integers and (a, b) are not both zero.

The given equation has a solution if and only if $d \mid c$ where $d = \gcd(a, b)$.

If x_0, y_0 is any particular solution of this equation then all other solutions are given by

$$x = x_0 + \left(\frac{b}{d}\right)t$$

$$y = y_0 - \left(\frac{a}{d}\right)t$$

where t is an arbitrary integer.

Proof : We shall prove this theorem in three parts.

(i) Suppose $ax + by = c$ has a solution.

Let x_0, y_0 be the solution.

Then, $$ax_0 + by_0 = c$$

Suppose $d = \gcd(a, b)$.

Then $$d \mid a \text{ and } d \mid b$$

Thus, there exist integers r and s such that

$$a = dr \text{ and } b = ds$$

Now, $$ax_0 + by_0 = c$$

or, $$(drx_0) + (dsy_0) = c$$

or, $$d(rx_0 + sy_0) = c$$

Hence, $$d \mid c$$

Thus, if $ax + by = c$ has a solution then $d \mid c$ where $d = \gcd(a, b)$.

(ii) Suppose $d \mid c$ where $d = \gcd(a, b)$.

As $d \mid c$, there exists integer t such that $c = dt$.

$$d = \gcd(a, b)$$

Hence, there exist integers x_0, y_0 such that $d = ax_0 + by_0$

Multiplying by t,

$$dt = ax_0t + by_0t$$

or, $$c = a(x_0t) + b(y_0t)$$

Thus, the given equation $ax + by = c$ has $x = x_0t$ and $y = y_0t$ as a particular solution.

Thus, if $d \mid c$, $ax + by = c$ has a solution.

By (i) and (ii), it is established that the given equation has a solution if and only if $d \mid c$ where $d = gcd(a, b)$.

(iii) Let x_0, y_0 be a solution of the given equation.

Let x', y' be any other solution.

Then, $$ax_0 + by_0 = c = ax' + by'$$

or, $$a(x' - x_0) = b(y_0 - y')$$

Let $$d = \gcd(a, b)$$

Then, there exist integers r and s such that

$$a = dr,\ b = ds$$

Also, r and s are relatively prime.

(Do you remember the result? If $\gcd(a, b) = d$, then $\gcd\left(\frac{a}{d}, \frac{b}{d}\right) = 1$)

Now, $a(x' - x_0) = b(y_0 - y')$

or, $dr(x' - x_0) = ds(y_0 - y')$

or, $r(x' - x_0) = s(y_0 - y')$

So, $r \mid s(y_0 - y')$ and $\gcd(r, s) = 1$

Hence, $r \mid y_0 - y'$

or, $y_0 - y' = rt$ for some integer t

$\therefore$ $x' - x_0 = st$

$\therefore$ $x' = x_0 + st = x_0 + \left(\frac{b}{d}\right)t$

$$y' = y_0 - rt = y_0 - \left(\frac{a}{d}\right)t$$

Now the proof of the theorem is complete.

You can verify that the values of x', y' given above satisfy the Diophantine equation.

$$ax' + by' = a\left[x_0 + \left(\frac{b}{d}\right)t\right] + b\left[y_0 - \left(\frac{a}{d}\right)t\right]$$

$$= (ax_0 + by_0) + \left(\frac{ab}{d}t - \frac{ab}{d}t\right)$$

$$= ax_0 + by_0 \qquad (\because x_0, y_0 \text{ is given solution})$$

$$= c$$

Solved Examples

1. Which of the following Diophantine equations has a solution?

(a) $3x + 12y = 16$ (b) $4x + 14y = 16$

(c) $9x + 15y = 26$ (d) $5x + 35y = 125$

Sol. (a) $3x + 12y = 16$

$\gcd(3, 12) = 3$

$3 \nmid 16$

Hence, this equation has no solution.

(b) $4x + 14y = 16$

$\gcd(4, 14) = 2$

$2 \mid 16$

Hence, this equation has a solution.

(c) $9x + 15y = 26$

$\gcd(9, 15) = 3$

$3 \nmid 26$

Hence, this equation has no solution.

(d) $5x + 35y = 125$

$\gcd(5, 35) = 5$

$5 \mid 125$

Hence, this equation has a solution.

2. Find solutions of the following Diophantine equation.

$$7x + 4y = 100$$

Sol. $7x + 4y = 100$

$\gcd(7, 4) = 1$

$1 \mid 100$

Hence, this equation has a solution.

You can see that $x = 0,\ y = 25$ is a solution of this equation.

$$7 \times 0 + 4 \times 25 = 100$$

Hence, all solutions are given by

$$x = x_0 + \left(\frac{b}{d}\right) t$$

$$y = y_0 - \left(\frac{a}{d}\right) t$$

where t is an arbitrary integer.

Here, $a = 7, b = 4$

$d = \gcd(a, b) = 1$

$x_0 = 0,\ y_0 = 25$

$\therefore$ $x = 0 + \left(\frac{4}{1}\right) t = 4t$

$$y = 25 - \left(\frac{7}{1}\right) t = 25 - 7t$$

Thus, $x = 4t,\ y = 25 - 7t$ satisfies given equation for any arbitrary integer t.

You can verify it for few values of t.

For $t = 0$, 0, 25 is the solution.

For $t = 1$, 4, 18 is the solution.

For $t = 2$, 8, 11 is the solution.

And so on.

3. Find solutions in positive integer of the equation $7x + 4y = 100$.

Sol. From the preceding example, we know that $x = 4t$, $y = 25 - 7t$ is a solution to this equation for any arbitrary integer t.

If we are looking for solutions in positive integers only,

$$x > 0, \ y > 0$$

or,
$$4t > 0, 25 - 7t > 0$$

or,
$$t > 0, t < \frac{25}{7}$$

or,
$$0 < t < \frac{25}{7}$$

Thus, $t = 1, 2, 3$ are only possible solutions.

Hence, (4, 18), (8, 11) and (12, 4) are only possible solutions in positive integers.

4. Solve the equation $56x + 72y = 40$.

Sol. $56x + 72y = 40$

First, we need to find gcd(56, 72).

$$72 = 56 \times 1 + 16$$
$$56 = 16 \times 3 + 8$$
$$16 = 8 \times 2 + 0$$

Hence gcd(56, 72) = gcd(56, 16) = gcd(16, 8) = 8

Also,
$$8 = 56 - 16 \times 3$$
$$= 56 - (72 - 56 \times 1) \times 3$$
$$= 56 - 72 \times 3 + 56 \times 3$$
$$= 56 \times 4 + 72 \times (-3)$$

or
$$8 = 56 \times 4 + 72 \times (-3)$$

Multiplying both sides by 5, we get

$$40 = 56 \times 20 + 72 \times (-15)$$

Hence, $x = 20$, $y = -15$ is a solution of the given equation.

Thus, all solutions of the given equation are as under:

$$x = x_0 + \left(\frac{b}{d}\right) t$$

$$y = y_0 - \left(\frac{a}{d}\right) t$$

Here $x_0 = 20$, $y_0 = -15$, $d = 8$, $a = 56$, $b = 72$.

Hence,
$$x = 20 + \left(\frac{72}{8}\right) t = 20 + 9t$$

$$y = -15 - \left(\frac{56}{8}\right)t = -15 - 7t$$

Thus, $x = 20 + 9t$, $y = -15 - 7t$ (t is any arbitrary integer) represents all solutions of the given equation.

5. Find all solutions in positive integers of the equation.

$$56x + 72y = 40$$

Sol. From the preceding example, we know that all solutions of this equation are represented by

$$x = 20 + 9t$$
$$y = -15 - 7t$$

for any arbitrary integer t.

For solutions in positive integers,

$$x > 0, y > 0$$

or, $$20 + 9t > 0, -15 - 7t > 0$$

or, $$t > -\frac{20}{9}, t < \frac{-15}{7}$$

or, $$\frac{-20}{9} < t < \frac{-15}{7}$$

or, $$\frac{-140}{63} < t < \frac{-135}{63}$$

or, $$\frac{-189}{63} < \frac{-140}{63} < t < \frac{-135}{63} < \frac{-126}{63}$$

or, $$-3 < \frac{-140}{63} < t < \frac{-135}{63} < -2$$

But there are no integers between -2 and -3.

Hence, this equation has no solution in positive integers.

6. Write 100 as a sum of two integers such that one is divisible by 7 and the other by 11.

Sol. Let $100 = m + n$ where m is divisible by 7 and n by 11.

Hence, $m = 7x$, $n = 11y$ for some integers x and y.

Thus, $$100 = 7x + 11y$$

$$\gcd(7, 11) = 1$$

$$1 \mid 100$$

Hence, this equation has a solution.

Let us apply Euclidean Algorithm to find $\gcd(7, 11)$.

$$11 = 7 \times 1 + 4$$
$$7 = 4 \times 1 + 3$$
$$4 = 3 \times 1 + 1$$

Hence, $\gcd(7, 11) = \gcd(7, 4) = \gcd(4, 3) = \gcd(3, 1) = 1$

Also,
$$\begin{aligned} 1 &= 4 - 3 \times 1 \\ &= 4 - (7 - 4 \times 1) \\ &= 4 \times 2 - 7 \\ &= (11 - 7 \times 1) \times 2 - 7 \\ &= 11 \times 2 - 7 \times 3 \\ &= 7 \times (-3) + 11 \times 2 \end{aligned}$$

Thus,
$$1 = 7 \times (-3) + 11 \times 2$$

Multiplying both sides by 100, we get
$$100 = 7 \times (-300) + 11 \times (200)$$

Thus, $x = -300$ and $y = 200$ is a solution of the given equation.

All other solutions are given by
$$x = x_0 + \left(\frac{b}{d}\right)t$$
$$y = y_0 - \left(\frac{a}{d}\right)t$$

Here, $x_0 = -300$, $y_0 = 200$, $a = 7$, $b = 11$, $d = 1$

$\therefore$
$$x = -300 + 11t$$
$$y = 200 - 7t, \qquad (t \text{ is any arbitrary integer})$$

represents all solutions of this equation.

Now,
$$\begin{aligned} 100 &= 7x + 11y \\ &= 7(-300 + 11t) + 11(200 - 7t) \end{aligned}$$

Please note that the first term is divisible by 7 whereas the second term is divisible by 11.

7. $\gcd(a, b) = 1$ and a, b are integers of opposite sign. Prove that $ax + by = c$ has infinitely many positive solutions for any integral value of c.

Sol. $\gcd(a, b) = 1$

$1 \mid c$ for any integer c.

Hence, the equation $ax + by = c$ has a solution x_0, y_0.

All other solutions are given by
$$x = x_0 + bt$$

or,
$$y = y_0 - at \qquad [\because d = \gcd(a, b) = 1]$$

For solution in positive integers,

$$x > 0,\ y > 0$$

or, $$x_0 + bt > 0,\ y_0 - at > 0,$$

or, $$bt > -x_0,\ at < y_0$$

Now 2 possibilities are there (∵ a and b are of opposite signs.)

(i) $a > 0, b < 0$

Then, $$bt > -x_0,\ at < y_0$$

or, $$t < \frac{-x_0}{b},\ t < \frac{y_0}{a}$$

So, if we take t lesser than the smaller of $\frac{-x_0}{b}$ and $\frac{y_0}{a}$, then we shall get a positive solution.

As there are infinitely many integers lesser than any given number, there are infinitely many positive solutions of the given equation.

(ii) $a < 0, b > 0$

Then, $$bt > -x_0,\ at < y_0$$

or, $$t > \frac{-x_0}{b},\ t > \frac{y_0}{a}$$

If we take t greater than the greater of $\frac{-x_0}{b}$ and $\frac{y_0}{a}$, then we shall get a positive solution.

As there are infinitely many integers greater than any given number, there are infinitely many positive solutions of the given equation.

Thus, in all cases, the given equation has infinitely many positive solutions.

8. Prove that $ax + by = a + c$ is solvable if and only if $ax + by = c$ is solvable.

Sol. Suppose $ax + by = a + c$ is solvable.

Then, $d \mid (a + c)$ where $d = \gcd(a, b)$

or, $a + c = dt$ for some integer t.

Also, $a = dr$ for some integer r as $d \mid a$. [∵ $d = \gcd(a, b)$]

Thus, $$dr + c = dt$$

or, $$d(t - r) = c$$

Hence, $$d \mid c$$

Thus, $ax + by = c$ is solvable.

Now suppose that $ax + by = c$ is solvable.

Then, $d \mid c$ where $d = \gcd(a, b)$

Also, $d \mid a$ $[\because d = \gcd(a, b)]$

$\therefore$ $d \mid (a + c)$

Hence, $ax + by = a + c$ is solvable.

9. Find the integral solution of the equation $13x - 7y = 0$ satisfying the condition $80 < x + y < 120$.

Sol. $13x - 7y = 0$

$$\gcd(13, 7) = 1$$

$$1 \mid 0$$

Hence, the equation has a solution.

$x = 0,\ y = 0$ is one solution of the equation.

Hence, all other solutions are represented by

$$x = x_0 + \left(\frac{b}{d}\right)t$$

$$y = y_0 - \left(\frac{a}{d}\right)t \qquad (t \text{ is any arbitrary integer})$$

Here, $a = 13, b = -7, d = 1, x_0 = 0, y_0 = 0$

$\therefore$
$$x = -7t$$
$$y = -13t$$
$$x + y = -20t$$
$$80 < x + y < 120$$

or, $$80 < -20t < 120$$

or, $$-4 > t > -6$$

Hence, only possible value of $t = -5$.

$\therefore$ $$x = 35,\ y = 65$$

Thus, $x = 35,\ y = 65$ is the only possible solution.

10. A dragonfly has 6 feet and a spider has 8 feet. Given that a certain group of dragonflies and spiders have in total 46 feet, find the number of dragonflies and the number of spiders.

Sol. Let x = Number of dragonflies

and y = Number of spiders

Then, $$6x + 8y = 46$$

or, $$3x + 4y = 23$$

$$\gcd(3, 4) = 1$$

$$1 \mid 23$$

Hence, this equation has a solution.

$$1 = 3 \times (-1) + 4 \times 1$$

Multiplying both sides by 23, we get

$$23 = 3 \times (-23) + 4 \times 23$$

Thus, $x = -23,\ y = 23$ is a solution.

Other solutions are represented by

$$x = x_0 + \left(\frac{b}{d}\right)t$$

$$y = y_0 - \left(\frac{a}{d}\right)t \qquad (t \text{ is any arbitrary integer})$$

Here, $x_0 = -23,\ y_0 = 23,\ a = 3,\ b = 4,\ d = 1$

$\therefore \qquad x = -23 + 4t$

$$y = 23 - 3t$$

Here we are looking for solutions in positive integers.

Hence, $\qquad x > 0,\ y > 0$

or, $\qquad -23 + 4t > 0,\ 23 - 3t > 0$

or, $\qquad t > \frac{23}{4},\ t < \frac{23}{3}$

or, $\qquad \frac{23}{4} < t < \frac{23}{3}$

or, $\qquad 5 < \frac{23}{4} < t < \frac{23}{3} < 8$

Hence, $t = 6$ or 7

For $t = 6,\ x = 1,\ y = 5$

For $t = 7,\ x = 5,\ y = 2$

Thus, $x = 1,\ y = 5$ and $x = 5,\ y = 2$ are two possible solutions.

Exercise

1. Which of the following Diophantine equations is solvable?
   (a) $33x + 14y = 115$ (b) $3x + 22y = 132$
   (c) $5x + 30y = 172$ (d) $6x + 42y = 225$
2. Find all solutions of $3x + 4y = 5$.
3. Find all solutions of $101x + 99y = 437$.
4. Find all solutions of in positive integer of $5x + 3y = 52$.
5. For how many pairs of positive integers (x, y) is $x + 3y = 100$?
6. A pen costs ₹ 11 and a notebook costs ₹ 13. Find the number of ways in which a person can spend exactly ₹ 1000 to buy pens and notebooks.
7. Whether the equation $101x + 37y = 3819$ has a positive solution in integers? If yes, find out all such positive solutions.
8. Let a, b, c be positive integers. Prove that there is no solution of $ax + by = c$ in positive integers if $a + b > c$.
9. a and b are relatively prime positive integers. Prove that the Diophantine equation $ax - by = c$ has infinitely many positive solutions.
10. We have an unknown number of coins. If you make 77 strings of them, you are 50 coins short. But if you make 78 strings, it is exact. How many coins are there?
11. If k is a positive integer such that the equation in x, $kx - 12 = 3k$ has an integral solution, then the number of such k is
    (a) 3 (b) 4 (c) 5 (d) 6 (e) 7
12. m, n are integers satisfying $3m + 2 = 5n + 3$ and $30 < 3m + 2 < 40$. Find the value of mn.
13. a, b are two relatively prime positive integers. Prove that the equation $ax + by = ab - a - b$ has no non-negative integral solution.

Answers

1. (a), (b) **2.** $x = -5 + 4t$, $y = 5 - 3t$, for any arbitrary integer t.

3. $x = -21413 + 99t$, $y = 21850 - 101t$, for any arbitrary integer t.

4. (2, 14), (5, 9), (8, 4). **5.** 33 **6.** 7

7. Yes, $x = 14$, $y = 65$ is the only positive solution.

10. $-78(50 + 77t)$, t is an integer, $t \leq -1$. **11.** (d) **12.** 84

06
Prime Numbers

1. We discussed about prime numbers and composite numbers in the chapter on divisibility.

Let us quickly refresh the concept of prime numbers.

1 and 5 are only divisors of 5.

Hence, 5 is a prime number.

1, 3 and 9 are divisors of 9.

Hence, 9 is a composite number.

1 and 13 are only divisors of 13.

Hence, 13 is a prime number.

1, 3, 5 and 15 are divisors of 15.

Hence, 15 is a composite number.

2. An integer $p > 1$ is called a prime number if its only positive divisors are 1 and p.

For example, 2, 3, 5, 7, 11, 13, 17, 19, 23 etc are prime numbers.

An integer $m > 1$ that is not a prime number is called a composite number.

For example, 4, 6, 8, 9, 10, 12, 14, 15, 16, 18, 20, 21, 22 etc are composite numbers.

3. Let us consider factorisation of few composite numbers.

$$4 = 2 \times 2$$

$$6 = 2 \times 3$$

$$8 = 2 \times 2 \times 2$$

$$9 = 3 \times 3$$

$$10 = 2 \times 5$$

$$12 = 2 \times 2 \times 3$$
$$14 = 2 \times 7$$
$$15 = 3 \times 5$$
$$16 = 2 \times 2 \times 2 \times 2$$
$$18 = 2 \times 3 \times 3$$
$$20 = 2 \times 2 \times 5$$
$$21 = 3 \times 7$$
$$22 = 2 \times 11$$

We can see that all these composite numbers can be written as the product of prime numbers.

In fact, every integer is either a prime or can be broken into unique prime factors.

This is a very significant result in number theory, called Fundamental Theorem of Arithmetic.

4. Theorem : If p is a prime and $p \mid ab$, then $p \mid a$ or $p \mid b$.

Proof : If $p \mid a$ there is nothing left to prove.

If $\quad p \nmid a$, $\gcd(p, a) = 1 \quad$ ($\because$ 1 and p are only divisors of p)

Now, $\quad \gcd(p, a) = 1$ and $p \mid ab$

Hence, by Euclid's lemma $p \mid b$

(Refer to theorem at para 47 in the Chapter 4 on "Divisibility".)

Thus, proof is complete.

5. Theorem : If p is a prime and $p \mid a_1 a_2 ... a_n$ then $p \mid a_k$ for some k, where $1 \leq k \leq n$.

Proof : We prove this result by the method of mathematical induction (Refer to Chapter 10 on "Mathematical Induction").

If $n = 1$, the result obviously holds true.

For $n = 2$, the result holds true by virtue of preceding theorem.

Now suppose that $n > 2$, and that whenever p divides a product of less than n factors, it divides at least one of the factors. ...(1)

Now, suppose that $p \mid a_1 a_2 ... a_n$

or, $\quad p \mid (a_1 a_2 ... a_{n-1}) a_n$

Hence by preceding theorem,

$$p \mid a_1 a_2 ... a_{n-1} \text{ or } p \mid a_n$$

If $p \mid a_n$ the result is proved.

If $p \mid a_1 a_2 ... a_{n-1}$, it follows from our assumption (refer to (1) above) that $p \mid a_k$ for some $k, 1 \leq k \leq n-1$.

In any case, p divides one of the integers $a_1, a_2, ..., a_n$.

Hence, the result is proved.

6. Theorem : If $p, q_1, q_2, ..., q_n$ are all prime and $p \mid q_1 q_2 ... q_n$, then $p = q_k$ for some k, where $1 \le k \le n$.

Proof : $p \mid q_1 q_2 \cdots q_n$

Hence, by preceding theorem $p \mid q_k$ for some k, where $1 \le k \le n$.

Since, q_k is prime, 1 and q_k are its only divisors.

$p > 1$ ($\because p$ is a prime.)

Hence, only possibility is that $p = q_k$

Thus, result is proved.

7. Let us consider one example of breaking down a composite number into prime factors.

$$18 = 2 \times 3 \times 3$$
$$= 3 \times 2 \times 3$$
$$= 3 \times 3 \times 2$$

So does 18 have three different prime factorisations?

If we ignore the sequence of factors, the factorisation of 18 into prime factors is unique.

8. Fundamental Theorem of Arithmetic

Every positive integer $n > 1$ is either a prime or a product of primes. If we ignore the sequence in which the factors occur, the representation as a product of primes is unique.

Proof : Every positive integer n is either prime or composite.

If n is prime, there is nothing more to prove.

If n is composite, then there exists an integer d satisfying $d \mid n$ and $1 < d < n$.

Let $S = \{r : r$ is a positive integer, $r \mid n$ and $1 < r < n\}$.

Obviously, S is a non-empty set. ($\because d \in S$)

Hence, by the well-ordering principle, S has a least element.

Let p_1 be the least element.

Then p_1 must be prime.

This is because if p_1 is not prime, there exists q, $1 < q < p_1$ such that $q \mid p_1$. But then $q \in S$ and $q < p_1$.

This is a contradiction.

Hence, p_1 is prime.

Thus, we can write $n = p_1 n_1$, where p_1 is a prime and $1 < n_1 < n$.

If n_1 is a prime, we have arrived at desired representation of n as a product of primes.

If n_1 is not a prime, we can as earlier find another prime number p_2 such that

$$n_1 = p_2 n_2, 1 < n_2 < n_1$$

or,

$$n = p_1 n_1$$

$$= p_1 p_2 n_2, 1 < n_2 < n_1 < n$$

If n_2 is a prime we have got the desired representation.

If n_2 is not a prime, we can find another prime number p_3 such that $n_2 = p_3 n_3$, $1 < n_3 < n_2$.

Hence, $n = p_1 p_2 p_3 n_3, 1 < n_3 < n_2 < n_1 < n$

The decreasing sequence $n > n_1 > n_2 > \ldots > 1$ cannot continue indefinitely.

Therefore, after a finite number of steps, say $k - 1$, we get a prime n_{k-1}. Let's call it p_k.

So, we get the prime factorisation

$$n = p_1 p_2 \cdots p_k$$

Thus, we have proved that every positive integer $n > 1$ is either a prime or a product of primes.

Now, we need to prove uniqueness of the prime factorisation.

Let us suppose that the integer n can be represented as a product of primes in two ways.

$$n = p_1 p_2 \cdots p_r$$

$$= q_1 q_2 \cdots q_s$$

where $p_1, p_2, \ldots, p_r, q_1, q_2, \ldots, q_s$ are all primes written in increasing order.

Let's assume that $r \leq s$.

Hence,

$$p_1 \leq p_2 \leq \ldots \leq p_r$$

$$q_1 \leq q_2 \leq \ldots \leq q_s$$

Because, $p_1 \mid q_1 q_2 \ldots q_s$, by theorem at para 6, it follows that $p_1 = q_n$ for some n.

$$q_n \geq q_1 \quad (\because \text{Numbers } q_1, q_2 \ldots \text{ are in increasing order.})$$

Hence,

$$p_1 \geq q_1$$

Similar reasoning for q_1 gives $q_1 \geq p_1$

Hence,

$$p_1 = q_1$$

We can cancel the common factor to obtain

$$p_2 \cdots p_r = q_2 \cdots q_s$$

We can repeat the same process to get $p_2 = q_2$

$\therefore$

$$p_3 \cdots p_r = q_3 \cdots q_s$$

$$r \leq s$$

If $r < s$, we eventually arrive at

$$1 = q_{r+1} q_{r+2} \cdots q_s$$

which is not possible because each $q_i > 1$.

Hence, $r = s$

Also,
$$p_1 = q_1$$
$$p_2 = q_2$$
$$\ldots\ldots$$
$$\ldots\ldots$$
$$p_r = q_r$$

Hence, the two different factorisations of n are identical.

Thus, uniqueness of factorisation is established.

9. $180 = 2 \times 2 \times 3 \times 3 \times 5$

Prime factors 2 and 3 are repeated in this factorisation.

We can write it as $180 = 2^2 \times 3^2 \times 5$

Accordingly, we can rephrase earlier theorem as follows:

Any positive integer $n > 1$ can be written uniquely in a canonical form

$$n = p_1^{k_1}\, p_2^{k_2} \ldots p_r^{k_r}$$

where $k_1, k_2, \ldots, k_r$ are positive integers and $p_1, p_2, \ldots, p_r$ are distinct prime numbers with $p_1 < p_2 < \ldots p_r$.

10. Find the greatest common divisor of 36 and 84.

Let us write prime factorisations of 36 and 84.

$$36 = 2^2 \times 3^2$$
$$84 = 2^2 \times 3 \times 7$$

The largest powers of prime numbers common to both 36 and 84 are 2^2 and 3.

Hence, $\gcd(36, 84) = 2^2 \times 3 = 4 \times 3 = 12$

Thus, prime factorisations provide another means of finding the greatest common divisor.

11. By Fundamental Theorem of Arithmetic (refer para 8), every positive integer greater than 1 is either a prime or a product of primes.

Hence, every composite number must have a prime factor lying between 1 and the number itself.

Determine whether 23 is prime or not.

2, 3, 5, 7, 11, 13, 17 and 19 are all prime numbers less than 23.

23 is not divisible by any of these prime numbers.

Hence, 23 is a prime number.

However, finding out the prime numbers lesser than a given number and verifying divisibility of the given number by all such prime numbers is a tedious task.

Is there a better way to determine whether a given number is prime or not?

12. A given integer $a > 1$ is composite.

Therefore, there exists an integer $b, 1 < b < a$ such that $b \mid a$.

Thus, there exists an integer c such that $a = bc$.

Let's assume that $b \le c$.

Then, $$b^2 \le bc$$

or, $$b^2 \le a$$

or, $$b \le \sqrt{a}$$

From the Fundamental Theorem of Arithmetic it follows that b has at least one prime factor $p, 1 < p \le b$.

Hence, $$1 < p \le \sqrt{a}$$

Thus, **we can conclude that every composite number a ($a > 1$) always has a prime divisor p satisfying $p \le \sqrt{a}$.**

Therefore, for testing primality of a given number $a > 1$, it is sufficient to verify divisibility of a by all primes not exceeding $\sqrt{a}$.

13. With this insight let's take up the problem of testing the primality of 23 once again.

$$4^2 < 23 < 5^2$$

$\therefore$ $$4 < \sqrt{23} < 5$$

Hence, for determining primality of 23, it is sufficient to verify divisibility of 23 by all primes less than or equal to 4.

2 and 3 are only primes less than or equal to 4.

23 is not divisible by either of 2 or 3.

Hence, 23 is a prime.

14. How do we find out all primes lesser than or equal to 100?

There is an intelligent way to find out solution of this problem.

Consider the sequence of consecutive integers 2, 3, 4, ...100.

2 is a prime. Cross out all multiples of 2 other than 2 from the list as such multiples are not primes. After crossing out, the first of the remaining integers (other than 2) is 3 which is a prime.

Now, strike out all multiples of 3 from the list except 3 itself.

The smallest integer other than 2 and 3 which has not been struck out is 5.

5 is not divisible by 2 or 3. Hence, 5 is a prime.

Now, strike out all multiples of 5 except 5 itself.

We continue this process up to 7, which is the largest prime lesser than or equal to $\sqrt{100} = 10$.

The integers that are left now (not struck out), *i.e.*, that do not fall through the "sieve" are primes.

The following picture represents the result of this exercise.

	2	3	~~4~~	5	~~6~~	7	~~8~~	~~9~~	~~10~~
11	~~12~~	13	~~14~~	~~15~~	~~16~~	17	~~18~~	19	~~20~~
~~21~~	~~22~~	23	~~24~~	~~25~~	~~26~~	~~27~~	~~28~~	29	~~30~~
31	~~32~~	~~33~~	~~34~~	~~35~~	~~36~~	37	~~38~~	~~39~~	~~40~~
41	~~42~~	43	~~44~~	~~45~~	~~46~~	47	~~48~~	~~49~~	~~50~~
~~51~~	~~52~~	53	~~54~~	~~55~~	~~56~~	~~57~~	~~58~~	59	~~60~~
61	~~62~~	~~63~~	~~64~~	~~65~~	~~66~~	67	~~68~~	~~69~~	~~70~~
71	~~72~~	73	~~74~~	~~75~~	~~76~~	~~77~~	~~78~~	79	~~80~~
~~81~~	~~82~~	83	~~84~~	~~85~~	~~86~~	~~87~~	~~88~~	89	~~90~~
~~91~~	~~92~~	~~93~~	~~94~~	~~95~~	~~96~~	97	~~98~~	~~99~~	~~100~~

Multiples of 2 are crossed out by /.

Multiples of 3 are crossed out by \.

Multiples of 5 are crossed out by —.

Multiples of 7 are crossed out by ×.

All the numbers in the table that are not crossed out are prime numbers.

Thus, 2, 3, 5, 7, 11, 13, 17, 19, 23, 29, 31, 37, 41, 43, 47, 53, 59, 61, 67, 71, 73, 79, 83, 89 and 97 are all prime numbers less than or equal to 100.

This clever technique of finding all primes below a given integer *n* is called the sieve of Eratosthenes.

Eratosthenes of Cyrene (276-194BC) was a Greek mathematician who found this technique of finding all primes below a given integer.

15. Consider integers 11, 111, 1111, 11111, ...

These integers are written as strings of 1's. These integers are called repunit.

$$\underbrace{111..1}_{n\text{ 1's}} = 1\times 10^{n-1} + 1\times 10^{n-2} + \ldots + 1$$

$$= \frac{10^n - 1}{10 - 1} \qquad \text{(Sum of geometric progression)}$$

$$= \frac{10^n - 1}{9}$$

We use the symbol R_n to denote the repunit consisting of n consecutive 1's.

Thus, $$R_n = \frac{10^n - 1}{9}$$

Are any of these repunit numbers primes?

So far only $R_2, R_{19}, R_{23}, R_{317}, R_{1031}, R_{49081}, R_{86453}, R_{109297}$ and R_{270343} have been identified as primes.

Primes of such special forms have always been a matter of interest.

16. Can we write every even integer greater than 4 as a sum of two odd prime numbers?

$$6 = 3 + 3$$
$$8 = 3 + 5$$
$$10 = 3 + 7$$
$$12 = 5 + 7$$
$$14 = 3 + 11 = 7 + 7$$
$$16 = 3 + 13 = 5 + 11$$
$$18 = 5 + 13 = 7 + 11$$
$$20 = 3 + 17 = 7 + 13$$

Thus, we can see that it is indeed possible to write even integers up to 20 as a sum of two odd prime numbers.

But is it true in general?

In a letter to Leonhard Euler in 1742, Christian Goldbach made the guess that every even integer is the sum of two numbers that are either prime or 1. A more general formulation is that "every even integer greater than 4 can be written as a sum of two odd primes". This statement is called Goldbach conjecture.

Till date we do not know whether this guess is correct or not.

Will you attempt to solve this problem which humanity has been trying to solve for last 100's of years?

Solved Examples

1. Write prime factorisation of following numbers.

(a) 128 (b) 324 (c) 676

Sol. (a) 128 is divisible by 8.

$$128 = 8 \times 16 = 2^3 \times 2^4 = 2^7$$

This is the desired prime factorisation.

(b) 324 is divisible by 4.

$$324 = 4 \times 81 = 2^2 \times 3^4$$

This is the desired prime factorisation.

(c) 676 is divisible by 4.

$$676 = 4 \times 169$$
$$= 2^2 \times 13^2$$

This is the desired prime factorization.

2. Determine whether the integer 329 is a prime number.

Sol. $18^2 = 324 < 329 < 361 = 19^2$

Therefore, to verify primality of 329, we need to verify divisibility of 329 by all prime numbers up to 18 *i.e.* by 2, 3, 5, 7, 11, 13, 17.

329 is divisible by 7.

Hence, 329 is not a prime number.

3. A natural number k is such that $k^2 < 2014 < (k+1)^2$. What is the largest prime factor of k?

Sol. $[\sqrt{2014}] = 44$ ([ ] denotes greatest integer function)

$\therefore$ $$44^2 < 2014 < 45^2$$

$\Rightarrow$ $$k = 44 = 2^2 \times 11$$

Thus, 11 is the largest prime factor of k.

4. Prove that 3999991 is not prime.

Sol. $3999991 = 4000000 - 9 = (2000)^2 - 3^2$

$$= (2000 + 3)(2000 - 3)$$
$$= 2003 \times 1997$$

Therefore, 3999991 is not prime.

5. Any prime number of the form $3n + 1$ is also of the form $6m + 1$. Prove.

Sol. Suppose that $3n + 1$ is prime.

n has one of the forms $2m$ or $2m + 1$.

If $n = 2m$, $3n + 1 = 6m + 1$

If $n = 2m + 1$, $3n + 1 = 6m + 4 = 2(3m + 2)$

But then $2(3m + 2)$ is divisible by 2.

Thus, it has a divisor different from 1 and $(6m + 4)$.

Therefore, it is not a prime.

Hence, only possible form of n is $2m$.

Thus, $$3n + 1 = 6m + 1$$

Hence, any prime number of the form $3m + 1$ is also of the form $6m + 1$.

6. Prove that any prime number (> 3) is always of the form $6n+1$ or $6n+5$.

Sol. Any integer has one of the forms $6n$, $6n+1$, $6n+2$, $6n+3$, $6n+4$ or $6n+5$.

$6n$ is always divisible by 6 *i.e.*, by 2 and 3.

Hence, a number of the form $6n$ can never be prime.

$6n+2\,[=2(3n+1)]$ is always divisible by 2. Hence, except for the value 2, $6n+2$ can never be a prime number.

$6n+3\,[=3(2n+1)]$ is always divisible by 3.

Hence, except for the value 3, $6n+3$ can never be a prime number.

$6n+4\,[=2(3n+2)]$ is always divisible by 2.

Hence, $6n+4$ can never be a prime number.

Only forms left now are $6n+1$ or $6n+5$.

Therefore, any prime number greater than 3 is always of the form $6n+1$ or $6n+5$.

7. Find out all prime numbers of the form n^3-1.

Sol. $n^3-1=(n-1)(n^2+n+1)$

For $n=1$, $\quad n^3-1=0$ which is not a prime.

For $n=2$, $\quad n^3-1=7$ which is a prime.

For all $n>2$, $\quad n-1>1$

$$n^2+n+1>1$$

Thus, n^3-1 has a factor $n-1$ lying between 1 and n^3-1.

Therefore, n^3-1 is a composite number for $n>2$.

Thus, 7 is the only prime number of the form n^3-1.

8. Each integer of the form $3n+2$ has a prime factor of this form. Prove.

Sol. Any integer has one of the forms $3k$, $3k+1$ or $3k+2$.

Therefore, prime factors of $3n+2$ have one of the forms $3k$, $3k+1$ or $3k+2$.

Suppose that $3n+2=p_1^{t_1}\ p_2^{t_2}\ \dots\ p_r^{t_r}$

where $p_1 p_2 \dots p_r$ are prime factors of $3n+2$.

Suppose that all prime factors of $3n+2$ have the form $3k$ or $3k+1$ only.

If a is of the form $3k$ and b is of the form $3k+1$, then ab is of the form $3k$.

If a and b both are of the form $3k$, then ab is of the form $3k$. If a and b both are of the form $3k+1$, then ab is of the form $3k+1$.

Hence, any power of $3k$ is of the form $3k$ only. Similarly, any power of $3k+1$ is of the form $3k+1$ only.

Thus, $p_1^{t_1}\ p_2^{t_2}\ \dots\ p_r^{t_r}=3n+2$ is of the form $3k$ or $3k+1$.

But this is a contradiction.

Therefore, our assumption of all prime factors being of the form $3k$ or $3k+1$ is incorrect.

Thus, an integer of the form $3n+2$ always has a prime factor of this form.

9. If $p>3$ is a prime number then p^2+2 is composite. Prove.

Sol. Any prime number greater than 3 is always of the form $6n+1$ or $6n+5$. (Refer to problem 6 of "Solved Examples")

$$(6n+1)^2 = 36n^2+12n+1 = 6(6n^2+2n)+1$$

$$(6n+5)^2 = 36n^2+60n+25 = 6(6n^2+10n+4)+1$$

Thus, if $p>3$ is a prime, p^2 is always of the form $6k+1$.

$\therefore$ $$p^2+2 = 6k+1+2 = 6k+3 = 3(2k+1)$$

Hence, p^2+2 is always divisible by 3.

Also, $$p^2+2>3$$

Thus, p^2+2 is a composite number.

10. p is a prime. $p|a^n$. Prove that $p^n|a^n$.

Sol. $p|a^n$

or, $$p|aa\ldots a \quad (n \text{ times})$$

$\therefore$ $$p|a \quad \text{(refer to the theorem at para 5 of this chapter)}$$

$\therefore$ $a=ps$ for some integer s

$\therefore$ $$a^n = (ps)^n$$

or, $$a^n = p^n s^n$$

Hence, $$p^n|a^n$$

11. Any integer of the form 8^n+1 where $n>1$, is composite. Prove.

Sol. We know that $a^3+b^3=(a+b)(a^2-ab+b^2)$

$\therefore$ $$8^n+1 = (2^3)^n+1 = (2^n)^3+1$$

$$= (2^n+1)(2^{2n}-2^n+1)$$

For $n>1$

$$2^n+1>1 \text{ and } 2^{2n}-2^n+1>1$$

Hence, 8^n+1 is composite for all $n>1$.

12. p and q are both primes $p>q>5$. Prove that $24|p^2-q^2$.

Sol. Any integer has one of the forms $3k$, $3k+1$ or $3k+2$.

As $p > q > 5$ and 3 is the only prime of the form $3k$, p and q are of one of the forms $3k+1$ or $3k+2$.

Thus, p^2 and q^2 are of the form $3k+1$.

Let $p^2 = 3m+1$ (for some integers m, n)

and $q^2 = 3n+1$

Then, $p^2 - q^2 = (3m+1) - (3n+1) = 3(m-n)$

$\therefore$ $3 \mid p^2 - q^2$

Similarly, any integer has one of the forms $8n$, $8n+1$, $8n+2$, $8n+3$, $8n+4$, $8n+5$, $8n+6$ or $8n+7$.

As p, q are primes, only possible forms of p, q are $8n+1$, $8n+3$, $8n+5$, $8n+7$.

$$(8n+1)^2 = 64n^2 + 16n + 1 = 8(8n^2 + 2n) + 1$$

$$(8n+3)^2 = 64n^2 + 48n + 9 = 8(8n^2 + 6n + 1) + 1$$

$$(8n+5)^2 = 64n^2 + 80n + 25 = 8(8n^2 + 10n + 3) + 1$$

$$(8n+7)^2 = 64n^2 + 112n + 49 = 8(8n^2 + 14n + 6) + 1$$

Hence, p^2 and q^2 are of the form $8n+1$ only.

Let $p^2 = 8r+1$

and $q^2 = 8s+1$ (for some integers r, s)

Hence, $p^2 - q^2 = (8r+1) - (8s+1) = 8(r-s)$

$\therefore$ $8 \mid p^2 - q^2$

Thus, both 3 and 8 are divisors of $p^2 - q^2$.

Also, $\gcd(3, 8) = 1$

Hence, $(3 \times 8) \mid p^2 - q^2$ (refer to the theorem at para 46 in the chapter 4- "Divisibility")

or, $24 \mid p^2 - q^2$

13. There is an infinite number of primes. Prove.

Sol. Suppose that the number of primes is finite.

Let's arrange these finite number of primes in ascending order.

Let $p_1 = 2$, $p_2 = 3$, $p_3 = 5$, $p_4 = 7$, ...

Suppose that p_n is the largest prime number.

Now consider the positive integer $P = p_1 p_2 \dots p_n + 1$

$$P > p_n$$

Therefore, P cannot be prime as $p_1, p_2, \dots, p_n$ are the only prime numbers.

Thus, P has a prime factor p.

Now, $p \mid P$ $(\because p \text{ is a factor of } P)$

Also, $p \mid p_1 p_2 \cdots p_n$

$(\because p$ is one of $p_1, p_2, ..., p_n$ because $p_1, p_2, ..., p_n$ are only prime numbers)

Hence, $p \mid (P - p_1 p_2 \cdots p_n)$ or $p \mid 1$.

But this is a contradiction as $p > 1$.

Hence, our assumption that the number of primes is finite is incorrect.

Therefore, there is an infinite number of primes. This proof was given by Greek mathematician Euclid in his book 'Elements'.

14. Let $p^{\#}$ be the product of all primes less than or equal to prime number p. Then the number of the form $p^{\#} + 1$ is called Euclidean number. Find first five Euclidean numbers.

Sol.

$$2^{\#} + 1 = 2 + 1 = 3$$

$$3^{\#} + 1 = 2 \times 3 + 1 = 7$$

$$5^{\#} + 1 = 2 \times 3 \times 5 + 1 = 31$$

$$7^{\#} + 1 = 2 \times 3 \times 5 \times 7 + 1 = 211$$

$$11^{\#} + 1 = 2 \times 3 \times 5 \times 7 \times 11 + 1 = 2311$$

Please note that the construct of Euclidean numbers has been used in the solution of the preceding problem 13.

Please also note that all these Euclidean numbers are primes.

However, Euclidean numbers are not prime in general.

For example, $13^{\#} + 1, 17^{\#} + 1$ and $19^{\#} + 1$ are not primes.

15. By Euclid's Theorem, there is an infinite number of primes.

Apart from the proof at para 13 above, is there any other way to prove it?

Sol. There is an interesting method to prove Euclid's Theorem.

Consider following infinite sequence of positive integers.

$$n_1 = 2$$

$$n_2 = n_1 + 1$$

$$n_3 = n_1 n_2 + 1$$

$$n_4 = n_1 n_2 n_3 + 1$$

$$\vdots$$

$$n_k = n_1 n_2 \ldots . n_{k-1} + 1$$

Let n_i, n_j be two different terms of this sequence with $i < j$.

Let $d = \gcd(n_i, n_j)$

Then, $d \mid n_i, d \mid n_j$

$n_j = n_1 n_2 \ldots n_{j-1} + 1$

$\therefore$ $d \mid n_1 n_2 \ldots n_{j-1}$ $(\because n_i$ appears in $n_1 n_2 \ldots n_{j-1}$ as $i < j)$

$\therefore$ $d \mid (n_j - n_1 n_2 \ldots n_{j-1})$

or $d \mid 1$

Hence, $\gcd(n_i, n_j) = 1$

Thus, no two different terms of the given sequence $n_1, n_2, \ldots, n_k$ have any common divisors other than 1.

Also, each term of the sequence has a prime divisor as each term is greater than 1.

Thus, there are at least as many distinct primes as the number of terms in the given sequence $n_1, n_2, \ldots, n_k$.

But the number of terms in the given sequence is infinitely many.

Hence, there are infinitely many prime numbers.

16. Consecutive primes 2, 3 appear at a gap of 1 whereas consecutive primes 23, 29 appear at a gap of 6. Prove that arbitrarily large gap occurs between consecutive primes.

Sol. Consider the integers.

$$(n+1)!+2, (n+1)!+3, \ldots., (n+1)!+(n+1)$$

k divides $[(n+1)!+k], 1 < k \leq n+1$

Hence, all n consecutive integers in the given set of integers are composite.

Therefore, for any arbitrary integer n, there is a set of n consecutive composite numbers.

Thus, it is established that arbitrarily large gap occurs between consecutive primes.

17. A pair of odd integers p and $p+2$ that are both primes is called twin primes. Find some twin primes.

Sol. (3, 5), (5, 7), (11, 13), (17, 19), (29, 31) etc. are few examples of twin primes.

We do not know yet whether there are infinitely many twin primes.

18. If 1 is added to the product of twin primes, perfect square is obtained. Prove.

Sol. Let p and $p+2$ be twin primes.

$$p(p+2)+1 = p^2 + 2p + 1 = (p+1)^2$$

Thus, a perfect square is obtained.

19. There is an infinite number of primes of the form $4n+3$. Prove.

Sol. Suppose that there exists only a finite number of primes of the form $4n+3$.

Let $q_1, q_2, \ldots, q_s$ be the only finite number of the primes of the form $4n+3$.

Now consider the integer

$$N = 4q_1q_2...q_s - 1 = 4(q_1q_2...q_s - 1) + 3$$

Let $N = r_1r_2...r_t$ be its prime factorisation.

N is an odd integer.

Hence, 2 cannot be its factor.

Thus, $r_1, r_2, ..., r_t$ are of the form $4n+1$ or $4n+3$.

The product of any number of integers of the form $4n+1$ is again an integer of the same form.

But N is of the form $4n+3$.

Therefore, for N to take $4n+3$ form, at least one prime factor must be of the form $4n+3$.

As $q_1, q_2, ..., q_s$ are only prime numbers of the form $4n+3$, one of them appears in the prime factorisation of N.

Therefore, $q_i \mid N$ for some $i, 1 \le i \le s$

Also, $\quad q_i \mid 4q_1q_2...q_s$

$\therefore \quad q_i \mid (N - 4q_1q_2...q_s)$

$\therefore \quad q_i \mid 1$

This is a contradiction as $q_i > 1$.

Hence, our assumption about finiteness of primes of the form $4n+3$ is incorrect.

Thus, there are an infinite number of primes of the form $4n+3$.

20. The number $\sqrt{2}$ is irrational. Prove.

Sol. Suppose that $\sqrt{2}$ is a rational number.

Let $\sqrt{2} = \frac{a}{b}$ where a and b are positive integers and $\gcd(a, b) = 1$.

$\therefore \quad a^2 = 2b^2$

If $b > 1$, by Fundamental Theorem of Arithmetic, b has a prime factor p.

$$p \mid b$$

Hence, $\quad p \mid a^2 \quad (\because a^2 = 2b^2)$

$\therefore p \mid a$ (refer to the theorem at para 4 of this chapter)

$\therefore \quad \gcd(a, b) \ge p$,

But this is a contradiction because we assumed that $\gcd(a, b) = 1$.

Hence, b cannot be greater than 1.

But if $b = 1$, $a^2 = 2$ for some integer a.

$$1^2 = 1$$

$$2^2 = 4$$

$$1^2 = 1 < 2 < 4 = 2^2$$

Thus, there is no integer which can be squared to get 2.

Therefore, out supposition that $\sqrt{2}$ is rational is not correct.

Hence, $\sqrt{2}$ is an irrational number.

21. Find all pairs of primes p and q satisfying $p - q = 3$.

Sol. Let us consider various possibilities for p and q when any of p and q is less than or equal to 3.

For, $$p = 5, q = 2$$
$$p - q = 3$$

This is the only possible solution for $p - q = 3$, where p and q are primes.

Now let us consider the possibilities when none of p and q is less than or equal to 3.

We know that any prime number greater than 3 is always of the form $6n + 1$ or $6n + 5$.

Hence, difference between any two consecutive primes can only be 2 (between, $6n + 5$ and $6n + 7$) or 4 (between $6n + 1$ and $6n + 5$), at the least.

Thus, if $p, q \geq 5$, $p - q \neq 3$ for any primes p, q.

Thus, $p = 5$, $q = 2$ are the only primes satisfying $p - q = 3$.

22. It was claimed that the quadratic polynomial $f(n) = n^2 + n + 41$ produces only prime numbers for $n = 0, 1, 2, \ldots$ Verify this claim.

Sol.
$$f(n) = n^2 + n + 41$$
$$f(0) = 41$$
$$f(1) = 43$$
$$f(2) = 47$$
$$f(3) = 53$$
$$f(4) = 61$$
$$f(5) = 71$$
$$f(6) = 83$$
$$f(7) = 97$$
$$f(8) = 113$$
$$f(9) = 131$$
$$f(10) = 151$$

All these numbers are prime numbers.

It was earlier believed that the quadratic polynomial $f(n) = n^2 + n + 41$ assumes only prime values.

It was shown to be false by Euler in 1772.

$f(n)$ does assume only prime values for $n = 0, 1, 2, ..., 39$.

$$\begin{aligned} f(40) &= 40^2 + 40 + 41 \\ &= 40(40+1) + 41 \\ &= 40 \times 41 + 41 \\ &= 41 \times 41 = 41^2 \end{aligned}$$

$$\begin{aligned} f(41) &= 41^2 + 41 + 41 \\ &= 41 \times (41+1) + 41 \\ &= 41 \times 42 + 41 \\ &= 41 \times 43 \end{aligned}$$

$f(40)$ and $f(41)$ are composite numbers.

Thus, $f(n)$ does not assume only prime values.

23. If all the n $(n > 2)$ terms of the Arithmetic progression p, $p+d$, $p+2d$, ..., $p+(n-1)d$ are prime numbers, then prove that the common difference d is divisible by every prime $q < n$.

Sol. Consider a prime number $q < n$.

Suppose that $q \nmid d$.

Now consider following q terms of the progression
p, $p+d$, $p+2d$, ..., $p+(q-1)d$.

Consider two different terms of the sequence: $p+jd$ and $p+kd$.

Suppose $p+jd$ and $p+kd$ leave the same remainder r when divided by q.

Then, $$\left.\begin{aligned} p+jd &= l \times q + r \\ p+kd &= m \times q + r \end{aligned}\right\} \quad \text{(for some integers } l \text{ and } m\text{)}$$

$\therefore$ $$(j-k)d = q(l-m)$$

$\therefore$ $$q \mid (j-k)d$$

Now, $$q \nmid d \qquad \text{(by assumption)}$$

$\therefore$ $$\gcd(q, d) = 1 \qquad (\because q \text{ is prime})$$

Hence, by Euclid's Lemma, $q \mid j-k$ which is not possible as

$$0 \le j, k \le q-1$$

$\therefore$ $$0 < |j-k| < q$$

Thus, all q terms of the progression p, $p+d$, $p+2d$, ..., $p+(q-1)d$ leave different remainders when divided by q.

There are q different terms in this progression and q possible values of the remainder are $0, 1, 2, ..., q-1$. This means that the remainder is 0 for some term $p+td$.

Therefore, $q \mid p + td$ for some $t, 0 \leq t \leq q - 1$.

Please also note that $n \leq p$. This is because if $n > p$ then the sequence $p, p + d$, $p + 2d, ..., p + (n-1)d$ will have a term $p + pd = p(1 + d)$ which is a composite number.

Hence, $n \leq p$.

Now, $$q < n \leq p \leq p + td \text{ and } q \mid p + td$$

$\therefore$ $p + td$ is a composite number.

But all terms of the given progression are prime.

Thus, we arrive at a contradiction.

Hence, our supposition was incorrect.

Therefore, $q \mid d$ for every prime $q < n$.

24. Find an arithmetic progression of 6 terms, each of which is a prime.

Sol. From the preceding problem, we know that if $p, p + d, ..., p + (n-1)d$ is an arithmetic progression with all terms prime then

(i) $q \mid d$ for every prime $q < 6$

(ii) $p \geq n$

Hence, for an arithmetic progression of 6 terms with all 6 terms being prime

(i) $q \mid d$ for every prime $q < 6$

$\therefore$ $$2 \mid d, 3 \mid d, 5 \mid d$$

or, $$2 \times 3 \times 5 \mid d$$

or, $$30 \mid d$$

(ii) $p \geq 6$

Hence, minimum possible value of $d = 30$.

Minimum possible value of $p = 7$.

With these values of p and q, we get the arithmetic progression 7, 37, 67, 97, 127, 157. All these terms of this progression are prime.

Thus, we get an arithmetic progression of 6 terms 7, 37, 67, 97, 127, 157 all of which are primes.

25. Determine all primes that can divide two successive integers of the form $k^2 + 3$.

Sol. Suppose that prime p has the desired property.

Thus, $$p \mid k^2 + 3 \text{ and } p \mid (k+1)^2 + 3$$

$\therefore$ $$p \mid [(k+1)^2 + 3] - [k^2 + 3]$$

or, $$p \mid 2k + 1$$

Let $2k + 1 = pn$ for some integer n.

Then, $(2k)^2 = (pn-1)^2$

or, $4k^2 = p^2n^2 - 2pn + 1$

or, $(4k^2 - 1) = p^2n^2 - 2pn$

$\therefore$ $p \mid 4k^2 - 1$

Also, $p \mid 4(k^2 + 3)$ $(\because p \mid k^2 + 3)$

$\therefore$ $p \mid [4(k^2 + 3) - (4k^2 - 1)]$

or, $p \mid 13$

Hence, $p = 13$

Please note that $13 \mid 6^2 + 3$ and $13 \mid 7^2 + 3$.

26. Determine all twin primes p and $q (q = p + 2)$ such that $pq - 2$ is also a prime.

Sol. For $p = 3$, $q = 5$

$$pq - 2 = 13$$

3, 5 and 13 are all primes.

Suppose $p > 3$.

p cannot be of the form $3n$ as p is prime.

Then, if p is of the form $3n + 1$, $q = 3n + 3$ is not a prime.

If p is of the form $3n + 2$, $q = 3n + 4$ and

$$pq - 2 = (3n + 2)(3n + 4) - 2$$
$$= 9n^2 + 18n + 6 = 3(3n^2 + 6n + 2)$$

Thus, $pq - 2$ is a composite number.

Hence, $p = 3$ and $q = 5$ are the only twin primes with the desired property.

27. Find the number of divisors of 72. Also find the sum of divisors.

Sol. Let's write prime factorisation 72.

$$72 = 2^3 \times 3^2$$

Any number of the form $2^m \times 3^n$ is a divisor of 72, with $0 \le m \le 3$ and $0 \le n \le 2$.

Number of possible ways in which m and n can be chosen is $4 \times 3 = 12$.

Hence, number of divisors of 72 = 12

Please also note that each term in the expanded form of $(1 + 2 + 2^2 + 2^3)$ $(1 + 3 + 3^2)$ is a divisor of 72.

Also, there is no divisor of 72 which does not appear in the expanded form.

Hence, sum of divisors

$$= (1 + 2 + 2^2 + 2^3)(1 + 3 + 3^2)$$

$$=\left(\frac{2^4-1}{2-1}\right)\left(\frac{3^3-1}{3-1}\right)$$

$$=15\times\frac{26}{2}=15\times 13=195$$

In general, let $N = p_1^{n_1} \times p_2^{n_2} \dots p_r^{n_r}$ where $p_1, p_2, \dots, p_r$ are distinct prime numbers and $n_1, n_2, \dots, n_r \geq 1$.

Then, the number of divisors of N.

$$= \text{Number of numbers of the form } p_1^{t_1}\ p_2^{t_2} \dots p_r^{t_r} \text{ with } \begin{bmatrix} 0 \le t_1 \le n_1 \\ 0 \le t_2 \le n_2 \\ \dots\dots\dots \\ 0 \le t_r \le n_r \end{bmatrix}$$

$$= (n_1+1)(n_2+1)\dots(n_r+1)$$

Please note that each term in the following expression is a divisor of N and there are no other divisors:

$$(1+p_1+\dots+p_1^{n_1})(1+p_2+\dots+p_2^{n_2})\dots(1+p_r+\dots+p_r^{n_r})$$

Hence, Sum of divisors of N

$$=\left(\frac{p_1^{n_1+1}-1}{p_1-1}\right)\left(\frac{p_2^{n_2+1}-1}{p_2-1}\right)\dots\left(\frac{p_r^{n_r+1}-1}{p_r-1}\right)$$

28. Find the positive integer n such that each of the numbers $n+1, n+3, n+7, n+9$, $n+13$ and $n+15$ is a prime number.

Sol. For $n=1$, $n+7=8$ which is composite number.

For $n=2$, $n+7=9$ which is composite number.

For $n=3$, $n+3=6$ which is composite number.

For $n=4$, 5, 7, 11, 13, 17 and 19 all are prime numbers.

For $n>4$, all of $n+1, n+3, n+7, n+9, n+13, n+15>5$

Any integer has one of the forms $5k, 5k+1, 5k+2, 5k+3$ or $5k+4$.

If n is of the form $5k$, $n+15$ is a composite number.

If n is of the form $5k+1$, $n+9$ is a composite number.

If n is of the form $5k+2$, $n+13$ is a composite number.

If n is of the form $5k+3$, $n+7$ is a composite number.

If n is of the form $5k+4$, $n+1$ is a composite number. ($\because k>0$ for $n\geq 5$)

Hence, $n+1, n+3, n+7, n+9, n+13$ and $n+15$ all are prime numbers only for $n=4$.

29. If A and B are twin primes with $A, B > 3$, then what is the largest number that would always divide $A + B$?

Sol. Any prime number > 3 is always of the form $6n + 1$ or $6n + 5$.

Form of $6n + 5$ is equivalent to the form of $6n - 1$. $(\because 6n + 5 = 6(n + 1) - 1)$

Hence, twin primes > 3 are always of the form $6n - 1$ and $6n + 1$.

$\therefore \quad A + B = (6n - 1) + (6n + 1) = 12n$

Thus, $A + B$ is always divisible by 12.

30. How many natural numbers below 660 are divisible by 5 and 11 but not by 3?

Sol. If a number is divisible by 5 and 11, it is divisible by $5 \times 11 = 55$. $(\because lcm(5, 11) = 55)$

Numbers of multiples of 55 less than 660 = 11 (55, 110, 165, ..., 550, 605)

Out of 11 multiples of 55, 3 multiples are divisible by 3 (55×3, 55×6 and 55×9).

Hence, number of natural numbers below 660 divisible by 5 and 11 but not by 3

$$= 11 - 3 = 8$$

31. N is the smallest number that has 7 factors. How many factors does $(N - 1)$ have?

Sol. We know that for $N = p_1^{n_1} p_2^{n_2} \ldots p_r^{n_r}$ (prime factorisation of N), number of factors of N

$$= (n_1 + 1)(n_2 + 1) \ldots (n_r + 1)$$

Hence, if N has 7 factors, prime factorisation of N has to be of the form p^6.

Thus, smallest such number $= 2^6 = 64$

$$N - 1 = 63$$

$$63 = 3^2 \times 7$$

Hence, number of factors of $63 = (2 + 1)(1 + 1) = 3 \times 2 = 6$

32. If p and $p^2 + 2$ are primes, then prove that $p^3 + 2$ is also a prime.

Sol. For $p = 2$, $p^2 + 2$ is not a prime.

$p = 3$, $p^2 + 2 = 11$ and $p^3 + 2 = 29$

Thus, for $p = 3$, p, $p^2 + 2$ and $p^3 + 2$ all are primes.

For $p > 3$, p has one of the forms $6k + 1$ or $6k + 5$.

Hence, p^2 is of the form $6n + 1$.

$\therefore \quad p^2 + 2 = 6n + 1 + 2 = 6n + 3 = 3(2n + 1)$

Thus, $p^2 + 2$ is a composite number.

Therefore, the only value of p for which both p and $p^2 + 2$ are primes, is $p = 3$ and in this case $p^3 + 2$ is also a prime.

33. Let n be the largest integer that is the product of exactly 3 distinct prime numbers, x, y and $10x + y$, where x and y are digits. What is the sum of the digits of n?

Sol. We have x, y, $10x + y$ as primes.

We need to maximize $xy(10x + y)$.

The product is maximum if x, y are as large as possible and preferably $x > y$.

Let us consider various choices for x and y.

We start from the largest prime integer *i.e.* 7. ($\because x$ and y are digits.)

The other number cannot be 5 as 57 and 75 both are composite.

Other number can be 3 as 73 is prime.

So, the desired three numbers are 3, 7, 73.

$$\text{Product} = 3 \times 7 \times 73 = 1533$$

Sum of digits of the product $= 1 + 5 + 3 + 3 = 12$

34. Prove that for every prime $p > 7$, $p^6 - 1$ is divisible by 504.

Sol. Since $504 = 2^3 3^2 7$, it is enough to show that $p^6 - 1$ is a multiple of $2^3, 3^2$ and 7.

Let us examine divisibility by 8.

$p^6 - 1 = (p^2 - 1)(p^4 + p^2 + 1)$

As $p > 7$, p is an odd integer.

Therefore, p is of the form $4k + 1$ or $4k + 3$.

If p is of the form $4k + 1$, $p - 1$ is a multiple of 4 and $p + 1$ is a multiple of 2.

If p is of the form $4k + 3$, $p - 1$ is a multiple of 2 and $p + 1$ is a multiple of 4.

Therefore, $p^2 - 1$ is always divisible by 8.

$p^6 - 1$ is divisible by $p^2 - 1$.

Hence, $p^6 - 1$ is divisible by 8.

Let us examine divisibility by 9.

As $p > 7$, p has to be of the form $3k + 1$ or $3k + 2$.

In either case, one of $p - 1$ and $p + 1$ is divisible by 3.

Therefore, $p^2 - 1$ is always divisible by 3.

Now, $$p^6 - 1 = (p^2 - 1)(p^4 + p^2 + 1)$$
$$= (p^2 - 1)\{(p^2 - 1)^2 + 3p^2\}$$

Since $p^2 - 1$ is divisible by 3, $(p^2 - 1)^2 + 3p^2$ is also divisible by 3.

Consequently $p^6 - 1$ is divisible by 9.

Now let us examine divisibility by 7.

As $p > 7$, p is of one of the forms $7k+1, 7k+2, 7k+3, 7k+4, 7k+5$ or $7k+6$.

Hence, p^2 is of one of the forms $7k+1$, $7k+2$ and $7k+4$.

Hence, p^6 can only be of the form $7k+1$.

Hence, $p^6 - 1$ is divisible by 7.

As $p^6 - 1$ is divisible by 8, 9 and 7 and the numbers 8, 9 and 7 are co-primes in pairs, it is divisible by $8 \times 9 \times 7$, *i.e.* 504.

Exercise

1. The only prime p for which $3p+1$ is a perfect square is $p = 5$. Prove.

2. Find out all primes of the form $n^2 - 4$.

3. a and b are positive integers.
$\gcd(a, b) = p$ where p is a prime. Find :

(i) $\gcd(a^2, b^2)$ (ii) $\gcd(a, b^2)$ (iii) $\gcd(a^2, b^3)$

4. If $n > 4$ is composite, then n divides $(n-1)!$. Prove.

5. Find the number of factors of 696.

6. Find the sum of factors of 924.

7. Every integer of the form $n^4 + 4$ with $n > 1$, is composite. Prove.

8. Every integer $n > 11$ can be written as the sum of two composite numbers. Prove.

9. Find five primes of the form $n^2 + 1$.

10. If $p \neq 5$ is an odd prime, prove that either $p^2 - 1$ or $p^2 + 1$ is divisible by 10.

11. Which of the following numbers are prime numbers?

(a) 629 (b) 787

(c) 889 (d) 1433

12. If $n > 1$ is an integer not of the form $6n+3$, prove that $n^2 + 2^n$ is a composite number.

13. Let $N = p_1^{n_1} p_2^{n_2} \dots p_r^{n_r}$, where $p_1, p_2, \dots, p_r$ are distinct prime numbers and n_1, $n_2, \dots, n_r > 1$. Prove that N is a square if and only if all $n_1, n_2, \dots, n_r$ are even integers.

14. An integer is said to be square-free if it is not divisible by the square of any integer greater than 1.

(i) Prove that an integer $n > 1$ is square-free if and only if n can be factored into a product of distinct primes.

(ii) Prove that every integer $n > 1$ is the product of a square-free integer and a perfect square.

15. A positive integer n is called square-full or powerful, if $p^2 \mid n$ for every prime factor p of n. If n is square-full, show that it can be written in the form $n = a^2 b^3$ where a and b are positive integers.

16. Find a positive integer n such that $\frac{n}{2}$ is a square $\frac{n}{3}$ is a cube and $\frac{n}{5}$ is a fifth power.

17. If $\gcd(a, b) = c$ then $\gcd(a^2, b^2) = c^2$. Prove.

18. a and b are positive integers. $\gcd(a, b) = 1$ and ab is a perfect square. Prove that a and b are perfect squares.

19. Prove that $n^2 - 81n + 1681$ is a prime for $n = 1, 2, 3, \dots 80$, but not for $n = 81$.

20. Prove that an odd integer $n > 1$ is a prime if and only if it is not expressible as a sum of three or more consecutive positive integers.

21. Given that $p \nmid n$ for all primes $p \le \sqrt[3]{n}$, show that $n > 1$ is either a prime or the product of two primes.

22. $\sqrt{p}$ is irrational for any prime p. Prove.

23. Any composite 3-digit number must have a prime factor less than or equal to 31. Prove.

24. If $n > 2$ then there exists a prime p satisfying $n < p < n!$. Prove.

25. For $n > 1$ prove that every prime divisor of $n! + 1$ is an odd integer that is greater than n.

26. Let p_n be the nth prime number. Prove that none of the integers $P_n = p_1 p_2 \cdots p_n + 1$ is a perfect square.

27. For repunits R_n, prove the following.

(i) If $n|m$, then $R_n \mid R_m$

(ii) If $q \mid R_n$ and $q \mid R_m$ then $q \mid R_{n+m}$

(iii) If $\gcd(n, m) = 1$, then $\gcd(R_n, R_m) = 1$

28. Are integers 1949 and 1951 twin primes?

29. Any integer $n > 9$ can be written as a sum of distinct odd primes. Express the integers 18, 35, 65 and 111 in this manner.

30. For $n > 1$, $n!$ is never a perfect square. Prove.

31. Find the value of $n \geq 1$ for which $n! + (n+1)! + (n+2)!$ is a perfect square.

32. What is the highest power of 2 contained in 50!?

33. $M = 2^5 \times 3^4 \times 5^6$, $N = 2^7 \times 3^2 \times 5^8$. What is the number of common factors of M and N?

34. If $n = x + 1$ where x is a product of four consecutive positive integers, then which of the following is (are) true?

(i) n is odd (ii) n is prime

(iii) n is a perfect square.

35. Find all primes which can be represented both as sums and difference of two primes.

36. For every even $n > 6$, there exist primes p and q such that $\gcd(n - p, n - q) = 1$. Prove.

37. Find all solutions of $x^2 + y^3 = z^4$ in prime numbers x, y, z.

38. Let k be a positive integer. Prove that the arithmetic progression $a, a + d, a + 2d, a + 3d, \ldots$ of positive integers, where $\gcd(a, d) = 1$, contains k consecutive terms that are composite.

39. Find all primes of the form $p^2 + 2^p$ where p is prime.

40. Show that $n^4 + 4$ is divisible by at least two primes for all $n > 1$.

41. Find all integers n for which $n^2 + n + 41$ is a perfect square.

42. Find all primes p and q such that $p^2 + 7pq + q^2$ is the square of an integer. p and q are distinct primes.

Answers

2. 5 **3.** (i) p^2 (ii) p (iii) p^2 **5.** 16 **6.** 2688

9. 2, 5, 17, 37, 101 **11.** (b), (d)

16. $2^{15(2p+1)} \cdot 3^{10(3q+1)} \cdot 5^{6(5r+1)}$, where p, q, r are integers, $p, q, r \geq 0$

28. Yes **31.** $n = 1$ **32.** 47 **33.** 126 **34.** (i), (iii)

35. 5 **37.** No such x, y, z **39.** 17 is only such prime.

41. $n = -41, 40$ **42.** $p = 3, q = 11$ and $p = 11, q = 3$ are only possible solutions.

07

The Theory of Congruences

"Mathematics is the queen of the sciences and number-theory the queen of mathematics."
—***Carl Friedrich Gauss***

1. Do you remember the question asked in the very first chapter of this book?

"What will be the remainder when 2^{981} is divided by 3?"

We also made the promise that you will be able to answer this question within seconds if you knew *"The Theory of Congruences"*. *"The Theory of Congruences"* is a very powerful tool of Number Theory.

Once you understand this tool, you will be able to answer the following questions very quickly.

- What will be the remainder when $1^5 + 2^5 + 3^5 + \ldots + 99^5 + 100^5$ is divided by 4?
- What is the last digit (unit digit) of 73^{73}?
- Last two digits of a number N are 67. What are the last two digit of N^2?
- What is the remainder when any odd power (> 1) of any odd number is divided by 8?
- A positive integer N leaves remainder 1, 2, 3, 4 when divided by 5, 7, 9, 11 respectively. What is the minimum value of N?

2. The theory of congruences is basically related to the properties of remainders.

Let us see a few examples to understand these properties.

- What is the remainder when 17 is divided by 8?

  → 1
- What is the remainder when 35 is divided by 8?

  → 3

- What is the remainder when 52 *i.e.*, $(17+35)$ is divided by 8?

  → 4 which is equal to $1+3$, (*i.e.* the sum of remainders in the two cases above)

Is it just a coincidence in this case?

Let us verify it for one more case.

- What is the remainder when 29 is divided by 11?

  → 7
- What is the remainder when 89 is divided by 11?

  → 1
- What is the remainder when 118 *i.e.* $(29+89)$ is divided by 11?

  → 8 which is equal to $7+1$, (*i.e.* the sum of remainders in the two cases above)

This property holds true in general.

What if the sum of remainders is greater than the divisor?

Let us take an example.

- What is the remainder when 27 is divided by 5?

  → 2
- What is the remainder when 39 is divided by 5?

  → 4
- What is the remainder when 66 (*i.e.* $27+39$) is divided by 5?

  → 1 which is equal to the remainder obtained when 6 (*i.e.*, $2+4$, the sum of remainders) in the two cases above is divided by 5.

3. In the preceding paragraph we noticed the relationship between the remainders obtained when two integers are separately divided by a particular integer and the remainder obtained when their sum is divided by the same integer.

Isn't it interesting to note that the remainders with respect to a particular divisor add just like the integers?

Is there any such relationship when two integers are multiplied?

Let us verify through some examples.

- What is the remainder when 7 is divided by 3?

  → 1
- What is the remainder when 17 is divided by 3?

  → 2
- What is the remainder when 119 (*i.e.* 7×17) is divided by 3?

  → 2 which is the product of remainders (*i.e.* 1×2) in the two cases above.

Let us take one more example.

- What is the remainder when 16 is divided by 7?

  $\to$ 2
- What is the remainder when 24 is divided by 7?

  $\to$ 3
- What is the remainder when 384 (*i.e.* 16×24) is divided by 7?

  $\to$ 6 which is the product of remainders (*i.e.* 2×3) in the two cases above.

It is really interesting to note that the remainders add and multiply just like the integers with respect to a particular divisor.

4. Let us see another interesting property of remainders.

- What is the remainder when 6 is divided by 5?

  $\to$ 1

Now add 1 to 6. We get 7.

- What is the remainder when 7 is divided by 5?

  $\to$ 2 which is the remainder obtained above as increased by 1

Add 2 to 6. We get 8.

- What is the remainder when 8 is divided by 5?

  $\to$ 3 which is the remainder obtained above as increased by 2

Thus, the remainder obtained by dividing an integer by a given divisor increases exactly as much as the given integer is increased. Is this statement true in all cases? Verify.

5. What happens when addition in para 4 above is replaced by multiplication?

Examples in the table below are with respect to divisor 5.

Divided by 5	**Remainder**	**Remarks**
6	1	
12 (*i.e.*, 6×2)	2	2 times the remainder when 6 is divided by 5 (*i.e.* 2×1)
18 (*i.e.*, 6×3)	3	3 times the remainder when 6 is divided by 5 (*i.e.* 3×1)
24 (*i.e.*, 6×4)	4	4 times the remainder when 6 is divided by 5 (*i.e.* 4×1)

Thus, we can see that the remainder obtained by dividing an integer by a given divisor gets multiplied by the same number as the given integer.

Is this statement true in all cases? Verify.

6. Now, let's examine the property of remainders in case of various powers of integers.

Examples in the table below are with respect to divisor 3.

Divided by 3	Remainder	Remarks
5	2	
5^2	1	Same as the remainder when 2^2 is divided by 3
5^3	2	Same as the remainder when 2^3 is divided by 3
5^4	1	Same as the remainder when 2^4 is divided by 3

Thus, we can see that when power is applied over a given integer, the remainder also follows the same pattern of power.

7. From the above discussion it is clear that the remainders with respect to a particular divisor add and multiply just like the integers. The theory of congruences is all about such properties of remainders.

8. Given a positive integer n, two integers a and b are said to be congruent modulo n, if n divides $a - b$ (*i.e.*, $a - b = kn$ for some integer k).

If a is congruent to b modulo n, it is denoted as $a \equiv b \pmod{n}$.

For example,

$8 \equiv 0 \pmod{2}$ (because 2 divides $8 - 0 = 8$)

$7 \equiv 1 \pmod{2}$ (because 2 divides $7 - 1 = 6$)

$11 \equiv 2 \pmod{3}$ (because 3 divides $11 - 2 = 9$)

$37 \equiv 1 \pmod{6}$ (because 6 divides $37 - 1 = 36$)

$58 \equiv 3 \pmod{11}$ (because 11 divides $58 - 3 = 55$)

9. Suppose $n > 1$ is a fixed integer. a, b, c and d are arbitrary integers. The following properties hold true.

(i) $a \equiv a \pmod{n}$.

(ii) If $a \equiv b \pmod{n}$, then $b \equiv a \pmod{n}$.

(iii) If $a \equiv b \pmod{n}$ and $b \equiv c \pmod{n}$ then $a \equiv c \pmod{n}$.

(iv) If $a \equiv b \pmod{n}$ and $c \equiv d \pmod{n}$ then $a + c \equiv b + d \pmod{n}$.

(v) If $a \equiv b \pmod{n}$ and $c \equiv d \pmod{n}$ then $ac \equiv bd \pmod{n}$.

(vi) If $a \equiv b \pmod{n}$ then $a + c \equiv b + c \pmod{n}$.

(vii) If $a \equiv b \pmod{n}$ then $ac \equiv bc \pmod{n}$.

(viii) If $a \equiv b \pmod{n}$ then $a^x \equiv b^x \pmod{n}$ for any positive integer x.

It is very easy to prove the properties above. Let us prove them one by one.

10. Theorem : $a \equiv a \pmod{n}$

Let us see few examples.

$$3 - 3 = 0 = 0 \times 5$$

Hence, $3 \equiv 3 \pmod{5}$

Similarly, $11 \equiv 11 \pmod{13}$

In general, $a - a = 0 = 0 \times n$

Hence, $a \equiv a \pmod{n}$

11. Theorem : If $a \equiv b \pmod{n}$, then $b \equiv a \pmod{n}$

Let us see few examples.

$$5 - 3 = 2 = 2 \times 1$$

Hence, $5 \equiv 3 \pmod{2}$

Now, $3 - 5 = -2 = 2 \times (-1)$

Hence, $3 \equiv 5 \pmod{2}$

Similarly, $27 \equiv 15 \pmod{6}$

Now, $15 - 27 = -12 = 6 \times (-2)$

Hence, $15 \equiv 27 \pmod{6}$

In general, if $a \equiv b \pmod{n}$

then $a - b = kn$ for some integer k

Hence, $b - a = -kn = (-k)n$

Hence, from the definition of congruence, it follows that $b \equiv a \pmod{n}$.

12. Theorem : If $a \equiv b \pmod{n}$ and $b \equiv c \pmod{n}$, then $a \equiv c \pmod{n}$.

Let us see few examples.

$$12 \equiv 7 \pmod{5}$$

Also, $7 \equiv 2 \pmod{5}$

Now, note that $12 \equiv 2 \pmod{5}$

because $12 - 2 = 10 = 5 \times 2$

In general, if $a \equiv b \pmod{n}$

then $a - b = kn$ for some integer k ...(i)

Similarly, if $b \equiv c \pmod{n}$

then $b - c = ln$ for some integer l .... (ii)

From equations (i) and (ii), we get

$$a - c = (a - b) + (b - c) = kn + ln = (k + l)n$$

Hence, $a \equiv c \pmod{n}$.

13. Theorem : If $a \equiv b \pmod{n}$ and $c \equiv d \pmod{n}$, then $(a + c) \equiv (b + d) \pmod{n}$.

Let us see few examples.

$$17 \equiv 1 \pmod{8}$$

$$35 \equiv 3 \pmod{8}$$

then, $$52 \equiv 4 \pmod{8} \qquad (52 = 17 + 35 \text{ and } 4 = 1 + 3)$$

In general, if $a \equiv b \pmod{n}$ and $c \equiv d \pmod{n}$

then, $a - b = kn$ and $c - d = \text{ln}$ for some integers k and l

Now, $$(a + c) - (b + d) = (a - b) + (c - d)$$

$$= kn + ln$$

$$= (k + 1)n$$

Hence, $$(a + c) \equiv (b + d) \pmod{n}$$

14. Theorem : If $a \equiv b \pmod{n}$ and $c \equiv d \pmod{n}$, then $ac \equiv bd \pmod{n}$.

Let us see few examples.

$$7 \equiv 1 \pmod{3}$$

$$17 \equiv 2 \pmod{3}$$

Now, $$7 \times 17 = 119 \text{ and } 119 \equiv 2 \pmod{3}$$

Please note that $$7 \times 17 = 1 \times 2 \pmod{3}$$

In general, if $a \equiv b \pmod{n}$ and $c \equiv d \pmod{n}$.

then, $a - b = kn$ and $c - d = ln$ for some integers k and l

or, $$a = b + kn \text{ and } c = d + ln$$

Hence, $$ac = (b + kn)\ (d + ln)$$

$$= bd + bln + kdn + kln^2$$

$$= bd + (bl + kd + kln)n$$

or, $$ac - bd = (bl + kd + kln)n$$

Hence, $$ac \equiv bd \pmod{n}$$

15. Theorem : If $a \equiv b \pmod{n}$, then $a + c \equiv b + c \pmod{n}$.

Let us see few examples.

$$6 \equiv 1 \pmod{5}$$

Please note that $$6 + 1 \equiv 1 + 1 \pmod{5}$$

or, $$7 \equiv 2 \pmod{5}$$

In general, if $$a \equiv b \pmod{n}$$

then $a - b = kn$ for some integer k.

Now, $$(a + c) - (b + c) = a - b = kn$$

Hence, $$a + c \equiv b + c \pmod{n}$$

16. Theorem : If $a \equiv b \pmod{n}$ then $ac \equiv bc \pmod{n}$.

Let us see few examples.

$$6 \equiv 1 \pmod 5$$
$$6 \times 2 = 12$$
$$1 \times 2 = 2$$

Please note that $12 \equiv 2 \pmod 5$

or, $6 \times 2 \equiv 1 \times 2 \pmod 5$

In general, if $a \equiv b \pmod n$ then $a - b = kn$ for some integer k.

Now,
$$(ac - bc) = (a - b)c$$
$$= knc$$
$$= (kc)n$$

Hence, $ac \equiv bc \pmod n$

17. Theorem : If $a \equiv b \pmod{n}$ then $a^x \equiv b^x \pmod{n}$ for any positive integer x.

Let us see few examples.

$$5 \equiv 2 \pmod 3$$
$$5^2 = 25$$
$$2^2 = 4$$

Please note that $25 \equiv 4 \pmod 3$

or, $5^2 \equiv 2^2 \pmod 3$

Similarly,
$$5^3 = 125$$
$$2^3 = 8$$

Please note that $5^3 \equiv 2^3 \pmod 3$

In general, if $a \equiv b \pmod n$, then $a - b = kn$ for some integer k.

We can prove this property by the method of mathematical induction.

If $x = 1$, then the given statement is trivially true.

Now, suppose that the given statement is true for $x = t$ *i.e.,* $a^t \equiv b^t \pmod n$ for some fixed integer t.

Hence, $a \equiv b \pmod n$ and $a^t \equiv b^t \pmod n$.

Now, by virtue of the property discussed at para 14 above,

$$a \times a^t \equiv b \times b^t \pmod n \text{ or } a^{t+1} \equiv b^{t+1} \pmod n$$

Thus, the theorem is proved.

18. Consider integers 0, 1, 2, 3 and 4.

$$0 \equiv 0 \pmod 5$$
$$1 \equiv 1 \pmod 5$$
$$2 \equiv 2 \pmod 5$$
$$3 \equiv 3 \pmod 5$$
$$4 \equiv 4 \pmod 5$$

Please also note that none of these integers are congruent to each other in pairs. For example,

$$0 \not\equiv 2 \pmod 5$$
$$4 \not\equiv 1 \pmod 5$$
$$3 \not\equiv 4 \pmod 5$$

and so on.

Please also note that 0, 1, 2, 3 and 4 are only possible remainders when any integer is divided by 5.

The set of five integers 0, 1, 2, 3, 4 is called the set of least non-negative residues modulo 5.

Can you find another set of five integers with the given properties?

Consider integers 5, 6, 7, 8 and 9.

$$5 \equiv 0 \pmod 5$$
$$6 \equiv 1 \pmod 5$$
$$7 \equiv 2 \pmod 5$$
$$8 \equiv 3 \pmod 5$$
$$9 \equiv 4 \pmod 5$$

The integers 5, 6, 7, 8 and 9 are congruent to 0, 1, 2, 3 and 4 respectively modulo 5. Further no two of the integers 5, 6, 7, 8 and 9 are congruent to each other modulo 5. The set of integers 5, 6, 7, 8 and 9 is said to form a complete set of residues or a complete system of residues.

19. In general, the set of n integers 0, 1, 2, ..., $n-1$ is called the set of least nonnegative residues modulo n.

20. In general, a collection of n integers $a_1, a_2, ..., a_n$ is said to form a complete set of residues or a complete system of residues modulo n if $a_1, a_2, ..., a_n$ are congruent to 0, 1, 2, ..., $n-1$ modulo n in some order.

21. Consider following set of integers.

26, 55, 68, 12, 19

$$26 \equiv 1 \pmod 5$$
$$55 \equiv 0 \pmod 5$$
$$68 \equiv 3 \pmod 5$$

$$12 \equiv 2 (\text{mod } 5)$$
$$19 \equiv 4 (\text{mod } 5)$$

Thus, the set of integers 26, 55, 68, 12 and 19 constitutes a complete set of residues modulo 5.

22. It is interesting to note here how division algorithm comes into picture.

Let n be the given integer ($n > 0$).

Then, for any arbitrary integer a, there exist integers q and r such that $a = qn + r$, $0 \leq r < n$

$\therefore$ $$a \equiv r \ (\text{mod } n)$$

There are n possible values for r: $0, 1, 2, \ldots, n-1$.

Hence, every integer a is congruent modulo n to exactly one of $0, 1, 2, \ldots, n-1$.

23. Theorem : For arbitrary integers a and b, $a \equiv b$ (mod n) if and only if a and b leave same non-negative remainder when divided by n.

Proof : Suppose $a \equiv b$ (mod n)

$\therefore$ $$n \mid a - b$$

Hence, $a - b = kn$ for some integer k.

Suppose quotient and remainder are q and r respectively when b is divided by n.

Hence, $b = qn + r$, where $0 \leq r < n$

$$a - b = kn$$

or, $$a = b + kn$$
$$= (qn + r) + kn$$
$$= (q + k)n + r$$

Thus, a leaves remainder r, same as in case of b, when divided by n.

Now suppose that a and b leave the same remainder r when divided by n.

Then, $a = q_1 n + r$

and $b = q_2 n + r$ (for some integers q_1 and q_2)

$\therefore$ $$a - b = (q_1 - q_2)n$$

$\therefore$ $$n \mid a - b$$

Hence, $$a \equiv b (\text{mod } n)$$

The proof of the theorem is complete.

24. $3 \times 4 \equiv 3 \times 1 \ (\text{mod } 9)$

But $4 \not\equiv 1 \ (\text{mod } 9)$

Thus, common factors cannot be cancelled in the arithmetic of congruences.

25. Theorem : If $ca \equiv cb \pmod{n}$, then $a \equiv b\left(\bmod \frac{n}{d}\right)$, where $d = \gcd(c, n)$.

Proof : $ca \equiv cb \pmod{n}$

Hence, $$n \mid (ca - cb)$$

$\therefore$ $$c(a - b) = nk \quad \text{(for some integer } k\text{)}$$

$$d = \gcd(c, n)$$

Hence, there exist relatively prime integers r and s satisfying

$$c = dr$$

$$n = ds$$

Now, $$c(a - b) = nk$$

or, $$(dr)(a - b) = (ds)k$$

or, $$r(a - b) = sk$$

Now, $s \mid r(a - b)$ and $\gcd(r, s) = 1$

Hence, by Euclid's lemma

$$s \mid (a - b)$$

or, $$\left(\frac{n}{d}\right) \mid a - b$$

$\therefore$ $$a \equiv b\left(\bmod \frac{n}{d}\right)$$

26. Following corollary follows from the preceding theorem.

If $ca \equiv cb \pmod{n}$ and $\gcd(c, n) = 1$, then $a \equiv b \pmod{n}$.

In other words, if common factor c is relatively prime to n, the common factor can be cancelled.

27. Corollary : If $ca \equiv cb \pmod{p}$ and $p \nmid c$, where p is *a* prime number, then $a \equiv b \pmod{p}$.

Proof : p is a prime and $p \nmid c$.

Hence, $\gcd(c, p) = 1$

Hence, it follows from corollary at para 26 that $a \equiv b \pmod{p}$.

28. $$6 \not\equiv 0 \pmod{12}$$

$$4 \not\equiv 0 \pmod{12}$$

However, $6 \times 4 \equiv 0 \pmod{12}$

Thus, two integers may not be congruent to zero modulo n.

However, their product may turn out to be congruent to zero modulo n.

29. An equation of the form $ax \equiv b \pmod{n}$ is called a linear congruence.

If for some integer x_0, $ax_0 \equiv b \pmod{n}$, then x_0 is a solution of the given linear congruence.

30. $ax \equiv b \pmod{n}$

By definition, $n \mid ax - b$

or, $\quad ax - b = ny \quad$ for integer y

$\therefore \quad ax - ny = b$

Thus, the problem of finding solution of linear congruence $ax \equiv b \pmod{n}$ is identical to that of finding solution of the linear Diophantine equation $ax - ny = b$.

31. Theorem : The linear congruence $ax \equiv b \pmod{n}$ has a solution if and only if $d \mid b$, where $d = \gcd(a, n)$.
If $d \mid b$, then it has d mutually incongruent solutions modulo n.

Proof : The given congruence is equivalent to the linear Diophantine equation $ax - ny = b$.

We know that this Diophantine equation can be solved if and only if $d \mid b$ where $d = \gcd(a, n)$.

Further, if this Diophantine equation is solvable and x_0, y_0 is one specific solution, then any other solution has the form

$x = x_0 - \frac{n}{d}t$, $y = y_0 - \frac{a}{d}t$ for arbitrary integer t

Without loss of generality, we can write $x = x_0 = \frac{n}{d}t$ as t is an arbitrary integer.

Thus, $x = x_0 + \frac{n}{d}t$ represents solution of the linear congruence $ax \equiv b \pmod{n}$.

Among various solutions, consider the solutions when $t = 0, 1, 2, ..., d - 1$.

$$x_0,\ x_0 + \frac{n}{d},\ x_0 + \frac{2n}{d}, ...,\ x_0 + \frac{(d-1)n}{d}$$

Suppose that one member of this set is congruent modulo n to some other member.

i.e. $x_0 + \frac{n}{d}t_1 \equiv x_0 + \frac{n}{d}t_2 \pmod{n}$ where $0 \le t_1 < t_2 \le d - 1$

Hence, $\quad \frac{n}{d}t_1 \equiv \frac{n}{d}t_2 \pmod{n}$

$\therefore \quad t_1 \equiv t_2 \pmod{d} \qquad$ (By Theorem at para 25)

$\therefore \quad d \mid t_2 - t_1$

But $\quad 0 < t_2 - t_1 < d$

This is a contradiction.

Thus, no two members of the given set of solutions are congruent modulo n to each other.

Now consider any arbitrary solution $x_0 + \frac{n}{d}t$ of the linear congruence $ax \equiv b \pmod{n}$.

By division algorithm, t can be written as $t = qd + r$, where $0 \le r \le d - 1$

Hence,
$$x_0 + \frac{n}{d}t = x_0 + \frac{n}{d}(qd + r)$$
$$= x_0 + nq + \frac{n}{d}r$$
$$\equiv x_0 + \frac{n}{d}r \pmod{n}$$

with $x_0 + \frac{n}{d}r$ being one of our d selected solutions

Thus, $x_0,\ x_0 + \frac{n}{d},\ x_0 + \frac{2n}{d},\ \ldots,\ x_0 + \frac{(d-1)n}{d}$ represent d mutually incongruent solutions modulo n.

32. From the preceding theorem, following corollary follows.

If $\gcd(a, n) = 1$, then the linear congruence $ax \equiv b \pmod{n}$ has a unique solution modulo n.

This solution is called the (multiplicative) inverse of a modulo n.

Solved Examples

1. What is the remainder when 3^5 is divided by 8?

Sol. $3^2 = 9 = 8 + 1$

Hence, $$3^2 \equiv 1 \pmod{8}$$

Squaring both sides, we get $(3^2)^2 \equiv (1)^2 \pmod{8}$ ..... (i)

($\because$ If $a \equiv b \pmod{n}$ then $a^k \equiv b^k \pmod{n}$ for any positive integer k)

Multiplying both sides of (i) by 3, we get $3 \times 3^4 \equiv 3 \times 1 \pmod{8}$

($\because$ If $a \equiv b \pmod{n}$ then $ac \equiv bc \pmod{n}$ for any integer c)

or, $$3^5 \equiv 3 \pmod{8}$$

$\therefore$ $$3^5 - 3 = 8q \qquad \text{for some integer } q$$

or, $$3^5 = 8q + 3$$

Hence, the remainder is 3 when 3^5 is divided by 8.

2. What is the remainder when 2^{18} is divided by 7?

Sol. $2^3 = 8 = 7 + 1$

Hence, $2^3 \equiv 1 \pmod 7$

$\therefore$ $(2^3)^6 \equiv (1)^6 \pmod 7$

or, $2^{18} \equiv 1 \pmod 7$

Hence, the remainder is 1 when 2^{18} is divided by 7.

3. What is the remainder when 2^{150} is divided by 7?

Sol. $2^3 \equiv 1 \pmod 7$

Hence, $(2^3)^{50} \equiv (1)^{50} \pmod 7$

or, $2^{150} \equiv 1 \pmod 7$

Hence, the remainder is 1 when 2^{150} is divided by 7.

4. What is the remainder when 41^{101} is divided by 7?

Sol. $41 \equiv -1 \pmod 7$

Hence, $(41)^{101} \equiv (-1)^{101} \pmod 7$

or, $41^{101} \equiv -1 \pmod 7$

$-1 \equiv 6 \pmod 7$

Hence, $41^{101} \equiv 6 \pmod 7$

($\because$ if $a \equiv b \pmod n$ and $b \equiv c \pmod n$, then $a \equiv c \pmod n$)

Thus, the remainder is 6 when 41^{101} is divided by 7.

5. What is the unit digit of 7^{31}?

Sol. Please note that if we divide any integer n by 10, we get unit digit of n as the remainder.

$7^2 = 49 = 50 + (-1)$

Hence, $7^2 \equiv -1 \pmod{10}$

$\therefore$ $(7^2)^{15} \equiv (-1)^{15} \pmod{10}$

or, $7^{30} \equiv -1 \pmod{10}$

or, $7 \times 7^{30} \equiv 7 \times (-1) \pmod{10}$

or, $7^{31} \equiv -7 \pmod{10}$

$-7 \equiv 3 \pmod{10}$

Hence, $7^{31} \equiv 3 \pmod{10}$

($\because$ if $a \equiv b \pmod n$ and $b \equiv c \pmod n$, then $a \equiv c \pmod n$)

Thus, $7^{31} - 3$ is divisible by 10.

Therefore, unit digit of $7^{31} - 3$ is 0.

Hence, unit digit of 7^{31} is 3.

6. What is the unit digit of 73^{73}?

Sol.
$$73 \equiv 3 \pmod{10}$$

$\therefore$
$$73^2 = 9 \pmod{10}$$

or,
$$73^2 \equiv -1 \pmod{10}$$

$\therefore$
$$73^{72} \equiv 1 \pmod{10}$$

$\therefore$
$$73^{73} \equiv 3 \pmod{10}$$

Hence, 10 divides $73^{73} - 3$.

Thus, unit digit of 73^{73} is 3.

7. What is the unit digit of 3^{400}?

Sol.
$$3^2 \equiv -1 \pmod{10}$$

$\therefore$
$$(3^2)^{200} \equiv (-1)^{200} \pmod{10}$$

or,
$$3^{400} \equiv 1 \pmod{10}$$

$\therefore$ $3^{400} - 1$ is divisible by 10.

Hence, unit digit of 3^{400} is 1.

8. What is the unit digit of 2^{400}?

Sol.
$$2^4 \equiv 6 \pmod{10}$$

$\therefore$
$$2^{400} \equiv 6^{100} \pmod{10}$$

or,
$$2^{400} \equiv 6 \pmod{10}$$

($\therefore$ any power of 6 always has unit digit 6)

Hence, 6 is the unit digit of 2^{400}.

9. Find the last two digits of 3^{400}.

Sol.
$$3^2 \equiv 9 \pmod{100}$$

$\therefore$
$$3^4 \equiv 81 \pmod{100}$$

$\therefore$
$$3^8 \equiv 61 \pmod{100}$$

$\therefore$
$$3^{16} \equiv 21 \pmod{100}$$

$\therefore$
$$3^{20} \equiv 01 \pmod{100}$$

$\therefore$
$$(3^{20})^{20} \equiv (01)^{20} \pmod{100}$$

$\therefore \qquad 3^{400} \equiv 1 \pmod{100}$

Thus, $3^{400} - 1$ is divisible by 100.

Hence, 01 are the last two digits of 3^{400}.

10. Is $2^{20} - 1$ divisible by 41?

Sol. $$2^5 = 32 = 41 + (-9)$$

Hence, $$2^5 \equiv (-9) \pmod{41}$$

or, $$(2^5)^2 \equiv (-9)^2 \pmod{41}$$

or, $$2^{10} \equiv 81 \pmod{41}$$

$$81 \equiv -1 \pmod{41}$$

Hence, $$2^{10} \equiv -1 \pmod{41}$$

or, $$(2^{10})^2 \equiv (-1)^2 \pmod{41}$$

or, $$2^{20} \equiv 1 \pmod{41}$$

Hence, 41 divides $2^{20} - 1$.

11. What is the remainder when 7^{198} is divided by 11?

Sol. $$7 \equiv -4 \pmod{11}$$

$\therefore$ $$7^2 \equiv 5 \pmod{11} \qquad \text{...(i)}$$

$\therefore$ $$7^4 \equiv 3 \pmod{11} \qquad \text{...(ii)}$$

$\therefore$ $$7^8 \equiv 9 \pmod{11}$$

$\therefore$ $$7^{16} \equiv 4 \pmod{11}$$

$\therefore$ $$7^{32} \equiv 5 \pmod{11}$$

$\therefore$ $$7^{64} \equiv 3 \pmod{11} \qquad \text{...(iii)}$$

$\therefore$ $$7^{128} \equiv 9 \pmod{11} \qquad \text{...(iv)}$$

Multiplying (iii) and (iv), we get

$$7^{128+64} \equiv 9 \times 3 \pmod{11}$$

[$\because$ if $a \equiv b \pmod{n}$ and $c \equiv d \pmod{n}$ then $ac \equiv bd \pmod{n}$]

or, $$7^{192} \equiv 5 \pmod{11} \qquad \text{...(v)}$$

Multiplying (i), (ii) and (v), we get

$$7^{2+4+192} \equiv 5 \times 3 \times 5 \pmod{11}$$

or, $$7^{198} \equiv 9 \pmod{11}$$

Hence, the remainder is 9 when 7^{198} is divided by 11.

12. What is the remainder when 4444^{4444} is divided by 9?

Sol.
$$4444 \equiv 7 \pmod 9$$
or,
$$4444 \equiv 16 \pmod 9$$
or,
$$4444 \equiv 2^4 \pmod 9$$
$\therefore$
$$4444^{4444} \equiv 2^{17776} \pmod 9$$
$$2^3 \equiv -1 \pmod 9$$
$$17776 = 3 \times 5925 + 1$$
$\therefore$
$$\begin{aligned} 4444^{4444} &\equiv 2^{17776} \pmod 9 \\ &\equiv (2^3)^{5925}\, 2 \pmod 9 \\ &\equiv (-1)\, 2 \pmod 9 \\ &\equiv 7 \pmod 9 \end{aligned}$$

Hence, the remainder is 7.

13. What is the remainder when $1! + 2! + 3! + 4! + \ldots + 100!$ is divided by 16?

Sol. $6! = 1 \times 2 \times 3 \times 4 \times 5 \times 6 = 45 \times 16$

Hence, $16 \mid 6!$

Thus, $16 \mid r!$ for all $r \geq 6$

Now,
$$\begin{aligned} &1! + 2! + 3! + 4! + \ldots + 100! \\ &\equiv 1 + 2! + 3! + 4! + 5! + 0 + 0 + \ldots + 0 \pmod{16} \\ &\equiv 1 + 2 + 6 + 8 + 8 \pmod{16} \\ &\equiv 9 \pmod{16} \end{aligned}$$

Hence, the remainder is 9 when $1! + 2! + 3! + \ldots + 100!$ is divided by 16.

14. Prove that if a is an odd integer, then $a^2 \equiv 1 \pmod 8$.

Sol. We know that any integer is of one of the forms $8k$, $8k+1$, $8k+2$, $8k+3$, $8k+4$, $8k+5$, $8k+6$ or $8k+7$.

If a is an odd integer, a is of one of the forms $8k+1$, $8k+3$, $8k+5$ or $8k+7$.

Hence,
$$a \equiv 1, 3, 5 \text{ or } 7 \pmod 8$$
or,
$$a^2 \equiv 1^2, 3^2, 5^2, \text{ or } 7^2 \pmod 8$$
or,
$$a^2 \equiv 1, 9, 25 \text{ or } 49 \pmod 8$$
$\therefore$
$$a^2 \equiv 1 \pmod 8$$

15. Prove that for any integer a, $a^4 \equiv 0$ or $1 \pmod 5$

Sol. Any integer is of one of the forms $5k$, $5k+1$, $5k+2$, $5k+3$, $5k+4$.

Hence,
$$a \equiv 0, 1, 2, 3 \text{ or } 4 \pmod 5$$

$$a^2 \equiv 0, 1, 4, 9 \text{ or } 16 \pmod 5$$

$\therefore$ $$a^2 \equiv 0, 1 \text{ or } 4 \pmod 5$$

$\therefore$ $$(a^2)^2 \equiv 0^2, 1^2 \text{ or } 4^2 \pmod 5$$

or, $$a^4 \equiv 0, 1 \text{ or } 16 \pmod 5$$

$\therefore$ $$a^4 \equiv 0 \text{ or } 1 \pmod 5$$

16. 13 divides $2^{42} + 3^{42}$. Prove.

Sol. $$64 \equiv -1 \pmod{13}$$

or, $$2^6 \equiv -1 \pmod{13}$$

or, $$(2^6)^7 \equiv (-1)^7 \pmod{13}$$

or, $$2^{42} \equiv -1 \pmod{13} \quad \text{...(i)}$$

$$27 \equiv 1 \pmod{13}$$

or, $$3^3 \equiv 1 \pmod{13}$$

or, $$(3^3)^{14} \equiv (1)^{14} \pmod{13}$$

or, $$3^{42} \equiv 1 \pmod{13} \quad \text{...(ii)}$$

From Eqs. (i) and (ii), we get

$$2^{42} + 3^{42} \equiv -1 + 1 \pmod{13}$$

or, $$2^{42} + 3^{42} \equiv 0 \pmod{13}$$

Hence, 13 divides $2^{42} + 3^{42}$.

17. Prove that 353 divides $1^{353} + 2^{353} + \ldots + 352^{353}$.

Sol. $$352 \equiv -1 \pmod{353}$$

or, $$(352)^{353} \equiv (-1)^{353} \pmod{353}$$

or, $$352^{353} \equiv -1 \pmod{353}$$

Similarly, $$351 \equiv -2 \pmod{353}$$

Hence, $$(351)^{353} \equiv (-2)^{353} \pmod{353}$$

or, $$351^{353} \equiv -2^{353} \pmod{353}$$

and so on.

Hence, $$1^{353} + 2^{353} + \ldots + 352^{353}$$

$$= (1^{353} + 352^{353}) + (2^{353} + 351^{353}) + \ldots$$

$$\equiv ((1^{353} - 1^{353}) + (2^{353} - 2^{353}) + \ldots) \pmod{353}$$

$$\equiv 0 \pmod{353}$$

Hence, 353 divides $1^{353} + 2^{353} + \ldots + 352^{353}$.

18. Find all integers n for which $2^n - 1$ is divisible by 7.

Also show that there is no positive integer n for which $2^n + 1$ is divisible by 7.

Sol. Any positive integers n is of one of the forms $3k$, $3k+1$ or $3k+2$ where k is an integer.

Now, $$8 \equiv 1 \pmod 7$$

Hence, $8^n \equiv 1 \pmod 7$ for any positive integer n

2^n is accordingly of the form $2^{3k}, 2^{3k+1}$ or 2^{3k+2} *i.e.*, $8^k, 2\times 8^k$ or 4×8^k

Hence, $$2^n \equiv 1, 2 \text{ or } 4 \pmod 7$$

$\therefore$ $$2^n - 1 \equiv 0, 1 \text{ or } 3 \pmod 7$$

and, $$2^n + 1 \equiv 2, 3 \text{ or } 5 \pmod 7$$

Hence, $2^n + 1$ is not divisible by 7 for any positive integer n.

Also, $$2^n - 1 \equiv 0 \pmod 7$$

when n is of the form $3k$.

Thus, $2^n - 1$ is divisible by 7 for all $n = 3k$, where k is a non-negative integer.

19. What will be the remainder when $1^5 + 2^5 + 3^5 + \ldots 99^5 + 100^5$ is divided by 4?

Sol. Any integer has one of the forms $4k$, $4k+1$, $4k+2$ or $4k+3$.

Hence, for any integer a,

$$a \equiv 0, 1, 2 \text{ or } 3 \pmod 4$$

$\therefore$ $$a^5 \equiv 0, 1, 32 \text{ or } 243 \pmod 4$$

or, $$a^5 \equiv 0, 1, 0 \text{ or } 3 \pmod 4$$

Now, $1^5 + 2^5 + 3^5 + \ldots + 99^5 + 100^5$

$$\equiv (1+0+3) + (0+1+0+3) + \ldots + (0+1+0+3) + 0 \pmod 4$$

$$\equiv 0\times 25 + 1\times 25 + 0\times 25 + 3\times 25 \pmod 4$$

$$\equiv 0+1+0+3 \pmod 4$$

$$\equiv 0 \pmod 4$$

Hence, the remainder is 0 when divided by 4.

20. Last two digits of a number N are 67. What are the last two digits of N^2?

Sol. Last two digits of N are 67.

Hence, $N - 67$ is divisible by 100.

$$N \equiv 67 \pmod{100}$$

$\therefore$ $$N^2 \equiv 67^2 \pmod{100}$$

or, $N^2 \equiv 4489 \pmod{100}$

$\therefore$ $N^2 \equiv 89 \pmod{100}$

Hence, last two digits of N^2 are 89.

21. Prove or disprove, if $a^2 \equiv b^2 \pmod{n}$ then $a \equiv b \pmod{n}$.

Sol. Let $a = 5, b = 4, n = 3$

$$a^2 - b^2 = 25 - 16 = 9$$

Hence, $a^2 \equiv b^2 \pmod{3}$

But $a \not\equiv b \pmod{3}$

Hence, the given statement is not true.

22. Prove that $13 \mid 3^{n+2} + 4^{2n+1}$ for any positive integer n.

Sol. $4^{2n+1} = 4 \times 4^{2n} = 4 \times 16^n$

$$16 \equiv 3 \pmod{13}$$

$\therefore$ $16^n \equiv 3^n \pmod{13}$

$\therefore$ $4^{2n+1} \equiv 4 \times 3^n \pmod{13}$

$$3^{n+2} + 4^{2n+1} = 3^2 \times 3^n + 4^{2n+1}$$

$$\equiv 9 \times 3^n + 4 \times 3^n \pmod{13}$$

$$\equiv 13 \times 3^n \pmod{13}$$

$$\equiv 0 \pmod{13}$$

Hence, $13 \mid 3^{n+2} + 4^{2n+1}$

23. Prove that if the integer a is not divisible by 2 or 3, then $a^2 \equiv 1 \pmod{24}$.

Sol. The integer a has one of the forms $8n, 8n+1, 8n+2, 8n+3, 8n+4, 8n+5, 8n+6$ or $8n+7$.

Since, a is not divisible by 2, it has one of the forms $8n+1, 8n+3, 8n+5$ or $8n+7$.

$\therefore$ $a \equiv 1, 3, 5$ or $7 \pmod{8}$

or, $a^2 \equiv 1, 9, 25$ or $49 \pmod{8}$

$\therefore$ $a^2 \equiv 1 \pmod{8}$ ...(i)

Also, a has one of the forms $3n, 3n+1$ or $3n+2$.

a is not divisible by 3.

Hence, it has one of the forms $3n+1$ or $3n+2$.

$\therefore$ $a \equiv 1$ or $2 \pmod{3}$

or, $a^2 \equiv 1$ or $4 \pmod{3}$

or, $$a^2 \equiv 1 \pmod{3} \qquad \text{...(ii)}$$

From Eqs. (i) and (ii), $8 \mid (a^2 - 1)$ and $3 \mid (a^2 - 1)$

Also, $$\gcd(3, 8) = 1$$
$$3 \times 8 = 24$$

Hence, $24 \mid (a^2 - 1)$

$\therefore$ $$a^2 \equiv 1 \pmod{24}$$

24. If $a_1, a_2, ..., a_n$ is a complete set of residues modulo n and $\gcd(a, n) = 1$, prove that $aa_1, aa_2, ..., aa_n$ is also a complete set of residues module n.

Sol. It suffices to show that no two numbers in $aa_1, aa_2, ..., aa_n$ are congruent to each other modulo n.

Suppose that any two numbers are congruent to each other modulo n.

So, $aa_i \equiv aa_j \pmod{n}$ with $1 \le i < j \le n$

$\therefore$ $$n \mid a(a_i - a_j)$$
$$\gcd(a, n) = 1$$

Hence, by Euclid's lemma,
$$n \mid (a_i - a_j)$$

or, $$a_i \equiv a_j \pmod{n}$$

But that is not possible because $a_1, a_2, \ldots, a_n$ constitute a complete set of residues modulo n.

Hence, by contradiction, it is proved that the numbers $aa_1, aa_2, ..., aa_n$ form a complete set of residues modulo n.

25. Verify that $0, 1, 2, 2^2, 2^3, ..., 2^9$ form a complete set of residues modulo 11. Also verify that $0, 1^2, 2^2, 3^2, ..., 10^2$ do not form a complete set of residues modulo 11.

Sol. $$0 \equiv 0 \pmod{11}$$
$$1 \equiv 1 \pmod{11}$$
$$2 \equiv 2 \pmod{11}$$
$$2^2 \equiv 4 \pmod{11}$$
$$2^3 \equiv 8 \pmod{11}$$
$$2^4 \equiv 5 \pmod{11}$$
$$2^5 \equiv 10 \pmod{11}$$
$$2^6 \equiv 9 \pmod{11}$$
$$2^7 \equiv 7 \pmod{11}$$
$$2^8 \equiv 3 \pmod{11}$$
$$2^9 \equiv 6 \pmod{11}$$

Thus, $0, 1, 2, 2^2, 2^3, ..., 2^9$ are congruent to 0, 1, 2, ..., 10 in some order. Hence, they form a complete set of residues modulo 11.

Now,
$$0 \equiv 0 \pmod{11}$$
$$1^2 \equiv 1 \pmod{11}$$
$$2^2 \equiv 4 \pmod{11}$$
$$3^2 \equiv 9 \pmod{11}$$
$$4^2 \equiv 5 \pmod{11}$$
$$5^2 \equiv 3 \pmod{11}$$
$$6^2 \equiv 3 \pmod{11}$$
$$7^2 \equiv 5 \pmod{11}$$
$$8^2 \equiv 9 \pmod{11}$$
$$9^2 \equiv 4 \pmod{11}$$
$$10^2 \equiv 1 \pmod{11}$$

You can see that
$$1^2 \equiv 10^2 \pmod{11}$$
$$2^2 \equiv 9^2 \pmod{11}$$
$$3^2 \equiv 8^2 \pmod{11}$$
$$4^2 \equiv 7^2 \pmod{11}$$
$$5^2 \equiv 6^2 \pmod{11}$$

Thus, the set $0, 1^2, 2^2, ..., 10^2$ does not form a complete set of residues modulo 11.

26. If $\gcd(a, n) = 1$, then the integers $c, c + a, c + 2a, ..., c + (n-1)a$ form a complete set of residues modulo n for any integer c. Prove.

Sol. $c, c + a, c + 2a, ..., c + (n-1)a$ is a set of n integers.

Suppose that any two members of this set are congruent to each other modulo n.

Then, $c + ia \equiv c + ja \pmod{n}$ where $0 \le i < j \le n-1$

or, $ia \equiv ja \pmod{n}$

$\therefore$ $n \mid (j-i)\, a$

$\gcd(a, n) = 1$

Hence, by Euclid's lemma, $n \mid j - i$

But, $0 < j - i \le n - 1$

This is a contradiction.

Hence, the members of the set $c, c + a, c + 2a, ..., c + (n-1)a$ are incongruent modulo n and therefore they form a complete set of residues modulo n.

27. Any n consecutive integers form a complete set of residues modulo n. Prove.

Sol. $\gcd(1, n) = 1$

Hence, by preceding example, $c, c+1, c+2, ..., c+(n-1)$ form a complete set of residues modulo n for any arbitrary integer c.

28. The product of any set of n consecutive integers is divisible by n. Prove.

Sol. By example at Sr. No. 27 above, any n consecutive integers $c, c+1, c+2, ...,$ $c+(n-1)$ form a complete set of residues modulo n.

Hence, $c+i \equiv 0 \pmod{n}$ for some i $0 \le i \le n-1$

Hence, $$c(c+1)\ldots(c+i)\ldots(c+n-1) \equiv 0 \pmod{n}$$

Hence, $$n \mid c(c+1)\ldots(c+n-1)$$

29. $a \equiv b \pmod{n_1}$ and $a \equiv b \pmod{n_2}$

Then $a \equiv b \pmod{n}$ where $n = lcm(n_1, n_2)$ Prove.

Sol. $n_1 \mid (a-b)$ and $n_2 \mid (a-b)$

Hence, $a-b$ is a common multiple of n_1 and n_2.

$\therefore$ $$n \mid (a-b) \text{ where } n = lcm(n_1, n_2)$$

30. As per divisibility criteria for 9, a number is divisible by 9 if and only if the sum of its digits is divisible by 9. Prove it using the theory of congruences.

Sol. Any integer N can be written as

$$N = a_m \times 10^m + a_{m-1} \times 10^{m-1} + \ldots + a_1 \times 10 + a_0$$

where $a_0, a_1, ..., a_m$ are digits of N.

Now, $$10 \equiv 1 \pmod{9}$$

Hence, $$10^i \equiv 1 \pmod{9} \quad \text{for any integer } i \ge 1$$

or, $$a_i \times 10^i \equiv a_i \pmod{9}$$

Hence, $$a_m \times 10^m + \ldots + a_1 \times 10 + a_0 \equiv a_m + \ldots + a_1 + a_0 \pmod{9}$$

or, $$N \equiv a_m + \ldots + a_1 + a_0 \pmod{9}$$

Hence, $N \equiv 0 \pmod{9}$ if and only if $a_m + \ldots + a_1 + a_0 \equiv 0 \pmod{9}$

Thus, a number is divisible by 9 if and only if the sum of its digits is divisible by 9.

31. As per divisibility criteria for 11, a number is divisible by 11 if and only if the alternating sum of its digits is divisible by 11. Prove it using the theory of congruences.

Sol. Any integer N can be written as

$N = a_m \times 10^m + a_{m-1} \times 10^{m-1} + \ldots + a_1 \times 10 + a_0$ where $a_0, a_1, ..., a_m$ are digits of N

Now, $10 \equiv -1 \pmod{11}$

Hence, $10^i \equiv (-1)^i \pmod{11}$ for any integer $i \geq 1$

or, $a_i 10^i \equiv a_i (-1)^i \pmod{11}$

Hence, $N \equiv 0 \pmod{11}$ if and only if $(-1)^m\, a_m + \ldots - a_1 + a_0 \equiv 0 \pmod{11}$

Thus, a number is divisible by 11 if and only if the alternating sum of its digits is divisible by 11.

32. What is the remainder when 2^{39} is divided by 31?

Sol. $39 = 32 + 4 + 2 + 1$

$$2^2 \equiv 4 \pmod{31}$$
$$2^4 \equiv 16 \pmod{31}$$
$$2^5 \equiv 1 \pmod{31}$$

Now,
$$2^{39} = 2^{32+4+2+1} = 2^{32} \times 2^4 \times 2^2 \times 2^1$$
$$\equiv 2^2 \times 2^4 \times 2^2 \times 2^1 \pmod{31}$$
$$\equiv 4 \times 16 \times 4 \times 2 \pmod{31}$$
$$\equiv 64 \times 8 \pmod{31}$$
$$\equiv 2 \times 8 \pmod{31}$$
$$\equiv 16 \pmod{31}$$

Hence, the remainder is 16 when 2^{39} is divided by 31.

This method to calculate the value of $a^k \pmod{n}$ is called the binary exponential algorithm.

33. The unit digit of any perfect square is 0, 1, 4, 5, 6 or 9. Prove.

Sol. For any integer a,

$$a \equiv 0, 1, 2, 3, 4, 5, 6, 7, 8 \text{ or } 9 \pmod{10}$$

$\therefore$ $a^2 \equiv 0, 1^2, 2^2, 3^2, 4^2, 5^2, 6^2, 7^2, 8^2 \text{ or } 9^2 \pmod{10}$

or, $a^2 \equiv 0, 1, 4, 9, 6, 5, 6, 9, 4 \text{ or } 1 \pmod{10}$

Hence, $a^2 \equiv 0, 1, 4, 5, 6 \text{ or } 9 \pmod{10}$

Thus, the unit digit of any perfect square is 0, 1, 4, 5, 6 or 9.

34. The unit digit of a^4 for any integer a is 0, 1, 5 or 6. Prove.

Sol. From preceding example, it follows that

$$a^2 \equiv 0, 1, 4, 5, 6 \text{ or } 9 \pmod{10}$$

$\therefore$ $a^4 \equiv 0, 1, 6, 5, 6 \text{ or } 1 \pmod{10}$

or $a^4 \equiv 0, 1, 5 \text{ or } 6 \pmod{10}$

Hence, the unit digit of a^4 is 0, 1, 5 or 6.

35. Find the last two digits of 9^{9^9}.

Sol. $9 \equiv 9 \pmod{10}$

$9^2 \equiv 1 \pmod{10}$

$9^8 \equiv 1 \pmod{10}$

$\therefore$ $9^9 \equiv 9 \pmod{10}$

Hence, $9^9 = 10n + 9$

Now, $9^{9^9} = 9^{10n+9} = 9^{10n} \times 9^9$

$9^2 \equiv 81 \pmod{100}$

or, $9^2 \equiv -19 \pmod{100}$

$\therefore$ $9^4 \equiv 61 \pmod{100}$

$\therefore$ $9^8 \equiv 21 \pmod{100}$

$9^{10} = 01 \pmod{100}$

$\therefore$ $9^{10n} \equiv 1 \pmod{100}$

Also, $9^9 \equiv 89 \pmod{100}$

Hence, $9^{9^9} = 9^{10n} \times 9^9$

$\equiv 1 \times 89 \pmod{100}$

$\equiv 89 \pmod{100}$

Hence, last two digits of 9^{9^9} are 89.

36. $2784x = x \times 5569$ where x is missing digit of the number $2784x$. Find the missing digit x.

Sol. $2784x \equiv 2 + 7 + 8 + 4 + x \pmod 9$ (refer to example at Sr. No. 30)

$\equiv 21 + x \pmod 9$

$\equiv 3 + x \pmod 9$

$x \times 5569 \equiv x \times (5 + 5 + 6 + 9) \pmod 9$

$\equiv x \times 7 \pmod 9$

$\therefore$ $3 + x \equiv 7x \pmod 9$

or, $6x \equiv 3 \pmod 9$

Possible values of x for which this relation holds true are 2, 5 and 8.

Now, $2784x \equiv 2 - 7 + 8 - 4 + x \pmod{11}$ (refer to example at Sr. No. 31)

$\equiv x - 1 \pmod{11}$

$5569 \equiv -5 + 5 - 6 + 9 \pmod{11}$

$\equiv 3 \pmod{11}$

$\therefore \quad x-1 \equiv 3x \pmod{11}$

or, $\quad 2x \equiv -1 \pmod{11}$

or, $\quad 2x \equiv 10 \pmod{11}$

or, $\quad 12x \equiv 60 \pmod{11}$

or, $\quad x \equiv 5 \pmod{11}$

Only possible value of x is 5.

Hence, $\quad x = 5$

37. For any integer a, $a^2 - a + 7$ ends in one of the digits 3, 7 or 9. Prove.

Sol. $\quad a \equiv 0, 1, 2, 3, 4, 5, 6, 7, 8 \text{ or } 9 \pmod{10}$

$\therefore \quad a-1 \equiv 9, 0, 1, 2, 3, 4, 5, 6, 7 \text{ or } 8 \pmod{10}$

Hence, $\quad a(a-1) \equiv 0, 0, 2, 6, 12, 20, 30, 42, 56 \text{ or } 72 \pmod{10}$

or, $\quad a(a-1) \equiv 0, 0, 2, 6, 2, 0, 0, 2, 6 \text{ or } 2 \pmod{10}$

Hence, $\quad a^2 - a \equiv 0, 2 \text{ or } 6 \pmod{10}$

$\therefore \quad a^2 - a + 7 \equiv 7, 9 \text{ or } 13 \pmod{10}$

or, $\quad a^2 - a + 7 \equiv 3, 7 \text{ or } 9 \pmod{10}$

Hence, $a^2 - a + 7$ ends in one of the digits 3, 7 or 9.

38. The sum of digits of an integer is 15. Prove that the integer cannot be a square or a cube.

Sol. Let a be an integer.

$$a \equiv 0, 1, 2, 3, 4, 5, 6, 7 \text{ or } 8 \pmod 9$$

$\therefore \quad a^2 \equiv 0, 1, 4, 9, 16, 25, 36, 49 \text{ or } 64 \pmod 9$

or, $\quad a^2 \equiv 0, 1, 4, 0, 7, 7, 0, 4 \text{ or } 1 \pmod 9$

or, $\quad a^2 \equiv 0, 1, 4 \text{ or } 7 \pmod 9$

Let N be the given integer.

Then, $\quad N \equiv \text{Sum of digits of } N \pmod 9$

(refer to example at Sr. No. 30)

or, $\quad N \equiv 15 \pmod 9$

or, $\quad N \equiv 6 \pmod 9$

However, $\quad a^2 \equiv 0, 1, 4 \text{ or } 7 \pmod 9$ (for any integer a)

Hence, N cannot be a perfect square.

Now, $\quad a \equiv 0, 1, 2, 3, 4, 5, 6, 7 \text{ or } 8 \pmod 9$

$\therefore \quad a^3 \equiv 0, 1, 8, 27, 64, 125, 216, 343 \text{ or } 512 \pmod 9$

or, $\quad a^3 = 0, 1, 8, 0, 1, 8, 0, 1 \text{ or } 8 \pmod 9$

or, $a^3 \equiv 0, 1 \text{ or } 8 \pmod 9$

But, $N \equiv 6 \pmod 9$

Hence, N cannot be a perfect cube.

Can you think about an alternative solution?

(***Hint :*** N is divisible by 3 but not by 9.)

39. Find the values of $n \geq 1$ for which $1! + 2! + 3! + \ldots + n!$ is a perfect square.

Sol. For any integer a

$$a \equiv 0, 1, 2, 3, 4, 5, 6, 7, 8 \text{ or } 9 \pmod{10}$$

$\therefore$ $$a^2 \equiv 0, 1, 4, 9, 16, 25, 36, 49, 64 \text{ or } 81 \pmod{10}$$

or, $$a^2 \equiv 0, 1, 4, 9, 6, 5, 6, 9, 4 \text{ or } 1 \pmod{10}$$

or, $$a^2 \equiv 0, 1, 4, 5, 6 \text{ or } 9 \pmod{10}$$

Thus, unit digit of a perfect square is 0, 1, 4, 5, 6 or 9.

Now for $n = 1$, $1! = 1$

$= 1^2$ which is a perfect square

For, $n = 2$, $1! + 2! = 1 + 2$

$= 3$ which is not a perfect square

For $n = 3$, $1! + 2! + 3!$

$= 1 + 2 + 6 = 9 = 3^2$ which is a perfect square

For $n = 4$, $1! + 2! + 3! + 4!$

$= 1 + 2 + 6 + 24 = 33$ which is not a perfect square

Now all integers from 5! onwards are divisible by 10 as both 2 and 5 are factors of $n!$ for $n \geq 5$.

Hence, unit digit of $(1! + 2! + \ldots + n!)$ for $n \geq 5$ is same as the unit digit of $(1! + 2! + 3! + 4!)$ *i.e.*, 3.

But $a^2 \equiv 0, 1, 4, 5, 6 \text{ or } 9 \pmod{10}$ for any integer a.

Hence, $n!$ cannot be a perfect square for any $n \geq 5$.

Thus, only values of n for which $(1! + 2! + \ldots + n!)$ is a perfect square are 1 and 3.

40. For a given integer N, let M be the integer formed by reversing the order of the digits of N. Prove that $N - M$ is divisible by 9.

Sol. Let $N = a_m \times 10^m + \ldots + a_2 \times 10^2 + a_1 \times 10 + a_0$ (where $a_0, a_1, a_2, \ldots, a_m$ are digits of N.)

Then, $M = a_0 \times 10^m + \ldots + a_{m-2} \times 10^2 + a_{m-1} \times 10 + a_m$

We know that $N \equiv a_m + \ldots + a_2 + a_1 + a_0 \pmod 9$

(refer to example at Sr. No. 30)

Also, $M \equiv a_0 + \ldots + a_{m-2} + a_{m-1} + a_m \pmod 9$

$\therefore\ N - M \equiv (a_m + \ldots + a_2 + a_1 + a_2) - (a_0 + \ldots + a_{m-2} + a_{m-1} + a_m) \pmod 9$

$\equiv 0 \pmod 9$

Hence, $N - M$ is divisible by 9.

41. Find solutions of the linear congruence $4x \equiv 10 \pmod 6$.

Sol. Refer to the theorem at para 31 of this chapter.

Theorem : The linear congruence $ax \equiv b \pmod n$ has a solution if and only if $d \mid b$ where $d = \gcd(a, n)$.

Further, if $d \mid b$, then it has d mutually incongruent solutions modulo n.

Here, $\gcd(4, 6) = 2$

$2 \mid 10$

Hence, this equation has a solution.

By inspection, $x = 4$ is one solution.

Hence, two solutions of this linear congruence ($\because d = 2$) are given by

$$x = 4 + \left(\frac{6}{2}\right)t, \quad t = 0, 1$$

$\therefore \quad x = 4, 7$

Therefore, $x = 1, 4$ are two incongruent solutions modulo 6.

42. Find solutions of the linear congruence $3x \equiv 7 \pmod{10}$.

Sol. $3x \equiv 7 \pmod{10}$

$\gcd(3, 10) = 1$

Hence, this linear congruence has a unique solution.

Multiplying both sides of $3x \equiv 7 \pmod{10}$ by 7, we get

$21x \equiv 49\ (\text{mol } 10)$

or, $x \equiv 9 \pmod{10}$

This is the desired solution.

43. Find solutions of the linear congruence $17x \equiv 9 \pmod{276}$.

Sol. $276 = 3 \times 4 \times 23$

3, 4 and 23 are relatively prime in pairs.

Hence, $17x \equiv 9 \pmod{276}$ is equivalent to $17x \equiv 9 \pmod 3$, $17x \equiv 9 \pmod 4$ and $17x \equiv 9 \pmod{23}$.

Multiplying both sides of $17x \equiv 9 \pmod 3$ by 2, we get

$$34x \equiv 18 \pmod{3}$$

or, $x \equiv 0 \pmod{3}$

$\therefore$ $x \equiv 3k$ for any integer k ....(i)

Now, $17x \equiv 9 \pmod{4}$

or, $x \equiv 1 \pmod{4}$

Substituting (i) into $x \equiv 1 \pmod{4}$, we get $3k \equiv 1 \pmod{4}$

Multiplying both sides of this equation by 3, we get

$$9k \equiv 3 \pmod{4}$$

or, $k \equiv 3 \pmod{4}$

$\therefore$ $k = 3 + 4m$ for any integer m ....(ii)

Now, last congruence gives

$$17x \equiv 9 \pmod{23}$$

or, $17 \times 3k \equiv 9 \pmod{23}$ [By (i) and (ii)]

or, $51 \times (3 + 4m) \equiv 9 \pmod{23}$

or, $204m + 153 \equiv 9 \pmod{23}$

or, $204m \equiv -144 \pmod{23}$

or, $-3m \equiv -6 \pmod{23}$

or, $3m \equiv 6 \pmod{23}$

or, $m \equiv 2 \pmod{23}$ [$\because \gcd(3, 23) = 1$]

$\therefore$ $m = 2 + 23n$ where n is an integer .... (iii)

Hence,
$$\left.\begin{aligned} x &= 3k = 3(3 + 4m) \\ &= 9 + 12m \\ &= 9 + 12(2 + 23n) \\ &= 276n + 33 \end{aligned}\right\} \quad \text{[By (i), (ii) and (iii)]}$$

Hence, $x \equiv 33 \pmod{276}$ provides solution to the given congruence $17x \equiv 9 \pmod{276}$.

This example is an application of the Chinese Remainder Theorem. The same is described as under.

Let $n_1, n_2, ..., n_r$ be positive integers such that $\gcd(n_i, n_j) = 1$ for $i \neq j$. Then the system of linear congruences

$$x \equiv a_1 \pmod{n_1}$$
$$x \equiv a_2 \pmod{n_2}$$
$$\vdots$$
$$x \equiv a_r \pmod{n_r}$$

has a simultaneous solution, which is unique modulo the integer $n_1 n_2 \ldots n_r$.

44. List all integers n in the range $1 \le n \le 100$ that satisfy $n \equiv 7 \pmod{17}$.

Sol. $n \equiv 7 \pmod{17}$

$\therefore$ $17 \mid n - 7$

or, $n - 7 = 17t$ for some integer t

or, $n = 7 + 17t$ $1 \le n \le 100$

or, $1 \le 7 + 17t \le 100$

or, $-6 \le 17t \le 93$

or, $\frac{-6}{17} \le t \le \frac{93}{17}$

$\therefore$ $0 \le t \le 5$

Hence, we get desired values of n for $t = 0, 1, 2, 3, 4, 5$

$\therefore$ $n = 7, 24, 41, 58, 75, 92$

45. 19 is not a divisor of $n^2 + 1$ for any integer n. Prove.

Sol. For any integer n,

$$n \equiv 0, 1, 2, 3, 4, 5, 6, 7, 8, 9, 10, 11, 12, 13, 14, 15, 16, 17, 18 \pmod{19}$$

$\therefore$ $n^2 \equiv 0, 1, 4, 9, 16, 25, 36, 49, 64, 81, 100, 121, 144, 169, 196, 225, 256, 289, 324 \pmod{19}$

$\therefore$ $n^2 \equiv 0, 1, 4, 9, 16, 6, 17, 11, 7, 5, 5, 7, 11, 17, 6, 16, 9, 4, 1 \pmod{19}$

or, $n^2 \equiv 0, 1, 4, 5, 6, 7, 9, 11, 16, 17 \pmod{19}$

$\therefore n^2 + 1 \equiv 1, 2, 5, 6, 7, 8, 10, 12, 17, 18 \pmod{19}$

Hence, $n^2 + 1$ is not divisible by 19 for any integer n.

46. $7 \mid (3^{2n+1} + 2^{n+2})$ for all integers n. Prove.

Sol. $3^2 \equiv 2 \pmod 7$

$\therefore$ $3^{2n} \equiv 2^n \pmod 7$

$3 \times 3^{2n} \equiv 3 \times 2^n \pmod 7$

or, $3^{2n+1} \equiv 3 \times 2^n \pmod 7$

$2^{n+2} \equiv 2^2 \times 2^n = 4 \cdot 2^n$

$\therefore$ $(3^{2n+1} + 2^{n+2}) \equiv 3 \times 2^n + 4 \times 2^n \pmod 7$

$\equiv 7 \times 2^n \pmod 7$

$\equiv 0 \pmod 7$

Thus, $7 \mid (3^{2n+1} + 2^{n+2})$

47. $\frac{n^5}{5}+\frac{n^3}{3}+\frac{7}{15}n$ is an integer for every integer n. Prove.

Sol. $\frac{n^5}{5}+\frac{n^3}{3}+\frac{7}{15}n=\frac{3n^5+5n^3+7n}{15}$

$$n \equiv 0, 1, 2 \pmod 3$$

$$n^2 \equiv 0, 1, 4 \pmod 3$$

or, $$n^2 \equiv 0, 1 \pmod 3$$

$$n^3 \equiv 0, 1, 8 \pmod 3$$

or, $$n^3 \equiv 0, 1, 2 \pmod 3$$

$$n^5 \equiv 0, 1, 2 \pmod 3$$

Now, $$3n^5 \equiv 0, 3, 6 \pmod 3$$

$$5n^3 \equiv 0, 5, 10 \pmod 3$$

$$7n \equiv 0, 7, 14 \pmod 3$$

Hence, $$3n^5+5n^3+7n \equiv 0, 15, 30 \pmod 3$$

$$\equiv 0 \pmod 3$$

$\therefore$ $3n^5+5n^3+7n$ is divisible by 3.

$$n \equiv 0, 1, 2, 3, 4 \pmod 5$$

$\therefore$ $$n^2 \equiv 0, 1, 4, 4, 1 \pmod 5$$

$$n^3 \equiv 0, 1, 3, 2, 4 \pmod 5$$

$$n^5 \equiv 0, 1, 2, 3, 4 \pmod 5$$

Now, $$3n^5+5n^3+7n \equiv 0, 15, 35, 40, 60 \pmod 5$$

$$\equiv 0 \pmod 5$$

$\therefore$ $3n^5+5n^3+7n$ is divisible by 5.

Thus, $3n^5+5n^3+7n$ is divisible by both 3 and 5.

$$\gcd(3, 5)=1$$

$$3\times 5=15$$

Hence, $3n^5+5n^3+7n$ is divisible by 15.

Therefore, $\frac{n^5}{5}+\frac{n^3}{3}+\frac{7}{15}n\left(=\frac{3n^5+5n^3+7n}{15}\right)$ is an integer for all integers n.

48. When a three-digit number is divided by 2, 3, 4, 5 and 7, the remainders are all 1. Find the minimum and maximum values of such three-digit numbers.

Sol. Let x be the number with desired property.

Then, $x-1$ is divisible by 2, 3, 4, 5 and 7.

Hence, $x-1$ is divisible by $lcm(2, 3, 4, 5, 7)$.

$\therefore$ $x-1$ is divisible by $3\times4\times5\times7=420$

$\therefore$ $x-1=420k$ for some integer k.

or, $x=420k+1$

Minimum value of $x=420\times1+1=421$

Maximum value of $x=420\times2+1=841$

49. 2726, 4472, 5054 and 6412 leave same remainder when they are divided by some 2-digit natural number m. Find the value of m.

Sol.

$$\left.\begin{aligned}2726&=a\times m+r\\4472&=b\times m+r\\5054&=c\times m\times r\\6412&=d\times m+r\end{aligned}\right\}\text{(for some integers } a, b, c, d, r)$$

Hence, $4472-2726=(b-a)\times m$

$\therefore$ $m\mid1746$

$5054-4472=(c-b)\times m$

$\therefore$ $m\mid582$

$6412-5054=(d-c)\times m$

$\therefore$ $m\mid1358$

$$1746=2\times3^2\times97$$

$$582=2\times3\times97$$

$$1358=2\times7\times97$$

$\therefore$ $\gcd(1746, 582, 1358)=2\times97=194$

Possible values of $m=1, 2, 97, 194$

As m is a 2-digit number, $m=97$

50. Find the smallest positive integer k such that $2^{69}+k$ is divisible by 127.

Sol.

$$2^7\equiv1 \pmod{127}$$

$\therefore$ $$(2^7)^9\equiv(1)^9 \pmod{127}$$

$\therefore$ $$2^{63}\equiv1 \pmod{127}$$

or, $$2^{69}\equiv2^6 \pmod{127}$$

or, $$2^{69}\equiv64 \pmod{127}$$

$\therefore$ $$2^{69}+k\equiv64+k \pmod{127}$$

$\therefore$ $2^{69}+k\equiv0 \pmod{127}$ if and only if $64+k\equiv0 \pmod{127}$

Hence, minimum possible value of $k=63$.

51. What is the remainder when $6^{273}+8^{273}$ is divided by 49?

Sol. In general, for odd positive integer n,

$$a^n+b^n=(a+b)(a^{n-1}-a^{n-2}b+a^{n-3}b^2-\ldots+b^{n-1})$$

$$\therefore \quad 6^{273}+8^{273}=(6+8)(6^{272}-6^{271}\times 8+6^{270}\times 8^2-\ldots+8^{272})$$

$$6\equiv -1 \pmod 7$$
$$8\equiv 1 \pmod 7$$

$$\therefore \quad 6^{272}-6^{271}\times 8+6^{270}\times 8^2-\ldots+8^{272}$$
$$\equiv(-1)^{272}-(-1)^{271}\times 1+\ldots+1^{272} \pmod 7$$
$$\equiv 1+1+\ldots+1 \pmod 7) \text{ (1 appears 273 times)}$$
$$\equiv 273 \pmod 7$$
$$\equiv 0 \pmod 7$$

Also, 7 divides first term as well ($\because 6+8=14$) in the expansion of $6^{273}+8^{273}$ given above.

Thus, 7 divides both first and second terms in the expansion of $6^{273}+8^{273}$

$$\therefore \quad 49 \mid 6^{273}+8^{273}$$

Thus, the desired remainder is 0.

52. What is the remainder when $2005^{2007^{2009}}$ is divided by 7?

Sol.

$$2005\equiv 3 \pmod 7$$
$$3^3\equiv 27\equiv 6 \pmod 7$$
$$\equiv -1 \pmod 7$$
$$\therefore \quad 3^6\equiv 1 \pmod 7$$

Now, $\quad 2007\equiv 3 \pmod 6$

$$\therefore \quad 2007^{2009}\equiv 3^{2009} \pmod 6$$
$$\equiv 3 \pmod 6$$

($\because$ Any power of 3 is congruent to 3 modulo 6)

$\therefore \quad 2007^{2009}=6n+3$ for some integer n

Now,
$$2005^{2007^{2009}}=2005^{6n+3}$$
$$\equiv 3^{6n+3} \pmod 7$$
$$\equiv 3^{6n}\times 3^3 \pmod 7$$
$$\equiv 1^n\times 27 \pmod 7$$
$$\equiv 6 \pmod 7$$

Hence, the required remainder is 6.

53. Find the last four digits of 7^{128}.

Sol.
$$7^4 = 2401 \equiv 2401 \pmod{10^4}$$
$$7^8 \equiv (2401)^2$$
$$\equiv (2400+1)^2 \pmod{10^4}$$
$$\equiv (2400)^2 + 4800 + 1 \pmod{10^4}$$
$$\equiv 4801 \pmod{10^4}$$
$$7^{16} = (4800+1)^2 \equiv 9601 \pmod{10^4}$$
$$7^{32} = (9600+1)^2 \equiv 9201 \pmod{10^4}$$
$$7^{64} = (9200+1)^2 \equiv 8401 \pmod{10^4}$$
$$7^{128} = (8400+1)^2 \equiv 6801 \pmod{10^4}$$

Therefore, the last four digits of 7^{128} are 6801.

54. A number leaves remainder 35 when divided by 222. Another number leaves remainder 47 when divided by 407. What is the remainder when the sum of these two numbers is divided by 37?

Sol.
$$x \equiv 35 \pmod{222}$$
$$y \equiv 47 \pmod{407}$$
$$222 = 37 \times 6$$
$$407 = 37 \times 11$$
$$\therefore \quad x = 37 \times 6 \times m + 35$$
$$y = 37 \times 11 \times n + 47 \qquad \text{for some integers } m \text{ and } n$$
$$\therefore \quad x + y = 37(6m + 11n) + 82$$
$$\therefore \quad x + y \equiv 82 \pmod{37}$$
$$\equiv 8 \pmod{37}$$

Hence, the required remainder is 8.

55. What is the unit digit of the number $6^{256} - 4^{256}$?

Sol. $6^n \equiv 6 \pmod{10}$ for any integer $n \geq 1$

$4^n \equiv 6 \pmod{10}$ for any even integer $n \geq 1$

Hence, for even n,
$$6^n - 4^n \equiv 0 \pmod{10}$$

Hence, $6^{256} - 4^{256}$ is divisible by 10.

Thus, unit digit of $6^{256} - 4^{256}$ is 0.

56. If m ends with the digit 5, then $1991 \mid 12^m + 9^m + 8^m + 6^m$. Prove.

Sol. Let
$$N = 12^m + 9^m + 8^m + 6^m$$
$$= (12^m + 8^m) + (9^m + 6^m)$$
$$= 4^m(3^m + 2^m) + 3^m(3^m + 2^m)$$
$$= (4^m + 3^m)(3^m + 2^m)$$

m ends with the digit 5.

Hence, $m = 10a + 5$ for some integer a.
$$4^m + 3^m = 4^{5(2a+1)} + 3^{5(2a+1)}$$

$\therefore\ 4^5 + 3^5 \mid 4^m + 3^m$

[$\because$ In general, for odd positive integer n, $a^n + b^n = (a+b)(a^{n-1} - a^{n-2}b + a^{n-3}b^2 - \ldots + b^{n-1})$]
$$3^m + 2^m = 3^{5(2a+1)} + 2^{5(2a+1)}$$

$\therefore\ 3^5 + 2^5 \mid 3^m + 2^m$
$$4^5 + 3^5 = 1024 + 243 = 1267 = 7 \times 181$$
$$3^5 + 2^5 = 243 + 32 = 275 = 25 \times 11$$
$$N = (4^m + 3^m)(3^m + 2^m)$$
$$4^m + 3^m \equiv 0 \pmod{181}$$
$$3^m + 2^m \equiv 0 \pmod{11}$$

Also, 181 and 11 are relatively prime.

Hence, $(4^m + 3^m)(3^m + 2^m) \equiv 0 \pmod{181 \times 11}$

or,
$$N \equiv 0 \pmod{1991}$$

57. Find the least positive integer n such that the product of 9999 and n contains only the digit 1 in decimal notation.

Sol. Let, $N = 9999$

and $R_k = 11\ldots1$ (digit 1 is repeated k times)

Now, $nN = R_k$ for some integer k
$$R_k \equiv \text{Sum of digits of } R_k \pmod 9$$
$$\equiv k \pmod 9$$

Also please note that
$$R_k = 11\ldots1 = 10^{k-1} + 10^{k-2} + \ldots + 1$$
$$= \frac{10^k - 1}{10 - 1}$$

$$N + 1 = 10000 = 10^4$$

Suppose $k = 4r + s$, where $s = 0, 1, 2$ or 3

Now, $$9Nn = 9R_k = 9 \times \frac{10^k - 1}{9}$$

$$= 10^k - 1 = 10^{4r+s} - 1$$

$$= (10^4)^r \times 10^s - 1 \qquad [\because 10^4 \equiv 1 (\text{mod } N)]$$

$$\equiv 10^s - 1 (\text{mod } N)$$

Hence, $$10^s - 1 \equiv 0 \ (\text{mod } N)$$

If $s = 1, 2$ or 3, $0 < 10^s - 1 < N$

But, $$10^s - 1 \equiv 0 \ (\text{mod } N)$$

Hence, $$s = 0$$

Thus, k is divisible by 4.

Also, $$R_k \equiv k \ (\text{mod } 9)$$

and $$R_k = nN \equiv 0 \ (\text{mod } 9)$$

$\therefore$ $$k \equiv 0 \ (\text{mod } 9)$$

Thus, k is divisible by 9.

Therefore, k is divisible by 36 as it is divisible by both 4 and 9.

Thus, the least possible value of k is 36.

$\therefore$ Least value of $n = \dfrac{R_k}{N} = \dfrac{(10^{36} - 1)}{9 \times (10^4 - 1)}$

Exercise

1. What is the remainder when 5^{127} is divided by 6?

2. What is the unit digit of 6^{937}?

3. What is the unit digit of $6^{901} - 4^{200}$?

4. Prove that $111^{333} + 333^{111}$ is divisible by 7.

5. Prove that for $n \geq 1$, $43 \mid 6^{n+2} + 7^{2n+1}$.

6. Prove that $41 \nmid 2^{25} - 1$.

7. Prove that $97 \mid 2^{48} - 1$.

8. Prove that $2222^{5555} + 5555^{2222}$ is divisible by 7.

9. Find the unit digit of 777^{777}.

10. $S = 1! + 2! + 3! + \ldots + 100!$

What is the remainder when S is divided by 12?

11. $ab \equiv cd \pmod{n}$

$b \equiv d \pmod{n}$

$\gcd(b, n) = 1$

Prove that $a \equiv c \pmod{n}$.

12. Compute $19^{53} \pmod{503}$.

13. Any one of the integers 0, 1, 2, 3, 4, 5, 6, 7, 8, 9 can occur as the unit digit of a^3 (for integer a). Prove.

14. $51840 \times 273581 = 1418243x040$. Find missing digit x by working modulo 9 or 11.

15. 495 divides $273x49y5$. Find missing digits x and y.

16. Find the last three digits of the number 7^{999}.

17. 2^n divides an integer N if and only if 2^n divides the number made up of the last n digits of N. Prove.

18. R_n is a repunit. A repunit is an integer written in decimal notation as a string of 1's such as 11, 111, 111 etc. R_n denotes the repunit consisting of n consecutive 1's. Prove that $9 \mid R_n$ if and only if $9 \mid n$.

19. R_n is a repunit. Prove that $11 \mid R_n$ if and only if n is even.

20. Prove that for any prime $p > 3, 13 \mid 10^{2p} - 10^p + 1$.

21. Solve the linear congruence $6x \equiv 15 \pmod{21}$.

22. Solve the linear congruence $140x \equiv 133 \pmod{301}$.

23. Solve the following sets of simultaneous linear congruences.

(i) $x \equiv 1 \pmod{3}, x \equiv 2 \pmod{5}, x \equiv 3 \pmod{7}$

(ii) $2x \equiv 1 \pmod{5}, 3x \equiv 9 \pmod{6}, 4x \equiv 1 \pmod{7}, 5x \equiv 9 \pmod{11}$

24. Solve the linear congruence $17n \equiv 3 \pmod{210}$ by solving the system

$$17n \equiv 3 \pmod{2}$$
$$17n \equiv 3 \pmod{3}$$
$$17n \equiv 3 \pmod{5}$$
$$17n \equiv 3 \pmod{7}$$

25. Obtain three consecutive integers each having a square factor.

26. Prove that $n^{13} - n$ is divisible by 2, 3, 5, 7 and 13 for any integer n.

27. Exhibit a complete residue system modulo 17 composed entirely of multiples of 3.

28. Find the number of positive integers n, such that the remainder is 7 when 2007 is divided by n.

29. Find the remainder of $47^{37^{27}}$ when it is divided by 11.

30. $n = 3 \times 7 \times 11 \times 15 \times 19 \times \ldots \times 2003$. Find the last three digits of n.

31. What is the unit digit of $3^{1999} \times 7^{2000} \times 17^{2001}$?

32. Find the last two digits of 2^{999}.

33. Find the last two digits of $14^{14^{14}}$.

34. Find the remainder of $(257^{33} + 46)^{26}$ when it is divided by 50.

35. What is the smallest positive integer $n > 1$ such that 3^n ends with 003?

36. Find all positive integers n, such that $n \times 2^n + 1$ is divisible by 3.

Answers

1. 5 **2.** 6 **3.** 0 **9.** 7 **10.** 9

12. 406 **14.** 9 **15.** $x = 7$, $y = 8$ **16.** 143

21. $x \equiv 6, 13, 20 \pmod{21}$ **22.** $x \equiv 16, 59, 102, 145, 188, 231, 274 \pmod{301}$

23. (i) $x \equiv 52 \pmod{105}$, (ii) $x \equiv 653 \pmod{770}$

24. $n \equiv 99 \pmod{210}$

25. n, $n+1$ and $n+2$ where $n = 548 + 900t$, t is an integer.

27. 3, 6, 9, 12, 15, 18, 21, 24, 27, 30, 33, 36, 39, 42, 45, 48, 51

28. 16 **29.** 5 **30.** 875 **31.** 9 **32.** 88

33. 36 **34.** 29 **35.** 81

36. All positive integers n of the forms $6k+1$ or $6k+2$

08

Fermat's Theorem

1. Consider the following numbers.

$$2^{3-1}-1=2^2-1=3$$

$$3^{3-1}-1=3^2-1=8$$

$$4^{3-1}-1=4^2-1=15$$

$$5^{3-1}-1=5^2-1=24$$

$$6^{3-1}-1=6^2-1=35$$

$$7^{3-1}-1=7^2-1=48$$

$$8^{3-1}-1=8^2-1=63$$

$$9^{3-1}-1=9^2-1=80$$

$$10^{3-1}-1=10^2-1=99$$

All these numbers except 8, 35 and 80 are divisible by 3.

Thus, $a^{3-1}-1$ is divisible by 3 for all a, $2 \leq a \leq 10$ except when a is divisible by 3 (*i.e.,* for $a = 3$, 6 and 9).

Is this result a coincidence?

This result follows from a famous theorem known as "Fermat's Little Theorem" or "Fermat's Theorem".

2. Fermat's Theorem : Let p be a prime. Suppose that $p \nmid a$. Then, $a^{p-1} \equiv 1 \pmod{p}$, for any integer a.

Proof : Consider following multiples of a

$$a, 2a, 3a, ..., (p-1)a$$

We claim that no two of these integers are congruent to each other modulo p.

Let two of these integers ra and sa be congruent to each other modulo p.

Then, $ra \equiv sa \pmod{p}$ $\quad 1 \le r, s \le p-1$

$\therefore$ $\quad p \mid (r-s)a$

It is given that $p \nmid a$.

Hence, $\gcd(a, p) = 1$

$\therefore$ By Euclid's Lemma, $p \mid r-s$

But $\quad -(p-2) \le r-s \le p-2,\ r-s \ne 0$

$\therefore$ $\quad 0 < |r-s| \le p-2$ and $p \mid r-s$

But this is obviously not possible.

Hence, no two of the integers $a, 2a, 3a, ..., (p-1)a$ are congruent to each other modulo p. Also, p cannot divide any of these integers.

Hence, none of these integers is congruent to 0 modulo p.

Thus, the set of integers, $a, 2a, ..., (p-1)a$ must be congruent to $1, 2, ..., p-1$ modulo p in some order.

$\therefore$ $\quad a \times 2a \times 3a \ldots (p-1)a \equiv 1 \times 2 \times 3 \ldots (p-1) \pmod{p}$

or, $\quad a^{p-1}(p-1)! \equiv (p-1)! \pmod{p}$

$\therefore$ $\quad a^{p-1} \equiv 1 \pmod{p}$ $\quad [\because p \nmid (p-1)!]$

3. Corollary : If p is a prime, then $a^p \equiv a \pmod{p}$ for any integer a.

If $\quad p \mid a,\ a^p \equiv 0 \pmod{p}$

Also, $\quad a \equiv 0 \pmod{p}$

$\therefore$ $\quad a^p \equiv a \pmod{p}$

If $p \nmid a$, then as per Fermat's theorem, $a^{p-1} \equiv 1 \pmod{p}$

Multiplying this congruence by a, we get $a^p \equiv a \pmod{p}$

Hence, $a^p \equiv a \pmod{p}$ for any integer a.

4. What is the remainder when 5^{27} is divided by 13?

By Fermat's theorem,

$$5^{12} \equiv 1 \pmod{13}$$

$\therefore$ $\quad 5^{24} \equiv 1 \pmod{13}$

$\therefore$ $\quad 5^{27} = 5^{24+3} = 5^{24} \times 5^3$

$$\equiv 1 \times 5^3 \pmod{13}$$

$$\equiv 25 \times 5 \pmod{13}$$

$$\equiv 8 \pmod{13}$$

Hence, the remainder is 8 when 5^{27} is divided by 13.

Fermat's theorem is very useful in calculations.

5. Find out whether 117 is a prime number.

Let's find out 2^{117} modulo 117.

$$2^7 = 128 \equiv 11 \pmod{117}$$

$$\begin{aligned}2^{117} &= 2^{7\times 16+5}\\ &= (2^7)^{16} \times (2^5)\\ &\equiv 11^{16} \times 32 \pmod{117}\\ &\equiv (121)^8 \times 32 \pmod{117}\\ &\equiv 4^8 \times 32 \pmod{117}\\ &\equiv 2^{21} \pmod{117}\\ &\equiv 11^3 \pmod{117} && [\because 2^7 \equiv 11 \pmod{117}]\\ &\equiv 4\times 11 \pmod{117}\\ &\equiv 44 \pmod{117}\end{aligned}$$

Thus, $2^{117} \not\equiv 2 \pmod{117}$

However, we know that for any prime p,

$$a^p \equiv a \pmod{p}$$

Hence, 117 cannot be a prime number.

In fact, on little inspection we find that

$$117 = 9 \times 13$$

Thus, Fermat's theorem also helps in testing the primality of a given integer.

6. Theorem : If p and q are distinct primes with $a^p \equiv a(\text{mod } q)$ and $a^q \equiv a(\text{mod } p)$, then $a^{pq} \equiv a(\text{mod } pq)$

Proof : $a^{pq} = (a^p)^q$

$\equiv a^p \pmod{q}$ (By Fermat's theorem)

Also, it is given that $a^p \equiv a \pmod{q}$

Hence, $a^{pq} \equiv a \pmod{q}$

Similarly, $a^{pq} \equiv a \pmod{p}$

Thus, $p \mid a^{pq} - a$ and $q \mid a^{pq} - a$

Also $\gcd(p, q) = 1$ [$\because p, q$ are distinct primes]

$\therefore$ $pq \mid a^{pq} - a$

$\therefore$ $a^{pq} \equiv a \pmod{pq}$

7. Find 2^{340} mod 341.

$$341 = 11 \times 31$$

$$2^{10} = 1024 = 31 \times 33 + 1$$

$\therefore$ $$2^{10} \equiv 1 (\text{mod } 31)$$

or, $$2^{11} \equiv 2 (\text{mod } 31)$$

Now, $$2^{31} = 2 \times (2^{10})^3 \equiv 2 \times 1^3 \ (\text{mod } 11)$$
$$\equiv 2 \ (\text{mod } 11)$$

Thus, for primes 11 and 31,

$$2^{11} \equiv 2 \ (\text{mod } 31)$$

$$2^{31} \equiv 2 \ (\text{mod } 11)$$

Hence, by preceding theorem at para 6 above,

$$2^{11 \times 31} \equiv 2 \ (\text{mod } 11 \times 31)$$

or, $$2^{341} \equiv 2 \ (\text{mod } 341)$$

or, $$2^{340} \equiv 1 \ (\text{mod } 341) \qquad (\because \gcd(2, 341) = 1)$$

Thus, $a^{p-1} \equiv 1 \ (\text{mod } p)$ for $p = 341$ and $a = 2$.

However, 341 is not a prime.

Thus, converse of Fermat's theorem is not true.

In other words, if $a^{n-1} \equiv 1 \ (\text{mod } n)$ for some integer a, then n need not be a prime.

8. There has been historical interest in the numbers of the form $2^n - 2$. Chinese mathematicians claimed over 2.5 centuries ago that n is prime if and only if $n \mid 2^n - 2$. In fact, this criterion is true for all integers $n \leq 340$.

However, for $n = 341$, the criterion fails.

$$341 \mid 2^{341} - 2$$

But 341 is not a prime. ($\because 341 = 11 \times 31$)

9. A composite integer n is called pseudoprime if $n \mid 2^n - 2$.

341 is the smallest pseudoprime.

In general, a composite integer n for which $a^n \equiv a \ (\text{mod } n)$ is called a pseudoprime to the base a. When $a = 2$, n is simply said to be a pseudoprime.

There are infinitely many pseudoprimes to any given base.

The composite numbers that are pseudoprimes to every base a, that is, $a^n \equiv a \ (\text{mod } n)$, are called "absolute pseudoprimes" or "Carmichael numbers".

10. Theorem : If n is an odd pseudoprime, then $m_n = 2^n - 1$ is also a pseudoprime.

Proof : n is a pseudoprime.

Hence, n is a composite number.

$\therefore \quad n = rs$ where $1 < r \leq s < n$

$$2^n - 1 = 2^{rs} - 1 = (2^r)^s - 1$$

$\therefore$
$$2^r - 1 \mid 2^n - 1$$

or,
$$2^r - 1 \mid m_n$$

$\therefore \quad m_n$ is a composite number.

As n is a pseudoprime, $n \mid 2^n - 2$.

$\therefore \quad 2^n - 2 = kn$ for some integer k

$$2^{m_n - 1} = 2^{2^n - 2} = 2^{kn}$$

Now,
$$\begin{aligned} 2^{m_n - 1} - 1 &= 2^{kn} - 1 \\ &= (2^n - 1)(2^{n(k-1)} + 2^{n(k-2)} + \ldots + 2^n + 1) \\ &= m_n (2^{n(k-1)} + 2^{n(k-2)} + \ldots + 2^n + 1) \\ &\equiv 0 \pmod{m_n} \end{aligned}$$

Multiplying both sides by 2, we get

$$2^{m_n} - 2 \equiv 0 \pmod{m_n}$$

or,
$$m_n \mid 2^{m_n} - 2$$

Hence, m_n is a pseudoprime.

11. Wilson's theorem : If p is a prime, then $(p-1)! \equiv -1 \pmod{p}$.

Proof : For $p = 2$, $(p-1)! = 1 \equiv -1 \pmod{2}$

For $p = 3$, $(p-1)! = 2! = 2 \equiv -1 \pmod{3}$

Hence, $(p-1)! \equiv -1 \pmod{p}$ for $p = 2$ and $p = 3$

Now, let us take $p > 3$.

Suppose that a is any one of the $p-1$ positive integers 1, 2, 3, ..., $p-1$.

Consider the linear congruence $ax \equiv 1 \pmod{p}$.

Then $\gcd(a, p) = 1$

Hence, the congruence $ax \equiv 1 \pmod{p}$ admits a unique solution modulo p.

Thus, there is a unique integer a', with $1 \leq a' \leq p-1$, satisfying $aa' \equiv 1 \pmod{p}$.

Suppose,
$$a = a'$$

Then,
$$a^2 \equiv 1 \pmod{p}$$

or, $(a-1)(a+1) \equiv 0 \pmod{p}$

Hence, $a = 1 \text{ or } p-1$

If we omit the numbers 1 and $p-1$ (from the given set of integers 1, 2, 3, ..., $p-1$), the remaining integers can be grouped into $\frac{p-3}{2}$ pairs, where $a \neq a'$, such that

$$aa' \equiv 1 \pmod{p}$$

When these $\frac{p-3}{2}$ congruence are multiplied and the factors are rearranged, we get

$$2 \times 3 \times \ldots \times (p-2) \equiv 1 \pmod{p}$$

or, $(p-2)! \equiv 1 \pmod{p}$

Multiplying both sides by $p-1$, we get $(p-1)! \equiv p-1 \equiv -1 \pmod{p}$

Thus, we get $(p-1)! \equiv -1 \pmod{p}$

12. Let us understand the proof of Wilson's theorem through an illustrative example.

For prime $p = 11$, consider following integers 2, 3, 4, 5, 6, 7, 8, 9

$$2 \times 6 \equiv 1 \pmod{11}$$
$$3 \times 4 \equiv 1 \pmod{11}$$
$$5 \times 9 \equiv 1 \pmod{11}$$
$$7 \times 8 \equiv 1 \pmod{11}$$

Thus, we get $\frac{p-3}{2} = 4$ pairs of integers, where product of each pair is congruent to 1 modulo 11.

Multiplying these congruences, we get

$$9! \equiv 1 \pmod{11}$$

$\therefore$ $10! \equiv 10 \pmod{11}$

or $10! \equiv -1 \pmod{11}$

13. Converse of Wilson's Theorem is also true. If $(n-1)! \equiv -1 \pmod{n}$, then n is a prime number.

Proof : $(n-1)! \equiv -1 \pmod{n}$

Suppose that n is not a prime. Then n has a divisor d with $1 < d < n$.

$\therefore$ $d \mid (n-1)!$

Also, $d \mid (n-1)! + 1$ $[\because n \mid [(n-1)! + 1] \text{ and } d \mid n]$

$\therefore$ $d \mid 1$ which is not possible

Hence, n is a prime.

14. A congruence of the form $ax^2 + bx + c \equiv 0 \pmod{n}$, with $a \not\equiv 0 \pmod{n}$ is called a quadratic congruence.

Wilson's theorem has important application in the study of quadratic congruences.

15. Theorem : The quadratic congruence $x^2 + 1 \equiv 0 \pmod{p}$, where p is an odd prime, has a solution if and only if $p \equiv 1 \pmod{4}$.

Proof : Let a be any solution of $x^2 + 1 \equiv 0 \pmod{p}$

$$\therefore \quad a^2 \equiv -1 \pmod{p}$$

$$\therefore \quad p \nmid a \qquad \text{(otherwise, } p \mid 1 \text{ which is not possible)}$$

Hence, by Fermat's Theorem $a^{p-1} \equiv 1 \pmod{p}$

$$\text{or,} \quad \left(a^{\frac{p-1}{2}}\right)^2 \equiv 1 \pmod{p}$$

$$\text{or,} \quad (a^2)^{\frac{p-1}{2}} \equiv 1 \pmod{p}$$

$$\text{or,} \quad (-1)^{\frac{p-1}{2}} \equiv 1 \pmod{p} \qquad [\because a^2 \equiv -1 \pmod{p}]$$

If p is of the form $4n+3$, $\dfrac{p-1}{2} = 2n+1$

$$\therefore \quad (-1)^{\frac{p-1}{2}} = (-1)^{2n+1} = -1 \equiv 1 \pmod{p}$$

$$\text{or,} \quad p \mid 2$$

which is not possible, as p is an odd prime.

Hence, p must be of the form $4n+1$.

Now, suppose that p is of the form $4n+1$.

$$(p-1)! = 1 \times 2 \ldots \frac{(p-1)}{2} \times \frac{(p+1)}{2} \ldots (p-2)\,(p-1)$$

$$p-1 \equiv -1 \pmod{p}$$

$$p-2 \equiv -2 \pmod{p}$$

$$\vdots \qquad \vdots \qquad \vdots$$

$$\frac{p+1}{2} \equiv -\left(\frac{p-1}{2}\right) \pmod{p}$$

$$\therefore \quad (p-1)! = 1\,(-1)\,2\,(-2) \ldots \left(\frac{p-1}{2}\right)\left(-\frac{p-1}{2}\right)$$

$$\equiv (-1)^{\frac{p-1}{2}} \left(1 \times 2 \ldots \frac{p-1}{2}\right)^2 \pmod{p}$$

By Wilson's theorem $(p-1)! \equiv -1 \pmod{p}$

$$\therefore \quad -1 \equiv (-1)^{\frac{p-1}{2}} \left[\left(\frac{p-1}{2}\right)!\right]^2 \pmod{p}$$

As p is of the form $4n+1$, $(-1)^{\frac{p-1}{2}}=1$

$\therefore$ $$-1 \equiv \left[\left(\frac{p-1}{2}\right)!\right]^2 \pmod{p}$$

$\therefore$ $\left(\frac{p-1}{2}\right)!$ satisfies the congruence $x^2+1 \equiv 0 \pmod{p}$.

Thus, the theorem is proved.

16. 13 is a prime number of the form $4n+1$.

$$\frac{(p-1)}{2}=6$$

$$6! = 720 \equiv 5 \pmod{13}$$

$\therefore$ $$(6!)^2+1 \equiv 5^2+1$$

$$\equiv 0 \pmod{13}$$

$\therefore$ $(6!)$ satisfies the congruence $x^2+1 \equiv 0 \pmod{13}$.

17. $(p-1)!+1$ is divisible by p (By Wilson's theorem).

Hence, $(p-1)!+1$ is a composite number.

As there are infinitely many primes, there are infinitely many composite numbers of the form $n!+1$.

Are there infinitely many prime numbers of the form $n!+1$?

18. What is the number of positive integers less than 12 that are relatively prime to 12?

1, 5, 7 and 11 are relatively prime to 12.

Thus, there are four such integers.

It turns out that the number of positive integers less than a given integer n and relatively prime to n has interesting mathematical properties.

19. Euler's Phi-function : For $n \geq 1$, $\varphi(n)$ denotes the numbers of positive integers not exceeding n that are relatively prime to n.

$\therefore$ $$\varphi(12)=4$$

You can verify that $\varphi(1)=1$, $\varphi(2)=1$, $\varphi(3)=2$, $\varphi(4)=2$, $\varphi(5)=4$, $\varphi(6)=2$, ...

Please note that $\varphi(1)=1$ because $\gcd(1, 1)=1$

The function φ is called the Euler's Phi-function.

20. For $n>1$, $\varphi(n)=n-1$ if and only if n is prime.

Proof : If n is prime, all integers 1, 2, ..., $n-1$ are relatively prime to n.

Hence, $$\varphi(n)=n-1$$

Now suppose that $\varphi(n)=n-1$

If n is composite, there exists $d, 1 < d < n$ such that $d \mid n$

Hence, $\varphi(n) \leq n - 2$

Thus, n cannot be composite and it has to be prime.

21. Theorem : If p is a prime and $n > 0$, then

$$\varphi(p^n) = p^n - p^{n-1} = p^n\left(1 - \frac{1}{p}\right)$$

Proof : It is evident that $\gcd(n, p^n) \neq 1$ if and only if $p \nmid n$.

The integers between 1 and p^n which are divisible by p are as under:

$$p, 2p, 3p, \ldots, (p^{n-1})p$$

Thus, there are p^{n-1} integers (including p^n) between 1 and p^n which are divisible by p.

Hence, the set $\{1, 2, \ldots, p^n\}$ contains exactly $p^n - p^{n-1}$ integers which are lesser than p^n and relatively prime to it.

Hence, by definition of phi-function, $\varphi(p^n) = p^n - p^{n-1}$.

22. Find $\varphi(16)$.

1, 3, 5, 7, 9, 11, 13 and 15 are relatively prime to 16.

Hence, $\varphi(16) = 8$

Also please note that $\varphi(16) = \varphi(2^4) = 2^4 - 2^3 = 16 - 8 = 8$

23. Lemma : Given integers a, b, c, $\gcd(a, bc) = 1$ if and only if $\gcd(a, b) = 1$ and $\gcd(a, c) = 1$

Proof : Suppose that $\gcd(a, bc) = 1$

Now suppose that $\gcd(a, b) = d$

$\therefore$ $d \mid a$ and $d \mid b$

Hence, $d \mid a$ and $d \mid bc$

$\therefore$ $\gcd(a, bc) \geq d$ or, $1 \geq d$ $[\because \gcd(a, bc) = 1]$

Hence, $d = 1$ or $\gcd(a, b) = 1$

By similar reasoning $\gcd(a, c) = 1$

Now suppose that $\gcd(a, b) = 1$ and $\gcd(a, c) = 1$

Let $\gcd(a, bc) = d$

Then, $d \mid a$, $d \mid bc$

Suppose that p is a prime factor of d.

Then $p \mid bc$

$\therefore$ $p \mid b$ or $p \mid c$

If $p \mid b$, $\gcd(a, b) \geq p$ which is a contradiction.
If $p \mid c$, $\gcd(a, c) \geq p$ which is a contradiction.
Hence, $d = 1$
Or, $\gcd(a, bc) = 1$

24. Theorem : The function φ is a multiplicative function.

Proof : We need to prove that $\varphi(mn) = \varphi(m)\,\varphi(n)$, whenever m and n are relatively prime.

If either of m or n is 1, then $\varphi(mn) = \varphi(m)\,\varphi(n)$ because $\varphi(1) = 1$

Now we need to prove the result when $m > 1$ and $n > 1$.

Let us arrange the integers from 1 to mn in m columns of n integers each, as under:

$$\begin{array}{ccccc} 1 & 2 & \ldots\ldots & r & \ldots\ldots\ m \\ m+1 & m+2 & \ldots\ldots & m+r & \ldots\ldots\ 2m \\ 2m+1 & 2m+2 & \ldots\ldots & 2m+r & \ldots\ldots\ 3m \\ \vdots & \vdots & \ldots\ldots & \vdots & \ldots\ldots\ \vdots \\ (n-1)m+1 & (n-1)m+2 & \ldots\ldots & (n-1)m+r & \ldots\ldots\ nm \end{array}$$

$\varphi(mn)$ = Number of entries in this array that are relatively prime to mn.
= Number of entries in this array that are relatively prime to both m and n
(By preceding Lemma at para 23).

Do you remember the following result from the chapter on Divisibility?

$$\gcd(qm + r, m) = \gcd(r, m)$$

Thus, $\gcd(qm + r, m) = 1$ if and only if $\gcd(r, m) = 1$

Hence, an entry in r^{th} column is relatively prime to m if and only if r itself is relatively prime to m. Further, if r is relatively prime to m, since there are m columns, there are exactly $\varphi(m)$ columns containing integers relatively prime to m.

Now suppose that r is relatively prime to m.

The entries in the rth columns are :

$$r,\ m + r,\ 2m + r,\ \ldots,\ (n-1)m + r$$

There are n integers in this sequence. Suppose that two entries of this sequence $jm + r$ and $km + r$ $(0 \leq j < k < n)$ are congruent to each other modulo n.

Then $\quad jm + r \equiv km + r \pmod{n}$

or, $\quad jm \equiv km \pmod{n}$

or, $\quad j \equiv k \pmod{n}$ $\quad [\because \gcd(m, n) = 1]$

$\therefore \quad n \mid k - j$

But $\quad 1 \leq k - j \leq n - 1$ $\quad [\because 0 \leq j < k < n]$

This is a contradiction.

Hence, no two members of the given sequence are congruent to each other modulo n.

Thus, the numbers in the rth column are congruent modulo n to $0, 1, 2, 3, \ldots, n-1$ in some order.

Now, we make the following claim.

If $s \equiv t \pmod{n}$ then $\gcd(s, n) = 1$ if and only if $\gcd(t, n) = 1$ .... (1)

($\because$ if $\gcd(s, n) = 1$ and $\gcd(t, n) \neq 1$, then some prime $p \mid t$, $p \mid n$ and thus $p \mid s$ as $s \equiv t \pmod{n}$. This is a contradiction.)

Hence, the number of integers in the rth column relatively prime to n

= Number of integers in the set $\{0, 1, 2, \ldots, n-1\}$ relatively prime to n

By definition the set $\{0, 1, 2, \ldots, n-1\}$ has exactly $\varphi(n)$ integers relatively prime to n.

Hence, r^{th} column has exactly $\varphi(n)$ integers relatively prime to n.

Now, we have following two results :

(i) There are exactly $\varphi(m)$ columns consisting of integers (all) relatively prime to m (for every column r where r is relatively prime to m).

(ii) In column r (r relatively prime to m), there are exactly $\phi(n)$ integers relatively prime to n.

Thus, there are exactly $\varphi(m)\,\varphi(n)$ integers in the given array relatively prime to both m and n.

Hence, there are exactly $\varphi(m)\,\varphi(n)$ integers relatively prime to mn.

$$\therefore \qquad \varphi(mn) = \varphi(m)\,\varphi(n)$$

25. Let us take few examples to discuss preceding result.

$$\varphi(2) = 1$$

$$\varphi(3) = 2$$

$$\varphi(6) = 2$$

$$\therefore \qquad \varphi(6) = \varphi(2)\,\varphi(3) \qquad [\because \gcd(2, 3) = 1]$$

$$\varphi(3) = 2$$

$$\varphi(5) = 4$$

$$\varphi(15) = 8$$

$$\therefore \qquad \varphi(15) = \varphi(3)\,\varphi(5) \qquad [\because \gcd(3, 5) = 1]$$

26. Theorem : If the integer $n > 1$ has the prime factorisation

$$n = p_1^{k_1} p_2^{k_2} \dots p_r^{k_r}, \text{ then}$$

$$\varphi(n) = (p_1^{k_1} - p_1^{k_1 - 1})(p_2^{k_2} - p_2^{k_2 - 1}) \dots (p_r^{k_r} - p_r^{k_r - 1})$$

$$= n\left(1 - \frac{1}{p_1}\right)\left(1 - \frac{1}{p_2}\right) \dots \left(1 - \frac{1}{p_r}\right)$$

Proof : $n = p_1^{k_1} p_2^{k_2} \dots p_r^{k_r}$

$$\varphi(n) = \varphi(p_1^{k_1} p_2^{k_2} \dots p_r^{k_r})$$

$$= \varphi(p_1^{k_1})\, \varphi(p_2^{k_2} \dots p_r^{k_r})$$

[$\because$ $\gcd(p_1^{k_1}, p_2^{k_2}, \dots, p_r^{k_r}) = 1$ as $p_1, p_2, \dots, p_r$ are distinct primes]

$$= \varphi(p_1^{k_1})\, \varphi(p_2^{k_2})\, \varphi(p_3^{k_3} \dots p_r^{k_r})$$

$$= \varphi(p_1^{k_1})\, \varphi(p_2^{k_2}) \dots \varphi(p_r^{k_r})$$

$$= (p_1^{k_1} - p_1^{k_1-1})(p_2^{k_2} - p_2^{k_2-1}) \dots (p_r^{k_r} - p_r^{k_r-1})$$

(By theorem at para 21)

$$= n\left(1 - \frac{1}{p_1}\right)\left(1 - \frac{1}{p_2}\right) \dots \left(1 - \frac{1}{p_r}\right)$$

27. Find $\varphi(120)$.

$$120 = 8 \times 3 \times 5 = 2^3 \times 3 \times 5$$

$$\therefore \quad \varphi(120) = 120\left(1 - \frac{1}{2}\right)\left(1 - \frac{1}{3}\right)\left(1 - \frac{1}{5}\right)$$

$$= 120 \times \frac{1}{2} \times \frac{2}{3} \times \frac{4}{5} = 32$$

28. Theorem : For $n > 2$, $\varphi(n)$ is an even integer.

Proof : Suppose that n is a power of 2.

Let $n = 2^k$, $k \geq 2$

Then by theorem at para 21, $\varphi(n) = 2^k\left(1 - \frac{1}{2}\right) = 2^{k-1}$

2^{k-1} is an even integer.

Now suppose that n is not a power of 2.

Then it must be divisible by some odd prime p.

Therefore, n can be written as

$n = p^k m$ where $k \geq 1$ and $\gcd(p^k, m) = 1$

Hence, by theorem at para 24,

$$\varphi(n) = \varphi(p^k)\,\varphi(m)$$
$$= (p^k - p^{k-1})\,\varphi(m)$$
$$= p^{k-1}(p-1)\,\varphi(m)$$
$$2 \mid p-1 \qquad (\because p \text{ is an odd prime.})$$

Hence, $\varphi(n)$ is an even integer.

29. Do you remember the Euclid's Theorem from the chapter on "Prime Numbers"? "There are infinitely many primes".

We can now prove this theorem in another way.

Suppose that there are finitely many primes $p_1, p_2, ..., p_r$.

Let $$a = p_1 p_2 \cdots p_r$$

Now consider any integer $n, 1 < n \le a$.

n is either a prime or has a prime divisor q.

In either case n has a factor common to a, as $p_1, p_2, ..., p_r$ are the only prime numbers.

Hence, $\gcd(n, a) \ne 1$ for all $n, 1 < n \le a$.

Therefore, $$\varphi(a) = 1$$

But by theorem at para 28, $\varphi(n)$ is an even integer for $n > 2$.

This is a contradiction.

Thus, it is established that there are infinitely many primes.

30. Lemma :

Let $n > 1$ and $\gcd(a, n) = 1$. If $a_1, a_2, ..., a_{\varphi(n)}$ are the positive integers less than n and relatively prime to n, then $aa_1, aa_2, ..., aa_{\varphi(n)}$ are congruent modulo n to $a_1, a_2, ..., a_{\varphi(n)}$ in some order.

Proof : Suppose that $$aa_i \equiv aa_j \pmod{n} \qquad [1 \le i < j \le \varphi(n)]$$

$$\therefore \quad a_i \equiv a_j \pmod{n} \qquad [\because \gcd(a, n) = 1]$$

$$\therefore \quad n \mid a_j - a_i$$

But, $$1 \le |a_j - a_i| \le n - 2$$

This is a contradiction.

Hence, no two of the integers $aa_1, aa_2, ... aa_{\varphi(n)}$ are congruent to each other modulo n.

Also, $$\gcd(a, n) = 1$$
$$\gcd(a_i, n) = 1, \qquad [1 \le i \le \varphi(n)]$$

Hence, by Lemma at para 23,

$$\gcd(aa_i, n) = 1$$

For any $aa_i, 1 \le i \le \varphi(n)$
there exists a unique integer $b, 0 \le b < n$ such that

$$aa_i \equiv b \pmod{n}$$

$$\therefore \qquad \gcd(b, n) = \gcd(aa_i, n) = 1$$

$\therefore$ b must be one of the integers $a_1, a_2, ..., a_{\varphi(n)}$.

Hence, $aa_1, aa_2, ..., a_{\varphi(n)}$ are congruent modulo n to $a_1, a_2, ..., a_{\varphi(n)}$ in some order.

31. Euler's Theorem : If $n \ge 1$ and $\gcd(a, n) = 1$, then $a^{\varphi(n)} \equiv 1 \pmod{n}$.

Proof : For $n = 1$, $a^{\varphi(1)} = 1 \pmod{1}$ which is trivially true.

Now suppose that $n > 1$.

Let $a_1, a_2, ..., a_{\varphi(n)}$ be the positive integers less than n that are relatively prime to n.

As $\gcd(a, n) = 1$, it follows from the preceding Lemma that $aa_1, aa_2, ... aa_{\varphi(n)}$ are congruent to $a_1, a_2, ..., a_{\varphi(n)}$ in some order.

Hence,

$$aa_1 \equiv a_1' \pmod{n}$$
$$aa_2 \equiv a_2' \pmod{n}$$
$$\dots\dots\dots\dots$$
$$\dots\dots\dots\dots$$
$$aa_{\varphi(n)} \equiv a_{\varphi(n)}' \pmod{n}$$

where $a_1', a_2', ..., a_{\varphi(n)}'$ are the integers $a_1, a_2, ..., a_{\varphi(n)}$ in some order.

Taking product of these $\varphi(n)$ congruences, we get

$$(aa_1) \times (aa_2) \times ... \times (aa_{\varphi(n)}) \equiv a_1' \times a_2' \times ... \times a_{\varphi(n)}' \pmod{n}$$
$$\equiv a_1 \times a_2 \times ... \times a_{\varphi(n)} \pmod{n}$$

or, $a^{\varphi(n)} (a_1 \times a_2 \times ... \times a_{\varphi(n)}) \equiv a_1 \times a_2 \times ... \times a_{\varphi(n)} \pmod{n}$

$\gcd(a_i, n) = 1$ for each i

Hence, $\gcd(a_1 a_2 ... a_{\varphi(n)}, n) = 1$ (By Lemma at para 23)

Therefore, the common factor may be cancelled to obtain $a^{\varphi(n)} \equiv 1 \pmod{n}$

32. Corollary : Fermat's Theorem- If p is a prime and $p \nmid a$, then $a^{p-1} \equiv 1 \pmod{p}$

Proof : If p is a prime and $p \nmid a$, $\gcd(a, p) = 1$

Also $\qquad \varphi(p) = p - 1$

Hence, by Euler's Theorem, $\qquad a^{p-1} \equiv 1 \pmod{p}$

Thus, Fermat's Theorem is a special case of Euler's Theorem.

Solved Examples

1. What is the remainder when 7^{33} is divided by 11?

Sol. By Fermat's theorem,

$$7^{10} \equiv 1 \pmod{11} \qquad (\because 11 \nmid 7)$$

$\therefore$ $$7^{30} \equiv 1 \pmod{11}$$

Also, $$7^2 \equiv 5 \pmod{11}$$

$$7^3 \equiv 35 \pmod{11}$$

or, $$7^3 \equiv 2 \pmod{11}$$

$\therefore$ $$7^{33} \equiv 2 \pmod{11}$$

Hence, the remainder is 2 when 7^{33} is divided by 11.

2. Find out whether 17 is a divisor of $11^{104}+1$ or not.

Sol. By Fermat's theorem,

$$11^{16} \equiv 1 \pmod{17} \qquad (\because 17 \nmid 11)$$

$\therefore$ $$11^{96} \equiv 1 \pmod{17}$$

Also, $$11 \equiv -6 \pmod{17}$$

$\therefore$ $$11^2 \equiv 2 \pmod{17}$$

$\therefore$ $$11^8 \equiv -1 \pmod{17}$$

Hence, $$11^{96+8} \equiv -1 \pmod{17}$$

or, $$11^{104}+1 \equiv 0 \pmod{17}$$

Hence, 17 divides $11^{104}+1$.

3. Prove that $8^{12} \equiv 1 \pmod{35}$.

Sol. $35 = 5 \times 7$

By Fermat's Theorem,

$$8^4 \equiv 1 \pmod{5} \qquad (\because 5 \nmid 8)$$

$\therefore$ $$8^{12} \equiv 1 \pmod{5}$$

Also, by Fermat's Theorem,

$$8^6 \equiv 1 \pmod{7} \qquad (\because 7 \nmid 8)$$

$\therefore$ $$8^{12} \equiv 1 \pmod{7}$$

Thus, $5 \mid 8^{12}-1$ and $7 \mid 8^{12}-1$

Also, $$\gcd(5, 7) = 1$$

Hence, $35 \mid 8^{12}-1$

$\therefore$ $$8^{12} \equiv 1 \pmod{35}$$

4. $\gcd(a, 42) = 1$. Prove that 168 divides $a^6 - 1$.

Sol.
$$42 = 2 \times 3 \times 7$$
$$\gcd(a, 42) = 1$$

Hence, by Fermat's Theorem,

$$a \equiv 1 \pmod{2}$$
$$a^2 \equiv 1 \pmod{3}$$
$$a^6 \equiv 1 \pmod{7}$$
$$168 = 2^3 \times 3 \times 7$$
$$\begin{aligned} a^6 - 1 &= (a^2)^3 - 1 \\ &= (a^2 - 1)(a^4 + a^2 + 1) \\ &= (a - 1)(a + 1)(a^4 + a^2 + 1) \end{aligned}$$

As a is an odd number ($\because a \equiv 1 \pmod{2}$), it is of one of the forms $4n + 1$ or $4n + 3$. In either case, $(a - 1)(a + 1)$ is divisible by 8.

Hence, $$a^6 \equiv 1 \pmod{8}$$

Also, $$a^6 \equiv 1 \pmod{3} \qquad [\because a^2 \equiv 1 \bmod 3]$$

and $$a^6 \equiv 1 \pmod{7}$$

8, 3 and 7 have no common factors in pairs.

Hence, $$a^6 \equiv 1 \pmod{8 \times 3 \times 7}$$

or, $$a^6 \equiv 1 \pmod{168}$$

5. $\gcd(a, 133) = \gcd(b, 133) = 1$. Prove that $133 \mid a^{18} - b^{18}$.

Sol. $133 = 7 \times 19$

By Fermat's Theorem,

$$a^6 \equiv 1 \pmod{7}$$
$$a^{18} \equiv 1 \pmod{19}$$

$\therefore$ $$a^{18} \equiv 1 \pmod{7}$$

$$\gcd(7, 19) = 1$$

Hence, $$a^{18} \equiv 1 \pmod{7 \times 19}$$

or, $$a^{18} \equiv 1 \pmod{133}$$

Similarly, $$b^{18} \equiv 1 \pmod{133}$$

Hence, $$a^{18} - b^{18} \equiv 0 \pmod{133}$$

or, $$133 \mid a^{18} - b^{18}$$

6. For any integer $n \geq 0, 13 \mid 11^{12n+6} + 1$. Prove.

Sol. By Fermat's theorem,

$$11^{12} \equiv 1 \pmod{13} \qquad (\because 13 \nmid 11)$$

$$\therefore \quad 11^{12n} \equiv 1 \pmod{13} \qquad (\text{for } n \geq 0)$$

$$11 \equiv -2 \pmod{13}$$

$$\therefore \quad 11^6 \equiv 64 \pmod{13}$$

$$\text{or,} \quad 11^6 \equiv -1 \pmod{13}$$

$$\therefore \quad 11^{12n+6} \equiv -1 \pmod{13}$$

$$\text{or,} \quad 11^{12n+6} + 1 \equiv 0 \pmod{13}$$

$$\text{Hence,} \quad 13 \mid 11^{12n+6} + 1$$

7. $a^{21} \equiv a \pmod{15}$ for all a. Prove.

Sol. By Fermat's Theorem,

$$a^5 \equiv a \pmod 5$$

$$\therefore \quad a^{20} \equiv a^4 \pmod 5$$

$$\therefore \quad a^{21} \equiv a^5 \pmod 5$$

$$\text{Hence,} \quad a^{21} \equiv a \pmod 5 \qquad [\because a^5 \equiv a \pmod 5]$$

$$\text{Also,} \quad a^3 \equiv a \pmod 3 \qquad (\text{By Fermat's Theorem})$$

$$\therefore \quad a^9 \equiv a^3 \pmod 3$$

$$\text{or,} \quad a^9 \equiv a \pmod 3$$

$$\text{or,} \quad a^{18} \equiv a^2 \pmod 3$$

$$\therefore \quad a^{21} \equiv a \pmod 3$$

$$\text{Thus,} \quad a^{21} \equiv a \pmod 5$$

$$\text{and} \quad a^{21} \equiv a \pmod 3$$

$$\therefore \quad a^{21} \equiv a \pmod{15} \qquad [\therefore \gcd(3, 5) = 1]$$

8. $a^9 \equiv 1 \pmod{30}$ for all a. Prove.

Sol. $30 = 2 \times 3 \times 5$

$$a^2 \equiv a \pmod 2 \qquad [\text{By Fermat's Theorem}]$$

$$\therefore \quad a^4 \equiv a^2 \pmod 2$$

$$\text{or,} \quad a^4 \equiv a \pmod 2$$

$$\therefore \quad a^8 \equiv a^2 \pmod 2$$

or, $a^8 \equiv a \pmod 2$

$\therefore$ $a^9 \equiv a^2 \pmod 2$

or, $a^9 \equiv a \pmod 2$

Again, by Fermat's Theorem,

$$a^3 \equiv a \pmod 3$$

$\therefore$ $a^9 \equiv a^3 \pmod 3$

$\therefore$ $a^9 \equiv a \pmod 3$

Again, by Fermat's Theorem,

$$a^4 \equiv 1 \pmod 5 \qquad [\text{if } 5 \nmid a]$$

$\therefore$ $a^8 \equiv 1 \pmod 5$

$\therefore$ $a^9 \equiv a \pmod 5$

If $5 \mid a$, then $a^9 \equiv a \pmod 5$

$\therefore$ $a^9 \equiv a \pmod 5$ for all a.

Thus, $a^9 \equiv a \pmod 2$

$$a^9 \equiv a \pmod 3$$

$$a^9 \equiv a \pmod 5$$

Numbers 2, 3 and 5 are relatively prime in pairs.

Hence, $a^9 \equiv a \pmod{2 \times 3 \times 5}$

or, $a^9 \equiv a \pmod{30}$

9. If $\gcd(a, 30) = 1$, prove that $60 \mid a^4 + 59$.

Sol. $30 = 2 \times 3 \times 5$

$$\gcd(a, 30) = 1$$

Hence, none of 2, 3 or 5 divide a.

Hence, by Fermat's Theorem,

$$a \equiv 1 \pmod 2$$

$\therefore$ $a \equiv 2k + 1$ for some integer k

$\therefore$ $a^2 \equiv 4k^2 + 4k + 1$

$\therefore$ $a^2 \equiv 1 \pmod 4$

$\therefore$ $a^4 \equiv 1 \pmod 4$

Again, by Fermat's Theorem,

$$a^2 \equiv 1 \pmod 3$$

∴ $$a^4 \equiv 1 \pmod 3$$

Again, by Fermat's Theorem,

$$a^4 \equiv 1 \pmod 5$$

Thus, $$a^4 \equiv 1 \pmod 4$$

$$a^4 \equiv 1 \pmod 3$$

$$a^4 \equiv 1 \pmod 5$$

3, 4 and 5 are relatively prime in pairs.

Hence, $$a^4 \equiv 1 \pmod{4 \times 3 \times 5}$$

or, $$a^4 \equiv 1 \pmod{60}$$

or, $$a^4 \equiv -59 \pmod{60}$$

∴ $$60 \mid a^4 + 59$$

10. Find the unit digit of 3^{100} by the use of Fermat's Theorem.

Sol. By Fermat's Theorem.

$$3 \equiv 1 \pmod 2$$

and $$3^4 \equiv 1 \pmod 5$$

∴ $$3^4 \equiv 1 \pmod 2$$

and $$3^4 \equiv 1 \pmod 5$$

2 and 5 are relatively prime.

Hence, $$3^4 \equiv 1 \pmod{2 \times 5}$$

or, $$3^4 \equiv 1 \pmod{10}$$

∴ $$3^{100} \equiv 1 \pmod{10}$$

Hence, the unit digit of 3^{100} is 1.

11. For any integer a, a^5 and a have the same unit digit. Prove.

Sol. $10 = 2 \times 5$

By Fermat's Theorem,

$$a^2 \equiv a \pmod 2$$

∴ $$a^4 \equiv a^2 \equiv a \pmod 2$$

∴ $$a^5 \equiv a^2 \equiv a \pmod 2$$

Also $\qquad a^5 \equiv a \pmod{5}$ [By Fermat's Theorem]

Thus, $\qquad a^5 \equiv a \pmod{2}$

and $\qquad a^5 \equiv a \pmod{5}$

2 and 5 are relatively prime.

Hence, $\qquad a^5 \equiv a \pmod{2 \times 5}$

or, $\qquad a^5 \equiv a \pmod{10}$

Thus, $\qquad 10 \mid a^5 - a$

Hence, a^5 and a have same unit digits.

12. $7 \nmid a$. Prove that either $a^3 + 1$ or $a^3 - 1$ is divisible by 7.

Sol. $7 \nmid a$.

Hence, by Fermat's Theorem.

$$a^6 \equiv 1 \pmod{7}$$

$\therefore \qquad 7 \mid a^6 - 1$

or, $\qquad 7 \mid (a^3)^2 - 1$

or, $\qquad 7 \mid (a^3 - 1)(a^3 + 1)$

Hence, either $a^3 - 1$ or $a^3 + 1$ is divisible by 7.

13. The three most recent appearances of Halley's comet were in the years 1835, 1910 and 1986. The next occurrence will be in 2061.

Prove that $1835^{1910} + 1986^{2061} \equiv 0 \pmod{7}$

Sol. $\qquad 1835 \equiv 1 \pmod{7}$

$\therefore \qquad 1835^{1910} \equiv 1 \pmod{7}$ ...(i)

$$1986 \equiv 5 \pmod{7}$$

$\therefore \qquad 1986^{2061} \equiv 5^{2061} \pmod{7}$

$5^6 \equiv 1 \pmod{7}$ [By Fermat's Theorem]

$\therefore \qquad 5^{2061} = 5^{6 \times 343 + 3}$

$$\equiv 1 \times 5^3 \pmod{7}$$

$\therefore \qquad 5^{2061} \equiv 6 \pmod{7}$

or, $\qquad 1986^{2061} \equiv 6 \pmod{7}$ ....(ii)

By (i) and (ii)

$$1835^{1910} + 1986^{2061} \equiv 0 \pmod{7}$$

14. Let p be a prime and $\gcd(a, p) = 1$. Prove that $n \equiv a^{p-2} b \pmod{p}$ is a solution of the linear congruence $ax \equiv b \pmod{p}$.

Sol. p is a prime and $\gcd(a, p) = 1$.

$$\therefore \quad a^{p-1} \equiv 1 \pmod{p} \qquad \text{[By Fermat's Theorem]}$$

$$n \equiv a^{p-2} b \pmod{p}$$

$$\therefore \quad an \equiv a^{p-1} b \pmod{p}$$

$$\equiv 1 \times b \pmod{p}$$

$$\equiv b \pmod{p}$$

Hence, $n \equiv a^{p-2} b \pmod{p}$ is a solution of the linear congruence $ax \equiv b \pmod{p}$

15. Solve congruence $3x \equiv 17 \pmod{29}$

Sol. By preceding result,

$n \equiv 3^{27} \cdot 17 \pmod{29}$ is the solution.

$$3^3 \equiv -2 \pmod{29}$$

$$\therefore \quad 3^{27} \equiv (-2)^9 \pmod{29}$$

$$\text{or,} \quad 3^{27} \equiv (-32) \times 16 \pmod{29}$$

$$\equiv -3 \times 16 \pmod{29}$$

$$\equiv 10 \pmod{29}$$

$$\therefore \quad 3^{27} \times 17 \equiv 10 \times 17 \pmod{29}$$

$$\equiv 25 \pmod{29}$$

$\therefore$ $n \equiv 25 \pmod{29}$ is solution of the given congruence $3x = 17 \pmod{29}$.

16. a and b are integers not divisible by the prime p.

Prove that if $a^p \equiv b^p \pmod{p}$, then $a \equiv b \pmod{p}$.

Sol. By Fermat's Theorem,

$$a^p \equiv a \pmod{p}$$

$$\text{And} \quad b^p \equiv b \pmod{p}$$

$$\therefore \quad (a^p - b^p) \equiv (a - b) \pmod{p} \qquad \text{....(i)}$$

$$\text{If} \quad a^p \equiv b^p \pmod{p}$$

$$\text{Then,} \quad a^p - b^p \equiv 0 \pmod{p}$$

Hence, by (i),

$$a - b \equiv 0 \pmod{p}$$

Thus, if $a^p \equiv b^p \pmod{p}$, then $a \equiv b \pmod{p}$

17. If p is an odd prime, prove that $1^p + 2^p + 3^p + \ldots + (p-1)^p \equiv 0 \pmod{p}$.

Sol. By Fermat's Theorem,

$$a^p \equiv a \pmod{p}$$

Hence, $1^p + 2^p + 3^p + \ldots + (p-1)^p$

$$\equiv 1 + 2 + 3 + \ldots + (p-1) \pmod{p}$$

$$\equiv \frac{p(p-1)}{2} \pmod{p}$$

$$\equiv 0 \pmod{p}$$

18. Let p and q be distinct odd primes such that $(p-1) \mid (q-1)$.

If $\gcd(a, pq) = 1$, prove that $a^{q-1} \equiv 1 \pmod{pq}$.

Sol. By Fermat's Theorem,

$$a^{p-1} \equiv 1 \pmod{p}$$

[$\because \gcd(a, pq) = 1$ implies that $\gcd(a, p) = 1$]

$$(p-1) \mid (q-1)$$

$\therefore\ q - 1 = (p-1)t$ for some integer t

$\therefore$ $$a^{(p-1)t} \equiv 1 \pmod{p}$$

or, $$a^{q-1} \equiv 1 \pmod{p} \quad \ldots\text{(i)}$$

Also, $$a^{q-1} \equiv 1 \pmod{q} \quad \ldots\text{(ii)}$$

(By Fermat's Theorem. $\gcd(a, pq) = 1$ implies that $\gcd(a, q) = 1$)

From (i) and (ii), it follows that

$$p \mid a^{q-1} - 1$$

And $$q \mid a^{q-1} - 1$$

Also $$\gcd(p, q) = 1 \quad [\because p \text{ and } q \text{ are distinct primes}]$$

$\therefore$ $$pq \mid a^{q-1} - 1$$

Hence, $$a^{q-1} \equiv 1 \pmod{pq}$$

19. Composite numbers n is called absolute pseudoprime or Carmichael number if $a^{n-1} \equiv 1 \pmod{n}$ for all integers a with $\gcd(a, n) = 1$. Verify that 1105 is an absolute pseudoprime.

Sol. $1105 = 5 \times 13 \times 17$

$\gcd(a, 1105) = 1$ implies that

$$\gcd(a, 5) = 1$$

$$\gcd(a, 13) = 1$$

$$\gcd(a, 17) = 1$$

Hence, by Fermat's theorem,

$$a^4 \equiv 1 \pmod 5$$
$$a^{12} \equiv 1 \pmod{13}$$
$$a^{16} \equiv 1 \pmod{17}$$

Now, $$a^{1104} = a^{4 \times 276}$$
$$\equiv 1 \pmod 5$$

Also, $$a^{1104} \equiv a^{12 \times 92} \pmod{13}$$
$$\equiv 1 \pmod{13}$$

Also, $$a^{1104} \equiv a^{16 \times 69} \pmod{17}$$
$$\equiv 1 \pmod{17}$$

$\therefore$ $$a^{1104} \equiv 1 \pmod{5 \times 13 \times 7}$$

or, $$a^{1104} \equiv 1 \pmod{1105}$$

Hence by definition, 1105 is an absolute pseudoprime.

20. Let $M_p = 2^p - 1$ where p is a prime.

If M_p is composite, prove that M_p is a pseudoprime.

Sol. $2^p \equiv 2 \pmod p$ (by Fermat's theorem)

$\therefore$ $2^p - 2 \equiv pt$ for some integer t

Now, $$2^{M_p - 1} - 1 = 2^{(2^p - 2)} - 1 = 2^{pt} - 1$$
$$= (2^p - 1)(2^{p(t-1)} + 2^{p(t-2)} + \ldots + 2^p + 1)$$

$\therefore$ $$= M_p(2^{p(t-1)} + 2^{p(t-2)} + \ldots + 2^p + 1)$$

$\therefore$ $$M_p \mid 2^{M_p - 1} - 1$$

$\therefore$ $$M_p \mid 2^{M_p} - 2$$

As M_p is a composite number, it is a pseudoprime.

21. What is the remainder when 15! is divided by 17?

Sol. By Wilson's theorem,

$$(17-1)! \equiv -1 \pmod{17}$$

or, $$16! \equiv -1 \pmod{17}$$

or, $$16! \equiv 16 \pmod{17}$$

or, $$16 \times 15! \equiv 16 \pmod{17}$$

We can cancel 16 on both sides as 16 is relatively prime to 17.

Hence, $$15! \equiv 1 \pmod{17}$$

Thus, we get remainder 1 when 15! is divided by 17.

22. What is the remainder when 2(26!) is divided by 29?

Sol. By Wilson's theorem,

$$(29-1)! \equiv -1 \pmod{29}$$

or, $$28! \equiv -1 \pmod{29}$$

or, $$28 \times 27! \equiv 28 \pmod{29}$$

We can cancel 28 on both sides as 28 is relatively prime to 29.

Hence, $$27! \equiv 1 \pmod{29}$$

or, $$27 \times 26! \equiv 1 \pmod{29}$$

or, $$(-2) \times 26! \equiv 1 \pmod{29}$$

or, $$2(26!) \equiv -1 \pmod{29}$$

or, $$2(26!) \equiv 28 \pmod{29}$$

Thus, we get remainder 28 when 2(26!) is divided by 29.

23. Determine whether 11 is a prime by examining whether $10! \equiv -1 \pmod{11}$.

Sol. $10! = 1 \times 2 \times 3 \times 4 \times 5 \times 6 \times 7 \times 8 \times 9 \times 10$

$$10 \equiv -1 \pmod{11}$$
$$9 \equiv -2 \pmod{11}$$
$$8 \equiv -3 \pmod{11}$$
$$7 \equiv -4 \pmod{11}$$
$$6 \equiv -5 \pmod{11}$$

$\therefore$ $$10! \equiv 1 \times 2 \times 3 \times 4 \times 5 \times (-5) \times (-4) \times (-3) \times (-2) \times (-1) \pmod{11}$$
$$\equiv -(1)^2\,(2)^2\,(3)^2\,(4)^2\,(5)^2 \pmod{11}$$
$$\equiv -4 \times 9 \times 16 \times 25 \pmod{11}$$
$$\equiv -4 \times (-2) \times 5 \times 3 \pmod{11}$$
$$\equiv 24 \times 5 \pmod{11} \equiv 2 \times 5 \pmod{11}$$
$$\equiv 10 \pmod{11} \equiv -1 \pmod{11}$$

Thus, $(11-1)! \equiv -1 \pmod{11}$

Hence, 11 is a prime.

24. Prove that $18! \equiv -1 \pmod{437}$.

Sol. $437 = 19 \times 23$

By Wilson's theorem, $$18! \equiv -1 \pmod{19} \quad \text{....(i)}$$
$$22! \equiv -1 \pmod{23}$$

or, $$22 \times 21 \times 20 \times 19 \times 18! \equiv -1 \pmod{23}$$

or, $$(-1) \times (-2) \times (-3) \times (-4) \times 18! \equiv -1 \pmod{23}$$

or, $$24\,(18!) \equiv -1 \pmod{23}$$

or, $$1 \times 18!! \equiv -1 \pmod{23}$$

or, $$18! \equiv -1 \pmod{23} \qquad ...(ii)$$

As 19 and 23 are relatively prime, by (i) and (ii), we get,

$$18! \equiv -1 \pmod{19 \times 23}$$

or, $$18! \equiv -1 \pmod{437}$$

25. If n is a composite integer, $(n-1)! \equiv 0 \pmod{n}$, except when $n = 4$. Prove.

Sol. For a composite integer $n > 4$, n can be written as $n = pq$ where $1 < p, q < n$.

If $p \neq q$, both p and q occur separately in $(n-1)!$

Hence, $pq \mid (n-1)!$ or $n \mid (n-1)!$

If $p = q$, then $n = p^2$.

For $n > 4$, at least one of p and q is greater than 2.

In this case, $p = q$ and $n = p^2$

Thus, $p > 2$

Hence, both p and $2p$ occur separately in $(n-1)!$.

Thus, $p^2 \mid (n-1)!$ or $n \mid (n-1)!$

Hence, in either case $n \mid (n-1)!$

$\therefore \quad (n-1)! \equiv 0 \pmod{n}$ for composite integer n except when $n = 4$

26. Find two solutions of the quadratic congruence $x^2 \equiv -1 \pmod{29}$.

Sol. By theorem at para 15 of this chapter, $\left(\frac{p-1}{2}\right)!$ satisfies the congruence

$x^2 + 1 \equiv 0 \pmod{p}$ for a prime p of the form $4k + 1$.

29 is a prime number of the form $4k + 1$.

Hence, $\left(\frac{29-1}{2}\right)!$ is a solution.

$$\left(\frac{29-1}{2}\right)! = 14!$$

$$= 1 \times 2 \times 3 \times 4 \times 5 \times 6 \times 7 \times 8 \times 9 \times 10 \times 11 \times 12 \times 13 \times 14$$

$$= (2 \times 14) \times (3 \times 13) \times (4 \times 12) \times (5 \times 11)$$

$$\times (6 \times 10) \times (7 \times 9) \times 8$$

$$\equiv (-1) \times 10 \times (-10) \times (-3) \times 2 \times 5 \times 8 \pmod{29}$$

$$\equiv -(10 \times 3 \times 2) \times (10 \times 5) \times 8 \pmod{29}$$

$$\equiv -2 \times (-8) \times 8 \pmod{29}$$

$$\equiv 2 \times 64 \pmod{29}$$

$$\equiv 2 \times 6 \pmod{29} \equiv 12 \pmod{29}$$

Hence, 12 and 41 $(29 + 12)$ are two solutions of the given quadratic congruence.

27. $4(29)! + 5!$ is divisible by 31. Prove.

Sol. By Wilson's theorem,

$$30! \equiv -1 \pmod{31}$$

or, $$30(29!) \equiv -1 \pmod{31}$$

or, $$30(29!) \equiv 30 \pmod{31}$$

$\therefore$ $$29! \equiv 1 \pmod{31}$$

$$4(29!) \equiv 4 \pmod{31}$$

$\therefore$ $$4(29!) + 5! \equiv 4 + 5! \pmod{31}$$

$$\equiv 4 + 120 \pmod{31}$$

$$\equiv 0 \pmod{31}$$

Hence, $31 \mid [4(29)! + 5!]$

28. Find the number of positive integers not exceeding 108 and relatively prime to 108.

Sol. The number of positive integers not exceeding 108 and relatively prime to 108 $= \varphi(108)$

$$108 = 2^2 \times 3^3$$

Hence, by theorem at para 26 of this chapter,

$$\varphi(108) = 108\left(1 - \frac{1}{2}\right)\left(1 - \frac{1}{3}\right) = 108 \times \frac{1}{2} \times \frac{2}{3} = 36$$

29. Find $\varphi(360)$.

Sol. $360 = 8 \times 9 \times 5 = 2^3 \times 3^2 \times 5$

$\therefore$ $$\varphi(360) = 360\left(1 - \frac{1}{2}\right)\left(1 - \frac{1}{3}\right)\left(1 - \frac{1}{5}\right)$$

$$= 360 \times \frac{1}{2} \times \frac{2}{3} \times \frac{4}{5} = 96$$

30. If n is an odd integer, then $\varphi(2n) = \varphi(n)$. Prove.

Sol. Suppose that integer n has prime factorisation $n = p_1^{k_1} \times p_2^{k_2} \times \ldots \times p_r^{k_r}$.

where, $p_i \neq 2, 1 \leq i \leq r$ as n is an odd integer.

$\therefore$ $$\varphi(n) = n\left(1 - \frac{1}{p_1}\right)\left(1 - \frac{1}{p_2}\right) \ldots \left(1 - \frac{1}{p_r}\right)$$

Now, $2n = 2^1 \times p_1^{k_1} \times p_2^{k_2} \times \ldots \times p_r^{k_r}$

This is the prime factorisation of $2n$.

Hence, $$\varphi(2n) = (2n)\left(1-\frac{1}{2}\right)\left(1-\frac{1}{p_1}\right)\left(1-\frac{1}{p_2}\right)\ldots\left(1-\frac{1}{p_r}\right)$$
$$= n\left(1-\frac{1}{p_1}\right)\left(1-\frac{1}{p_2}\right)\ldots\left(1-\frac{1}{p_r}\right) = \varphi(n)$$

31. If n is an even integer, then $\varphi(2n) = 2\varphi(n)$. Prove.

Sol. n has the prime factorisation
$$n = 2^{k_1} \times p_2^{k_2} \times \ldots \times p_r^{k_r}$$
$$p_i \neq 2, 2 \leq i \leq r$$
$\therefore$ $$\varphi(n) = n\left(1-\frac{1}{2}\right)\left(1-\frac{1}{p_2}\right)\ldots\left(1-\frac{1}{p_r}\right)$$
$$= \left(\frac{n}{2}\right)\left(1-\frac{1}{p_2}\right)\ldots\left(1-\frac{1}{p_r}\right)$$
Now, $$2n = 2^{k_1+1} \times p_2^{k_2} \times \ldots \times p_r^{k_r}$$
$\therefore$ $$\varphi(2n) = (2n)\left(1-\frac{1}{2}\right)\left(1-\frac{1}{p_2}\right)\ldots\left(1-\frac{1}{p_r}\right)$$
$$= n\left(1-\frac{1}{p_2}\right)\ldots\left(1-\frac{1}{p_r}\right) = 2\varphi(n)$$

32. $\varphi(3n) = 3\varphi(n)$ if and only if $3 \mid n$. Prove.

Sol. Suppose that $3 \mid n$.

Suppose n has the prime factorisation
$$n = 3^{k_1} \times p_2^{k_2} \times \ldots \times p_r^{k_r}, \ p_i \neq 3, 2 \leq i \leq r$$
$\therefore$ $$\varphi(n) = n\left(1-\frac{1}{3}\right)\left(1-\frac{1}{p_2}\right)\ldots\left(1-\frac{1}{p_r}\right)$$
$$= \left(\frac{2n}{3}\right)\left(1-\frac{1}{p_2}\right)\ldots\left(1-\frac{1}{p_r}\right)$$
$$3n = 3^{k_1+1} \times p_2^{k_2} \times \ldots \times p_r^{k_r}$$
$\therefore$ $$\varphi(3n) = (3n)\left(1-\frac{1}{3}\right)\left(1-\frac{1}{p_2}\right)\ldots\left(1-\frac{1}{p_r}\right)$$
$$= 3\left(\frac{2n}{3}\right)\left(1-\frac{1}{p_2}\right)\ldots\left(1-\frac{1}{p_r}\right) = 3\varphi(n)$$

Now, suppose that $\varphi(3n) = 3\varphi(n)$

Let's assume to the contrary that $3 \nmid n$.

n has a prime factorisation $n = p_1^{k_1} \times p_2^{k_2} \times \ldots \times p_r^{k_r}$ where $p_i \neq 3, 1 \leq i \leq r$.

$$\therefore \quad \varphi(n) = n\left(1-\frac{1}{p_1}\right)\left(1-\frac{1}{p_2}\right)\ldots\left(1-\frac{1}{p_r}\right)$$

$3n$ has the prime factorization $3n = 3 \times p_1^{k_1} \times p_2^{k_2} \times \ldots \times p_r^{k_r}$.

$$\therefore \quad \varphi(3n) = (3n)\left(1-\frac{1}{3}\right)\left(1-\frac{1}{p_1}\right)\left(1-\frac{1}{p_2}\right)\ldots\left(1-\frac{1}{p_r}\right)$$

$$= 2n\left(1-\frac{1}{p_1}\right)\left(1-\frac{1}{p_2}\right)\ldots\left(1-\frac{1}{p_r}\right) = 2\varphi(n)$$

But $\varphi(3n) = 3\varphi(n)$

This is a contradiction.

Hence, our assumption was incorrect.

Therefore, $3 \mid n$

Thus, it is proved that $\varphi(3n) = 3\varphi(n)$ if and only if $3 \mid n$.

33. Prove that the equation $\varphi(n) = \varphi(n+2)$ is satisfied by $n = 2(2p-1)$ whenever p and $2p-1$ are both odd primes.

Sol. Suppose p and $2p-1$ are both odd primes.

$$n = 2(2p-1)$$

$$\therefore \quad \varphi(n) = n\left(1-\frac{1}{2}\right)\left(1-\frac{1}{2p-1}\right)$$

$$= \frac{n}{2}\left(\frac{2p-2}{2p-1}\right) = \frac{2(2p-1)}{2}\frac{(2p-2)}{(2p-1)} = 2p-2$$

$$n+2 = 2(2p-1)+2 = 4p$$

$$\varphi(n+2) = (n+2)\left(1-\frac{1}{2}\right)\left(1-\frac{1}{p}\right)$$

$$= (4p)\left(\frac{1}{2}\right)\left(\frac{p-1}{p}\right) = 2p-2$$

$$\therefore \quad \varphi(n) = \varphi(n+2)$$

34. There are infinitely many integers n for which $\varphi(n)$ is a perfect square. Prove.

Sol. Let $n = 2^{2r+1}, r \geq 1$

$$\therefore \quad \varphi(n) = n\left(1-\frac{1}{2}\right) = 2^{2r+1} \times \frac{1}{2}$$

$$= 2^{2r} = (2^r)^2$$

Thus, $\varphi(n)$ is a perfect square for all n of the form $2^{2r+1}, r \geq 1$.

As there are infinitely many integers of the form 2^{2r+1}, the desired result follows.

35. Find the last two digits of 3^{256}.

Sol. $\gcd(3, 100) = 1$

Hence, by Euler's theorem,

$$3^{\varphi(100)} \equiv 1 \pmod{100}$$

$$\varphi(100) = \varphi(2^2 \times 5^2)$$

$$= 100\left(1 - \frac{1}{2}\right)\left(1 - \frac{1}{5}\right) = 40$$

$\therefore$ $$3^{40} \equiv 1 \pmod{100}$$

Now, $$3^{256} = 3^{240+16} = 3^{6\times 40+16}$$

$$\equiv (3^{40})^6 \times 3^{16} \pmod{100}$$

$$\equiv 3^{16} \pmod{100}$$

$$3^2 \equiv 9 \pmod{100}$$

$$3^4 \equiv 81 \pmod{100}$$

$$3^8 \equiv 61 \pmod{100}$$

$$3^{16} \equiv 21 \pmod{100}$$

$\therefore$ $$3^{256} \equiv 21 \pmod{100}$$

Hence, last 2 digits of 3^{256} are 21.

36. For any integer $n \geq 0$, $51 \mid 10^{32n+9} - 7$. Prove.

Sol. $51 = 3 \times 17$

$$\varphi(51) = 51\left(1 - \frac{1}{3}\right)\left(1 - \frac{1}{17}\right) = 32$$

$$\gcd(10, 51) = 1$$

Hence, by Euler's theorem,

$$10^{\varphi(51)} \equiv 1 \pmod{51}$$

or, $$10^{32} \equiv 1 \pmod{51}$$

Now, $$10^{32n+9} - 7 = 10^{32n} \times 10^9 - 7 \pmod{51}$$

$$\equiv 10^9 - 7 \pmod{51}$$

$$10^2 \equiv -2 \pmod{51}$$

$$\therefore \quad 10^8 \equiv 16 \pmod{51}$$

$$\therefore \quad 10^9 \equiv 160 \pmod{51} \equiv 7 \pmod{51}$$

Now, $$10^{32n+9} - 7 \equiv 10^9 - 7 \pmod{51}$$

$$\equiv 7 - 7 \pmod{51}$$

$$\equiv 0 \pmod{51}$$

Hence, $51 \mid 10^{32n+9} - 7$

37. Find the remainder when 17^{341} is divided by 8.

Sol. $\gcd(8, 17) = 1$

Hence, by Euler's theorem,

$$17^{\varphi(8)} \equiv 1 \pmod 8$$

$$\varphi(8) = 8\left(1 - \frac{1}{2}\right) = 4$$

$$\therefore \quad 17^4 \equiv 1 \pmod 8$$

$$\therefore \quad (17^4)^{85} \equiv 1 \pmod 8$$

or, $$17^{340} \equiv 1 \pmod 8$$

or, $$17^{341} \equiv 17 \pmod 8$$

or, $$17^{341} \equiv 1 \pmod 8$$

Hence, the remainder is 1 when 17^{341} is divided by 8.

38. What is the remainder when $6^{83} + 8^{83}$ is divided by 49?

Sol. $\gcd(6, 49) = 1$

$\gcd(8, 49) = 1$

Hence, by Euler's theorem,

$$6^{\varphi(49)} \equiv 1 \pmod{49}$$

$$8^{\varphi(49)} \equiv 1 \pmod{49}$$

$$\varphi(49) = 49\left(1 - \frac{1}{7}\right) = 42$$

$$\therefore \quad 6^{42} \equiv 1 \pmod{49}$$

and $$8^{42} \equiv 1 \pmod{49}$$

$$\therefore \quad 6^{84} \equiv 1 \pmod{49}$$

Let $$6^{83} \equiv x \pmod{49}$$

Then, $$6^{84} \equiv 6x \pmod{49} \equiv 1 \pmod{49}$$

$\therefore \quad x \equiv -8$

$\therefore \quad 6^{83} \equiv -8 \pmod{49}$

Similarly, let $\quad 8^{83} \equiv x \pmod{49}$

Then, $\quad 8^{84} \equiv 8x \pmod{49} \equiv 1 \pmod{49}$

$\therefore \quad x = -6$

$\therefore \quad 6^{83} + 8^{83} \equiv -14 \pmod{49}$

$$= 35 \pmod{49}$$

Hence, the remainder is 35 when $6^{83} + 8^{83}$ is divided by 49.

39. What is the remainder when 2^{2017} is divided by 31?

Sol. By Fermat's theorem,

$$2^{30} \equiv 1 \pmod{31}$$

$\therefore \quad (2^{30})^{67} \equiv 1 \pmod{31}$

or, $\quad 2^{2010} \equiv 1 \pmod{31}$

$\therefore \quad 2^{2017} \equiv 2^7 \pmod{31}$

$$\equiv 128 \pmod{31} \equiv 4 \pmod{31}$$

Hence, the remainder is 4 when 2^{2017} is divided by 31.

40. Find the last three digits of 7^{9999}.

Sol. For finding the last 3 digits of 7^{9999}, we need to obtain $7^{9999} \pmod{1000}$.

$$\gcd(7, 1000) = 1$$

Hence, by Euler's theorem,

$$7^{\varphi(1000)} \equiv 1 \pmod{1000}$$

$$1000 = 2^3 \times 5^3$$

$\therefore \quad \varphi(1000) = 1000\left(1 - \frac{1}{2}\right)\left(1 - \frac{1}{5}\right) = 400$

$\therefore \quad 7^{400} \equiv 1 \pmod{1000}$

$\therefore \quad (7^{400})^{25} \equiv 1 \pmod{1000}$

$\therefore \quad 7^{10000} \equiv 1 \pmod{1000}$

Let $\quad 7^{9999} \equiv x \pmod{1000}$

Then, $\quad 7x \equiv 7^{10000} \pmod{1000}$

$$\equiv 1 \pmod{1000}$$

This is equivalent to solving the Diophantine equation

$$7x - 1000y = 1$$

We can use Euclidean Algorithm to solve it.

Here, we see that

$$1001 = 7 \times 11 \times 13$$

or, $1001 \equiv 1 \pmod{1000}$

or, $143 \times 7 \equiv \pmod{1000}$

$\therefore$ $x = 143$

Thus, $7^{9999} \equiv 143 \pmod{1000}$

Hence, 143 are the last three digits of 7^{9999}.

41. Find the sum of all integers less than N and relatively prime to it in terms of N and $\varphi(N)$.

Sol. Let n be an integer less than N and relatively prime to it.

Then, obviously, $N - n$ is also an integer less than N and relatively prime to it.

Let $1, n_1, n_2, n_3, \ldots$ be the sequence consisting of all integers less than N and relatively prime to it.

Then, sum of all such integers

$$= 1 + n_1 + n_2 + n_3 + \ldots + (N - n_1) + (N - n_2) + (N - n_3) + \ldots + (N - 1)$$

$$= [1 + (N-1)] + [n_1 + (N - n_1)] + [n_2 + (N - n_2)] + [n_3 + (N - n_3)] + \ldots.$$

[The number of terms in this sum is obviously $\varphi(N)$.]

$$= N + N + \ldots \quad \left(\frac{\phi(N)}{2} \text{ times}\right)$$

$$= \frac{1}{2}\,\phi(N)\,N$$

42. Find all odd n such that $n \mid 3^n + 1$.

Sol. For $n = 1, 3^n + 1 = 4$

$$1 \mid 4$$

Thus, for $n = 1$, $n \mid 3^n + 1$

Now suppose that $n > 1$ is the least odd integer for which $n \mid 3^n + 1$.

If $3 \mid n$, $\quad 3 \mid (3^n + 1) - 3^n$

or, $\quad 3 \mid 1$ which is not possible.

Hence, $\quad 3 \nmid n$

or, $\quad \gcd(3, n) = 1$

Hence, by Euler's theorem,

$$3^{\phi(n)} \equiv 1 \pmod{n} \quad \ldots\text{(i)}$$

Also, $3^n \equiv -1 \pmod{n}$ ...(ii)

Let $d = \gcd(\phi(n), n)$

Thus, there exist integers x and y such that

$$x\phi(n) + yn = d$$

$$\therefore \quad 3^d = 3^{x\phi(n) + yn}$$

$$= (3^{\phi(n)})^x (3^n)^y$$

$$\equiv 1 \times (-1)^y \pmod{n} \quad \text{...(iii)}$$

Also, $\phi(n) = dr$ and $n = ds$ for some integers r and s.

$$\therefore \quad 3^n = 3^{ds}$$

$$\equiv (-1)^{ys} \pmod{n} \quad \text{...(iv)} \quad \text{(By (iii))}$$

If y is even, $3^n \equiv 1 \pmod{n}$ ...(v)

By (ii) and (v) we get $1 \equiv -1 \pmod{n}$

or, $2 \equiv 0 \pmod{n}$

or, $n \mid 2$

or, $n = 2$ $(\because n > 1)$

But it is given that n is an odd integer.

Hence, $n = 2$ is not possible.

If y is odd, $3^d \equiv -1 \pmod{n}$ (By (iii)

$$d = \gcd(\phi(n), n)$$

$$\phi(n) \le n - 1 \text{ for } n > 1$$

$$\therefore \quad 1 \le d < n$$

If $d = 1$, $3 \equiv -1 \pmod{n}$ or, $n \mid 4$ which is not possbile as n is odd.

Also, d cannot be even as $d \mid n$.

Hence, d is an odd integer (> 1) lesser than n and $d \mid 3^d + 1$ $(\because d \mid n)$

But we assumed that n is the least odd integer (> 1) for which $n \mid 3^n + 1$.

This is a contradiction.

Hence, there is no odd integer n (> 1) for which $n \mid 3^n + 1$.

Thus, $n = 1$ is the only odd integer for which $n \mid 3^n + 1$.

43. What is the remainder when 10! is divided by 13?

Sol. By Wilson's theorem,

$$12! \equiv -1 \pmod{13}$$

or, $12 \times 11! \equiv 12 \pmod{13}$

or, $11! \equiv 1 \pmod{13}$ $[\because \gcd(12, 13) = 1]$

or, $$11 \times 10! \equiv 1 \pmod{13}$$
or, $$66 \times 10! \equiv 6 \pmod{13}$$
or, $$1 \times 10! \equiv 6 \pmod{13}$$
or, $$10! \equiv 6 \pmod{13}$$
Hence, the remainder is 6 when 10! is divided by 13.

44. For any prime *p*, if $a^p \equiv b^p \pmod{p}$, then $a^p \equiv b^p \pmod{p^2}$. Prove.

Sol. *p* is a prime.

Hence, by Fermat's theorem,
$$a^p \equiv a \pmod{p}$$
and $$b^p \equiv b \pmod{p}$$
∴ $$a^p - b^p \equiv a - b \pmod{p}$$
It is given that $a^p - b^p \equiv 0 \pmod{p}$.

Hence, $$a - b \equiv 0 \pmod{p}$$
or, $$a \equiv b \pmod{p}$$
Now, $$a^p - b^p = (a-b)(a^{p-1} + a^{p-2}b + \ldots + ab^{p-2} + b^{p-1})$$
As $$a \equiv b \pmod{p}$$
$$a^k \equiv b^k \pmod{p}, \qquad \text{for } k \geq 1$$
Hence, each term in $(a^{p-1} + a^{p-2}b + \ldots + ab^{p-2} + b^{p-1})$ is of the from
$$a^{p-1-k}b^k \equiv a^{p-1-k}a^k \pmod{p}$$
$$\equiv a^{p-1} \pmod{p}$$
Hence, $$(a^{p-1} + a^{p-2}b + \ldots + ab^{p-2} + b^{p-1}) \equiv pa^{p-1} \pmod{p}$$
$$\equiv 0 \pmod{p}$$
Also, $a - b \equiv 0 \pmod{p}$

Thus, both factors $a - b$ and $(a^{p-1} + a^{p-2}b + \ldots + ab^{p-2} + b^{p-1})$ are divisible by *p*. Hence, their product is divisible by p^2.

Thus, $(a-b)(a^{p-1} + a^{p-2}b + \ldots + ab^{p-2} + b^{p-1}) \equiv 0 \pmod{p^2}$

or, $$a^p - b^p \equiv 0 \pmod{p^2}$$
or, $$a^p \equiv b^p \pmod{p^2}$$

45. Find the last two digits in the decimal representation of $3^{1001} + 2^{1001}$.

Sol. We have to find $3^{1001} + 2^{1001} \pmod{100}$.
$$\gcd(3, 100) = 1$$

$$\varphi(100) = 100\left(1-\frac{1}{2}\right)\left(1-\frac{1}{5}\right) \qquad [\because 100 = 2^2 \times 5^2]$$

$$= 40$$

Hence, by Euler's theorem,

$$3^{\varphi(100)} \equiv 1 \pmod{100}$$

or, $$3^{40} \equiv 1 \pmod{100}$$

or, $$3^{1000} \equiv 1 \pmod{100}$$

or, $$3^{1001} \equiv 3 \pmod{100} \qquad \text{.... (i)}$$

$$\gcd(2, 100) \neq 1$$

Hence, we cannot apply Euler's theorem.

$$2^5 \equiv 32 \pmod{25}$$

$\therefore$ $$2^{10} \equiv 1024 \pmod{25}$$

$$\equiv -1 \pmod{25}$$

or, $$2^{20} \equiv 1 \pmod{25}$$

$\therefore$ $$2^{1000} \equiv 1 \pmod{25}$$

or, $$2 \times 2^{999} \equiv 1 \pmod{25}$$

or, $$(13 \times 2) \times 2^{999} \equiv 13 \pmod{25}$$

or, $$26 \times 2^{999} \equiv 13 \pmod{25}$$

or, $$2^{999} \equiv 13 \pmod{25}$$

$\therefore$ $$2^{999} \equiv 25n + 13 \quad \text{for some integer } n$$

or, $$2^{1001} \equiv 52 \pmod{100} \qquad \text{.... (ii)}$$

By (i) and (ii),

$$3^{1001} + 2^{1001} \equiv 55 \pmod{100}$$

Hence, the last two digits of $3^{1001} + 2^{1001}$ are 55.

46. Prove that $\frac{1}{2}\sqrt{n} \leq \varphi(n) \leq n$ for all $n \geq 1$.

Sol. $\varphi(1) = 1$

$$\frac{1}{2} \leq 1 \leq 1$$

Hence, $\frac{1}{2}\sqrt{n} \leq \phi(n) \leq n \quad$ for $n = 1$

For $n > 1$, by definition

$$\varphi(n) \leq n - 1$$

Hence, $\varphi(n) \le n$ for all n.

Let $n = 2^l \times m$, where $l \ge 0$ and m is odd.

Let $m = p_1^{k_1} \, p_2^{k_2} \ldots p_r^{k_r}$ (prime factorisation of m, where p_i is odd prime)

$$\varphi(m) = m\left(1-\frac{1}{p_1}\right)\left(1-\frac{1}{p_2}\right)\ldots\left(1-\frac{1}{p_r}\right)$$

$$= p_1^{k_1}\left(1-\frac{1}{p_1}\right)p_2^{k_2}\left(1-\frac{1}{p_2}\right)\ldots p_r^{k_r}\left(1-\frac{1}{p_r}\right)$$

$$= p_1^{k_1-1}(p_1-1)\,p_2^{k_2-1}(p_2-1)\ldots p_r^{k_r-1}(p_r-1)$$

$\therefore$ $$p_i - 1 > \sqrt{p_i} \qquad (\because p_i \ge 3 \text{ for } 1 \le i \le r)$$

$\therefore$ $$p_i^{k_i-1}(p_i-1) > p_i^{k_i-1}\sqrt{p_i}$$

$$= p_i^{\left(k_i - \frac{1}{2}\right)}$$

$$k_i - \frac{1}{2} \ge \frac{k_i}{2} \text{ for } k_i \ge 1$$

Hence, $$p_i^{(k_i-1)}(p_i-1) > p_i^{k_i/2}$$

Hence, $$\varphi(m) \ge p_1^{k_1/2}\,p_2^{k_2/2}\ldots p_r^{k_r/2} = \sqrt{m} \qquad \text{.... (i)}$$

$$\varphi(2^l) = 1 \text{ if } l = 0 \text{ and } \varphi(2^l) = 2^{l-1} \text{ if } l \ge 1 \qquad \text{....(ii)}$$

Now, $$\phi(n) = \varphi(2^l \times m)$$

$$= \varphi(2^l)\,\varphi(m) \qquad (\because 2^l \text{ and } m \text{ are relatively prime})$$

$$2 \times \varphi(n) = 2\varphi(2^l)\,\varphi(m)$$

$$\ge 2^l\sqrt{m} \qquad \text{(By (i) and (ii))}$$

$$\ge \sqrt{2^l m} \qquad \left(\because 2^l \ge \sqrt{2^l}\right)$$

$$= \sqrt{n}$$

Hence, $$\varphi(n) \ge \frac{1}{2}\sqrt{n}$$

Thus, $\frac{1}{2}\sqrt{n} \le \phi(n) \le n$ for all $n \ge 1$.

47. For a given integer n, the equation $\varphi(x) = n$ has only a finite number of solutions. Prove.

Sol. Refer to the preceding problem 46.

$$\frac{1}{2}\sqrt{x} \le \varphi(x) \le x$$

or, $$\frac{1}{2}\sqrt{x} \le n$$

or, $$\sqrt{x} \le 2n$$

or, $$x \le 4n^2$$

As n is given and $x \le 4n^2$, x can take only finite number of integral values less than or equal to $4n^2$.

Thus, $\phi(x) = n$ has only a finite number of solutions.

48. Find all positive integers n for which $\varphi(n) \equiv 2 \pmod 4$.

Sol. $$\varphi(n) \equiv 2 \pmod 4$$

$\therefore$ $\varphi(n) - 2 = 4k$ for some integer k

$$\therefore \quad \varphi(n) = 4k + 2$$

$$\therefore \quad \frac{\varphi(n)}{2} = 2k + 1$$

Thus, $\frac{\varphi(n)}{2}$ is an odd integer.

If n has an odd prime divisor p, then n can be written as $n = p^t m$, where m is not divisible by p.

$$\therefore \quad \varphi(n) = \varphi(p^t)\,\varphi(m) \qquad [\because p^t \text{ and } m \text{ are relatively prime}]$$

$$= p^t\left(1 - \frac{1}{p}\right)\phi(m)$$

$$= p^{t-1}(p-1)\,\phi(m)$$

$$\therefore \quad \frac{\varphi(n)}{2} = \left(\frac{p-1}{2}\right)p^{t-1}\varphi(m)$$

$\frac{\varphi(n)}{2}$ is odd.

$\therefore$ $\frac{p-1}{2} = 2s + 1$ for some integer s.

or, $$p = 4s + 3$$

Also $\varphi(m)$ is an even integer for $m > 2$.

Hence, $m = 1$ or 2.

Thus, possible values of n are p^t and $2p^t$ where p is a prime of the from $4s + 3$.

If n has no odd prime divisor, then

$$n = 2^r$$

$$\therefore \quad \varphi(n) = 2^{r-1}$$

and $$\frac{\varphi(n)}{2} = 2^{r-2}$$

2^{r-2} is odd if and only if $r = 2$.

Hence, $$n = 4$$

Thus, the desired values of n are 4, p^t and $2p^t$ where p is a prime number of the from $4s + 3$. It can be verfied that $\phi(n) \equiv 2 \pmod 4$ for these values of n.

49. N is an even number not divisible by 10. What digit is in the ten's place of the number N^{20}?

Sol. Let $N = 2n$

N is not divisible by 10.

Hence, n is not divisible by 5.

$$\therefore \quad \gcd(n, 5) = 1$$

$$\therefore \quad \gcd(n, 25) = 1$$

$$\varphi(25) = 25\left(1 - \frac{1}{5}\right) = 20$$

Hence, by Euler's Theorem,

$$n^{\varphi(25)} \equiv 1 \pmod{25}$$

or, $$n^{20} \equiv 1 \pmod{25}$$

$\therefore \ n^{20} \equiv 25k + 1$ for some integer k

Now, $$N^{20} = 2^{20} n^{20} = 2^{20}(25k + 1)$$

$$= 2^{20} \times 25k + 2^{20}$$

$$= 2^{18}(100k) + 2^{20}$$

$$\equiv 2^{20} \pmod{100}$$

$$2^{10} = 1024$$

$$\equiv 24 \pmod{100}$$

$$\therefore \quad 2^{20} \equiv 576 \pmod{100}$$

$$\equiv 76 \pmod{100}$$

Hence, $$N^{20} \equiv 76 \pmod{100}$$

Thus, last two digits of N^{20} are 76.

Hence, 7 is the digit at ten's place of the number N^{20}.

50. Let $n = 2p$ where p is an odd prime. Prove that $a^{n-1} \equiv a \pmod{n}$ for any a.

Sol. If $p \mid a$, then $p \mid (a^{n-1} - a)$ ($\because n \geq 6$ as p is an odd prime)

Also, $a^{n-1} - a$

$= a(a^{n-2} - 1)$ which is always divisible by 2.

Hence, $2p \mid (a^{n-1} - a)$ ($\because \gcd(2, p) = 1$)

or, $n \mid a^{n-1} - a$

$\therefore$ $a^{n-1} \equiv a \pmod{n}$

Now suppose that $p \nmid a$.

Hence, by Fermat's theorem,

$$a^{p-1} \equiv 1 \pmod{p}$$

$$a^{n-2} = a^{2p-2} = (a^{p-1})^2$$

$$\equiv 1 \pmod{p}$$

$\therefore$ $a^{n-1} - a = a(a^{n-2} - 1)$ is divisible by p for all a.

$a(a^{n-2} - 1)$ is always divisible by 2.

Thus, $a^{n-1} - a = a(a^{n-2} - 1)$ is divisible by both p and 2 and hence, by $2p$.

Thus, $a^{n-1} \equiv a \pmod{n}$ for all a.

51. An absolute pseudoprime or Carmichael number is square-free. Prove.

Sol. Let n be an absolute pseudoprime.

By definition, $a^n \equiv a \pmod{n}$ for every integer a.

Suppose that $k^2 \mid n$ for some $k > 1$.

Now, let us put $a = k$

$$k^n \equiv k \pmod{n}$$

Thus, $k^2 \mid k^n - k$

Hence, $k^2 \mid k$

But this is not possible.

Hence, n must be square-free.

52. Let n be a composite square-free integer. Suppose $n = p_1 p_2 \dots p_r$, where the p_i's are distinct primes. If $p_i - 1 \mid n - 1$ for $i = 1, 2, \dots r$, then n is an absolute pseudoprime or Carmichael number. Prove.

Sol. Suppose that a is an integer satisfying $\gcd(a, n) = 1$.

Thus, $\gcd(a, p_i) = 1$ for each i

By Fermat's theorem, $p_i \mid a^{p_i - 1} - 1$

Also $p_i - 1 \mid n - 1$

Hence, $p_i \mid a^{n-1} - 1$

$p_i \mid a^{n-1} - 1$, and therefore $p_i \mid a^n - a$ for all a and $i = 1, 2, \dots, r$

As p_i's are relatively prime to each other, $n \mid a^n - a$.

If $\gcd(a, n) \neq 1$, $p_i \mid a$ for some i.

Thus, $p_i \mid (a^n - a)$

For any p_k for which $p_k \nmid a$, $\gcd(a, p_k) = 1$

Therefore, $p_k \mid a^n - a$

Hence, $n \mid a^n - a$

($\because p_i \mid a^n - a$ and $p_k \mid a^n - a$ for any i where $p_i \mid a$ and for any k where $p_k \nmid a$)

Thus, $n \mid a^n - a$ for all a

Thus, n is an absolute pseudoprime or Carmichael number.

The converse of this result is also true, *i.e.*, if n is an absolute pseudoprime and $n = p_1 p_2 \dots p_r$, where the p_i's are distinct primes, then $p_i - 1 \mid n - 1$ for $i = 1, 2, \dots, r$.

53. Let p, q be prime numbers such that $n^{3pq} - n$ is a multiple of $3pq$ for all positive integers n. Find the least possible value of $p + q$.

Sol. $3pq \mid n^{3pq} - n$ for all positive integers n.

Thus, $3pq$ is an absolute pseudoprime or Carmichael number.

So, 3, p, q must be distinct primes, and we must have,

$$2 \mid (3pq - 1)$$

$$(p - 1) \mid (3pq - 1)$$

$$(q - 1) \mid (3pq - 1)$$

From the first divisibility condition it follows that both p, q are odd primes.

Other conditions are equivalent to

$$(p-1) \mid [3\{(p-1)+1\}q - 1],\ (q-1) \mid [3p\{(q-1)+1\} - 1]$$

$$\Rightarrow \quad (p-1) \mid 3\{(p-1)q + 3q - 1\},\ (q-1) \mid 3p\{(q-1) + 3p - 1\}$$

$\Rightarrow \qquad (p-1) \mid (3q-1), (q-1) \mid (3p-1)$

So, we need to find the smallest distinct primes p, q greater than 3 satisfying both the above conditions.

Now, as p, q are neither even nor multiples of 3, only possible forms of p, q are $6k+1$ or $6k+5$.

For $k=0$, let $p=6k+5=5$, then $(q-1) \mid 14$

But there is no possible odd prime q in this case.

For $k=1$, let $p=6k+1=7$, then $(q-1) \mid 20$

Thus, $\qquad q=5$ or 11

But for $q=5$, $p-1=6$ which does not divide $((3\times 5)-1)$

Also, for $q=11$, $p-1=6$, which does not divide $((3\times 11)-1)$

For $k=1$, let $p=6k+5=11$, then $(q-1) \mid 32$

Thus, $\qquad q=5$ or 17

But for $q=5$, $p-1=10$, which does not divide $((3\times 5)-1)$

Also, for $q=17, 10 \mid ((3\times 17)-1)$

Thus, $\qquad p=11, q=17$

It follows from the preceding problem at Sr. No. 52 that $3\times 11\times 17$ is an absolute pseudoprime.

Therefore, the least value of $p+q$ is 28.

54. For each positive integer n, consider the greatest common divisor d_n of the two integers $n!+1$ and $(n+1)!$. For $n<100$, find the largest value of d_n.

Sol. By Wilson's theorem,

$n! \equiv -1 \pmod{n+1}$ if $n+1$ is a prime

Hence, $\qquad n+1 \mid n!+1$

Also, $\qquad n+1 \mid (n+1)!$

Any divisor of $(n+1)!$ is an integer $t \le n+1$.

But any integer $1<t\le n$ cannot be a divisor of $(n!+1)$ because otherwise $t \mid n!$ and $t \mid (n!+1)$. Thus, $t \mid 1$ which is not possible.

Hence, $\qquad \gcd((n!+1), (n+1)!) = n+1$

Any divisor of $(n+1)!$ is an integer $t \le n+1$.

If $n+1$ is not a prime, $\qquad (n+1) \nmid (n!+1)$

Also, any integer $1<t\le n$ cannot be a divisor of $(n!+1)$.

Hence, $\qquad \gcd((n!+1), (n+1)!) = 1$

As 97 is the highest prime less than 100, we can take $n+1=97$ and $n=96$.

Both $96!+1$ and $97!$ are divisible by 97.

Hence, the largest value of d_n for $n<100 = 97$

Exercise

1. What is remainder when 8^{92} is divided by 19?

2. Prove that 35 divides $16^{120} - 1$.

3. $a^7 \equiv a \pmod{42}$ for all a. Prove.

4. If p is an odd prime, then $1^{p-1} + 2^{p-1} + 3^{p-1} + \ldots + (p-1)^{p-1} \equiv -1 \pmod{p}$. Prove.

5. If p and q are distinct primes, prove that $p^{q-1} + q^{p-1} \equiv 1 \pmod{pq}$.

6. Verify that 2821 and 2465 are absolute pseudoprimes or Carmichael numbers.

7. For $n = 195$, prove that $a^{n-2} \equiv a \pmod{n}$ for any integer a.

8. $561 \mid 2^{561} - 2$ and $561 \mid 3^{561} - 3$. Prove.

9. $2222^{5555} + 5555^{2222} \equiv 0 \pmod{7}$. Prove.

10. Arrange the integers 2, 3, 4, ..., 14, 15 in pairs x and y that satisfy $xy \equiv 1 \pmod{17}$.

11. Prove that an integer $n > 1$ is prime if and only if $(n-2)! \equiv 1 \pmod{n}$.

12. Given a prime number p, prove that $(p-1)! \equiv p-1 \pmod{1+2+3+\ldots+(p-1)}$.

13. If p is a prime, prove that for any integer a, $p \mid a^p + (p-1)!\, a$ and $p \mid (p-1)!\, a^p + a$.

14. For any odd prime p, $1^2 \times 3^2 \times 5^2 \times \ldots \times (p-2)^2 \equiv (-1)^{(p+1)/2} \pmod{p}$. Prove.

15. If p is a prime number of the form $4k+3$, then prove that either $\left(\frac{p-1}{2}\right)! \equiv 1 \pmod{p}$ or, $\left(\frac{p-1}{2}\right)! \equiv -1 \pmod{p}$

16. How many integers from 1 to 1000, do not have a common factor (other than 1) with 1000?

17. Find $\varphi(24)$, $\varphi(72)$ and $\varphi(1008)$.

18. $\varphi(3n) = 2\varphi(n)$ if and only if $3 \nmid n$. Prove.

19. $\varphi(n) = \frac{n}{2}$ if and only if $n = 2^k$ for some $k \geq 1$. Prove.

20. If n has r distinct prime divisors, then $\varphi(n) \geq \frac{n}{2^r}$. Prove.

21. If n has r distinct odd prime divisors, then $\varphi(n)$ is divisible by 2^r. Prove.

22. If p is prime, then $\varphi(n) = 2p$ has a solution if and only if $2p+1$ is prime.

23. Prove that there is no solution for the equation $\varphi(x) = 14$. What is the next smallest even integer n such that $\varphi(x) = n$ has no solution?

24. Determine all positive integers n such that $\varphi(n) = \frac{n}{2}$.

25. Determine all positive integer n such that $\varphi(n) = \frac{n}{3}$.

26. If $n > 1$ is a composite number, then $\varphi(n) \leq n - \sqrt{n}$. Prove.

27. If n and $n+2$ are a pair of twin primes, then $\varphi(n+2) = \varphi(n) + 2$. Prove.

28. If p and $2p+1$ are both odd primes, then $n = 4p$ satisfies $\varphi(n+2) = \varphi(n) + 2$. Prove.

29. If $\varphi(n) \mid n-1$, prove that n is a square-free integer.

30. $m \mid n$. Prove that $\varphi(m) \mid \varphi(n)$.

31. There is no integer n for which $\varphi(n) = \frac{n}{4}$. Prove.

32. What is the remainder when 21^{802} is divided by 16?

33. $\gcd(a, n) = \gcd(a-1, n) = 1$. Prove that $1 + a + a^2 + \ldots + a^{\varphi(n)-1} \equiv 0 \pmod{n}$.

34. m and n are relatively prime positive integers. Prove that $m^{\varphi(mn)} + n^{\varphi(mn)} \equiv 1 \pmod{mn}$.

35. Let $f(n)$ = sum of the positive integers less than n and relatively prime to n. Prove that $f(m) = f(n)$ implies that $m = n$.

36. m and n are distinct natural numbers. Suppose that, in their decimal representations, the last three digits of 1978^m are equal, respectively to the last three digits of 1978^n. Find m, n, such that $m+n$ has the least value.

37. Find all solutions of $\varphi(x) = 24$.

38. Prove that an absolute pseudoprime or Carmichael number is necessarily odd.

Answers

1. 7

10. (2, 9), (3, 6), (4, 13), (5, 7), (8, 15), (10, 12), (11, 14)

16. 400

17. 8, 24, 288

23. 26

24. All integers n of the form 2^r, $r \geq 1$

25. All integers n of the form $2^l \times 3^m$, $l, m \geq 1$

32. 9

36. 106

37. $x = 35, 39, 45, 52, 56, 70, 72, 78, 84, 90$

09

Properties of Squares and Cubes

1. Many problems in number theory involve application of concepts relating to the properties of squares and cubes. Let's discuss these concepts.

2. **The unit digit of a perfect square :**

   0, 1, 4, 5, 6 and 9 are only possible unit digits of a perfect square.

   Let N be an integer.

   If unit digit of $N = 0$, unit digit of $N^2 = 0$.

   If unit digit of $N = 1, 9$, unit digit of $N^2 = 1$.

   If unit digit of $N = 2, 8$, unit digit of $N^2 = 4$.

   If unit digit of $N = 3, 7$, unit digit of $N^2 = 9$.

   If unit digit of $N = 4, 6$, unit digit of $N^2 = 6$.

   If unit digit of $N = 5$, unit digit of $N^2 = 5$.

3. Last two digits of a perfect square :

Last digit of a perfect square	**Corresponding last two digits**
0	00
1	01, 21, 41, 61, 81
4	04, 24, 44, 64, 84
5	25
6	16, 36, 56, 76, 96
9	09, 29, 49, 69, 89

How do you find the last two digits of a perfect square?

If the last digit of a perfect square N^2 is 1, last digit of N must be 1 or 9. Hence, possible values of last two digits of N and N^2 are as under:

Last two digits of N	**Last two digits of N^2**
01	01
11	21
21	41
31	61
41	81
51	01
61	21
71	41
81	61
91	81
09	81
19	61
29	41
39	21
49	01
59	81
69	61
79	41
89	21
99	01

Thus, if the last digit of a perfect square is 1, possible values of its last two digits are 01, 21, 41, 61 and 81.

In the similar manner you can find the last two digits in other cases.

4. It can be seen that when the last digit of a perfect square is 0, 1, 4, 5 or 9, the second last digit is always even. However, when the last digit is 6, the second last digit is always odd. (Refer to para 3 above.)

How do we get this interesting result?

Any positive integer N can be written as $N = ab$ where b is the last digit of N and a is the number formed by remaining digits of N.

For example, for $N = 342$, $a = 34$ and $b = 2$

Thus, $$N = 10a + b$$
$$N^2 = 100a^2 + 20ab + b^2$$

$100a^2 + 20ab$ has 0 as the last digit.

$100a^2 + 20ab$ has an even number as the second last digit because otherwise $100a^2 + 20ab$ won't be divisible by 4.

For $b = 0, 1, 2, 3, 5, 7, 8$ and 9, second last digit of b^2 is always even (including cases of 0 as second last digit for $b = 0, 1, 2,$ and 3).

Thus, the second last digit of $N^2 (= 100a^2 + 20ab + b^2)$ is always even in these cases.

However, for $b = 4$ and 6, second last digit of b^2 is odd.

Hence, the second last digit of N^2 is odd in these cases.

Please note that in both these cases (for $b = 4$ and 6) the last digit of N^2 is 6.

5. Suppose a natural number N has the prime factorization $N = p_1^{k_1} p_2^{k_2} \ldots p_r^{k_r}$. Then N is a perfect square if and only if each k_i $(1 \leq i \leq r)$ is even.

For example, $$36 = 2^2 \times 3^2$$

Hence, 36 $(= 6^2)$ is a perfect square.

$$1000 = 2^3 \times 5^3$$

Hence, 1000 is not a perfect square.

6. Remainders of N^2 modulo certain numbers :

(i) $N^2 \equiv 0$ or 1 (mod 3)

Proof : $N \equiv 0, 1$ or 2 (mod 3)

Hence, $$N^2 \equiv 0, 1 \text{ or } 4 \pmod 3$$

Thus, $$N^2 \equiv 0 \text{ or } 1 \pmod 3$$

(ii) $N^2 \equiv 0$ or 1 (mod 4)

Proof : $N \equiv 0, 1, 2$ or 3 (mod 4)

Hence, $$N^2 \equiv 0, 1, 4 \text{ or } 9 \pmod 4$$

Thus, $$N^2 \equiv 0 \text{ or } 1 \pmod 4$$

(iii) $N^2 \equiv 0, 1,$ or 4 (mod 8)

Proof : $N \equiv 0, 1, 2, 3, 4, 5, 6$ or 7 (mod 8)

Hence, $$N^2 \equiv 0, 1, 4, 9, 16, 25, 36 \text{ or } 49 \pmod 8$$

Thus, $$N^2 \equiv 0, 1 \text{ or } 4 \pmod 8$$

7. There is no perfect square between any two consecutive perfect squares.

Proof : Let k^2 and $(k+1)^2$ be two consecutive perfect squares.

Suppose that n is a perfect square lying between these two perfect squares.

Let $$n = m^2$$

Then, $$k^2 < m^2 < (k+1)^2$$

It implies that m is an integer lying between k and $(k+1)$.

However, the same is not possible.

Thus, there is no perfect square between any two consecutive perfect squares.

8. Every perfect square has an odd number of factors.

We know that if $a \mid b$ $(a \neq 0)$, then there exists an integer c such that $b = ac$.

For example, $3 \mid 12$

$$12 = 3 \times 4$$

Thus, divisors occur in pairs. For every divisor a of b, there exists another divisor c such that $b = ac$.

Given the fact that the divisors occur in pairs, can we conclude that any integer has an even numbers of divisors (or factors)?

Let us see few examples.

$$12 = 1 \times 12 = 2 \times 6 = 3 \times 4$$

Thus, 12 has total six factors 1, 2, 3, 4, 6 at 12.

Hence, 12 has an even number of factors.

$$28 = 1 \times 28 = 2 \times 14 = 4 \times 7$$

Thus, 28 has total 6 factors which is again an even number.

Now, what about 16?

$$16 = 1 \times 16 = 2 \times 8 = 4 \times 4$$

16 has total 5 factors 1, 2, 4, 8 and 16.

Thus, 16 has an odd number of factors.

So, what is unique about 16?

You can see that the factor 4 is repeated in this case.

$$16 = 4 \times 4$$

That is why we got an odd number of factors.

16 is a perfect square $(16 = 4^2)$.

In general, $c = ab$

Suppose $a = b$

Then $c = a^2$ *i.e.* c is a perfect square.

In case of a perfect square, a factor is repeated twice.

Therefore, a perfect square has an odd number of factors.

Thus, any integer has an even number of factors except when it is a perfect square.

Alternate proof : Suppose that N has the following prime factorization:

$$N = p_1^{k_1} p_2^{k_2} \dots p_r^{k_r}$$

Then $$N^2 = p_1^{2k_1} p_2^{2k_2} \dots p_r^{2k_r}$$

Number of factors of $N^2 = (2k_1 + 1)(2k_2 + 1)\dots(2k_r + 1)$

Each term in this product is an odd number.

Hence, the number of factors of a perfect square is odd.

9. Properties of cubes : Cubes of numbers have many interesting properties. The following two properties regarding cubes are especially very interesting.

(i) $a^3 \equiv 0, 1, 6 \pmod 7$

(ii) $a^3 = 0, 1, 8 \pmod 9$

Can you prove these results?

Solved Examples

1. M is a perfect square. Prove that $M \equiv 0, 1, 4$ or $7 \pmod 9$

Sol. $N \equiv 0, 1, 2, 3, 4, 5, 6, 7$ or $8 \pmod 9$

Hence, $N^2 \equiv 0, 1, 4, 9, 16, 25, 36, 49$ or $64 \pmod 9$

or, $N^2 \equiv 0, 1, 4, 0, 7, 7, 0, 4$ or $1 \pmod 9$

Thus, $N^2 \equiv 0, 1, 4$ or $7 \pmod 9$

2. Prove that there exists no positive integer n such that $n^2 + 4n + 6$ is a perfect square.

Sol. $$(n+2)^2 = n^2 + 4n + 4$$

$$(n+3)^2 = n^2 + 6n + 9$$

Thus, $$(n+2)^2 < n^2 + 4n + 6 < (n+3)^2$$

But there cannot be a perfect square between two consecutive perfect squares.

Hence, $n^2 + 4n + 6$ can never be a perfect square.

3. The sum of squares of three consecutive natural numbers cannot be a perfect square. Prove.

Sol. For any natural number n, $n \equiv 0, 1$ or $2 \pmod 3$

Hence, $n^2 \equiv 0, 1$ or $4 \pmod 3$

Thus, $n^2 \equiv 0, 1 \text{ or } 1 \pmod 3$

Accordingly, $(n+1)^2 \equiv 1, 1, 0 \pmod 3$

$(n+2)^2 \equiv 1, 0, 1 \pmod 3$

Thus, for any natural number n,

$$n^2 + (n+1)^2 + (n+2)^2$$
$$\equiv 2 \pmod 3$$

But we know that for any perfect square k, $k \equiv 0 \text{ or } 1 \pmod 3$

Hence, the sum of squares of three consecutive natural numbers cannot be a perfect square.

4. The sum of squares of four consecutive integers cannot be a perfect square. Prove.

Sol. For any integer n, $n \equiv 0, 1, 2 \text{ or } 3 \pmod 4$

Hence, $n^2 \equiv 0, 1, 0 \text{ or } 1 \pmod 4$

Accordingly, $(n+1)^2 \equiv 1, 0, 1 \text{ or } 0 \pmod 4$

$(n+2)^2 \equiv 0, 1, 0 \text{ or } 1 \pmod 4$

$(n+3)^2 \equiv 1, 0, 1 \text{ or } 0 \pmod 4$

Thus, for any integer n,

$$n^2 + (n+1)^2 + (n+2)^2 + (n+3)^2 \equiv 2 \pmod 4$$

But we know that for any perfect square k, $k \equiv 0 \text{ or } 1 \pmod 4$

Hence, the sum of squares of four consecutive integers cannot be a perfect square.

5. M = Sum of two squares, say $M = p^2 + q^2$

N = Sum of two squares, say $N = x^2 + y^2$

Then, MN can also be expressed as a sum of two squares. Prove.

Sol. $M = p^2 + q^2$

$N = x^2 + y^2$

Then,
$$MN = (p^2 + q^2)(x^2 + y^2)$$
$$= (px)^2 + (py)^2 + (qx)^2 + (qy)^2$$
$$= [(px)^2 + (qy)^2 + 2pxqy] + [(py)^2 + (qx)^2 - 2pyqx]$$
$$= (px + qy)^2 + (py - qx)^2$$

Thus, MN can also be expressed as a sum of two squares.

6. The product of two consecutive natural numbers cannot be a perfect square. Prove.

***Sol*.** Let $N = k(k+1)$ where k is a natural number

Then, $$N = k^2 + k < k^2 + 2k + 1 = (k+1)^2$$

Thus, $$k^2 < N < (k+1)^2$$

There cannot be a perfect square between any two consecutive perfect squares.

Hence, N cannot be a perfect square.

7. The product of three consecutive natural numbers cannot be a perfect square. Prove.

Sol. Let $N = (k-1)(k)(k+1)$ where k is a natural number and $k-1 \geq 1$

$$= k(k^2 - 1) \qquad \text{.....(i)}$$

Suppose that $d \mid k$ and $d \mid k^2 - 1$

Then, $d \mid 1$

$\therefore$ $$d = 1$$

Hence, k and $k^2 - 1$ are relatively prime.

Thus, $k(k^2 - 1)$ can be a perfect square if and only if both k and $(k^2 - 1)$ are perfect squares.

$$(k-1)^2 < k^2 - 1 < k^2$$

But there cannot be a perfect square between two consecutive perfect squares.

Thus, $(k^2 - 1)$ cannot be a perfect square.

Hence, $k(k^2 - 1)$ cannot be a perfect square.

8. The product of four consecutive natural numbers cannot be a perfect square. Prove.

Sol. Let $N = k(k+1)(k+2)(k+3)$ where k is a natural number

Now, $$\begin{aligned} N &= [k(k+3)][(k+1)(k+2)] \\ &= (k^2 + 3k)(k^2 + 3k + 2) \\ &= (k^2 + 3k + 1 - 1)(k^2 + 3k + 1 + 1) \\ &= (T-1)(T+1) \qquad \text{where } T = k^2 + 3k + 1 \\ &= T^2 - 1 \end{aligned}$$

From preceding example at Sr. No. 7, it follows that $(T^2 - 1)$ cannot be a perfect square.

Hence, the product of four consecutive natural numbers cannot be a perfect square.

9. Prove that the sum of digits of a perfect square cannot be 15.

Sol. Any natural number n can be written as

$n = a_k 10^k + a_{k-1} 10^{k-1} + ... + a_1 10 + a_0$ where $a_0, a_1, ... a_{k-1}, a_k$ are digits of n

$$10 \equiv 1 \pmod 9$$

$$\therefore \quad 10^i \equiv 1 \pmod 9$$

$$\therefore \quad a_i 10^i \equiv a_i \pmod 9$$

Hence, $\quad n \equiv a_k + a_{k-1} + ... a_1 + a_0 \pmod 9$

or, $\quad n \equiv$ Sum of digits of n (mod 9)

Let $S(n^2)$ be the sum of digits of n^2.

Then, $\quad n^2 \equiv S(n^2) \pmod 9$

If $S(n^2) = 15$ then

$$S(n^2) \equiv 6 \pmod 9 \quad ...(i)$$

For any natural number N, $N \equiv 0, 1, 2, 3, 4, 5, 6, 7$ or $8 \pmod 9$

Hence, $\quad N^2 \equiv 0, 1, 4, 9, 16, 25, 36, 49$ or $64 \pmod 9$

Thus, $\quad N^2 \equiv 0, 1, 4$ or $7 \pmod 9$

However, by (i), $\quad S(n^2) \equiv 6 \pmod 9$

This is not possible.

Hence, there can be no perfect square for which the sum of digits is 15.

10. Let $n = a^2 + b^2$ where a and b are whole numbers. Prove that the sum of digits of n cannot be 15.

Sol. Let $S(n) =$ Sum of digits of n

From preceding example at Sr. No. 9, it follows that

$$S(n) \equiv n \pmod 9$$

Hence, $\quad S(n) \equiv (a^2 + b^2) \pmod 9$

From preceding example, it also follows that

$$a^2 \equiv 0, 1, 4 \text{ or } 7 \pmod 9$$

$$b^2 \equiv 0, 1, 4 \text{ or } 7 \pmod 9$$

$$\therefore \quad a^2 + b^2 \equiv 0, 1, 2, 4, 5, 7 \text{ or } 8 \pmod 9$$

If the sum of digits of n is 15, $a^2 + b^2 \equiv 6 \pmod 9$ which is not possible.

Hence, the sum of digits of n cannot be 15.

11. For any perfect square number n, the number of its tail zeros (*i.e.* the digit 0's on its right end) must be even. Prove.

Sol. Let $n = m\underbrace{00\ldots0}_{r \text{ times}}$

Unit digit of m is not zero.

There are r tail 0's in n. m is the number formed by remaining digits.

Hence, $$n = m \times 10^r$$

Hence, m can be divisible by 5 only if its unit digit is 5. Also, in that case m is not divisible by 2.

Hence, $n = 2^r 5^r m$ where m is not divisible by 2

Thus, the exponent of 2 contained in $n = r$

We know that the exponent of any prime number contained in the prime factorization of a perfect square is even.

Hence, r must be even.

Now, suppose that m is not divisible by 5.

Hence, $n = 2^r 5^r m$ where m is not divisible by 5

Thus, the exponent of 5 contained in $n = r$

We know that the exponent of any prime number contained in the prime factorization of a perfect square is even.

Hence, r must be even.

Thus, in all cases, r must be even.

12. An odd perfect square greater than 9 must have an even tens digit (second last digit). Prove.

Sol. Suppose that n is an odd perfect square.

Let $n = 10a + b$ where b is the unit digit of n.

$$n^2 = (10a + b)^2 = 100a^2 + 20ab + b^2$$

The number $100a^2 + 20ab$ has 0 as the unit digit and an even tens digit.

($\because$ it is divisible by 4.)

As n is odd, b is odd *i.e.,* 1, 3, 5, 7, 9.

Thus, the tens digit of b^2 is even (*i.e.,* 01, 09, 25, 49, 81).

Now, tens digit of both $100a^2 + 20ab$ and b^2 are even.

Therefore, the tens digit of n^2 $(= 100a^2 + 20ab + b^2)$ must be even.

13. Prove that any positive integer $n \geq 10$ cannot be a perfect square number if it is formed by the same digits.

Sol. If the used digit is odd, then the conclusion follows from the preceding example at Sr. No. 12.

If the used digit is 2 or 8, the conclusion simply follows from the fact that 2 and 8 cannot be the unit digit of a perfect square.

If the used digit is 6, the conclusion follows from the fact that if unit digit of a perfect square is 6, then the tens digit must be odd (refer to para 4 of this chapter).

Finally, if the used digit is 4, let $n^2 = \underbrace{44....44}_{k \text{ times}}$ with $k \geq 2$

Then $\quad n = 2m \quad$ ($\because$ n has to be even.)

Thus, $\quad n^2 = 4m^2$

So, $\quad m^2 = \underbrace{11...11}_{k \text{ times}}$

But we just proved that any positive integer formed by the same odd digit cannot be a perfect square.

This is a contradiction.

Thus, the result is established for all possible cases.

14. Among the following numbers, which one can never be a perfect square?

(A) $3n^2 - 3n + 3$,

(B) $4n^2 + 4n + 4$,

(C) $5n^2 - 5n - 5$,

(D) $7n^2 - 7n + 7$,

(E) $11n^2 + 11n - 11$.

Sol. $3n^2 - 3n + 3 = 3(n^2 - n + 1)$ which is 3^2 when $n = 2$

$5n^2 - 5n - 5 = 5(n^2 - n - 1) = 5^2$ when $n = 3$

$7n^2 - 7n + 7 = 7(n^2 - n + 1) = 7^2$ when $n = 3$

$11n^2 + 11n - 11 = 11(n^2 + n - 1) = 11^2$ when $n = 3$

Therefore, (A), (C), (D) and (E) are ruled out.

$(2n + 1)^2 = 4n^2 + 4n + 1 < 4n^2 + 4n + 4 < 4n^2 + 8n + 4 = (2n + 2)^2$

There cannot be a perfect square between two consecutive perfect squares.

Hence, $4n^2 + 4n + 4$ cannot be a perfect square.

Thus, (B) is the desired answer.

15. 5-digit number $\overline{2x9y1}$ is a perfect square. x and y are digits. Find the value of $3x + 7y$.

Sol. Let $A^2 = \overline{2x9y1}$

$141^2 = 19881 < A^2$ and $175^2 = 30625 > A^2$

So, $141^2 < A^2 < 175^2$

The unit digit of A^2 is 1.

Hence, the unit digit of A is 1 or 9 only.

Therefore, it is sufficient to check $151^2, 161^2, 171^2, 149^2, 159^2, 169^2$ only.

We find that $161^2 = 25921$ satisfies all the requirements and other numbers do not satisfy all the requirements.

Thus, $x = 5,\ y = 2$

Hence, $3x + 7y = 15 + 14 = 29$

16. Find the number of the pairs (x, y) of two positive integers, such that $N = 23x + 92y$ is a perfect square number less than or equal to 2392.

Sol. $N = 23x + 92y = 23(x + 4y)$

23 is a prime number.

Hence, $x + 4y = 23m^2$ for some positive integer m

$$N = 23^2 m^2 \le 2392$$

$$\therefore \quad m^2 \le \frac{2392}{23^2} = \frac{104}{23} < 5$$

Hence, $$m^2 = 1 \text{ or } 4$$

$$\therefore \quad m = 1 \text{ or } 2$$

When $m^2 = 1$, then $x + 4y = 23$ or $x = 23 - 4y$

Since x, y are positive integers, $y = 1, 2, 3, 4, 5$ and $x = 19, 15, 11, 7, 3$ in order.

When $m^2 = 4$, then $x + 4y = 92$ or $x = 92 - 4y$

So, y can take each positive integral value from 1 through 22, and x can take the corresponding positive integral values given by $x = 92 - 4y$.

Thus, the number of desired pairs (x, y) is 27 $(= 5 + 22)$.

17. Find all the natural numbers n such that $n^2 - 19n + 91$ is a perfect square.

Sol. (i) When $n > 10$, $n - 9 > 0$ and $10 - n < 0$

$$n^2 - 19n + 91 = n^2 - 20n + 100 + (n - 9)$$
$$= (n - 10)^2 + (n - 9) > (n - 10)^2$$

and $n^2 - 19n + 91 = n^2 - 18n + 81 + (10 - n)$

$$= (n-9)^2 + (10-n) < (n-9)^2$$

$\therefore \quad (n-10)^2 < n^2 - 19n + 91 < (n-9)^2$

But there cannot be a perfect square between two consecutive perfect squares.

Hence, $n^2 - 19n + 91$ is not a perfect square.

(ii) When $n < 9$, then $n^2 - 19n + 91 = (10-n)^2 + (n-9) < (10-n)^2$

and $\qquad n^2 - 19n + 91 = (9-n)^2 + 10 - n > (9-n)^2$

$\therefore \qquad (9-n)^2 < n^2 - 19n + 91 < (10-n)^2$

Hence, $n^2 - 19n + 91$ cannot be a perfect square.

(iii) When $n = 9$, then $n^2 - 19n + 91 = 1$

When, $n = 10$, then

$$n^2 - 19n + 91 = 1$$

Thus, $n^2 - 19n + 91$ is a perfect square for $n = 9$ and 10.

Exercise

1. Suppose a natural number N has the prime factorization $N = p_1^{k_1} p_2^{k_2} \ldots p_r^{k_r}$. Prove that N is a perfect square if and only if each k_i $(1 \le i \le r)$ is even.

2. For any odd integer N, $N^2 \equiv 1 \pmod 8$. Prove.

3. For any integer N, $N^2 \equiv 0, 1, 4$ or $9 \pmod{16}$. Prove.

4. For any integer n, $n^3 \equiv 0, 1, 6 \pmod 7$. Prove.

5. For any integer n, $n^3 \equiv 0, 1, 8 \pmod 9$. Prove.

6. Prove that for any integer k, the numbers of the forms $3k+2$, $4k+2$, $4k+3$, $5k+2$, $5k+3$, $8k \pm 2$, $8k \pm 3$, $8k \pm 7$ cannot be perfect squares.

7. Sum of squares of five consecutive integers cannot be a perfect square. Prove.

8. Sum of squares of six consecutive numbers cannot be a perfect square. Prove.

9. Sum of squares of nine consecutive integers cannot be a perfect square. Prove.

10. Prove that the sum of 1 and the product of any four consecutive integers must be a perfect square.

11. Prove that 2006 cannot be expressed as the sum of ten odd perfect square numbers.

12. Determine if there is a natural number k such that the sum of the two numbers $3k^2 + 3k - 4$ and $7k^2 - 3k + 1$ is a perfect square.

13. If $(x-1)(x+3)(x-4)(x-8) + m$ is a perfect square, then m is.

(a) 32 (b) 24

(c) 98 (d) 196

14. $n + 20$ and $n - 21$ are both perfect squares. n is a natural number. Find n.

15. If the sum of 2009 consecutive positive integers is a perfect square, find the minimum value of the maximal number of the 2009 numbers.

16. Prove that for any positive integer n, $n^4 + 2n^3 + 2n^2 + 2n + 1$ is not a perfect square.

17. If a 9-digit number is formed by the nine non-zero digits, and its unit digit is 5, prove that it must not be a perfect square.

18. Prove that the equation $a^2 + b^2 - 8c = 6$ has no integer solution.

19. Show that if x and y are positive integers such that $x^2 + y^2 - x$ is divisible by $2xy$, then x is a perfect square.

20. Find the number of ordered pairs (m, n) of two integers with $1 \le m, n \le 99$, such that $(m+n)^2 + 3m + n$ is a perfect square number.

21. Given that p is a prime number, and the sum of all positive divisors of p^4 is a perfect square, find the number of such primes p.

22. Prove that the number $3^n + 2 \times 17^n$, where n is a non-negative integer, is never a perfect square.

Answers

12. No such natural number k

13. (d)

14. 421 **15.** 2029 **20.** 98

21. Only one prime $p = 3$

10

Mathematical Induction

1. Are you familiar with the following formula?

Sum of integers from 1 to n $(n \geq 1)$ *i.e.* $1+2+\ldots+n=\dfrac{n(n+1)}{2}$

You can verify this result for few values of n.

Let $s=1+2+\ldots+n$

For $n=1$, $s=1$ and $\dfrac{n(n+1)}{2}=\dfrac{1\times 2}{2}=1=s$

For, $n=2$, $s=1+2=3$ and $\dfrac{n(n+1)}{2}=\dfrac{2\times 3}{2}=3=s$

For $n=3$, $s=1+2+3=6$ and $\dfrac{n(n+1)}{2}=\dfrac{3\times 4}{2}=6=s$

For $n=4$, $s=1+2+3+4=10$ and $\dfrac{n(n+1)}{2}=\dfrac{4\times 5}{2}=10=s$

Thus, the given formula appears to be true.

But how do we prove it?

2. Let $s=\boxed{1}+\boxed{2}+\boxed{3}+\ldots+\boxed{(n-1)}+\boxed{n}$

or, $s=\boxed{n}+\boxed{(n-1)}+\boxed{(n-2)}+\ldots+\boxed{2}+\boxed{1}$

(writing the terms in increasing and decreasing order)

Please note that the sum of two terms lying in a given box '$\square$' is always $n+1$.

$\therefore\ 2s=(n+1)+(n+1)+(n+1)+\ldots+(n+1)+(n+1)$ (n times)

Hence, $2s=n(n+1)$

or, $s=\dfrac{n(n+1)}{2}$

Thus, we have established the given formula.

3. Can you think about any other way to prove the given formula?

There is a very interesting way to prove it.

Let's articulate it in terms of a statement.

Statement : $1+2+\ldots+n=\dfrac{n(n+1)}{2}$ for any positive integer $n\geq 1$

For $n=1$, the given statement is evidently true. .... (i)

Suppose that the given statement is true for any positive integer k.

i.e. $\qquad 1+2+\ldots+k=\dfrac{k(k+1)}{2}$

Now, $\qquad 1+2+\ldots+k+(k+1)$

$$=[1+2+\ldots+k]+(k+1)$$
$$=\frac{k(k+1)}{2}+(k+1)$$
$$=\frac{(k+1)}{2}[k+2]$$
$$=\frac{(k+1)(k+2)}{2}$$
$$=\frac{(k+1)\{(k+1)+1\}}{2}$$

Thus, the given statement is true for $n=k+1$ if it is true for $n=k$. ...(ii)

What are the implications of inferences (i) and (ii)?

If the given statement is true for $n=k$, it is true for $n=k+1$.

Also the given statement is true for $n=1$.

Hence, we can conclude that the given statement is also true for $n=1+1=2$. (This follows from (ii).)

But again by (ii), it is obvious that the given statement is true for $n=2+1=3$.

And again, it is obvious that the statement is true for $n=3+1=4$ and so on.

Thus, by (i) and (ii), we can conclude that the given statement *i.e.* formula $\left(1+2+\ldots+n=\dfrac{n(n+1)}{2}\right)$ is true for all positive integers $n\geq 1$.

This method of proof is called mathematical induction.

Inference (i) (that the given statement is true for a particular integer) is called the basis for the induction.

Inference (ii) (that the given statement is true for $n=k+1$ if it is true for $n=k$) is known as the induction step.

4. Let us prove one more result using the method of mathematical induction.

$$1^2 + 2^2 + 3^2 + \ldots + n^2 = \frac{n(n+1)(2n+1)}{6} \text{ for positive integer } n \geq 1.$$

Proof : For $n = 1$,

$$\text{LHS (Left Hand Side)} = 1^2 = 1$$

$$\text{RHS (Right Hand Side)} = \frac{n(n+1)(2n+1)}{6} = \frac{1 \times 2 \times 3}{6} = 1$$

Thus, the given formula is true for $n = 1$.

Suppose that the given formula is true for $n = k$.

i.e. $$1^2 + 2^2 + \ldots + k^2 = \frac{k(k+1)(2k+1)}{6}$$

Now, for $n = k + 1$

$$\begin{aligned}1^2 + 2^2 + \ldots + k^2 + (k+1)^2 &= \frac{k(k+1)(2k+1)}{6} + (k+1)^2 \\ &= (k+1)\left[\frac{2k^2 + k + 6k + 6}{6}\right] \\ &= \frac{(k+1)}{6}[2k^2 + 7k + 6] \\ &= \frac{(k+1)}{6}[2k^2 + 4k + 3k + 6] \\ &= \frac{(k+1)}{6}[2k(k+2) + 3(k+2)] \\ &= \frac{(k+1)(k+2)(2k+3)}{6} \\ &= \frac{(k+1)\{(k+1)+1\}\{2(k+1)+1\}}{6}\end{aligned}$$

Thus, the given formula is true for $n = k + 1$ if it is true for $n = k$.

Hence, by the method of mathematical induction we have proved that the given formula is true for all positive integers $n \geq 1$.

5. Mathematical induction is a standard technique to prove statements about positive integers. However, one disadvantage of this technique is that it is of no use in formulating such statements.

We have seen some beautiful patterns of numbers in chapter 2.

For identifying such patterns, we need to observe carefully. Then we can use the technique of mathematical induction to prove the statements underlying these patterns.

For example, let us examine the following pattern of numbers.

$$1=1$$
$$1+2=3$$
$$1+2+2^2=7$$
$$1+2+2^2+2^3=15$$
$$1+2+2^2+2^3+2^4=31$$
$$1+2+2^2+2^3+2^4+2^5=63$$

Can we express it in terms of some formula?

Please note that

$$1=2^1-1$$
$$3=2^2-1$$
$$7=2^3-1$$
$$15=2^4-1$$
$$31=2^5-1$$
$$63=2^6-1$$

So, in general, we can write the formula as $1+2+2^2+\ldots+2^{n-1}=2^n-1$ for $n\geq 1$.

Thus, we have arrived at the statement by observing the pattern.

Now, let us prove it using the technique of mathematical induction.

For $n=1$,

$$\text{LHS}=1$$
$$\text{RHS}=2^n-1=2^1-1=1$$

Hence, the given statement is true for $n=1$.

Suppose that the given statement is true for $n=k$.

i.e., $$1+2+2^2+..+2^{k-1}=2^k-1$$

Now, $$1+2+2^2+\ldots+2^{k-1}+2^k=(2^k-1)+2^k$$
$$=2\times 2^k-1=2^{k+1}-1$$

Thus, the given statement is true for $n=k+1$ if it is true for $n=k$.

Hence, by the method of mathematical induction, we have established the result.

You can see that the technique of mathematical induction is very useful once you are able to guess formulas or statements from the given pattern of numbers.

6. The technique of proof by mathematical induction consists of two parts. For any statement S, we need to prove that

(i) S is true for some integer $n=k$.

(ii) If S is true for $n=k$, it is true for $n=k+1$.

(i) is called the basis for the induction and (ii) is called the induction step.

Please note that for proving any statement, we need to prove both (i) and (ii).

If either of the conditions (i) or (ii) fail, then the result is not established.

7. Consider following formula $1+3+5+\ldots+(2n-1)=n^2+3$.

Suppose that the given statement is true for $n=k$.

So, $\quad 1+3+5+\ldots+(2k-1)=k^2+3$

Now, for $n=k+1$,

$$\begin{aligned}1+3+5+\ldots+(2k-1)+(2k+1)\\ &=(k^2+3)+(2k+1)\\ &=(k^2+2k+1)+3\\ &=(k+1)^2+3\end{aligned}$$

Thus, it is true for $n=k+1$.

We have established the induction step.

But what about the basis for the induction?

For $n=1$,

LHS (of formula) = 1

RHS (of formula) $=1^2+3=4$

$$1 \neq 4$$

For $n=2$,

$$\text{LHS } =1+3=4$$
$$\text{RHS } =2^2+3=7$$
$$4 \neq 7$$

For $n=3$,

$$\text{LHS } =1+3+5=9$$
$$\text{RHS } =3^2+3=12$$
$$9 \neq 12$$

We can't find any integer n for which the given statement is true.

Hence, the basis for the induction fails.

Therefore, the given statement is not true. It is a false or incorrect formula.

8. An analogy can be drawn between the technique of mathematical induction and an infinite row of bricks.

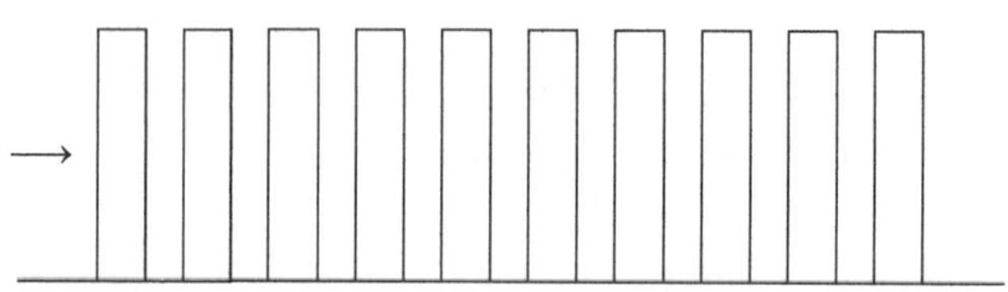

If you knock one brick on the left side to the right side, entire set of bricks gets knocked down.

However, if you do not knock the brick, the set of bricks does not get knocked down.

The failure to knock the brick is similar to the failure of the basis for the induction (see preceding para 7).

The process of knocking down does not start unless you knock one brick.

Also, if the spacing between bricks is too large, the set of bricks does not get knocked down even if you knock one brick on the left.

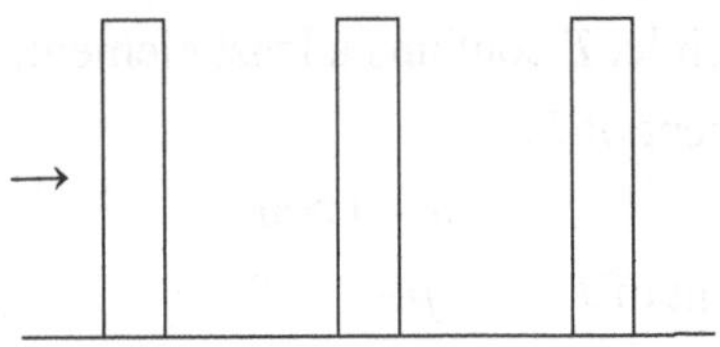

This is similar to the induction step.

Isn't this analogy interesting?

9. Well-ordering Principle : Every non-empty set S of non-negative integers contains a least element.

In other words, there is some integer a in S such that $a \leq b$ for all b's belonging to S.

10. Theorem :

Archimedean property : If a and b are any positive integers, then there exists a positive integer n such that $na \geq b$.

Proof : Suppose that the Archimedean property is not true.

Thus, $na < b$ for every positive integer n.

Now, consider the following set

$$S = \{b - na \mid n \text{ is a positive integer}\}$$

S consists of only positive integers

($\because na < b \Rightarrow b - na > 0$ for all positive integers n)

By well-ordering principle, S consists of a least element.

Let $b - ka$ be the least element of S.

Now, consider the number $b - (k+1)a$.

By very definition of S, $b - (k+1)\,a \in S$

Also, $$b - (k+1)a = b - ka - a < b - ka$$

But this is a contradiction because $b - ka$ is the least element of S.

This contradiction arose from our original assumption that the Archimedean property is not true.

Hence, by contradiction, it is established that the Archimedean property is true.

11. Using well-ordering principle, we can prove the principle of mathematical induction in a more formal way.

First principle of finite induction : Let S be a set of positive integers with the following properties:

(i) The integer m belongs to S.

(ii) Whenever the integer n is in S, the next integer $n+1$ must also be in S.

Then S is the set of all positive integers $\geq m$.

Proof : Let T be the set of all positive integers ($\geq m$) not in S.

Suppose that T is non-empty.

By well-ordering principle, T contains a least element.

Let p be the least element of T.

As $m \in S, p > m$, $\quad p-1 \geq m$

As p is the least element of T, $\quad p-1 \notin T$

Hence, $\quad p-1 \in S$

But we know that if $(p-1) \in S, (p-1)+1 \in S$ or $p \in S$.

But this is a contradiction because $p \in T$.

This contradiction arose because of our original assumption that T is a non-empty set.

Hence, by contradiction it is established that T is an empty set.

Thus, S is the set of all positive integers $\geq m$.

12. Many times we use a variant of the induction principle, known as the second principle of finite induction.

Second principle of finite induction : Let S be a set of positive integers with the following properties

(i) The integer m belongs to S.

(ii) If n is a positive integer such that $1,, 2, \ldots, n$ belong to S, then $n+1$ must also be in S.

Then S is the set of all positive integers $\geq m$.

The second principle can be formally proved in the same manner as the first principle.

13. As discussed in the preceding paras mathematical induction can be used as a method of proof. It can also be used as a method of definition.

Are you familiar with the symbol $n!$?

$n!$ is pronounced as "n factorial".

$n!$ is defined as the product of all positive integers from 1 to n.

i.e. $$n! = 1 \times 2 \times \ldots \times n$$

$\therefore$ $$1! = 1$$

$$2! = 1 \times 2 = 2$$
$$3! = 1 \times 2 \times 3 = 6$$
$$4! = 1 \times 2 \times 3 \times 4 = 24$$
$$5! = 1 \times 2 \times 3 \times 4 \times 5 = 120$$

and so on.

$n!$ can also be defined using mathematical induction as under.

(i) $1! = 1$

(ii) $n! = n \times \{(n-1)!\}$ for $n > 1$

Thus,
$$2! = 2 \times 1! = 2 \times 1$$
$$3! = 3 \times 2! = 3 \times 2 \times 1$$
$$4! = 4 \times 3! = 4 \times 3 \times 2 \times 1$$

and so on.

14. Consider following sequence of integers.

$$a_1 = 1$$
$$a_2 = 3$$
$$a_n = a_{n-1} + a_{n-2} \text{ for } n \geq 3$$

By definition,
$$a_3 = a_2 + a_1 = 3 + 1 = 4$$
$$a_4 = a_3 + a_2 = 4 + 3 = 7$$
$$a_5 = a_4 + a_3 = 7 + 4 = 11$$
$$a_6 = a_5 + a_4 = 11 + 7 = 18$$

and so on.

This sequence of integers 1, 3, 4, 7, 11, 18, ... is called Lucas sequence.

15. Let a_n be a term of Lucas sequence. Then $a_n < \left(\frac{7}{4}\right)^n$ for every positive integer n.

Proof : For $n = 1$

$$a_1 = 1 < \left(\frac{7}{4}\right)^1$$

For $n = 2$

$$a_2 = 3 < \left(\frac{7}{4}\right)^2 = \frac{49}{16}$$

Now suppose that the given inequality holds true for all integers $n =$ 1, 2, ..., k where $k \geq 2$.

$$\therefore \qquad a_{k-1} < \left(\frac{7}{4}\right)^{k-1} \text{ and } a_k < \left(\frac{7}{4}\right)^k$$

Now, by definition of Lucas sequence, $a_{k+1} = a_k + a_{k-1}$

$$< \left(\frac{7}{4}\right)^k + \left(\frac{7}{4}\right)^{k-1}$$

$$= \left(\frac{7}{4}\right)^{k-1} \times \left(\frac{7}{4}+1\right) = \left(\frac{7}{4}\right)^{k-1} \times \frac{11}{4}$$

$$< \left(\frac{7}{4}\right)^{k-1} \times \left(\frac{7}{4}\right)^2 \qquad \left[\because \frac{11}{4} < \left(\frac{7}{4}\right)^2\right]$$

$$= \left(\frac{7}{4}\right)^{k+1}$$

Thus, the given inequality is true for $n = k+1$ whenever it is true for $n = 1, 2, ..., k$. Hence, we can conclude by the second principle of finite induction that

$$a_n < \left(\frac{7}{4}\right)^n \text{ for all } n \geq 1$$

Please note that this problem cannot be solved using the first principle of finite induction.

Solved Examples

1. $1+3+5+\ldots+(2n-1) = n^2$ for all $n \geq 1$. Prove.

Sol. For $n = 1$,

LHS $= 1$,

RHS $= n^2 = 1^2 = 1$

Thus, the statement (or formula) is true for $n = 1$. ....(i)

Suppose that the given statement is true for $n = k$.

i.e. $\quad 1+3+5+\ldots+(2k-1) = k^2$

Now, for $n = k+1$,

$$1+3+5+\ldots+(2k-1)+(2(k+1)-1)$$
$$= [1+3+5+\ldots+(2k-1)] + (2k+1)$$
$$= k^2 + 2k + 1 = (k+1)^2$$

Thus, the given statement is true for $n = k+1$ whenever it is true for $n = k$. ...(ii)

As we have established (i) and (ii), it follows from the first principle of mathematical induction that the given statement is true for all positive integers.

i.e. $1+3+5+\ldots+(2n-1) = n^2$ for all $n \geq 1$.

2. $1\times2+2\times3+3\times4+\ldots+n\times(n+1)=\dfrac{n(n+1)(n+2)}{3}$ for all $n\geq1$. Prove.

Sol. For $n=1$,

$$\text{LHS}=1\times2=2$$

$$\text{RHS}=\frac{n(n+1)(n+2)}{3}=\frac{1\times2\times3}{3}=2$$

Hence, the given statement (or formula) is true for $n=1$. ...(i)

Now, suppose that the given statement is true for $n=k$.

i.e. $1\times2+2\times3+3\times4+\ldots+k\times(k+1)=\dfrac{k(k+1)(k+2)}{3}$

Now, for $n=k+1$

$$1\times2+2\times3+3\times4+\ldots+k\times(k+1)+(k+1)\times(k+2)$$

$$=[1\times2+2\times3+3\times4+\ldots+k\times(k+1)]+(k+1)\times(k+2)$$

$$=\frac{k(k+1)(k+2)}{3}+(k+1)(k+2)$$

$$=(k+1)(k+2)\left[\frac{k}{3}+1\right]$$

$$=\frac{(k+1)(k+2)(k+3)}{3}$$

This is the expression obtained when we substitute $n=k+1$ in the given formula.

Thus, the given statement is true for $n=k+1$ whenever it is true for $n=k$. ....(ii)

As we have established (i) and (ii), it follows from the first principle of mathematical induction that the given statement is true for all positive integers.

i.e. $1\times2+2\times3+3\times4+\ldots+n\times(n+1)=\dfrac{n(n+1)(n+2)}{3}$ for all $n\geq1$.

3. $1^3+2^3+3^3+\ldots+n^3=\left[\dfrac{n(n+1)}{2}\right]^2$ for all $n\geq1$.

Sol. For $n=1$,

$$\text{LHS}=1^3=1$$

$$\text{RHS}=\left[\frac{n(n+1)}{2}\right]^2=\left[\frac{1\times2}{2}\right]^2=1$$

Hence, the given statement (or formula) is true for $n=1$. ...(i)

Suppose that the given statement is true for $n=k$.

i.e. $1^3+2^3+3^3+\ldots+k^3=\left[\dfrac{k(k+1)}{2}\right]^2$

Now, for $n = k + 1$,

$$1^3 + 2^3 + 3^3 + \ldots + k^3 + (k+1)^3 = [1^3 + 2^3 + 3^3 + \ldots + k^3] + (k+1)^3$$

$$= \left[\frac{k(k+1)}{2}\right]^2 + (k+1)^3$$

$$= (k+1)^2\left[\frac{k^2}{4} + k + 1\right]$$

$$= (k+1)^2\,\frac{(k^2 + 4k + 4)}{4}$$

$$= \frac{(k+1)^2\,(k+2)^2}{4}$$

$$= \left[\frac{(k+1)(k+2)}{2}\right]^2$$

This is the expression obtained when we substitute $n = k + 1$ in the given formula.

Thus, the given statement is true for $n = k + 1$ whenever it is true for $n = k$. ...(ii)

As we have established (i) and (ii), it follows from the principle of mathematical induction that the given statement is true for all positive integers.

i.e. $\quad 1^3 + 2^3 + 3^3 + \ldots + n^3 = \left[\frac{n(n+1)}{2}\right]^2$ for all $n \geq 1$.

4. $n! > n^2$ for every integer $n \geq 4$. Prove.

Sol. For $n = 4$,

$$\text{LHS} = n! = 4 \times 3 \times 2 \times 1 = 24$$

$$\text{RHS} = n^2 = 4^2 = 16$$

$$24 > 16$$

Thus, $n! > n^2$ for $n = 4$ ...(i)

Suppose that the given inequality is true for $n = k$ $(k \geq 4)$.

i.e. $\quad k! > k^2$

Now, $\quad (k+1)! = (k!)\,(k+1)$

$$> k^2(k+1) \quad \text{...(ii)}$$

$$k^2(k+1) - (k+1)^2 = (k+1)(k^2 - k - 1)$$

$$= (k+1)\left[\left(k - \frac{1}{2}\right)^2 - \frac{5}{4}\right]$$

$$\left(k-\frac{1}{2}\right)^2 \geq \left(4-\frac{1}{2}\right)^2 = \frac{49}{4} \qquad \text{(for } k \geq 4)$$

$$\therefore \qquad \left(k-\frac{1}{2}\right)^2 - \frac{5}{4} \geq \frac{49}{4} - \frac{5}{4} > 0 \qquad \text{(for } k \geq 4)$$

Hence, $\quad k^2(k+1)-(k+1)^2 > 0$

or, $\quad k^2(k+1) > (k+1)^2$ ...(iii)

From (ii) and (iii) it follows that $(k+1)! > (k+1)^2$

Thus, the given inequality is true for $n = k+1$ whenever it is true for $n = k$. ....(iv)

As we have established (i) and (iv), it follows from the principle of mathematical induction that the given statement is true for all positive integers $n \geq 4$.

i.e. $n! > n^2$ for every integer $n \geq 4$.

5. $a^n - 1 = (a-1)(a^{n-1} + a^{n-2} + \ldots + a + 1)$ for all $n \geq 1$. Prove.

Sol. For $n = 1$,

$$\text{LHS} = a^n - 1 = a - 1$$

$$\text{RHS} = (a-1) \times 1 = a - 1$$

Thus, the statement is true for $n = 1$.

For $n = 2$,

$$\text{LHS} = a^n - 1 = a^2 - 1 = (a-1)(a+1)$$

$$\text{RHS} = (a-1)(a+1)$$

Thus, the statement is true for $n = 2$.

Therefore, the given statement is true for $n = 1$ and $n = 2$. ....(i)

Now, suppose that the given statement is true for $n = 1, 2, \ldots, k$ $(k \geq 2)$.

Now, $a^{k+1} - 1 = (a+1)(a^k - 1) - a(a^{k-1} - 1)$

$$= (a+1)(a-1)(a^{k-1} + a^{k-2} + \ldots + a + 1) - a(a^{k-1} - 1)$$

$$= (a^2 - 1)(a^{k-1} + a^{k-2} + \ldots + a + 1) - (a^k - a)$$

$$= a^2(a^{k-1} + a^k + \ldots + a + 1) - (a^{k-1} + a^{k-2} + \ldots + a + 1) - a^k + a$$

$$= (a^{k+1} + a^k + \ldots + a^2 + a) - (a^k + a^{k-1} + a^{k-2} + \ldots + a + 1)$$

$$= a(a^k + a^{k-1} + \ldots + a + 1) - (a^k + a^{k-1} + \ldots + a + 1)$$

$$= (a-1)(a^k + a^{k-1} + \ldots + 1)$$

Thus, the given statement is true for $n = k+1$ whenever it is true for $n = 1, 2, .., k$ ...(ii)

As we have established (i) and (ii), it follows from the second principle of finite induction that the given statement is true for all $n \geq 1$.

i.e. $a^n - 1 = (a-1)(a^{n-1} + a^{n-2} + \ldots + a + 1)$ for all $n \geq 1$.

6. Prove that $(3!)^n$ divides $(3n!)$ for all $n \geq 1$.

Sol. For $n = 1$,

$$(3!)^1 = 1 \times 2 \times 3 = 6$$

$$(3n)! = (3 \times 1)! = 1 \times 2 \times 3 = 6$$

Thus, $(3!)^n$ divides $(3n)!$ for $n = 1$. ...(i)

Suppose that $(3!)^n$ divides $(3n)!$ for $n = k$.

i.e. $\dfrac{(3n)!}{(3!)^k} = m$ where m is a positive integer.

Now, for $n = k + 1$

$$\frac{(3(k+1))!}{(3!)^{k+1}} = \frac{(3k+3)!}{(3!)^{k+1}}$$

$$= \frac{(3k+3)(3k+2)(3k+1)[(3k)]!}{(3!)(3!)^k}$$

$$= \left[\frac{(3k+3)(3k+2)(3k+1)}{1 \times 2 \times 3}\right]\left[\frac{(3k)!}{(3!)^k}\right]$$

$$= \frac{(3k+1)(3k+2)(k+1)m}{2} \qquad \left[\because \frac{(3k)!}{(3!)^k} = m\right]$$

As $3k + 1$ and $3k + 2$ are consecutive integers, one of them is definitely an even integer divisible by 2.

Hence, $\dfrac{(3(k+1))!}{(3!)^{k+1}} = \dfrac{(3k+1)(3k+2)(k+1)m}{2}$ is an integer.

Thus, $\dfrac{(3n)!}{(3!)^n}$ is an integer for $n = k + 1$ whenever it is an integer for $n = k$ ...(ii)

Hence, from the principle of mathematical induction, it follows from (i) and (ii) that $(3!)^n$ divides $(3n)!$ for all $n \geq 1$.

7. a is an odd integer. Prove that $a^{2^n} \equiv 1 \pmod{2^{n+2}}$ for $n \geq 1$.

Sol. For $n = 1$, we need to prove that

$$a^2 \equiv 1 \pmod 8$$

As a is an odd integer, it has one of the forms $8k + 1$, $8k + 3$, $8k + 5$ or $8k + 7$.

Hence, $\qquad a \equiv 1, 3, 5 \text{ or } 7 \pmod 8$

$\therefore \qquad a^2 \equiv 1, 9, 25 \text{ or } 49 \pmod 8$

$\therefore \qquad a^2 \equiv 1 \pmod 8$

Thus, the given statement is true for $n = 1$. ...(i)

Now, suppose that the given statement is true for $n = k$.

i.e. $a^{2^k} \equiv 1 (\text{mod}\, 2^{k+2})$ ...(ii)

Now, $a^{2^{k+1}} - 1 = (a^{2^k})^2 - 1$

$$= (a^{2^k} + 1)(a^{2^k} - 1)$$

As a is an odd integer, $2 \mid a^{2^k} + 1$

Also, $2^{k+2} \mid a^{2^k} - 1$ (by (ii))

Hence, $2 \times 2^{k+2} \mid (a^{2^k} + 1)(a^{2^k} - 1)$

or, $2^{k+3} \mid a^{2^{k+1}} - 1$

$\therefore$ $a^{2^{k+1}} \equiv 1 (\text{mod}\, 2^{(k+1)+2})$

Thus, the given statement is true for $n = k + 1$ whenever is true for $n = k$. ...(iii)

Hence, from the principle of mathematical induction, it follows from (i) and (iii) that $a^{2^n} \equiv 1 (\text{mod}\, 2^{n+2})$ for all $n \geq 1$.

8. Prove that $n^2 + n$ is even for all positive integers $n \geq 1$.

Sol. For $n = 1$,

$$n^2 + n = 1^2 + 1 = 2$$

2 is an even number.

Hence, the given statement is true for $n = 1$. ...(i)

Suppose that the given statement is true for $n = k$.

i.e. $k^2 + k$ is even.

Let $k^2 + k = 2t$ for some integer t ...(ii)

Now, for $n = k + 1$

$$(k+1)^2 + (k+1) = k^2 + 2k + 1 + k + 1$$

$$= (k^2 + k) + 2k + 2$$

$$= (k^2 + k) + 2(k + 1)$$

$$= 2t + 2(k+1) \quad \text{[by (ii)]}$$

$$= 2(t + k + 1) \text{ which is an even integer}$$

Hence, the given statement is true for $n = k + 1$ whenever is true for $n = k$. ...(iii)

Thus, from the principle of mathematical induction, it follows from (i) and (iii) that $n^2 + n$ is even for all positive integers $n \geq 1$.

Exercise

1. $1^2 + 3^2 + 5^2 + \ldots + (2n-1)^2 = \dfrac{n(2n-1)(2n+1)}{3}$ for all $n \geq 1$. Prove.

2. Prove that for any positive integer n,

$$a + ar + ar^2 + \ldots + ar^n = \frac{a(r^{n+1} - 1)}{r - 1}, \quad (r \neq 1)$$

3. The cube of any integer can be expressed as the difference of two squares. Prove.

4. $n! > n^3$ for every integer $n \geq 6$. Prove.

5. $1(1!) + 2(2!) + 3(3!) + \ldots + n(n!) = (n+1)! - 1$ for all $n \geq 1$. Prove.

6. $\dfrac{1}{1^2} + \dfrac{1}{2^2} + \dfrac{1}{3^2} + \ldots + \dfrac{1}{n^2} \leq 2 - \dfrac{1}{n}$ for all $n \geq 1$. Prove.

7. The expression $\dfrac{(2n)!}{(2^n n!)}$ is an integer for all $n \geq 1$. Prove.

8. Let $a_1 = 1, a_2 = 2, a_3 = 3$ and $a_n = a_{n-1} + a_{n-2} + a_{n-3}$ for all $n \geq 4$. Prove that $a_n < 2^n$ for all $n \geq 1$.

9. Prove that $2^{3n} - 1$ is a multiple of 7 for all $n \geq 1$.

10. $(-13)^{n+1} \equiv (-13)^n + (-13)^{n-1} \pmod{181}$ for all $n \geq 1$. Prove.

11
Pigeonhole Principle

1. Have you seen such pigeonholes?

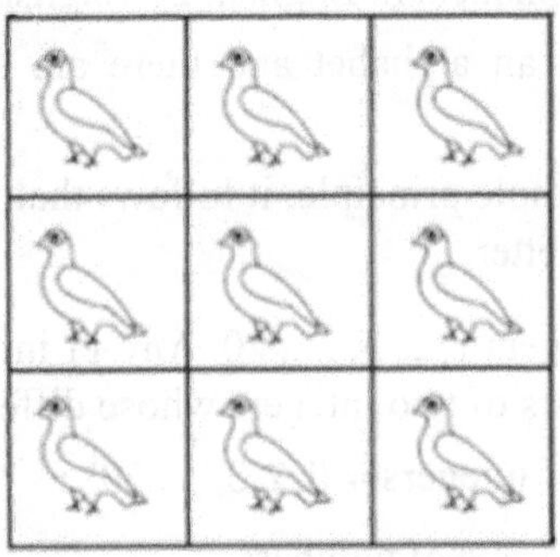

In this picture, there are 9 pigeons in 9 pigeonholes.
Now suppose that you have 10 pigeons to be kept in these 9 pigeonholes.

So, you will need to keep at least two pigeons in one pigeonhole.
Thus, if you have 10 pigeons and 9 pigeonholes, you will need to keep more than one pigeon in at least one pigeonhole.
This is called pigeonhole principle.

2. More formally, the pigeonhole principle is stated as under.

When $m+1$ pigeons enter m pigeonholes, there must be at least one hole having more than 1 pigeon. (m is a positive integer.)

Proof : This statement can be easily proved by using the method of contradiction.

Suppose that each hole consists of 1 or less pigeon.

Since there are m pigeonholes, total number of pigeons $\leq 1 \times m = m$

But it is given that there are $m+1$ pigeons.

This is a contradiction.

Hence our assumption (that each hole contains 1 or less pigeon) is incorrect.

In other words, there is at least one hole having more than 1 pigeon.

3. 27 English words are given. There must be at least two words among the given words that begin with the same letter. Prove.

Proof : There are 26 alphabets in English. 27 English words are given.

Each word starts with an alphabet and there are 26 possible values for the alphabet.

Hence, from the pigeonhole principle, it follows that there are at least two words starting with the same letter.

4. Consider the set of integers 1, 2, 3, ..., 20. Any 11 integers are selected from this set. Then this set consists of two integers whose difference is 2. Prove.

Proof : The given set of integers = $\{1, 2, 3, \ldots, 20\}$

Now consider following sets of numbers.

(1, 3), (2, 4), (5, 7), (6, 8), (9, 11), (10, 12), (13, 15), (14, 16), (17, 19), (18, 20)

We have 10 sets of numbers. Each set consists of exactly 2 numbers whose difference is 2. Each number in the set $\{1, 2, 3, ..., 20\}$ appears exactly once in one of these 10 sets.

Now we have to select 11 numbers from the given set $\{1, 2, 3, ..., 20\}$.

This selection is equivalent to selecting 11 numbers from the given 10 sets.

Therefore, it follows from the pigeonhole principle that at least two numbers are selected from the same set.

But in that case the difference of those two numbers is 2.

Thus, it is established that the selection of 11 integers consists of two integers whose difference is 2.

5. Now let us consider another form of pigeonhole principle. Suppose that there are 4 pigeonholes and 9 pigeons.

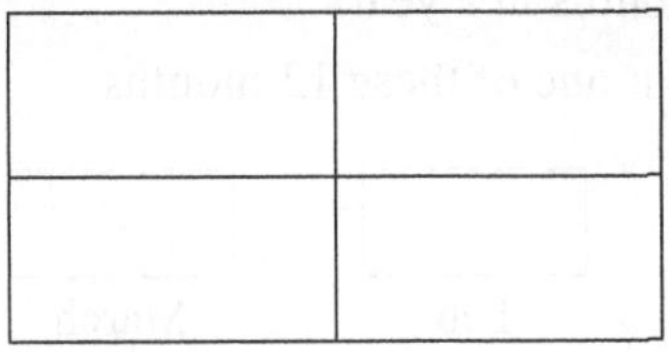

So how do you place 9 pigeons into 4 pigeonholes?

One pigeonhole must contain at least 3 pigeons to accommodate 9 pigeons.

In other words, one pigeonhole must contain at least $\left[\frac{9-1}{4}\right]+1$ pigeons.

6. More formally, we can state it as under.

When $m+1$ pigeons enter n pigeonholes, there must be one hole having at least $\left[\frac{m}{n}\right]+1$ pigeons.

Proof : Suppose that each pigeonhole consists of $\left[\frac{m}{n}\right]$ or less pigeons.

As there are n pigeonholes,

Total numbers of pigeons $\leq n\left[\frac{m}{n}\right]$,

$\therefore$ Total numbers of pigeons $\leq n\left(\frac{m}{n}\right) < m+1$ $\qquad \left(\because \left[\frac{m}{n}\right] \leq \frac{m}{n}\right)$

But total numbers of pigeons $= m+1$. This is a contradiction.

Thus, our assumption of each pigeonhole consisting of $\left[\frac{m}{n}\right]$ or less pigeons is incorrect.

Hence, there is at least one pigeonhole consisting of $\left[\frac{m}{n}\right]+1$ pigeons.

7. In a class, there are 100 students. At least how many people were born in the same month?

Proof : There are 12 months in a year.

Each student was born in one of these 12 months.

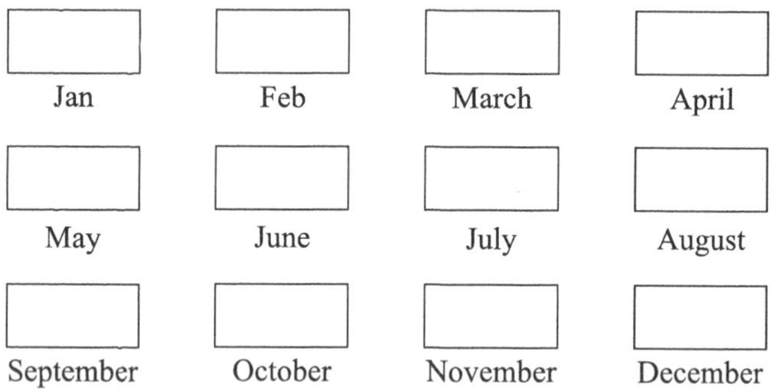

As we have to find an arrangement in which the least possible number of students have their birthdays in the same month, let's keep the months of birth distributed among 12 months to the extent possible.

So, in each month, we can keep 8 students.

$$12 \times 8 = 96$$

(Please note that we cannot keep more than 8 students in a month.)

Still 4 students are left who need to be further distributed among these 12 months.

These 4 students can be distributed among 4 different months.

So, at least 9 students $(8+1)$ were born in the same month.

We can also obtain this result by directly applying pigeonhole principle.

i.e.
$$\left[\frac{100-1}{12}\right]+1=\left[\frac{99}{12}\right]+1=8+1=9$$

Solved Examples

1. In an examination, students can get one of the four possible grades A, B, C or D. There is a group of 5 students. Prove that at least two students get the same grade.

Sol.

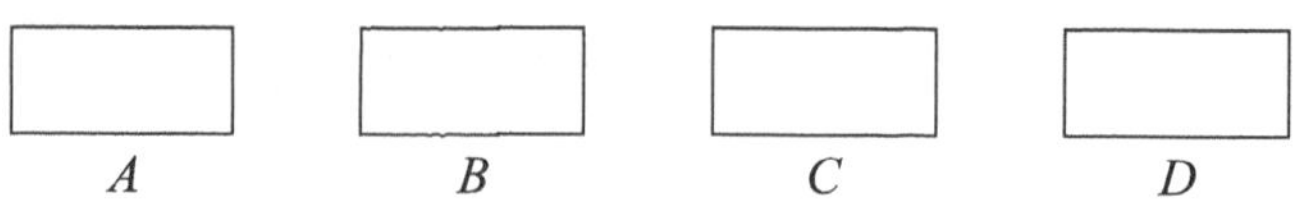

There are four possible grades A, B, C, D.

Each student gets exactly one of these grades.

Since there are 5 students, all of them cannot get different grades as there are only four possible grades.

Hence, it follows from the pigeonhole principle that at least two students must get the same grade.

2. In an examination, students are graded on a scale of 0 to 10. A student can get any of the grades 0, 1, 2, 3, 4, 5, 6, 7, 8, 9 or 10. How many students must appear in the examination to guarantee that at least two students receive the same grade?

Sol. There are 11 possible grades. Hence, if 12 students appear in the examination, at least two students will receive the same grade.

Hence, least possible number of students such that at least two students receive the same grade = 12

3. Prove that if seven distinct numbers are selected from $\{1, 2, ..., 11\}$, then we can find two numbers in the selection whose sum is 12.

Sol. Let's consider following six sets of numbers formed from the numbers $\{1, 2, ..., 11\}$.

$$\{1, 11\}, \{2, 10\}, \{3, 9\}, \{4, 8\}, \{5, 7\}, \{6, 6\}$$

If first six numbers are selected in such a way that any two of them belong to the same set from the given six sets, then obviously their sum is 12 and the claim is proved.

So, let's assume that the first six numbers are selected in such a way that no two numbers belong to the same set *i.e.* exactly one number is selected from each of the given six sets.

Therefore, seventh number is bound to be selected from one of the first five sets ($\because$ Sixth set has only one element which is already selected).

But in that case the selection of seven numbers consists of two numbers from the same set (out of the first five sets).

Therefore, the sum of these two numbers is 12.

Thus, the claim is proved.

4. There is a group of 20 people. Among them friendship is mutual. Show that there exist two people who have the same numbers of friends.

Sol. Each person can have 0 to 19 friends.

If any person has 0 friends, then nobody can have 19 friends ($\because$ friendship is mutual).

Hence, possible numbers of friends = 0, 1, 2, 3, …., 18.

If no person has 0 friends, then possible number of friends = 1, 2, 3, ..., 19.

In either case, possible number of friends = 19.

As there are 20 people, it follows from the pigeonhole principle that at least two persons have the same number of friends.

5. A bag contains 200 marbles. There are 60 red ones, 60 blue ones, 60 green ones and the remaining 20 consist of yellow and white ones. If marbles are chosen from the bag without looking, what is the smallest number of marbles one must pick in order to ensure that, among the chosen marbles, at least 20 are of the same colour?

Sol. In the worst possible case of selection, there may be 19 marbles of red colour, 19 blue, 19 green and 20 yellow and white.

So, if we choose 77 (= 19 + 19 + 19 + 20) marbles, it is still possible that we do not have 20 marbles of the same colour. But if we choose 78 marbles, 78th marble is found to be of red, blue or green colour (assuming worst possible case of selection).

Accordingly, we will have 20 marbles of the same colour (red, blue or green depending upon the colour of 78th marble).

Hence, the smallest number of marbles to be picked = 78.

6. Among any set of 21 decimal digits, there must be at least 3 digits which are same. Prove.

Sol. There are 10 decimal digits 0, 1, 2, 3, 4, 5, 6, 7, 8, 9.

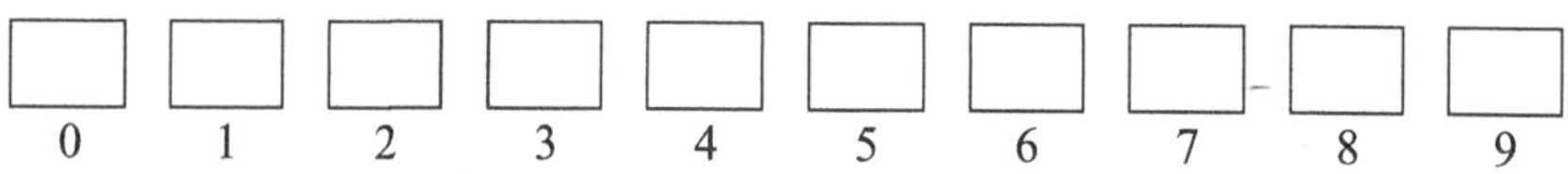

In the worst possible case (worst from the perspective of maximizing number of same digits), each of the 10 digits may get repeated twice in the set of 21 decimal digits.

However, 21st digit then has to be one of those 10 digits and accordingly, that particular digit appears thrice in the set of 21 digits.

Alternatively, by applying pigeonhole principle, at least one digit appears

$$\left[\frac{21-1}{10}\right]+1=3 \text{ times}$$

7. There are five possible grades in an examination A, B, C, D and F. What is the minimum number of students that must appear in the examination to ensure that at least six students receive the same grade?

Sol.

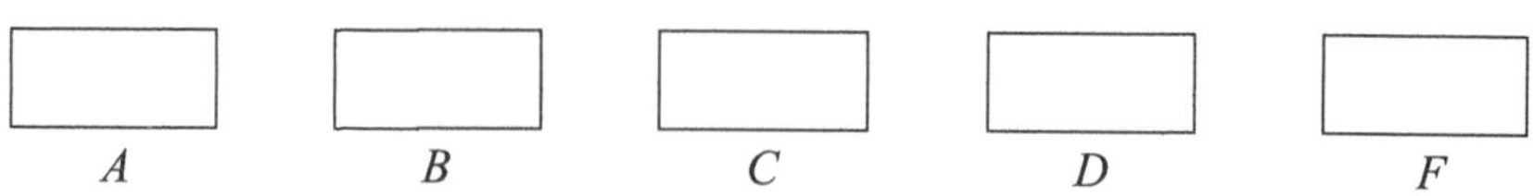

In the worst possible case (worst from the perspective of maximizing number of students with the same grade), each student gets a different grade, to the extent possible.

If 5 students appear, each one may get a different grade.

If 10 students appear, exactly 2 students may correspond to each grade.

Similarly, if 25 students appear, exactly 5 students may correspond to each grade.

However, if 26 (25 + 1) students appear, there is bound to be one grade to which at least six students correspond.

Thus if 26 students appear in the examination, it is guaranteed that at least six students will receive the same grade.

8. Any collection of 6 integers consists of two integers such that their difference is divisible by 5. Prove.

Sol. Any integer $x \equiv 0, 1, 2, 3$ or $4 \pmod 5$

Hence, any collection of 6 integers consists of two integers x and y such that they are congruent to the same integer (0, 1, 2, 3 or 4) modulo 5.

i.e.
$$x \equiv a \pmod 5$$
$$y \equiv a \pmod 5$$

where $a = 0, 1, 2, 3$ or 4

Hence, $$x - y \equiv 0 \pmod 5$$

Thus, their difference is divisible by 5.

9. If 51 numbers are arbitrarily taken out from the first 100 natural numbers {1, 2, ..., 100}, there must be two numbers drawn such that one is a multiple of the other. Prove.

Sol. Let $A = \{1, 2, 3, ..., 100\}$

A consists of 50 odd numbers 1, 3, 5, 7, ..., 97, 99.

You can see that any number in A can be written uniquely in the from $2^m q$ where $m \geq 0$ and q is one of the 50 odd numbers 1, 3, 5, 7, ..., 97, 99.

Let's partition set A into 50 sets where any set has fixed value of q.

i.e.
$$A_1 = \{2^0 \times 1, 2^1 \times 1, 2^2 \times 1, 2^3 \times 1, 2^4 \times 1, 2^5 \times 1, 2^6 \times 1\}$$
$$A_3 = \{2^0 \times 3, 2^1 \times 3, 2^2 \times 3, 2^3 \times 3, 2^4 \times 3, 2^5 \times 3\}$$
$$\vdots$$
$$A_{97} = \{2^0 \times 97\}$$
$$A_{99} = \{2^0 \times 99\}$$

As 51 numbers are arbitrarily chosen, at least two numbers (say, x and y) belong to the same set A.

Hence, $x = 2^{n_1} q$

$y = 2^{n_2} q$

for some odd number q and integers n_1 and n_2. But then $x \mid y$ or $y \mid x$ depending upon whether $n_2 \geq n_1$ or $n_1 > n_2$.

Thus, one of the two numbers is a multiple of the other.

10. For any given 50 positive integers, it is always possible to select four numbers a_1, a_2, a_3 and a_4 from them, such that $(a_2 - a_1)(a_4 - a_3)$ is divisible by 2009.

Sol. $2009 = 49 \times 41$

Any integer $a \equiv 0, 1, 2, 3, ..., 48 \pmod{49}$

Hence, in the given set of 50 positive integers, it follows from the pigeonhole principle that there are two integers a_1 and a_2 such that

$$a_1 \equiv x \pmod{49}$$

$$a_2 \equiv x \pmod{49}$$

where $x = 0, 1, 2, 3, ..., 48$

Hence, $a_2 - a_1 \equiv 0 \pmod{49}$

or $49 \mid a_2 - a_1$ ...(i)

Once we select such two numbers a_1 and a_2, now 48 numbers are left.

Proceeding in the similar manner, we can select two integers a_3 and a_4 from the remaining 48 number such that

$$41 \mid a_4 - a_3 \qquad \text{...(ii)}$$

It follows from (i) and (ii) that $(49 \times 41) \mid (a_2 - a_1)(a_4 - a_3)$

or, $2009 \mid (a_2 - a_1)(a_4 - a_3)$

11. Five points are taken at random from within a square of side 1. Prove that there must be two of them such that the distance between them is not greater than $\frac{\sqrt{2}}{2}$.

Sol.

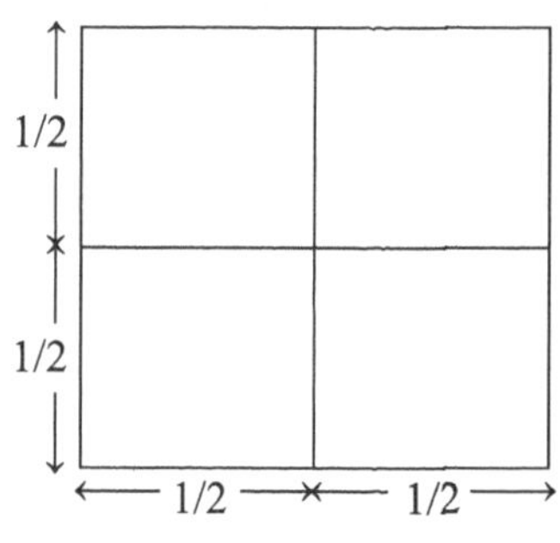

Mid-points of opposite sides are connected. We get four squares of side 1/2 each.

As five points are taken at random, it follows from the pigeonhole principle that at least two of them are in the same square of side 1/2.

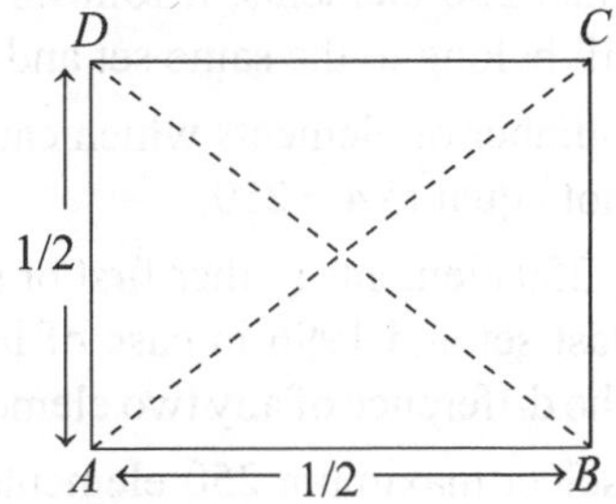

Diagonal $AC = BD$

$$= \sqrt{\left(\frac{1}{2}\right)^2 + \left(\frac{1}{2}\right)^2} = \frac{1}{\sqrt{2}} = \frac{\sqrt{2}}{2}$$

This square (of side 1/2) is circumscribed by a circle with same centre as the square and radius of $\frac{\sqrt{2}}{4}$.

Hence, the distance between any two points in this circle cannot be greater than the diameter which is $\frac{\sqrt{2}}{2}$.

12. Determine the maximum number of elements of a subset L of $\{1, 2, 3, ..., 1999\}$ such that the difference of any two distinct elements of L is not equal to 4.

Sol. Let $A = \{1, 2, 3, ..., 1999\}$

Any integer $a \equiv 0, 1, 2$ or 3 (mod 4)

Let's partition A into four subsets L_0, L_1, L_2 and L_3 in such a way that the elements in a given subset are congruent to exactly one of 0, 1, 2 or 3 modulo 4.

i.e. $L_0 = \{4, 8, 12, 16, ..., 1996\}$ (each element in $L_0 \equiv 0 \pmod 4$)

$L_1 = \{1, 5, 9, ..., 1997\}$ (each element in $L_1 \equiv 1 \pmod 4$)

$L_2 = \{2, 6, 10, ..., 1998\}$ (each element in $L_2 \equiv 2 \pmod 4$)

and $L_3 = \{3, 7, 11, ..., 1999\}$ (each element in $L_3 \equiv 3 \pmod 4$)

Please note that each of L_1, L_2 and L_3 has 500 elements whereas L_0 has 499 elements.

Also note that if the difference of two integers is 4, then the two integers must belong to exactly one of the subsets

$$L_0, L_1, L_2 \text{ or } L_3 \qquad \text{... (i)}$$

Now consider the set L_0.

$$L_0 = \{4, 8, 12, ..., 1996\}$$

Let's consider following sets of numbers formed from elements of L_0.

$(4, 8), (12, 16), (20, 24), ..., (1988, 1992), (1996)$ (total 250 sets)

Last one has only one element as L_0 has 499 elements.

If we select more than 250 elements, it follows from the pigeonhole principle that two of them will belong to the same set and their difference will be 4.

Hence, maximum number of elements which can be selected from L_0 such that their difference is not equal to $4 = 250$.

If we select exactly 250 elements (either first or second element in case of each set other than the last set and 1996 in case of last set), we can obtain a set of numbers such that the difference of any two elements is not equal to 4. ...(ii)

Similarly, we can select maximum 250 elements from each of the sets L_1, L_2 and L_3 as well such that the difference of any two (of the 250 elements) is not equal to 4. ... (iii)

Thus, we can construct subset L by selecting 250 elements from each of the subsets L_0, L_1, L_2 and L_3 as defined above. ....(iv)

From (i), (ii), (iii) and (iv), it follows that maximum numbers of elements of $L = 1000$.

Exercise

1. A function f from a set A with $k+1$ elements to a set B with k elements cannot be one-to-one. Prove.

2. Among 13 people, there are at least two persons who have their birthdays in the same month. Prove.

3. There are n married couples. How many of the $2n$ people must be selected in order to guarantee that one has selected a married couple?

4. In any group of n people there are at least two persons who have the same number of friends. Prove. (You can assume that the friendship is mutual.)

5. A basket of fruits is being arranged out of apples, bananas and oranges. What is the smallest number of fruits that must be randomly put in the basket in order to guarantee that there are at least 8 apples or at least 6 bananas or at least 9 oranges?

6. If $n+1$ numbers are selected from $\{1, 2, ..., 2n-1\}$, then some two of these numbers sum to $2n$. Prove.

7. If $n+1$ integers are selected from $\{1, 2, ..., 2n\}$, then the selection consists of two integers a and b such that $a \mid b$. Prove.

8. If $n+1$ integers are selected from the set $\{1, 2, ..., 2n\}$, then the selection consists of two integers a and b such that $\gcd(a, b) = 1$. Prove.

9. If four points are selected from the interior of a unit circle, then there are at least two points whose distance apart is less than $\sqrt{2}$. Prove.

10. In a set containing n positive integers, there must be a subset such that the sum of all numbers in it is divisible by n. Prove.

11. Among any $n+1$ integers, there must be at least two which are congruent modulo n. Prove.

12. Prove that in the 2009 numbers $1, 11, \ldots, \underbrace{111......111}_{2009 \text{ times } 1\text{'s}}$ there is at least one number that is divisible by 2009.

13. Among any seven distinct integers, there must be two such that their sum or difference is divisible by 10. Prove.

14. Let A be a set formed by choosing 20 numbers arbitrarily from the arithmetic sequence 1, 4, 7, ..., 100. Prove that there must be two numbers in A such that their sum is 104.

15. On the blackboard some student has written 17 natural numbers and their unit digits are inside the set $\{0, 1, 2, 3, 4\}$. Prove that one can always select 5 numbers from them such that their sum is divisible by 5.

16. Prove that from a set of ten distinct two-digit numbers (in the decimal system) it is possible to select two disjoint subsets whose members have the same sum.

Answers

3. $n+1$ **5.** 21

12

Binomial Theorem

1. Are you familiar with the symbol $n!$?

$n!$ is pronounced as "n factorial".

$n!$ is defined as the product of all positive integers from 1 to n.

i.e., $$n! = 1 \times 2 \times \ldots \times n$$

For example,

$$1! = 1$$

$$2! = 1 \times 2 = 2$$

$$3! = 1 \times 2 \times 3 = 6$$

$$4! = 1 \times 2 \times 3 \times 4 = 24$$

$$5! = 1 \times 2 \times 3 \times 4 \times 5 = 120$$

$0!$ is defined to be 1.

2. For any positive integer n and any integer k satisfying $0 \leq k \leq n$, binomial coefficient $\binom{n}{k}$ is defined as

$$\binom{n}{k} = \frac{n!}{k!(n-k)!}$$

$$\therefore \quad \binom{2}{1} = \frac{2!}{1!\,(2-1)!} = \frac{2}{1 \times 1} = 2$$

$$\binom{3}{2} = \frac{3!}{2!\,(3-2)!} = \frac{1 \times 2 \times 3}{1 \times 2 \times 1} = 3$$

$$\binom{6}{2} = \frac{6!}{2!\,(6-2)!} = \frac{1 \times 2 \times 3 \times 4 \times 5 \times 6}{(1 \times 2) \times (1 \times 2 \times 3 \times 4)} = 15$$

Also note that, $\binom{n}{0} = \frac{n!}{0!(n-0)!} = \frac{n!}{1 \times n!} = 1$

$$\binom{n}{n} = \frac{n!}{n!(n-n)!} = \frac{n!}{n! \times 0!} = 1$$

3. Suppose that there are 3 fruits in a basket- one apple, one orange and one banana. You are asked to choose any two fruits out of them. In how many ways can you make the choice?

You can choose in the following three ways :

(i) one apple and one orange

(ii) one apple and one banana

(iii) one orange and one banana

In terms of symbols, "the number of subsets consisting of 2 distinct elements of the given set with 3 elements" is denoted as C_2^3 or ${}^3C_2$.

Please note that C_2^3 or ${}^3C_2 = 3$.

($\because$ The number of such subsets is the same as the number of ways in which 2 fruits can be chosen out of the given 3 fruits as discussed above.)

In general, a k-combination of a set S with n elements ($k \leq n$) is a subset consisting of k distinct elements of S.

The number of such subsets with k elements is denoted as C_k^n or ${}^nC_k$.

C_k^n or ${}^nC_k$ is equal to the binomial coefficient $\binom{n}{k}$. Can you prove it?

4. We discussed following identities in Chapter 3 (refer para 12):

$$(a+b)^1 = a+b$$

$$(a+b)^2 = a^2 + 2ab + b^2$$

$$(a+b)^3 = a^3 + 3a^2b + 3ab^2 + b^3$$

$$(a+b)^4 = a^4 + 4a^3b + 6a^2b^2 + 4ab^3 + b^4$$

You can obtain these expressions by simple multiplication.

Let's arrange the coefficients of these expressions in the following way:

Coefficients in $(a+b) \rightarrow$ 1 1

Coefficients in $(a+b)^2 \rightarrow$ 1 2 1

Coefficients in $(a+b)^3 \rightarrow$ 1 3 3 1

Coefficients in $(a+b)^4 \rightarrow$ 1 4 6 4 1

Do you see any pattern here?

Please refer to the picture below to understand the pattern.

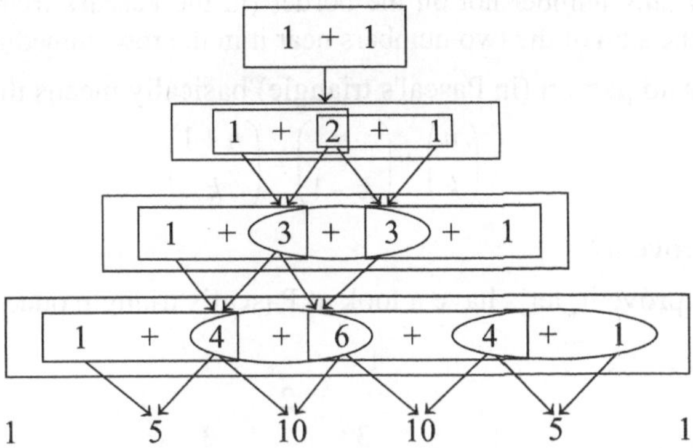

The borders in this picture are composed of 1's. Any number not on the border is the sum of the two numbers near it in the row immediately above. This configuration is known as the Pascal's triangle.

Using pascal's triangle, you can find expansion of $(a+b)^n$ without actual multiplication, for any n.

For example, let's find $(a+b)^6$.

1 1
1 2 1
1 3 3 1
1 4 6 4 1
1 5 10 10 5 1
1 6 15 20 15 6 1

$$\therefore \quad (a+b)^6 = a^6 + 6a^5b + 15a^4b^2 + 20a^3b^3 + 15a^2b^4 + 6ab^5 + b^6$$

Please note that

$$\binom{1}{0} = 1 \text{ and } \binom{1}{1} = 1 \qquad \text{[refer to the coefficients in } (a+b)]$$

$$\binom{2}{0} = 1, \binom{2}{1} = 2 \text{ and } \binom{2}{2} = 1 \quad \text{[refer to the coefficients in } (a+b)^2]$$

and so on.

You can see that the coefficients in the expansion of $(a+b)^n$ are $\binom{n}{0}, \binom{n}{1}, \binom{n}{2}, \ldots,$

$\binom{n}{n}$. How do coefficients of $(a+b)^n$ give rise to such a pattern?

5. You can see from the pattern above that the expansion of $(a+b)^n$ can be written as

$$(a+b)^n = \binom{n}{0}a^n + \binom{n}{1}a^{n-1}b + \binom{n}{2}a^{n-2}b^2 + \ldots + \binom{n}{n-1}ab^{n-1} + \binom{n}{n}b^n.$$

6. As we saw, any number not on the border (in the Pascal's triangle, refer to para 4 above), is the sum of the two numbers near it in the row immediately above.

Thus, the said pattern (in Pascal's triangle) basically means that

$$\binom{n}{k}+\binom{n}{k-1}=\binom{n+1}{k}$$

Can you prove it?

Before we prove it, let's have a look at Pascal's triangle once more.

$$\begin{array}{ccccccccccccc}
 & & & & & 1 & & 1 & & & & & \\
 & & & & 1 & & 2 & & 1 & & & & \\
 & & & 1 & & 3 & & 3 & & 1 & & & \\
 & & 1 & & 4 & & 6 & & 4 & & 1 & & \\
 & 1 & & 5 & & 10 & & 10 & & 5 & & 1 & \\
1 & & 6 & & 15 & & 20 & & 15 & & 6 & & 1
\end{array}$$

Let's recap few facts.

(i) Numbers in the nth row are $\binom{n}{0},\binom{n}{1},\binom{n}{2},\ldots,\binom{n}{n}$ in order.

For example,

In the 1st row, numbers are 1, 1.

$$\binom{1}{0}=1$$

$$\binom{1}{1}=1$$

In the 2nd row, numbers are 1, 2, 1.

$$\binom{2}{0}=1$$

$$\binom{2}{1}=2$$

$$\binom{2}{2}=1$$

In the 3rd row, numbers are 1, 3, 3, 1.

$$\binom{3}{0}=1$$

$$\binom{3}{1}=3$$

$$\binom{3}{2}=3$$

$$\binom{3}{3}=1$$

In the 4th row, numbers are 1, 4, 6, 4, 1.

$$\binom{4}{0}=1$$

$$\binom{4}{1}=4$$

$$\binom{4}{2}=6$$

$$\binom{4}{3}=4$$

$$\binom{4}{4}=1$$

and so on.

(ii) Numbers in the nth row represent coefficients in the expansion of $(a+b)^n$ in order.

For example,
$$(a+b)^1 = a+b$$
$$(a+b)^2 = a^2 + 2ab + b^2$$
$$(a+b)^3 = a^3 + 3a^2b + 3ab^2 + b^3$$
$$(a+b)^4 = a^4 + 4a^3b + 6a^2b^2 + 4ab^3 + b^4$$

and so on.

Let's prove the identity now.

$$\binom{n}{k}+\binom{n}{k-1}=\binom{n+1}{k} \qquad 1 \le k \le n$$

$$\binom{n}{k}+\binom{n}{k-1}=\frac{n!}{k!(n-k)!}+\frac{n!}{(k-1)!(n-k+1)!}$$

$$=\frac{n!}{(k-1)!(n-k)!}\left[\frac{1}{k}+\frac{1}{n-k+1}\right]$$

$$= \frac{n!}{(k-1)!\,(n-k)!}\left[\frac{n-k+1+k}{k(n-k+1)}\right]$$

$$= \frac{n!}{(k-1)!\,(n-k)!} \cdot \frac{(n+1)}{k(n-k+1)}$$

$$= \frac{[n!(n+1)]}{[(k-1)!k][(n-k)!\,(n-k+1)]}$$

$$= \frac{(n+1)!}{k!\,(n+1-k)!}$$

$$= \binom{n+1}{k}$$

7. We observed that the coefficients in the expansion of $(a+b)^n$ are $\binom{n}{0}, \binom{n}{1}, \binom{n}{2}, \ldots, \binom{n}{n}$ in order.

In general,

$$(a+b)^n = \binom{n}{0}a^n + \binom{n}{1}a^{n-1}b + \binom{n}{2}a^{n-2}b^2 + \ldots + \binom{n}{n-1}ab^{n-1} + \binom{n}{n}b^n$$

or, $$(a+b)^n = \sum_{k=0}^{n}\binom{n}{k}a^{n-k}b^k$$

This is known as the binomial theorem.

Let's prove it formally.

Proof : For $n = 1$,

$$\text{LHS} = (a+b)^1 = a+b$$

$$\text{RHS} = \sum_{k=0}^{n}\binom{n}{k}a^{n-k}b^k$$

$$= \binom{1}{0}a^1b^0 + \binom{1}{1}a^0b^1 = a+b$$

Hence, the given statement or formula is true for $n = 1$. ...(i)

Suppose that the given formula is true for some positive integer m.

i.e. $$(a+b)^m = \sum_{k=0}^{m}\binom{m}{k}a^{m-k}b^k$$

Now, $$(a+b)^{m+1} = (a+b)(a+b)^m$$

$$= a(a+b)^m + b(a+b)^m$$

$$= a\sum_{k=0}^{m}\binom{m}{k} a^{m-k}b^{k} + b\sum_{k=0}^{m}\binom{m}{k}a^{m-k}b^{k}$$

$$= \sum_{k=0}^{m}\binom{m}{k} a^{m-k+1}b^{k} + \sum_{k=0}^{m}\binom{m}{k} a^{m-k}b^{k+1}$$

$$= \left[a^{m+1} + \sum_{k=1}^{m}\binom{m}{k}a^{m-k+1}b^{k}\right] + \left[\sum_{k=0}^{m-1}\binom{m}{k} a^{m-k}b^{k+1} + b^{m+1}\right]$$

$$= \left[a^{m+1} + \sum_{k=1}^{m}\binom{m}{k}a^{m-k+1}b^{k}\right] + \left[\sum_{j=1}^{m}\binom{m}{j-1} a^{m-j+1}b^{j} + b^{m+1}\right]$$

(Substitute $j = k+1$)

$$= a^{m+1} + \sum_{k=1}^{m}\left[\binom{m}{k} + \binom{m}{k-1}\right] a^{m-k+1}b^{k} + b^{m+1}$$

$$= a^{m+1} + \sum_{k=1}^{m}\binom{m+1}{k} a^{(m+1)-k}b^{k} + b^{m+1} \qquad \left[\because \binom{n}{k} + \binom{n}{k-1} = \binom{n+1}{k}\right]$$

$$= \sum_{k=0}^{m+1}\binom{m+1}{k} a^{m+1-k}b^{k}$$

which is precisely the formula in the case of $n = m+1$. ...(ii)

Thus, by virtue of (i) and (ii), we have established the binomial theorem by induction.

Solved Examples

1. $\binom{n}{k}\binom{k}{r} = \binom{n}{r}\binom{n-r}{k-r}$ $n \geq k \geq r \geq 0$. Prove.

Sol. Left hand side of expression

$$= \binom{n}{k}\binom{k}{r}$$

$$= \frac{n!}{k!\,(n-k)!} \cdot \frac{k!}{r!\,(k-r)!}$$

$$= \frac{n!}{r!\,(k-r)!\,(n-k)!} \qquad \text{...(i)}$$

Right hand side of expression

$$= \binom{n}{r}\binom{n-r}{k-r}$$

$$= \frac{n!}{r!(n-r)!} \cdot \frac{(n-r)!}{(k-r)!(n-k)!}$$

$$= \frac{n!}{r!(k-r)!(n-k)!} \quad \ldots(ii)$$

From (i) and (ii), it follows that

$$\binom{n}{k}\binom{k}{r} = \binom{n}{r}\binom{n-r}{k-r}$$

2. $\binom{n}{0} + \binom{n}{1} + \binom{n}{2} + \ldots + \binom{n}{n} = 2^n$ for $n \geq 1$. Prove.

Sol. $(a+b)^n = \sum_{k=0}^{n} \binom{n}{k} a^{n-k} b^k$

Let's substitute $a = b = 1$ in this formula.

Now, we get
$$2^n = \sum_{k=0}^{n} \binom{n}{k} \times 1 \times 1$$
$$= \binom{n}{0} + \binom{n}{1} + \binom{n}{2} + \ldots + \binom{n}{n}$$

3. $\binom{n}{0} - \binom{n}{1} + \binom{n}{2} + \ldots + (-1)^n \binom{n}{n} = 0$ for $n \geq 1$. Prove.

Sol. $(a+b)^n = \sum_{k=0}^{n} \binom{n}{k} a^{n-k} b^k$

Let's substitute $a = 1$, $b = -1$ in this formula.

Now, we get
$$0 = \sum_{k=0}^{n} \binom{n}{k} \times 1 \times (-1)^k$$
$$= \binom{n}{0} - \binom{n}{1} + \binom{n}{2} - \ldots + (-1)^n \binom{n}{n}$$

4. $\binom{n}{1} + 2\binom{n}{2} + 3\binom{n}{3} + \ldots + n\binom{n}{n} = n2^{n-1}$ for $n \geq 1$. Prove.

Sol. $n(a+b)^{n-1}$

$$= n\sum_{k=0}^{n-1} a^{n-1-k} b^k \binom{n-1}{k}$$

$$= \sum_{k=0}^{n-1} n \binom{n-1}{k} a^{n-1-k} b^k \quad \text{...(i)}$$

Now, $$n\binom{n-1}{k} = n \frac{(n-1)!}{k!(n-1-k)!}$$

$$= \frac{n!}{k!(n-k-1)!}$$

$$= (k+1) \frac{n!}{(k+1)!(n-k-1)!}$$

$$= (k+1)\binom{n}{k+1} \quad \text{...(ii)}$$

By (i) and (ii), we get

$$n(a+b)^{n-1} = \sum_{k=0}^{n-1} (k+1)\binom{n}{k+1} a^{n-1-k} b^k$$

On substituting $a = b = 1$, we get

$$n2^{n-1} = \sum_{k=0}^{n-1} (k+1)\binom{n}{k+1} \times 1 \times 1$$

$$= \binom{n}{1} + 2\binom{n}{2} + 3\binom{n}{3} + \ldots + n\binom{n}{n}$$

5. Prove that $\binom{n}{r} = \binom{n}{r+1}$ if and only if n is an odd integer and $r = \frac{1}{2}(n-1) \cdot\ (n \geq 1)$

Sol. Suppose that

$$\binom{n}{r} = \binom{n}{r+1}$$

or, $$\frac{n!}{r!(n-r)!} = \frac{n!}{(r+1)!(n-r-1)!}$$

or, $$\frac{1}{n-r} = \frac{1}{r+1}$$

or, $$r+1 = n-r$$

or, $$2r = n-1$$

It has a solution if and only if $n-1$ is even, *i.e.*, n is an odd integer.

Also, $$r = \frac{1}{2}(n-1)$$

6. For $n \geq 1$, prove that $1^2 + 3^2 + 5^2 + \ldots + (2n-1)^2 = \binom{2n+1}{3}$

Sol. Let's prove it by induction on n.

For $n = 1$, Left hand side of the formula $= 1^2 = 1$

Right hand side of the formula $= \binom{3}{3} = 1$

Hence, the formula is true for $n = 1$. ...(i)

Let's assume that the formula is true for $n = k$.

i.e. $$1^2 + 3^2 + 5^2 + \ldots + (2k-1)^2 = \binom{2k+1}{3}$$

Now, for $n = k+1$

$$1^2 + 3^2 + \ldots + (2k-1)^2 + (2k+1)^2 = \binom{2k+1}{3} + (2k+1)^2$$

$$= \frac{(2k+1)!}{3!(2k-2)!} + (2k+1)^2$$

$$= (2k+1)\left[\frac{2k!}{3!(2k-2)!} + (2k+1)\right]$$

$$= (2k+1)\left[\frac{(2k-1)2k}{3!} + (2k+1)\right]$$

$$= (2k+1)\left[\frac{(2k-1)k}{3} + 2k+1\right]$$

$$= \frac{(2k+1)[2k^2 - k + 6k + 3]}{3}$$

$$= \frac{(2k+1)[2k^2 + 5k + 3]}{3} \quad \text{....(ii)}$$

$$\binom{2k+3}{3} = \frac{(2k+3)!}{3!(2k)!} = \frac{(2k+1)(2k+2)(2k+3)}{1 \times 2 \times 3}$$

$$= \frac{(2k+1)}{3}[(k+1)(2k+3)]$$

$$= \frac{(2k+1)}{3}(2k^2 + 5k + 3) \quad \text{...(iii)}$$

From (ii) and (iii), it follows that the formula is true for $n = k+1$ ....(iv)

By virtue of (i) and (iv), we have proved the given formula by induction.

7. Find the constant term in the expansion of $\left(x^2+\frac{1}{x^2}\right)^6$.

Sol. The general term in the expansion of $\left(x^2+\frac{1}{x^2}\right)^6$ is

$$\binom{6}{r}(x^2)^{6-r}\left(\frac{1}{x^2}\right)^r=\binom{6}{r}x^{12-2r}\left(\frac{1}{x^{2r}}\right)$$

$$=\binom{6}{r}x^{12-4r}$$

This term will be a constant when $12-4r=0$, *i.e.*, when $r=3$.

Hence, the constant term in the expansion of $\left(x^2+\frac{1}{x^2}\right)^6$ is $\binom{6}{3}=20$.

8. Find the coefficient of x^5 in the expansion of $(1-2x+3x^2)^5$.

Sol. $(1-2x+3x^2)^5=[(1-2x)+3x^2]^5$

$$=(1-2x)^5+5(1-2x)^4(3x^2)+10(1-2x)^3(3x^2)^2+\ldots$$

Please note that all terms subsequent to the third term consist of power of x higher than 5.

- The coefficient of x^5 in $(1-2x)^5$ is $(-2)^5=-32$.
- The coefficient of x^5 in $5(1-2x)^4(3x^2)$ is $15\binom{4}{3}(-2)^3=-480$.
- The coefficient of x^5 in $10(1-2x)^3(3x^2)^2$ is $90\binom{3}{1}(-2)=-540$.
- The remaining terms do not contain x^5.

Therefore, the required coefficient is $-32-480-540=-1052$.

9. Find the greatest coefficient in the expansion of $(1+3x)^{21}$.

Sol. The general term of this expansion is $\binom{21}{k}(3x)^k$.

The coefficient of this term is $\binom{21}{k}3^k$.

The next coefficient is $\binom{21}{k+1}3^{k+1}$.

The ratio of the two coefficients is

$$\frac{\binom{21}{k+1}3^{k+1}}{\binom{21}{k}3^{k}} = \frac{21!}{(20-k)!\,(k+1)!} \times \frac{(21-k)!\,k!}{21!} \times 3$$

$$= \frac{63-3k}{k+1}$$

$$\frac{63-3k}{k+1} > 1 \Rightarrow k < 15\frac{1}{2}$$

Thus, the coefficients are increasing for $k = 0, 1, 2, ..., 14, 15$ and decreasing for $k = 16, ..., 21$.

Therefore, the coefficient is greatest when $k = 16$.

Hence, the greatest coefficient

$$= \binom{21}{16}3^{16}$$

10. Find the remainder when 7^{103} is divided by 25.

Sol. $7^{103} = (7^2)^{51} \times 7 = 49^{51} \times 7 = (50-1)^{51} \times 7$

$$= \left[\binom{51}{0}(50)^{51} + \binom{51}{1}(50)^{50}(-1)^1 \ldots + \binom{51}{50}(50)^1(-1)^{50} + \binom{51}{51}(-1)^{51}\right] \times 7$$

Please note that all terms other than the last term is divisible by 25.

Hence, the remainder on division by 25 is -1×7 *i.e.* 18.

11. Find the last three digits of 17^{256}.

Sol. $17^{256} = (17^2)^{128} = (289)^{128} = (290-1)^{128}$

$$= \binom{128}{0}(290)^{128} + \binom{128}{1}(290)^{127}(-1)^1 + \ldots + \binom{128}{125}(290)^3(-1)^{125}$$

$$+ \binom{128}{126}(290)^2(-1)^{126} + \binom{128}{127}(290)^1(-1)^{127} + \binom{128}{128}(-1)^{128}$$

Please note that all terms except last three terms are divisible by 1000.

The last three terms add up to $\frac{128 \times 127}{2} \times (290)^2 - 128 \times 290 + 1.$

Hence, the remainder on division by 1000

$$= 800 - 120 + 1$$

$$= 681$$

12. Find the number of irrational terms in $(\sqrt[8]{5}+\sqrt[6]{2})^{100}$.

Sol. The general term in the expansion is $\binom{100}{r}(5)^{\frac{100-r}{8}}(2)^{\frac{r}{6}}$.

This term becomes rational when $\frac{100-r}{8}$ and $\frac{r}{6}$ both are integers.

For both to be integers, r should be a multiple of 6 and $100-r$ should be a multiple of 8.

It is easy to verify that both conditions are satisfied for following values of r.

$r=12, 36, 60, 84$

Therefore, the number of rational terms equals 4.

Please note that the total number of terms in the expansion is 101.

Thus, the number of irrational terms $=101-4=97$

Exercise

1. $\binom{n}{k}=\left[\frac{n-k+1}{k}\right]\binom{n}{k-1}$ $n\geq k\geq 1$. Prove.

2. $\binom{n}{0}+2\binom{n}{1}+2^2\binom{n}{2}+\ldots+2^n\binom{n}{n}=3^n$ for $n\geq 1$. Prove.

3. $\binom{n}{0}+\binom{n}{2}+\binom{n}{4}+\ldots=\binom{n}{1}+\binom{n}{3}+\binom{n}{5}+\ldots=2^{n-1}$ for $n\geq 1$. Prove.

4. $\binom{2}{2}+\binom{3}{2}+\binom{4}{2}+\ldots+\binom{n}{2}=\binom{n+1}{3}$ for $n\geq 2$. Prove.

5. $\binom{2}{2}+\binom{4}{2}+\binom{6}{2}+\ldots+\binom{2n}{2}=\frac{n(n+1)(4n-1)}{6}$ for $n\geq 1$. Prove.

6. $\binom{2n}{n}=\frac{1\times 3\times 5\times\ldots\times(2n-1)}{2\times 4\times 6\times\ldots\times 2n}2^{2n}$ for $n\geq 1$. Prove.

7. Find the number of rational terms in the expansion of $(\sqrt{2}+\sqrt[3]{3})^{15}$.

8. Find the number of terms in the expansion of $(2x+3y)^4\times(3x-2y)^4$.

9. Find the last 3 digit of 3^{2024}.

10. Which one is bigger: $(1.0001)^{10000}$ or 2?

Answers

7. 3

8. 9

9. 481

10. $(1.0001)^{10000}$

13 Greatest Integer Function

1. Consider following numbers.

3.2, – 0.8, 1.7, $\sqrt{2}$, π, 6, – 8

Each of these numbers is either an integer or lies between two consecutive integers.

$$3 < 3.2 < 4$$
$$-1 < -0.8 < 0$$
$$1 < 1.7 < 2$$
$$1 < \sqrt{2} < 2$$
$$3 < \pi < 4$$
$$6$$
$$-8$$

Thus, 3 is the greatest integer less than or equal to 3.2.
– 1 is the greatest integer less than or equal to – 0.8.
1 is the greatest integers less than or equal to 1.7 and so on.
Such integers are of special significance and they are denoted by $[x]$.

For example,
$$[3.2] = 3$$
$$[-0.8] = -1$$
$$[1.7] = 1$$
$$[\sqrt{2}] = 1$$
$$[\pi] = 3$$
$$[6] = 6$$
$$[-8] = -8$$

$[x]$ is called the greatest integer function.

2. For a real number x, $[x]$ denotes the largest integer less than or equal to x.

$[x]$ is the unique integer that satisfies following condition.

$$x-1<[x]\leq x$$

For example, 3 is the largest integer less than or equal to 3.2.

Hence, $[3.2]=3$

Please also note that $2.2 < 3 < 3.2$.

Similarly, -1 is the largest integer less than or equal to -0.8.

Hence, $[-0.8]=-1$

Please also note that $-1.8 < -1 < -0.8$.

3. Every real number can be written in the form $x=[x]+\{x\}$ where $[x]$ is the greatest integer function and $0\leq \{x\} < 1$. $\{x\}$ is called fractional part of x.

For example,

$$\begin{aligned} 3.2 &= 3+0.2 \\ &= [3.2]+\{3.2\} \qquad 0\leq 0.2<1 \\ -0.8 &= -1+0.2 \\ &= [-0.8]+\{-0.8\} \qquad 0\leq 0.2<1 \\ 6 &= 6+0 \\ &= [6]+\{6\} \qquad 0\leq 0<1 \end{aligned}$$

4. We know that $n!=1\times 2\times 3\times \ldots \times n$ ($n!$isread as factorial n.)

So,

$$\begin{aligned} 1! &= 1 \\ 2! &= 1\times 2=2 \\ 3! &= 1\times 2\times 3=6 \\ 4! &= 1\times 2\times 3\times 4=24 \text{ and so on.} \end{aligned}$$

Now, let's investigate the following question.

How many times primes 2, 3, 5 and 7 appear in $8!$?

$$\begin{aligned} 8! &= 1\times 2\times 3\times 4\times 5\times 6\times 7\times 8 \\ &= (2\times 4\times 6\times 8)\times(3\times 5\times 7) \\ &= (2^7\times 3)\times(3\times 5\times 7) \\ &= 2^7\times 3^2\times 5\times 7 \end{aligned}$$

Thus, 2, 3, 5 and 7 appear 7, 2, 1 and 1 times respectively in $8!$.

Apart from brute multiplication, is there any other way to find it out?

To find out the number of times 2 appears in $8!$, we need to find out the following.

(i) Which numbers out of 1, 2, 3, 4, 5, 6, 7 and 8 are divisible by 2?

(ii) Which numbers out of 1, 2, 3, 4, 5, 6, 7 and 8 are divisible by $2^2=4$?

(iii) Which numbers out of 1, 2, 3, 4, 5, 6, 7 and 8 are divisible by $2^3=8$?

Please note that the numbers 1, 2, 3, 4, 5, 6, 7 and 8 are not divisible by any higher power of 2.

2, 4, 6 and 8 are four integers divisible by 2. .... (i)

4 and 8 are two integers divisible by $2^2 = 4$. .... (ii)

Please note that 4 and 8 are divisible by 2 as well.

Thus, they already appeared in (i).

Therefore, we count them only once (and not twice) as far as counting of power of 2 in 8! is concerned.

8 is the only integer divisible by $2^3 = 8$. ...(iii)

Please note that 8 is divisible by 2^2 as well.

Hence, it already appeared in (ii).

Thus, by (i), (ii) and (iii), the number of times 2 appears in 8!

$$= 4 + 2 + 1 = 7$$

Please also note that the number of times 2 appears in 8!

$$= \left[\frac{8}{2}\right] = 4$$

The number of times 2^2 appears in 8!

$$= \left[\frac{8}{2^2}\right] = 2$$

The number of times 2^3 appears in 8!

$$= \left[\frac{8}{2^3}\right] = 1$$

$\therefore$ The number of times 2 appears in 8!

$$= \left[\frac{8}{2}\right] + \left[\frac{8}{2^2}\right] + \left[\frac{8}{2^3}\right]$$

$$= 4 + 2 + 1 = 7$$

Similarly, 3 and 6 are divisible by 3.

None of 1, 2, 3, 4, 5, 6, 7 and 8 are divisible by $3^2 = 9$.

Hence, the number of times 3 appears in 8!

$$= 2 = \left[\frac{8}{3}\right]$$

Similarly, we can find the number of times 5 and 7 appear in 8!.

This example leads us to the following general result.

5. Theorem : If n is a positive integer and p is a prime, then the exponent of the highest power of p that divides $n!$ is

$$\sum_{k=1}^{\infty}\left[\frac{n}{p^k}\right]$$

Please note that this summation has finite number of terms because $\left[\frac{n}{p^k}\right]=0$ for $p^k > n$.

Proof : By definition, $n! = 1\times 2\times 3\times \ldots \times n$

Among the integers 1, 2, 3, …, n, those divisible by p are $p, 2p, \ldots, tp$ where t is the largest integer such that $tp \le n$.

$$\therefore \qquad t \le \frac{n}{p}$$

Thus, t is the largest integer less than or equal to $\frac{n}{p}$.

Hence, by definition of greatest integer function,

$$t = \left[\frac{n}{p}\right]$$

Thus, there are exactly $\left[\frac{n}{p}\right]$ multiples of p occurring in the product $1\times 2\times \ldots \times n$ i.e. $n!$.

These multiples are as under.

$$p, 2p, \ldots, \left[\frac{n}{p}\right]p \qquad \ldots\text{(i)}$$

Similarly, multiples of p^2 that occur in $n!$ are as under.

$$p^2, 2p^2, \ldots, \left[\frac{n}{p^2}\right]p^2 \qquad \ldots\text{(ii)}$$

Please note that all these terms are multiples of p as well.

Hence, they already appeared in (i).

Hence, we count these terms only once (and not twice) as far as counting of power of p in $n!$ is concerned.

Similarly, multiples of p^3 that occur in $n!$ are as under.

$$p^3, 2p^3, \ldots, \left[\frac{n}{p^3}\right]p^3$$

Please note that this process cannot continue indefinitely as $\left[\frac{n}{p^k}\right]=0$ for some positive integer k.

Hence, after a finite number of steps we get the exponent of the highest power of p that divides $n!$ and the said exponent is equal to

$$\left[\frac{n}{p}\right]+\left[\frac{n}{p^2}\right]+\ldots+\left[\frac{n}{p^{k-1}}\right] \qquad \left(\text{assuming}\left[\frac{n}{p^k}\right]=0\right)$$

$$=\sum_{k=1}^{\infty}\left[\frac{n}{p^k}\right]$$

6. What is the number of zeros with which the decimal representation of 42! terminates?

Proof : Exponent of 2 in 42!

$$=\left[\frac{42}{2}\right]+\left[\frac{42}{2^2}\right]+\left[\frac{42}{2^3}\right]+\left[\frac{42}{2^4}\right]+\left[\frac{42}{2^5}\right]$$

$$=21+10+5+2+1=39$$

Exponent of 5 in 42!

$$=\left[\frac{42}{5}\right]+\left[\frac{42}{5^2}\right]=8+1=9$$

Hence, the power of 10 by which 42! is divisible

= Lesser of the exponent of 2 and 5 in 42!

$=9$

Thus, 42! terminates in 9 zeros.

7. Consider following examples:

(i) $[3]=3$

$[5]=5$

$[3+5]=[8]$

$=8=[3]+[5]$

(ii) $[2]=2$

$[0.8]=0$

$[2+0.8]=[2.8]$

$=2=[2]+[0.8]$

(iii) $[1.2]=1$

$[-0.8]=-1$

$[1.2+(-0.8)]=[0.4]=0$

$=[1.2]+[-0.8]$

(iv) $[1.1]=1$

$[2.9]=2$

$$[1.1+2.9]=[4]$$
$$=4>3$$
$$=[1.1]+[2.9]$$

(v) $[-0.7]=-1$

$[-1.6]=-2$

$$[(-0.7)+(-1.6)]=[-2.3]$$
$$=-3$$
$$=[-0.7]+[-1.6]$$

(vi) $[-0.2]=-1$

$[-0.1]=-1$

$$[(-0.2)+(-0.1)]=[-0.3]$$
$$=-1>-2$$
$$=[-0.2]+[-0.1]$$

Thus, we can see that $[a+b]\geq[a]+[b]$ for real numbers a and b. Is this result true in general?

8. Theorem : $[a+b]\geq[a]+[b]$ where a and b are arbitrary real numbers.

Proof : Let $a=[a]+\{a\}$ where $[a]$ is the greatest integer function and $\{a\}$ is the fractional part of a.

Let $x=\{a\}, 0\leq x<1$

and $p=[a]$

Similarly, $b=[b]+\{b\}$

Let $y=\{b\}, 0\leq y<1$

and $q=[b]$

Now,
$$[a+b]=[p+x+q+y]$$
$$=[(p+q)+(x+y)]$$

p and q are integers.

$$x+y\geq 0$$

Hence, by definition of the greatest integer function,

$$[a+b]\geq p+q$$

or,
$$[a+b]\geq[a]+[b]$$

9. Theorem : n and r are positive integers. $1 \le r < n$. Consider binomial coefficient $\binom{n}{r} = \dfrac{n!}{r!(n-r)!}$ $\binom{n}{r}$ is also an integer.

Proof : By theorem at para 5 above, the exponent of the highest power of p that divides $n!$ is $\sum_{k=1}^{\infty}\left[\frac{n}{p^k}\right]$.

Similarly, the exponent of the highest primes of p that divide $r!$ is

$$\sum_{k=1}^{\infty}\left[\frac{r}{p^k}\right]$$

Also, the exponent of the highest power of p that divides $(n-r)!$ is

$$\sum_{k=1}^{\infty}\left[\frac{n-r}{p^k}\right]$$

By preceding theorem at para 8,

$$[a+b] \ge [a]+[b]$$

Hence,
$$\left[\frac{n}{p^k}\right] \ge \left[\frac{r}{p^k}\right] + \left[\frac{(n-r)}{p^k}\right]$$

$\therefore$
$$\sum_{k=1}^{\infty}\left[\frac{n}{p^k}\right] \ge \sum_{k=1}^{\infty}\left[\frac{r}{p^k}\right] + \sum_{k=1}^{\infty}\left[\frac{(n-r)}{p^k}\right]$$

Thus, any prime p appears in $n!$ at least as many times as in $(r!)\,(n-r)!$ and this is true for every prime divisor of $r!(n-r)!$.

$\therefore$ $(r!)\,(n-r)!$ divides $n!$.

Hence, $\dfrac{n!}{r!\,(n-r)!}$ is an integer.

10. Consider following products of three consecutive integers.

(i) $1 \times 2 \times 3 = 6$ (ii) $3 \times 4 \times 5 = 60$

(iii) $10 \times 11 \times 12 = 1320$ (iv) $5 \times 6 \times 7 = 210$

Please note that all these products are divisible by 3! *i.e.* 6.

Now consider following products of four consecutive integers.

(i) $1 \times 2 \times 3 \times 4 = 24$ (ii) $2 \times 3 \times 4 \times 5 = 120$

(iii) $5 \times 6 \times 7 \times 8 = 1680$ (iv) $9 \times 10 \times 11 \times 12 = 11880$

Please note that all these products are divisible by 4! *i.e.* 24.

So, can we say that the product of r consecutive positive integers is divisible by $r!$?

11. Theorem : For any positive integer r, the product of any r consecutive positive integers is divisible by $r!$.

Proof : Consider following r consecutive positive integers.

$$n, (n-1), (n-2), \ldots, (n-r+1)$$

Product of these integers

$$= n(n-1)(n-2)\ldots(n-r+1)$$

$$= \frac{n(n-1)(n-2)\ldots(n-r+1)[(n-r)\ldots1]}{[(n-r)\ldots1]}$$

$$= \frac{n!}{(n-r)!} = \left[\frac{n!}{r!(n-r)!}\right] r! = \binom{n}{r} r!$$

By theorem at para 9 above, $\binom{n}{r}$ is an integer.

Thus, $r!$ divides $n(n-1)(n-2)\ldots(n-r+1)$.

Hence, the product of any r consecutive positive integers is divisible by $r!$.

Solved Examples

1. Find

(a) $[\sqrt{5}]$ (b) $[-3.8]$

(c) $[\sqrt{2}+\sqrt{3}]$ (d) $[1-\sqrt{3}]$

Sol. (a) $2^2 < 5 < 3^2$

$$\therefore \quad 2 < \sqrt{5} < 3$$

Thus, 2 is the largest integer less than or equal to $\sqrt{5}$.

$$\therefore \quad [\sqrt{5}] = 2$$

(b) -4 is the largest integer less than or equal to -3.8.

$$\therefore \quad [-3.8] = -4$$

(c) $3 < \sqrt{2}+\sqrt{3} < 4$

$$\therefore \quad [\sqrt{2}+\sqrt{3}] = 3$$

(d) $-1 < 1-\sqrt{3} < 0$

$$\therefore \quad [1-\sqrt{3}] = -1$$

2. $[x] \leq 5$

What are the possible values of x?

Sol. For any real number $x < 6$,

$$[x] \leq 5$$

Hence, desired values of x are

$$x < 6$$

3. $[x]^2 - 5[x] + 6 > 0$

What are the possible values of x?

Sol. Let $y = [x]$

$$y^2 - 5y + 6 > 0$$

or, $y^2 - 2y - 3y + 6 > 0$

or, $(y-2)(y-3) > 0$

This is possible only if both terms $(y-2)$ are $(y-3)$ are of same sign.

Hence, $(y-2) > 0$ and $(y-3) > 0$

or, $(y-2) < 0$ and $(y-3) < 0$

$\therefore$ $y > 3$ or $y < 2$

$\therefore$ $[x] > 3$ or $[x] < 2$

Hence, $x \geq 4$ or $x < 2$

4. $[x]^2 = [x+2]$

What are the possible values of x?

Sol. $[x]^2 = [x+2]$

or, $[x]^2 = [x] + 2$

Let $[x] = y$

Now, $y^2 = y + 2$

or, $y^2 - y - 2 = 0$

or, $y^2 - 2y + y - 2 = 0$

or, $(y-2)(y+1) = 0$

$\therefore$ $y = 2$ or $y = -1$

or, $[x] = 2$ or $[x] = -1$

$\therefore$ $2 \leq x < 3$ or $-1 \leq x < 0$

5. $\dfrac{5[x]+4}{11[x]+7} \geq 3$

What are the possible values of x?

Sol. $\dfrac{5[x]+4}{11[x]+7} \geq 3$

Let $[x] = y$

$\therefore$ $\dfrac{5y+4}{11y+7} \geq 3$

Suppose, $11y+7>0$

Then, $5y+4 \geq 3(11y+7)$

or, $28y+17 \leq 0$

$\therefore$ $y \leq -\dfrac{17}{28}$

Also, $11y+7>0$

$\therefore$ $y > -\dfrac{7}{11}$

$\therefore$ $-\dfrac{7}{11} < y \leq -\dfrac{17}{28}$

But there is no integer between $-\dfrac{7}{11}$ and $-\dfrac{17}{28}$. [$\because y = [x]$ is an integer]

Hence, there is no solution in this case.

Now, suppose $11y+7<0$

$\therefore$ $5y+4 \leq 3(11y+7)$

$\therefore$ $28y+17 \geq 0$

$\therefore$ $y \geq -\dfrac{17}{28}$

Also, $11y+7<0$

$\therefore$ $y < -\dfrac{7}{11}$

But $-\dfrac{17}{28} > -\dfrac{7}{11}$

Hence, again there is no solution in this case.

Thus, there is no solution for x.

6. $0 < x < 1000$ and $\left[\dfrac{x}{2}\right]+\left[\dfrac{x}{3}\right]+\left[\dfrac{x}{5}\right] = \dfrac{31}{30}x$

What are the possible values of x?

Sol. We know that

$$\left[\frac{x}{2}\right]+\left[\frac{x}{3}\right]+\left[\frac{x}{5}\right]\leq\left[\frac{x}{2}+\frac{x}{3}+\frac{x}{5}\right]=\left[\frac{31x}{30}\right]$$

or,
$$\frac{31x}{30}\leq\left[\frac{31x}{30}\right] \quad \ldots\text{(i)}$$

Also, by definition of greatest integer function $\left[\frac{31x}{30}\right]\leq\frac{31x}{30}$ ...(ii)

Hence, by (i) and (ii)

$$\left[\frac{31x}{30}\right]=\frac{31x}{30}$$

$\therefore\ \frac{31x}{30}$ is an integer.

Hence, x is a multiple of 30.

As $0<x<1000$, there are 33 multiples of x in this range.

Hence, there are 33 possible solutions for x.

7. $2^k \mid 17!$ where k is a positive integer. What is the maximum possible value of k?

Sol. The exponent of the highest power of 2 that divides 17!

$$=\left[\frac{17}{2}\right]+\left[\frac{17}{2^2}\right]+\left[\frac{17}{2^3}\right]+\left[\frac{17}{2^4}\right]$$

$$=8+4+2+1=15$$

Hence, maximum possible value of $k=15$.

8. What is the number of zeros with which the decimal representation of 100! terminates?

Sol. The exponent of the highest power of 2 that divides 100!

$$=\left[\frac{100}{2}\right]+\left[\frac{100}{2^2}\right]+\left[\frac{100}{2^3}\right]+\left[\frac{100}{2^4}\right]+\left[\frac{100}{2^5}\right]+\left[\frac{100}{2^6}\right]$$

$$=50+25+12+6+3+1=97$$

The exponent of the highest power of 5 that divides 100!

$$=\left[\frac{100}{5}\right]+\left[\frac{100}{5^2}\right]=20+4=24$$

Hence, the exponent of the highest power of $10\,(=2\times5)$ that divides 100!

$$=\text{Lesser of 97 and 24}$$

$$=24$$

Hence, 100! terminates with 24 zeros.

9. For real number x and integer n, $[x+n]=[x]+n$. Prove.

Sol. Let $x=[x]+\{x\}$ where $[x]$ is the greatest integer function and $\{x\}$ represents the fractional part of x.

Let $\quad [x]=p$ and $\{x\}=y$

So, $\quad x=p+y, 0\le y<1$

Now
$$\begin{aligned}[x+n] &=[p+y+n]\\ &=[p+n+y]\\ &=p+n \qquad [\because p \text{ and } n \text{ are integers and } 0\le y<1]\\ &=[x]+n\end{aligned}$$

10. For any real number x, $[x]+[-x]=\begin{cases}0, & \text{if } x \text{ is an integer}\\ -1, & \text{if } x \text{ is not an integer}\end{cases}$.

Prove.

Sol. For any real number x,

$$x=[x]+\{x\}$$

where $[x]$ is the greatest integer function and $\{x\}$ is the fractional part of x.

Let $\quad y=\{x\}$

By definition, $\quad 0\le y<1$

$\therefore \quad -1<-y\le 0$

$$\therefore \quad [-y]=\begin{cases}0, & \text{if } y=0\\ -1, & \text{if } y>0\end{cases} \qquad \text{...(i)}$$

Also, y is 0 if and only if x is an integer. ...(ii)

Now, $\quad x=[x]+y$

$\therefore \quad -x=-[x]-y$

or, $\quad [-x]=-[x]+[-y]$

Hence, by (i) and (ii),

$$[-x]=\begin{cases}-[x], & \text{if } x \text{ is an integer}\\ -[x]-1, & \text{if } x \text{ is not an integer}\end{cases}$$

Hence, $$[x]+[-x]=\begin{cases}0, & \text{if } x \text{ is an integer}\\ -1, & \text{if } x \text{ is not an integer}\end{cases}$$

11. For positive real numbers x and y, $[x][y]\le[xy]$. Prove.

Sol. We can write

$$x=[x]+p$$
$$y=[y]+q$$

where p and q are fractional parts of x and y respectively.

Hence, $0 \leq p, q < 1$

Now, $xy = ([x] + p)([y] + q)$

$= [x][y] + [x]q + [y]p + pq$

$[x]q + [y]p + pq \geq 0$ [$\because x$ and y are positive real numbers]

Hence, $[xy] = [[x][y] + [x]q + [y]p + pq]$

$= [x][y] + [[x]q + [y]p + pq]$

$\geq [x][y]$

12. For an integer $n \geq 0$, $\left[\frac{n}{2}\right] - \left[-\frac{n}{2}\right] = n$. Prove.

Sol. For $n = 0$, it is obviously true.

So, let's examine the case of $n > 0$.

Any integer has one of the forms $2k$ or $2k + 1$.

(i) Suppose $n = 2k$ where k is a positive integer.

Now, $\left[\frac{n}{2}\right] - \left[-\frac{n}{2}\right] = \left[\frac{2k}{2}\right] - \left[-\frac{2k}{2}\right]$

$= [k] - [-k]$

$= k - (-k) = 2k = n$

(ii) Suppose $n = 2k + 1$, where k is a non-negative integer.

Now, $\left[\frac{n}{2}\right] - \left[-\frac{n}{2}\right] = \left[\frac{2k+1}{2}\right] - \left[-\frac{2k+1}{2}\right]$

$= \left[k + \frac{1}{2}\right] - \left[-k - \frac{1}{2}\right]$

$= k - (-k - 1)$

$= 2k + 1 = n$

Thus, $\left[\frac{n}{2}\right] - \left[-\frac{n}{2}\right] = n$ for all $n \geq 0$.

13. $\frac{(2n)!}{(n!)^2}$ is an even integer for any positive integer n. Prove.

Sol. We know that for positive integers n and r with $1 \leq r \leq n$, the binomial coefficient $\binom{n}{r}$ is always an integer.

Hence, $\binom{2n}{n} = \frac{(2n)!}{(n!)^2}$ is an integer.

Now, we also need to prove that $\frac{(2n)!}{(n!)^2}$ is even.

Let k be the greatest integer such that $2^k \mid n$

Hence, $\quad 2^{k+1} \nmid n$

$\therefore \quad \left[\frac{n}{2^k}\right] = 1$ and $\left[\frac{n}{2^{k+1}}\right] = 0$

Let $x =$ The exponent of the highest power of 2 that divides $n!$.

Then, $$x = \left[\frac{n}{2}\right] + \left[\frac{n}{2^2}\right] + \ldots + \left[\frac{n}{2^k}\right]$$

Let $y =$ The exponent of the highest power of 2 that divides $(2n!)$

Then, $$y = \left[\frac{2n}{2}\right] + \left[\frac{2n}{2^2}\right] + \ldots + \left[\frac{2n}{2^k}\right] + \left[\frac{2n}{2^{k+1}}\right]$$

$\therefore$ The exponent of the highest power of 2 that divides $\frac{(2n)!}{(n!)^2} = y - 2x$

$$= \left(\left[\frac{2n}{2}\right] + \left[\frac{2n}{2^2}\right] + \ldots + \left[\frac{2n}{2^k}\right] + \left[\frac{2n}{2^{k+1}}\right]\right) - 2\left(\left[\frac{n}{2}\right] + \left[\frac{n}{2^2}\right] + \ldots + \left[\frac{n}{2^k}\right]\right)$$

$$= \left(\left[\frac{2n}{2}\right] - 2\left[\frac{n}{2}\right]\right) + \left(\left[\frac{2n}{2^2}\right] - 2\left[\frac{n}{2^2}\right]\right) + \ldots + \left(\left[\frac{2n}{2^k}\right] - 2\left[\frac{n}{2^k}\right]\right) + \left[\frac{2n}{2^{k+1}}\right]$$

Each term in this expression (except the last term) ≥ 0 $\quad (\because [x]\,[y] \leq [xy])$

Hence, $$y - 2x \geq 0 + 0 + \ldots + 0 + \left[\frac{2n}{2^{k+1}}\right] = \left[\frac{n}{2^k}\right] = 1$$

Hence, the highest power of 2 that divides $\frac{(2n)!}{(n!)^2}$ is greater than or equal to 1.

Hence, $\frac{(2n)!}{(n!)^2}$ is an even integer.

14. $x = \left[\frac{3^{31} + 2^{31}}{3^{29} + 2^{29}}\right]$

Find the value of $[x]$.

Sol. $3^2(3^{29} + 2^{29}) = 3^{31} + 3^2 \times 2^{29}$

$> 3^{31} + 2^2 \times 2^{29}$

$= 3^{31} + 2^{31}$

$\therefore \quad \frac{3^{31} + 2^{31}}{3^{29} + 2^{29}} < 9$

or, $x<9$ ...(i)

Now, if we can prove that $x>8$, then obviously $[x]=8$.

Now, $3^{31}+2^{31}-8(3^{29}+2^{29})=9\times 3^{29}+2^{31}-8\times 3^{29}-2\times 2^{31}$

$$=3^{29}-2^{31}$$

We know that $3^4>2^6$

$\therefore$ $(3^4)^7>(2^6)^7$

or, $3^{28}>2^{42}$

or, $3^{29}>3\times 2^{42}$

Obviously, $3\times 2^{42}>2^{31}$

$\therefore$ $3^{29}-2^{31}>0$

$\therefore$ $3^{31}+2^{31}-8(3^{29}+2^{29})>0$

$\therefore$ $\dfrac{3^{31}+2^{31}}{3^{29}+2^{29}}>8$

or, $x>8$ ...(ii)

By (i) and (ii), $8<x<9$

Hence, $[x]=8$

15. Let n be a natural number. Prove that $\left[\frac{n}{1}\right]+\left[\frac{n}{2}\right]+\left[\frac{n}{3}\right]+\ldots\left[\frac{n}{n}\right]+[\sqrt{n}]$ is even.

Sol. Let $f(n)=\left[\frac{n}{1}\right]+\left[\frac{n}{2}\right]+\left[\frac{n}{3}\right]+\ldots+\left[\frac{n}{n}\right]+[\sqrt{n}]$

Then $f(1)=2$ which is even.

Now, suppose that $f(n)$ is even for some $n\geq 1$.

Then, $f(n+1)=\left[\frac{n+1}{1}\right]+\left[\frac{n+1}{2}\right]+\left[\frac{n+1}{3}\right]+\ldots\left[\frac{n+1}{n+1}\right]+[\sqrt{n+1}]$

$$\left[\frac{n+1}{k}\right]=\begin{cases}\left[\frac{n}{k}\right]+1, & \text{if } k\mid n+1\\ \left[\frac{n}{k}\right], & \text{if } k\nmid n+1\end{cases}$$

Hence, $f(n+1)=\left[\frac{n}{1}\right]+\left[\frac{n}{2}\right]+\left[\frac{n}{3}\right]+\ldots+\left[\frac{n}{n}\right]+[\sqrt{n+1}]+\sigma(n+1)$, where $\sigma(n+1)$ denotes the number of positive divisors of $n+1$.

Please also note that $[\sqrt{n+1}]=[\sqrt{n}]$ unless $(n+1)$ is a square, in which case $[\sqrt{n+1}]=[\sqrt{n}]+1$

On the other hand, $\sigma(n+1)$ is odd if and only if $(n+1)$ is a square.

Thus, if $n+1$ is a perfect square,

$$f(n+1) = f(n) + 1 + \sigma(n+1) = f(n) + \text{even integer}$$

$\therefore$ $f(n+1)$ is an even integer.

If $n+1$ is not a perfect square,

$$f(n+1) = f(n) + \sigma(n+1) = f(n) + \text{even integer}$$

$\therefore$ $f(n+1)$ is an even integer.

Thus, the result is established by the principle of mathematics induction.

16. Find all real numbers x such that $[x^2 + 2x] = [x]^2 + 2[x]$

Sol. Adding 1 to both sides, the equation reduces to

$$[x^2 + 2x] + 1 = [x]^2 + 2[x] + 1$$

or, $$[x^2 + 2x + 1] = [x]^2 + 2[x] + 1 \quad [\because [x] + m = [x + m] \text{ for any integer } m]$$

or, $$[(x+1)^2] = ([x]+1)^2$$

or, $$[(x+1)^2] = ([x+1])^2$$

Suppose, $x + 1 \le 0$

Then, $[x+1] \le x + 1 \le 0$

Thus, $([x+1])^2 \ge (x+1)^2 \ge [(x+1)^2] = ([x+1])^2$

This is possible only if $x+1$ is an integer.

Also, $x + 1 \le 0$

Hence, $x \in \{-1, -2, -3, \ldots\}$

Now, suppose $x + 1 > 0$

$$(x+1)^2 \ge [(x+1)^2] = ([x+1])^2$$

Also, $$(x+1)^2 < 1 + [(x+1)^2]$$

$$= 1 + ([x+1])^2$$

$\therefore$ $$([x+1]^2) \le (x+1)^2 < 1 + ([x+1])^2$$

$\therefore$ $$[x+1] \le x + 1 < \sqrt{1 + ([x+1])^2}$$

$\therefore$ $$[x] \le x < \sqrt{1 + ([x]+1)^2} - 1$$

This shows that $x \in \left(n, \sqrt{1+(n+1)^2} - 1\right)$ where $n \ge -1$ is an integer.

Thus, the solution set is

$$\{-1, -2, -3, \ldots\} \cup \left\{\cup_{n=-1}^{\infty} \left(n, \sqrt{1+(n+1)^2} - 1\right)\right\}$$

17. Determine all positive integers n such that $[\sqrt{n}]$ divides n.

Sol. Let $m = [\sqrt{n}]$

$\therefore$ $$m \le \sqrt{n} < m+1$$

If $m \mid n$, let $n = am$

Then, $$m^2 \le n < (m+1)^2$$

or, $$m^2 \le am < (m+1)^2$$

$\therefore$ $$m \le a < m+2+\frac{1}{m}$$

Hence, $a = m$, $m+1$ and $m+2$.

Thus, the desired values of n are of the form m^2, $m(m+1)$, $m(m+2)$ for positive integers m.

18. Determine all positive integers n, not a perfect square, such that $[\sqrt{n}]^3$ divides n^2.

Sol. Let $m = [\sqrt{n}]$

$\therefore$ $m < \sqrt{n} < m+1$

If $m^3 \mid n^2$, let $n^2 = am^3$

Then, $\left(\dfrac{n}{m}\right)^2$ is an integer and so, $\dfrac{n}{m}$ is an integer.

Since n is not a perfect square, it follows from the preceding example that (i) $n = m(m+1)$ or (ii) $n = m(m+2)$.

In case (i), $$am^3 = n^2 = m^2(m+1)^2$$

$\therefore$ $$am = (m+1)^2 = m^2 + 2m + 1$$

This implies that $m \mid 1$ and hence, $m = 1$, $n = m(m+1) = 2$

In case (ii), $$am^3 = n^2 = m^2(m+2)^2$$

$\therefore$ $$am = (m+2)^2 = m^2 + 4m + 4$$

This implies that $m \mid 4$.

Hence, $m = 1$, 2 or 4 and $n = m(m+2) = 1\times 3, 2\times 4$ or 4×6.

Thus, the desired values of n are 2, 3, 8 and 24.

19. Prove that $[3x]+[3y] \ge [x]+[y]+2[x+y]$ for all real numbers x, y.

Sol. Let $a = [x]$, $b = [y]$, $u = x - a$ and $v = y - b$. Then, $0 \le u, v < 1$.

Since, $[N+t] = N+[t]$ for integers N,

$$[3x]+[3y] = 3a+[3u]+3b+[3v]$$

And $$[x+y] = a+b+[u+v]$$

So, the inequality to be proved reduces to

$$[3u]+[3v]\geq 2[u+v] \quad \text{...(i)}$$

We know that $[\alpha+\beta]=[\alpha]+[\beta]$ or $[\alpha]+[\beta]+1$, for all real α, β.

$$\therefore \quad [3u]\geq [u+v]+[2u-v]$$

$$[3v]\geq [u+v]+[2v-u]$$

$$[2u-v]+[2v-u]\geq [(2u-v)+(2v-u)]-1=[u+v]-1$$

Combining these inequalities, we get

$$[3u]+[3v]\geq 2[u+v]+[u+v]-1 \quad \text{...(ii)}$$

$$[u+v]=0 \text{ or } 1$$

If $(u+v)=0$,

(ii) reduces to $\quad [3u]+[3v]\geq -1$

And (i) reduces to $\quad [3u]+[3v]\geq 0$

Hence, (i) is trivially true.

If $[u+v]=1$

(ii) reduces to $\quad [3u]+[3v]\geq 2$

And (i) reduces to $\quad [3u]+[3v]\geq 2$

Hence, the result gets established.

20. Find all natural numbers n such that $\left[\dfrac{n^2}{5}\right]$ is prime.

Sol. For $n = 1, 2, ..., 9$, the values of $\left[\dfrac{n^2}{5}\right]$ are 0, 0, 1, 3, 5, 7, 9, 12, 16 respectively.

Of these, only 3, 5 and 7 are prime. These correspond to $n = 4$, 5 and 6.

Let $n = 5k + r$, where $k\geq 2$ and $0\leq r\leq 4$.

Then, $$\left[\frac{n^2}{5}\right]=\left[5k^2+2kr+\frac{r^2}{5}\right]=\begin{cases}5k^2+2kr & \text{for } r=0,1,2\\ 5k^2+6k+1 & \text{for } r=3\\ 5k^2+8k+3 & \text{for } r=4\end{cases}$$

Now, $$5k^2+2kr=k(5k+2r)$$

$$5k^2+6k+1=(k+1)(5k+1)$$

And $$5k^2+8k+3=(k+1)(5k+3)$$

As $k\geq 2$, all of these are composite.

Hence, the desired values of n are 4, 5 and 6.

21. Show that there is a natural number n such that $n!$ when written in decimal notation ends in exactly 1993 zeros.

Sol. We have to show that there exists n such that the highest power of 10 that divides $n!$ is 10^{1993}. The highest power of 5 that divides $n!$ is 5^e where

$$e = \left[\frac{n}{5}\right] + \left[\frac{n}{5^2}\right] + \left[\frac{n}{5^3}\right] + \ldots$$

Similarly, the highest power of 2 that divides $n!$ is 2^f where

$$f = \left[\frac{n}{2}\right] + \left[\frac{n}{2^2}\right] + \left[\frac{n}{2^3}\right] + \ldots$$

Since, $$2\left[\frac{n}{5^i}\right] \le 2\frac{n}{5^i} < \frac{n}{2^i}2 \qquad \text{for } i \ge 1$$

We see that $2e \le f$.

Hence, if n is divisible by 5^e, then it will also be divisible by 2^e.

Let's write representation of n in base 5.

Let $n = a_0 + a_1 5 + a_2 5^2 + a_3 5^3 + \ldots + a_k 5^k$ where $0 \le a_i \le 4$, $a_k \ne 0$.

Then, $$\left[\frac{n}{5}\right] = a_1 + a_2 5 + a_3 5^2 + \ldots + a_k 5^{k-1}$$

$$\left[\frac{n}{5^2}\right] = a_2 + a_3 5 + \ldots + a_k 5^{k-2}$$

and so on.

Adding, $$e = a_1 + a_2(5+1) + \ldots + a_k(5^{k-1} + 5^{k-2} + \ldots + 1)$$

If $1 + 5 + \ldots + 5^i = b_i$, then

$$b_1 = 6,\ b_2 = 31,\ b_3 = 156,\ b_4 = 781,\ \ldots$$

We have to find n such that $e = 1993$, that is,

$$1993 = a_1 + 6a_2 + 31a_3 + 156a_4 + 781a_5 + \ldots$$

Since, $b_5 > 5^5 > 1993$ and $2 \times 781 < 1993 < 3 \times 781$, we see that $k = 5$, $a_5 = 2$, and $a_1 + 6a_2 + 31a_3 + 156a_4 = 1993 - 2 \times 781 = 431$

We find successively, that $a_4 = 2$, $a_3 = 3$, $a_2 = 4$ and $a_1 = 2$

Hence, we have

$n = a_0 + 2 \times 5 + 4 \times 5^2 + 3 \times 5^3 + 2 \times 5^4 + 2 \times 5^5 = a_0 + 7985$, where $0 \le a_0 \le 4$.

If n has any of these five values, then $n!$ ends in exactly 1993 zeros.

Exercise

1. Find

(a) $[\sqrt{17}]$ (b) $[-6.812]$

(c) $[\sqrt{11}-\sqrt{2}]$ (d) $[-\sqrt{13}+2]$

2. $[x] \le -5.3$

What are the possible values of x?

3. $2[x]+3 = 3[x-2]+5$

$y = 2[x]+3$

Then what is the value of $[x + y]$?

4. Find the complete set of values of x satisfying $[x]^2 - 3[x] + 2 \le 0$.

5. $[x+[x+[x]]] \le 3$

What are the possible values of x?

6. Solve $\dfrac{[x]+3}{[x]-2} \ge \dfrac{[x]+1}{[x]-3} - 1$

7. What is the highest power of 11 that divides 1000!

8. What is the number of zeros in which 175! terminates?

9. For what values of n does $n!$ terminate in 45 zeros?

10. For a real number x and positive integer n, $\left[\dfrac{x}{n}\right] = \left[\dfrac{[x]}{n}\right]$. Prove.

11. For positive integers n, m and k, $\left[\dfrac{nm}{k}\right] \ge n\left[\dfrac{m}{k}\right]$. Prove.

12. For real numbers x and y, $[x]+[y]+[x+y] \le [2x]+[2y]$. Prove.

13. In the prime factorisation of $\dfrac{(2n)!}{(n!)^2}$ $(n \ge 1)$, the exponent of any prime p such that $n < p < 2n$ is equal to 1. Prove.

14. $x[x[x[x]]] = 2001$. What is the value of x?

15. $\{x\} + \{y\} = 1$ if and only if x and y both arc non-intcgcrs and $x + y$ is an integer. Prove.

16. $\{x\} + \{x^2\} = 1$. What is the value of x?

17. For any real number x and any positive integer n,
$[x]+\left[x+\frac{1}{n}\right]+\ldots+\left[x+\frac{n-1}{n}\right]=[nx]$. Prove.

18. Prove that $[4x]+[4y]\geq[x]+[y]+[2x+y]+[2y+x]$ for all real numbers x, y.

19. Determine all real numbers x satisfying the equation
$[x]+[2x]+[4x]+[8x]+[16x]+[32x]=12345$

20. Determine all positive integers k with the property that $[kx]+[ky]\geq[x]+[y]+[(k-2)x+y]+[(k-2)y+x]$ for all real numbers x and y.

Answers

1. (a) 4 (b) -7 (c) 1 (d) -2 **2.** $x < -5$ **3.** 15 **4.** $1 \le x < 3$

5. $x < 2$ **6.** $x < 0$ or $x > 5$ **7.** 98 **8.** 43

9. 185, 186, 187, 188 and 189

14. $x = \dfrac{2001}{286}$

16. $x = \dfrac{-1 \pm \sqrt{1+4k}}{2}$ where k is a positive integer and $4k+1$ is not a perfect square

19. No Solution

20. $k = 1, 2, 3, 4, 5$

14 Rational and Irrational Numbers

1. When we talk about numbers, what comes to our mind?

1, 2, 3, 4, 5, 6, ….

The set of numbers starting from 1 and then continuing infinitely to 2, 3, 4, 5, 6, …… is called natural numbers.

In day-to-day life, we use these numbers for counting purposes. The set of natural numbers is normally denoted by N.

So, $N = \{1, 2, 3, 4, 5, 6, \ldots\}$

What if we add 0 to this set?

0, 1, 2, 3, 4, 5, 6, ….

This set of numbers is called whole numbers.

The set of whole numbers is normally denoted by W.

So, $W = \{0, 1, 2, 3, 4, 5, 6, \ldots\}$

Now, suppose we add negative numbers as well to this set.

…., – 6, – 5, – 4, – 3, – 2, – 1, 0, 1, 2, 3, 4, 5, 6, …

This set of numbers is called integers.

The set of integers is normally denoted by I.

So, $I = \{\ldots, -6, -5, -4, -3, -2, -1, 0, 1, 2, 3, 4, 5, 6, \ldots\}$

1, 2, 3, 4, 5, 6, …. are called positive integers whereas ………, – 6, – 5, – 4, – 3, – 2, – 1 are called negative integers.

0 is neither a positive integer nor a negative integer.

2. As we know, various operations are defined with respect to numbers.

For example, addition $(+)$, subtraction $(-)$, multiplication $(\times)$, division $(\div)$ etc.

You can easily verify that the sum of any two natural numbers is a natural number. We express this feature of the set of natural numbers by saying that "the set of natural numbers is closed with respect to addition''.

Now, what about the operation of subtraction? Is the difference of two natural numbers always a natural number?

$$5-3=2$$

2 is a natural number.

$$17-11=6$$

6 is a natural number.

$$18-21=-3$$

-3 is not a natural number.

Thus, the set of natural numbers is not closed with respect to subtraction. The set of whole numbers is also not closed with respect to subtraction.

What about the set of integers?

$$5-7=-2$$

$$3+8=11$$

$$-3-7=-10$$

You can verify that the difference of any two integers is also an integer.

Thus, the set of integers is closed with respect to subtraction.

Now, with respect to the operation of multiplication, you can easily verify that all three sets, natural numbers, whole numbers and integers are closed with respect to multiplication.

What about the operation of division?

3. **Number line :**

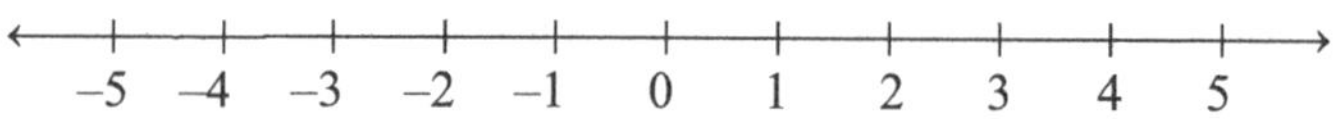

The geometrical concept of line and the concept of numbers have many things in common.

The most important commonality is that there are infinitely many numbers (natural numbers, whole numbers, integers etc.) and there are infinitely many points on a line. Thus, a line can be used to represent numbers.

Any point on a line can be chosen to represent 0.

Then, by convention, positive integers are represented on the right-hand side of 0 whereas negative integers are represented on the left-hand side of 0.

4. Now let's examine whether the set of integers is closed with respect to division.

$$8 \div 2 = 4$$

$$-12 \div 3 = -4$$

$$16 \div (-2) = -8$$

What about $2 \div 3$?

Let $\quad 2 \div 3 = x$

Then, $\quad 3x = 2$

It is evident that there is no integer x which will yield 2, when multiplied by 3.

Thus, x *i.e.* $2 \div 3$ is not an integer.

Similarly, $1 \div 2$, $3 \div 4$ and $-2 \div 3$ are not integers.

Thus, it is evident that the set of integers is not closed with respect to the operation of division.

5. Now it's time to define numbers in a new way so as to expand its scope.

A rational number is defined as a number of the form $\frac{p}{q}$ where p and q are integers and $q \neq 0$.

$\frac{2}{3}, \frac{4}{5}, \frac{-2}{3}, \frac{14}{16}$ etc are all examples of rational numbers.

Please also note that all integers are covered within the definition of rational numbers as any integer p can be written as $\frac{p}{1}$.

Thus, all integers are rational numbers.

6. Now let us examine closure of rational numbers with respect to various operations.

Let $\frac{p}{q}$ and $\frac{r}{s}$ be two rational numbers. p, q, r, s are integers and $q, s \neq 0$

Now, $\quad \frac{p}{q} + \frac{r}{s} = \frac{ps + rq}{qs}$

Both $ps + rq$ and qs are integers as p, q, r, s are integers.

($\because$ The set of integers is closed with respect to the operations of addition and multiplication.)

Further, $\quad qs \neq 0$ as $q, s \neq 0$

Hence, by definition of rational numbers, $\frac{p}{q} + \frac{r}{s}$ is also a rational number.

Similarly, $\frac{p}{q} - \frac{r}{s} = \frac{ps - qr}{qs}$ is a rational number.

$\frac{p}{q} \times \frac{r}{s} = \frac{pr}{qs}$ is also a rational number.

Thus, just like the set of integers, the set of rational numbers is also closed with respect to the operations of addition, subtraction and multiplication.

What about the operation of division?

Before we discuss closure property with respect to division, it is important to note that division by 0 is not defined.

So, for given rational numbers $\frac{p}{q}$ and $\frac{r}{s}$ we need to make one more assumption

i.e. $\frac{r}{s} \neq 0$ or $r \neq 0$.

Now, $$\frac{p}{q} \div \frac{r}{s} = \frac{ps}{qr}$$

Both ps and qr are obviously integers.

Also $$qr \neq 0 \qquad [\because q \neq 0, r \neq 0]$$

Hence, $\frac{ps}{qr}$ is a rational number.

Thus, the set of rational numbers is closed with respect to the operation of division. Please note that by generalizing the concept of numbers, moving from integers to rational numbers, we have obtained a more "complete" set of numbers.

This set of numbers is more "complete" in the sense that unlike integers, the set of rational numbers is closed with respect to the operation of division as well.

7. Can we represent rational numbers on the number line?

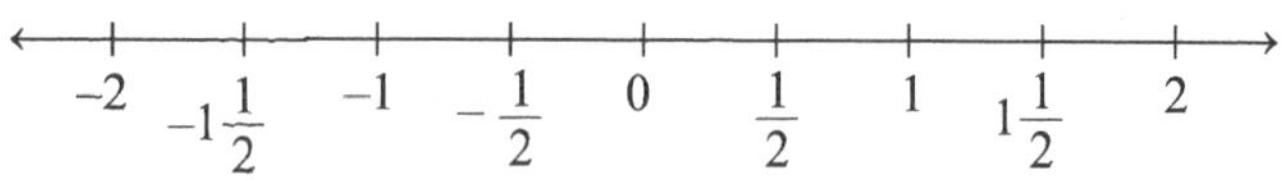

Just like the integers, you can represent rational numbers as well on the number line.

For example, the point exactly midway between 0 and 1 represents $\frac{1}{2}$.

Similarly, the point exactly midway between – 1 and – 2 represents $-1\frac{1}{2}$ or $-\frac{3}{2}$.

In the similar manner, all rational numbers can be represented on the number line.

By convention, positive numbers are represented on the right-hand side of 0 whereas negative numbers are represented on the left-hand side of 0.

8. Representation of rational numbers in decimal form:

Consider rational number $\frac{1}{2}$.

There is another representation for this rational numbers $\frac{1}{2}$, *i.e.* 0.5.

How do we obtain this decimal form?

$$\begin{array}{r} 0.5 \\ 2\overline{)1.0} \\ \underline{10} \\ \underline{0} \end{array}$$

This decimal form of $\frac{1}{2}$ *i.e.* 0.5 is an example of terminating decimal. The decimal form is terminating in the sense that there is a finite number of digits after decimal (only one digit, 5 after decimal) in the decimal form of $\frac{1}{2}$.

Now let's obtain decimal form of $\frac{7}{5}$.

$$\begin{array}{r} 1.4 \\ 5\overline{)\ 7} \\ \underline{5} \\ 20 \\ \underline{20} \\ 0 \end{array}$$

Again, decimal form of $\frac{7}{5}$ *i.e.,* 1.4 is a terminating decimal.

Now, let's obtain decimal form of $\frac{5}{6}$.

$$\begin{array}{r} 0.8333 \\ 6\overline{)\ 5.0} \\ \underline{48} \\ 20 \\ \underline{18} \\ 20 \\ \underline{18} \\ 20 \\ \underline{18} \\ 2 \end{array}$$

Thus, the decimal form of $\frac{5}{6}$ is 0.8333 …. where 3 keeps on repeating infinitely many times. This is an example of non-terminating decimal as the digits after decimal keep on repeating infinitely many times. These digits repeat in a definite pattern.

Therefore, it is called non-terminating recurring decimal. Decimal form of $\frac{5}{6}$ is symbolically represented as $0.8\overline{3}$.

Now, let's obtain decimal form of $\frac{3}{7}$.

$$
\begin{array}{r|l}
 & 0.42857142 \\
\hline
7 & 3.0 \\
 & \underline{28} \\
 & 20 \\
 & \underline{14} \\
 & 60 \\
 & \underline{56} \\
 & 40 \\
 & \underline{35} \\
 & 50 \\
 & \underline{49} \\
 & 10 \\
 & \underline{7} \\
 & 30 \\
 & \underline{28} \\
 & 20 \\
 & \underline{14} \\
 & \underline{6}
\end{array}
$$

Again, this is an example of non-terminating recurring decimal.

$$\frac{3}{7} = 0.\overline{428571}$$

Please note that if any number is divided by 7, only possible remainders are 0, 1, 2, 3, 4, 5 and 6. Therefore, we are bound to obtain a recurring pattern after certain steps.

9. Representation of rational numbers in the form of $\frac{p}{q}$ is not unique.

For example, $\frac{1}{2} = \frac{2}{4} = \frac{3}{6} = \frac{-4}{-8} = ...$

Thus, a rational number can be represented in the form of $\frac{p}{q}$ in infinitely many ways.

For the sake of simplicity, normally a rational number $\frac{p}{q}$ is represented in its lowest form *i.e.*, the when the greatest common divisor of p and q is equal to 1.

In the example above, $\frac{1}{2}$ is the representation in its lowest form.

10. Now let's summarize the results obtained in para 8 above.

Let $\frac{p}{q}$ be a rational number in its lowest form.

To obtain representation of $\frac{p}{q}$ in decimal form, we divide p iteratively by q.

When we divide by q, only possible remainders are $0, 1, \ldots, q-1$. Hence, there are only two possibilities:

(i) We obtain 0 after certain numbers of divisions. In this case we get a terminating decimal.
Division by q can lead to 0 remainder only if q is of the form $2^m 5^n$ where m, n are integers and $m, n \geq 0$.

(ii) We obtain a recurring pattern after certain number of divisions. In this case we get a non-terminating recurring decimal.

Thus, the decimal form of a rational number is always a terminating decimal or non-terminating recurring decimal.
In other words, a terminating decimal and a non-terminating recurring decimal represent rational numbers.

11. The set of rational numbers appears to be complete in the sense that it is closed with respect to all four basic operations: addition, subtraction, multiplication and division.
But is it really complete with respect to other operations as well?
Let's obtain square root of few integers.

$$\sqrt{16} = 4 \quad (\because\ 4^2 = 16.\ \text{Hence, 4 is the square root of } 16)$$

$$\sqrt{9} = 3$$

$$\sqrt{25} = 5$$

What about the square root of 2?

$$1^2 = 1$$

$$2^2 = 4$$

$$1^2 = 1 < 2 < 4 = 2^2$$

Thus, there is no integer which will yield 2 when squared.
So, let's assume that the square root of 2 is a rational number $\frac{p}{q}$ which is not an integer.

Let's also assume that $\frac{p}{q}$ is in its lowest form.

Thus, $\gcd(p, q) = 1$

Also, we can assume that $q > 1$ as $\frac{p}{q}$ is not an integer.

Now, $\sqrt{2} = \frac{p}{q}$

$\therefore$ $2 = \left(\frac{p}{q}\right)^2$

or $p^2 = 2q^2$

Thus, $2 \mid p$ ...(i)

Suppose, $p = 2t$ for some integer t

Now, $(2t)^2 = 2q^2$

or, $4t^2 = 2q^2$

or, $q^2 = 2t^2$

Thus, $2 \mid q$ .... (ii)

From, (i) and (ii), it follows that $\gcd(p, q) \geq 2$.

But this is a contradiction as we assumed that $\gcd(p, q) = 1$.

This contradiction arose from our assumption that $\sqrt{2}$ is a rational number.

Hence, the square root of 2 is not a rational number.

Thus, the set of rational numbers is not really "complete" if we have to obtain square roots.

12. Discovery of irrational numbers led to death!!![1]

Can you believe it?

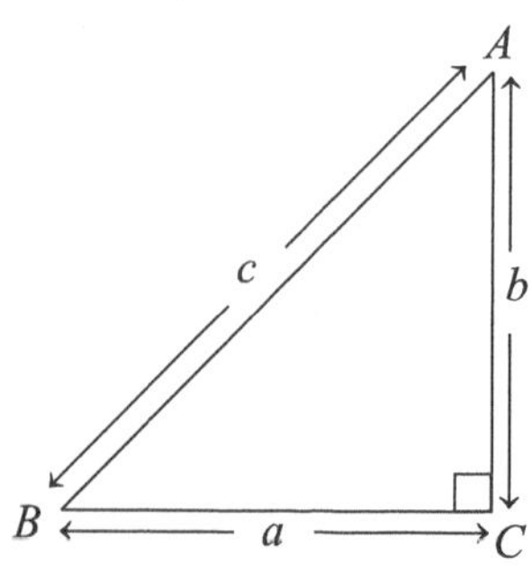

For a right–angled triangle ABC, $a^2 + b^2 = c^2$

[1] https://brilliant.org/wiki/history-of-irrational-numbers/

This is called Pythagoras theorem.

Around 2500 years ago, there was a Greek mathematician, named Pythagoras.

Pythagoras made important contributions to numbers theory.

For Pythagoras and his followers, numbers were not just numbers but held special philosophical significance.

For example, all even numbers were considered female because they divided. Odd numbers were considered male. Pythagoras believed that all numbers can be expressed as the ratio of two integers (*i.e.,* as rational numbers).

Therefore, when subsequently it was discovered that square root 2 cannot be expressed as the ratio of two integers, Hippassus, a Greek philosopher and follower of Pythagoras was shocked.

It is said that Hippassus died at sea as a result of punishment by gods for this discovery which went against Pythagorean beliefs.

13. Representation of irrational numbers on number line :

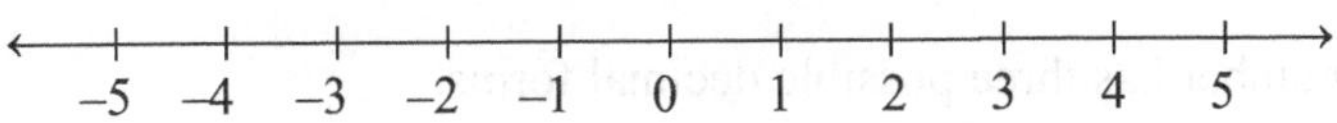

How do we represent an irrational number like $\sqrt{2}$ on number line?

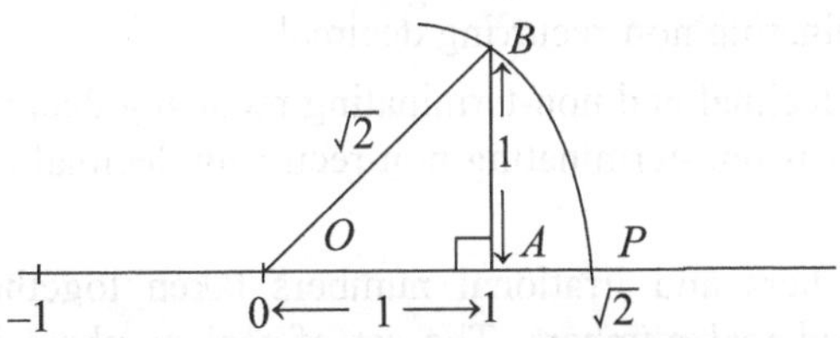

From Pythagoras theorem it follows that the length of diagonal OB

$$= \sqrt{1^2 + 1^2} = \sqrt{2}$$

Now, using our compass, we can find a point P on the number line such that $OP = OB = \sqrt{2}$

Thus, point P represents $\sqrt{2}$ on the number line.

Similarly, we can represent other irrational numbers like $\sqrt{3}$, $\sqrt{5}$, $\sqrt{7}$ etc on the number line.

14. We have seen that the representation of rational numbers in decimal form is invariably a terminating decimal or non-terminating recurring decimal.

Now, what about a non-terminating non-recurring decimal number 0.101001000100001....?

This number can be represented on number line as the point of convergence of the following chain of points.

$$0.1$$
$$0.101$$
$$0.101001$$
$$0.1010010001$$

And so on.

This number 0.101001000100001... again represents an irrational number.

What is the value of $\sqrt{2}$ *in decimal form?*

$$\sqrt{2} = 1.4142135623...$$

It is again a non-terminating non-recurring decimal.

15. Every number on the number line represents either a rational number or an irrational number.

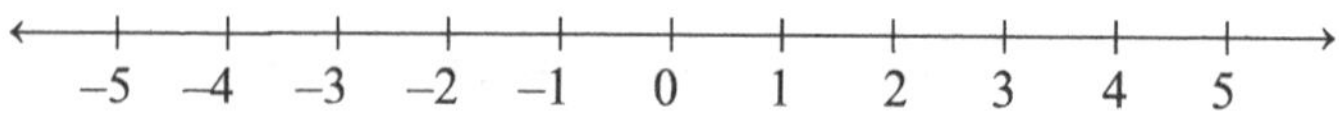

Any number has three possible decimal forms.

(a) Terminating decimal

(b) Non–terminating recurring decimal

(c) Non–terminating non-recurring decimal

Terminating decimal and non-terminating recurring decimal represent a rational number whereas non-terminating non-recurring decimal represents an irrational number.

Rational numbers and irrational numbers taken together represent a set of numbers called real numbers. The set of real numbers is denoted by R. The number line given above is called real number line. Please note that every real number corresponds to a point on the number line.

Conversely, every point on the number line corresponds to a real number. Thus, there is one–to–one correspondence between the set of real numbers and the number line.

Please also note that one-to-one correspondence is not there for any other sets of numbers such as natural numbers, whole numbers, integers and rational numbers.

16. Now we have sufficiently expanded the scope of numbers and arrived at the set of real numbers. This set of real numbers appears to be complete also in the sense that unlike the sets of natural numbers, integers and rational numbers there is now one–to–one correspondence between the number line and the real numbers. But is the set of real numbers really complete with respect to all types of operations? Think!!!

Solved Examples

1. Which of the following is not a rational number?

(a) 3 (b) $-\frac{5}{11}$

(c) 1.222.... (d) $\sqrt{2}$

Sol. (a) 3 is an integer.

Hence, by definition, 3 is a rational number.

(b) $-\frac{5}{11}$ is again a rational number.

(c) 1.222... is a non-terminating recurring decimal. Hence, it is a rational number.

(d) We know that $\sqrt{2}$ is not a rational number.

Hence, among the four given numbers, only $\sqrt{2}$ is not a rational number.

2. Which of the following rational numbers are terminating decimal?

(a) $\frac{9}{5}$

(b) $\frac{7}{12}$

Sol. (a) $\frac{9}{5}$

$$\begin{array}{r|l} & 1.8 \\ \hline 5 & 9 \\ & \underline{5} \\ & 40 \\ & \underline{40} \\ & \underline{0} \end{array}$$

$\therefore$ $\frac{9}{5} = 1.8$

Hence, $\frac{9}{5}$ is a terminating decimal.

(b) $\frac{7}{12}$

$$\begin{array}{r} 0.5833 \\ 12\overline{)\;70} \\ \underline{60} \\ 100 \\ \underline{96} \\ 40 \\ \underline{36} \\ 40 \\ \underline{36} \\ 4 \end{array}$$

$\therefore$ $$\frac{7}{12} = 0.58333... = 0.58\bar{3}$$

Hence, $\frac{7}{12}$ is a non-terminating decimal.

We can infer it even without actual division.

In $\frac{9}{5}$, prime divisors of 5 are 5 only.

Hence, it is a terminating decimal.

In $\frac{7}{12}$, prime divisors of 12 are 2 and 3.

Since 12 has a prime divisor 3 (other than 2 and 5), $\frac{7}{12}$ is a non-terminating decimal.

3. Represent each of the following in decimal form :

(a) $\frac{4}{15}$

(b) $2\frac{5}{12}$

(c) $3\frac{1}{7}$

Sol. (a) $\frac{4}{15}$

$$\begin{array}{r|l} 15 & 4.0 \; (0.266 \\ & \underline{30} \\ & 100 \\ & \underline{\;\;90} \\ & \;\;100 \\ & \underline{\;\;\;\;90} \\ & \;\;\;\;10 \end{array}$$

Hence, $\frac{4}{15} = 0.2666...$

$= 0.2\bar{6}$

(b) $2\frac{5}{12}$

$$\begin{array}{r|l} 12 & 5.0 \; (0.4166 \\ & \underline{48} \\ & 20 \\ & \underline{12} \\ & \;80 \\ & \underline{\;72} \\ & \;80 \\ & \underline{\;72} \\ & \;\;8 \end{array}$$

Hence, $\frac{5}{12} = 0.41666...$

$= 0.41\bar{6}$

Thus, $2\frac{5}{12} = 2.41\bar{6}$

(c) $3\frac{1}{7}$

$$
\begin{array}{l}
\qquad 0.142857142857 \\
7\,\overline{)\;10} \\
\quad \underline{7} \\
\quad\; 30 \\
\quad\; \underline{28} \\
\qquad 20 \\
\qquad \underline{14} \\
\qquad\; 60 \\
\qquad\; \underline{56} \\
\qquad\quad 40 \\
\qquad\quad \underline{35} \\
\qquad\quad\; 50 \\
\qquad\quad\; \underline{49} \\
\qquad\qquad 10 \\
\qquad\qquad \underline{7} \\
\qquad\qquad\; 30 \\
\qquad\qquad\; \underline{28} \\
\qquad\qquad\quad 20 \\
\qquad\qquad\quad \underline{14} \\
\qquad\qquad\quad\; 60 \\
\qquad\qquad\quad\; \underline{56} \\
\qquad\qquad\qquad 40 \\
\qquad\qquad\qquad \underline{35} \\
\qquad\qquad\qquad\; 50 \\
\qquad\qquad\qquad\; \underline{49} \\
\qquad\qquad\qquad\; \underline{\;\;1}
\end{array}
$$

Hence, $\frac{1}{7} = 0.142857142857...$

$= 0.\overline{142857}$

Thus, $3\frac{1}{7} = 3.\overline{142857}$

4. Express each of the following as a rational number in the form $\frac{p}{q}$ where p,q are integers and $q \neq 0$.

(a) $0.\overline{4}$ (b) $0.\overline{27}$

(c) $0.2\overline{13}$ (d) $0.1\overline{523}$

Sol. (a) Let $x = 0.\bar{4} = 0.4444...$ ..... (i)

Multiplying both sides of equation (i) by 10, we get

$$10x = 4.4444... \quad ...(ii)$$

Subtracting equation (i) from equation (ii), we get

$$\begin{array}{r} 10x = 4.4444... \\ - \underline{\quad x = 0.4444...} \end{array}$$

$\therefore \quad 9x = 4$

$\therefore \quad x = \dfrac{4}{9}$

(b) Let $x = 0.\overline{27} = 0.27272727...$ ....(i)

Multiplying both sides of equation (i) by 100, we get

$$100x = 27.27272727... \quad ...(ii)$$

Subtracting equation (i) from equation (ii), we get

$$\begin{array}{r} 100x = 27.27272727... \\ - \underline{\quad x = 0.27272727...} \end{array}$$

$\therefore \quad 99x = 27$

$\therefore \quad x = \dfrac{27}{99}$

or, $\quad \boxed{x = \dfrac{3}{11}}$

(c) Let $x = 0.21\bar{3} = 0.213333...$ ...(i)

Multiplying both sides of equation (i) by 100, we get

$$100x = 21.3333... \quad ...(ii)$$

Multiplying both sides of equation (i) by 1000, we get

$$1000x = 213.3333... \quad ...(iii)$$

Subtracting equation (ii) from equation (iii), we get

$$\begin{array}{r} 1000x = 213.3333... \\ - \underline{\ 100x = 21.3333...} \end{array}$$

$\therefore \quad 900x = 192$

$\therefore \quad x = \dfrac{192}{900} = \dfrac{16}{75}$

(d) Let $x = 0.1\overline{523} = 0.1523523...$ ... (i)

Multiplying both sides of equation (i) by 10000, we get

$$10000x = 1523.523523... \quad ...(ii)$$

Multiplying both sides of equation (i) by 10000000, we get

$$10000000x = 1523523.523... \quad ...(iii)$$

Subtracting equation (ii) from equation (iii), we get

$$\begin{aligned} 10000000x &= 1523523.523... \\ - \quad 10000x &= 1523.523... \\ \hline 9990000x &= 1522000 \end{aligned}$$

$$\therefore \quad x = \frac{1522}{9990} = \frac{761}{4995}$$

5. Find a rational number between rational numbers a and b $(a \neq b)$.

Sol. Let $c = \dfrac{a+b}{2}$

Let's assume that $a < b$.

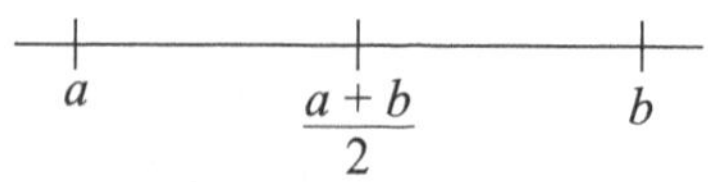

It is easy to see that $\dfrac{a+b}{2}$ lies between a and b.

$$\because \quad \frac{a+b}{2} < \frac{b+b}{2} = b$$

And $$\frac{a+b}{2} > \frac{a+a}{2} = a$$

Thus, $$a < \frac{a+b}{2} < b$$

Also, we know that the set of rational numbers is closed with respect to the operations of addition and division.

Hence, $a + b$ is a rational number ($\because$ a, b are rational numbers).

Thus, $\dfrac{a+b}{2}$ is a rational number.

$\therefore$ $\dfrac{a+b}{2}$ is a rational number between a and b.

6. Find two rational numbers lying between $\dfrac{1}{3}$ and $\dfrac{1}{2}$.

Sol. $\dfrac{1}{2}\left(\dfrac{1}{3} + \dfrac{1}{2}\right) = \dfrac{1}{2} \times \dfrac{5}{6} = \dfrac{5}{12}$

Now, $$\frac{1}{3} < \frac{5}{12} < \frac{1}{2}$$

$$\frac{1}{2}\left(\frac{5}{12} + \frac{1}{2}\right) = \frac{1}{2} \times \frac{11}{12} = \frac{11}{24}$$

Now, $$\frac{5}{12} < \frac{11}{24} < \frac{1}{2}$$

$\therefore$ $$\frac{1}{3} < \frac{5}{12} < \frac{11}{24} < \frac{1}{2}$$

Thus, $\frac{5}{12}$ and $\frac{11}{24}$ are two rational numbers lying between $\frac{1}{3}$ and $\frac{1}{2}$.

7. Prove that the odd integers are not closed with respect to the operation of subtraction.

Sol. Consider odd integers 5 and 3.

$$5 - 3 = 2$$

2 is an even integer.

Thus, the set of odd integers is not closed with respect to the operation of subtraction.

8. Prove that the integers of the form $3n + 2$ are not closed under multiplication.

Sol. $3a + 2$ and $3b + 2$ are two integers of the form $3n + 2$.

$$(3a + 2)(3b + 2) = 9ab + 6a + 6b + 4$$
$$= 3k + 1$$

Where, $$k = 3ab + 2a + 2b + 1$$

Thus, the product is not of the form $3n + 2$.

Hence, the integers of the form $3n + 2$ are not closed under multiplication.

9. a is a rational number whereas b is an irrational number. Prove that $a + b$ and ab are irrational numbers. $(a \neq 0)$

Sol. Let $c = a + b$

Suppose that c is a rational number. It is given that a is a rational number.

We know that the set of rational numbers is closed with respect to the operation of subtraction.

Hence, $c - a$ is a rational number.

or, $(a + b) - a = b$ is a rational number.

But we know that b is an irrational number.

This is a contradiction.

Hence, our assumption that c is a rational number is incorrect.

Thus, $a + b$ is an irrational number.

Now, let $$d = ab$$

Again, let's assume that d is a rational number. It is given that a is a rational number.

Hence, $\frac{d}{a}$ $(a \neq 0)$ is a rational number.

or, b is a rational number.

But we know that b is an irrational number.

This is a contradiction.

Hence, our assumption that d is a rational number is incorrect.

Thus, ab is an irrational number.

10. $\sqrt{5}$ is an irrational number. Prove.

Sol. $2^2 = 4 < 5 < 9 = 3^2$

$\therefore \quad 2 < \sqrt{5} < 3$

Hence, $\sqrt{5}$ cannot be an integer.

Suppose that $\sqrt{5}$ is a rational number.

Let $$\sqrt{5} = \frac{p}{q}$$

where p, q are integers and $\frac{p}{q}$ is in the lowest form ($q > 1$ and $\gcd(p, q) = 1$).

Now, $$\sqrt{5} = \frac{p}{q}$$

or, $$p^2 = 5q^2$$

Hence, $$5 \mid p$$

Let $$p = 5m$$

Hence, $$(5m)^2 = 5q^2$$

or, $$25m^2 = 5q^2$$

or, $$q^2 = 5m^2$$

Hence, $5 \mid q$

Thus, 5 divides both p and q.

$$\therefore \quad \gcd(p, q) \geq 5$$

But this is a contradiction.

Hence, our assumption that $\sqrt{5}$ is a rational number is incorrect.

Thus, $\sqrt{5}$ is an irrational number.

11. $\sqrt{2} + \sqrt{3}$ is an irrational number. Prove.

Sol. Let $a = \sqrt{2} + \sqrt{3}$

Suppose that a is a rational number.

Then, a^2 is also a rational number.

Now, $$a^2 = (\sqrt{2}+\sqrt{3})^2$$
$$= 2 + 3 + 2\sqrt{2} \times \sqrt{3} = 5 + 2\sqrt{6}$$

It is easy to prove that $\sqrt{6}$ is an irrational number.

Hence, $2\sqrt{6}$ is an irrational number.

Therefore, $5 + 2\sqrt{6}$ is an irrational number.

But this is a contradiction.

Hence, our assumption that $\sqrt{2}+\sqrt{3}$ is a rational number is incorrect.

Thus, $\sqrt{2}+\sqrt{3}$ is an irrational number.

12. Find two irrational numbers between 0 and 1.

Sol. $0 < 0.1010010001... < 1$

Also, $0 < 0.110111011110... < 1$

Both 0.1010010001... and 0.110111011110... are non-terminating non-recurring decimals and thus irrational numbers.

13. Rationalize the denominators and simplify following numbers.

(i) $\dfrac{1}{3-\sqrt{5}}$ (ii) $\dfrac{1}{2\sqrt{5}-\sqrt{3}}$

Sol. (i) $$\frac{1}{3-\sqrt{5}} = \frac{1}{(3-\sqrt{5})} \times \frac{(3+\sqrt{5})}{(3+\sqrt{5})} = \frac{3+\sqrt{5}}{3^2-(\sqrt{5})^2} = \frac{3+\sqrt{5}}{9-5} = \frac{3+\sqrt{5}}{4}$$

(ii) $$\frac{1}{2\sqrt{5}-\sqrt{3}} = \frac{1}{(2\sqrt{5}-\sqrt{3})} \times \frac{(2\sqrt{5}+\sqrt{3})}{(2\sqrt{5}+\sqrt{3})} = \frac{2\sqrt{5}+\sqrt{3}}{(2\sqrt{5})^2-(\sqrt{3})^2}$$
$$= \frac{2\sqrt{5}+\sqrt{3}}{20-3} = \frac{2\sqrt{5}+\sqrt{3}}{17}$$

14. There is a number x such that x^2 is irrational but x^4 is rational. Does such a number exist?

Sol. Let $x = \sqrt[4]{2}$

Now, $x^2 = \sqrt{2}$ which is an irrational number

$x^4 = 2$ which is a rational number

Thus, such a number exists.

Exercise

1. There are infinitely many rational as well as irrational numbers between any two rational numbers.

   (a) True (b) False

2. The product of any two irrational numbers is always irrational.

   (a) True (b) False

3. Which of the following is an irrational number?

   (a) $\sqrt{81}$ (b) $\dfrac{\sqrt{9}}{\sqrt{16}}$ (c) $\sqrt{5}$ (d) $\sqrt{\dfrac{108}{12}}$

4. Prove that the integers of the form $3n+1$ are not closed under addition.

5. Prove that the following sets are closed under the indicated operations:

   (a) the integers of the form $3n+1$, under multiplication.

   (b) the integers of the form $3n$, under addition.

   (c) the integers of the form $3n$, under multiplication.

6. Which of the following sets are closed under the indicated operation? Please give a proof in each case.

   (a) the integers of the form $6n+3$, under addition.

   (b) the integers of the form $6n+3$, under multiplication.

   (c) the integers of the form $6n$, under addition.

   (d) the integers of the form $6n+1$, under subtraction.

   (e) the integers of the form $6n+1$, under multiplication.

   (f) the integers of the form $3n$, under multiplication.

   (g) the integers not of the form $3n$, under multiplication.

7. Let x be a rational number and y be an irrational number. $x \neq 0$. Prove that $x - y$ and $\dfrac{x}{y}$ are always irrational numbers.

8. For a positive integer n, there does not exist any integer p such that $p^2 = n$. Prove that $\sqrt{n}$ is an irrational number.

9. $\dfrac{5+2\sqrt{3}}{7+4\sqrt{3}} = a - 6\sqrt{3}$

   Find the value of a.

10. Let $a = 2 + \sqrt{3}$

Find the value of $a - \frac{1}{a}$.

11. Let $a = \frac{3 + \sqrt{5}}{2}$

Find the value of $a^2 + \frac{1}{a^2}$.

12. Which of the following is an irrational number?

(a) π (b) e

(c) ϕ

13. Which of the following rational numbers are terminating decimal?

(a) $\frac{6}{21}$ (b) $\frac{12}{50}$ (c) $\frac{13}{500}$ (d) $\frac{7}{12}$

14. Represent each of the following as a rational number in the form of $\frac{p}{q}$, where p, q are integers.

(a) $0.7\bar{1}$ (b) $0.21\overline{35}$ (c) $0.\overline{155}$

15. Find a rational number between 0.1010010001.... and 0.110111011110....

16. $\sqrt{7} - \sqrt{5}$ is an irrational number. Prove.

17. Rationalize the denominator and simplify following numbers.

(a) $\frac{1}{1 + \sqrt{5} + \sqrt{3}}$ (b) $\frac{1}{\sqrt{6} + \sqrt{5} - \sqrt{11}}$

18. $\frac{4\sqrt{5} + 3\sqrt{2}}{3\sqrt{5} - 2\sqrt{2}} = a + b\sqrt{10}$

Find the value of a and b.

19. Let a, b, n be integers such that $n = ab$. We know that $\sqrt{n} = \sqrt{ab}$ is an irrational number. Then, prove that $\sqrt{a} + \sqrt{b}$ is also irrational.

20. Given that α (alpha) is an irrational number, prove that $\alpha^{-1} = \frac{1}{\alpha}$ is also irrational.

21. If $\sqrt{5 + 2\sqrt{6}} = a\sqrt{3} + b\sqrt{2}$ then find a and b.

Answers

1. (a) **2.** (b) **3.** (c) **6.** (b), (e), (f), (g)

9. 11 **10.** $2\sqrt{3}$ **11.** 7 **12.** (a), (b)

13. (b), (c) **14.** (a) $\frac{32}{45}$, (b) $\frac{1057}{4950}$, (c) $\frac{155}{999}$ **15.** 0.102

17. (a) $\frac{7+3\sqrt{3}-\sqrt{5}-2\sqrt{15}}{11}$ (b) $\frac{6\sqrt{5}+5\sqrt{6}+\sqrt{330}}{60}$

18. $a=\frac{72}{37},\ b=\frac{17}{37}$ **21.** $a=b=1$

15

Special Types of Numbers

15.1 Numbers have very interesting patterns and properties.

Let's see the following patterns and properties.

(i) 1, 2, 3 and 6 are divisors of 6.sss

Sum of divisors $= 1 + 2 + 3 + 6 = 12$

Sum of proper divisors of 6 (excluding 6)

$$= 1 + 2 + 3 = 6$$

Thus, the sum of proper divisors of 6 is equal to 6 itself.

The numbers with this beautiful property are called perfect numbers.

(ii) Consider the 3-digit number 153.

1, 5 and 3 are digits of 153.

$$1^3 = 1$$

$$5^3 = 125$$

$$3^3 = 27$$

$$1^3 + 5^3 + 3^3 = 153$$

Thus, the sum of cubes of digits of 153 is equal to 153 itself.

Such numbers are called Armstrong numbers.

These numbers are special in the sense that they have some interesting and peculiar properties.

Let's discuss few special types of numbers.

15.2 Pythagorean Triple

15.2.1. Find integral solutions of the following equation.

$$x^2 + y^2 = z^2$$

You can see that this equation is satisfied for

(i) $x=3,\ y=4,\ z=5$ i.e. $3^2+4^2=5^2$

(ii) $x=6,\ y=8,\ z=10$ i.e. $6^2+8^2=10^2$

(iii) $x=5,\ y=12,\ z=13$ i.e. $5^2+12^2=13^2$

Thus, the equation $x^2 + y^2 = z^2$ has integral solutions.

In other words, we can find integral values of x, y, z such that $x^2 + y^2 = z^2$.

15.2.2. Does $x^3 + y^3 = z^3$ have integral solutions?

Does $x^4 + y^4 = z^4$ have integral solutions?

It turns out that $x^n + y^n = z^n$ has no integral solutions for $n > 2$.

This result is known as the Fermat's Last Theorem.

15.2.3. Now let's discuss the equation $x^2 + y^2 = z^2$.

Let $x_0,\ y_0,\ z_0$ be a solution to this equation.

i.e., $$x_0^2 + y_0^2 = z_0^2$$

Then the set of integers $x_0,\ y_0,\ z_0$ is called a Pythagorean triple.

Thus, (3, 4, 5), (6, 8, 10) and (5, 12, 13) are examples of Pythagorean triple.

The triple is said to be primitive Pythagorean triple if $\gcd(x, y, z) = 1$.

Thus, (3, 4, 5) and (5, 12, 13) are primitive Pythagorean triples whereas (6, 8, 10) is not primitive.

15.2.4. (6, 8, 10) is not a primitive Pythagorean triple.

$$\gcd(6, 8, 10) = 2$$

$$6 = 2\times 3$$

$$8 = 2\times 4$$

$$10 = 2\times 5$$

$$6^2+8^2=10^2$$

or, $$2^2\times 3^2+2^2\times 4^2=2^2\times 5^2$$

$\therefore$ $$3^2+4^2=5^2$$

Please note that (3, 4, 5) is a primitive Pythagorean triple.

In general, let (x, y, z) be a Pythagorean triple.

i.e., $$x^2 + y^2 = z^2$$

Let, $d = \gcd(x, y, z)$

So, $x = dx_1$, $y = dy_1$, $z = dz_1$ for some integers x_1, y_1, z_1

Now, $$x_1^2 + y_1^2 = \left(\frac{x}{d}\right)^2 + \left(\frac{y}{d}\right)^2 = \frac{x^2 + y^2}{d^2} = \frac{z^2}{d^2} = z_1^2$$

Also $\gcd(x_1, y_1, z_1) = 1$

Thus, (x_1, y_1, z_1) form a primitive Pythagorean triple.

15.2.5. Theorem :

If x, y, z is a primitive Pythagorean triple, then one of the integers x or y is even, while the other is odd.

Proof : Suppose that both x and y are even.

Then, $2 \mid x$

$\therefore$ $2 \mid x^2$

$2 \mid y$

$\therefore$ $2 \mid y^2$

$\therefore$ $2 \mid (x^2 + y^2)$

or, $2 \mid z^2$

$\therefore$ $2 \mid z$

Thus, $\gcd(x, y, z) \geq 2$

But this is not possible because x, y, z is a primitive Pythagorean triple.

Hence, $\gcd(x, y, z) = 1$

Now let's assume that both x and y are odd.

Then, $x^2 \equiv 1 \pmod 4$

$y^2 \equiv 1 \pmod 4$

$\therefore$ $z^2 \equiv x^2 + y^2 \equiv 2 \pmod 4$

But this is not possible because square of any integer is congruent to 0 or 1 mod 4.

Thus, only option left is that one of x, y is even while the other is odd.

15.2.6. Let x, y, z be a primitive Pythagorean triple. By virtue of the preceding theorem, one of x, y is even while the other is odd.

Let x be even and y be odd.

Then $$z^2 = x^2 + y^2$$
$$= \text{even} + \text{odd}$$
$$= \text{An odd integer}$$

Hence, z is odd.

Thus, in a primitive Pythagorean triple x, y, z, two of the integers is always odd while one is even. z is always odd.

15.2.7. Can we have a primitive Pythagorean triple x, y, z where all of x, y, z are prime numbers?

Suppose that such a primitive Pythagorean triple exists.

Then x is even while y and z are odd.

2 is the only even prime number.

Hence, $\quad x = 2$

Now, $\quad x^2 + y^2 = z^2$

or, $\quad z^2 - y^2 = 4 \qquad \ldots(i)$

As both y and z are odd, $\quad z \geq y + 2$

$$\therefore \quad z^2 - y^2 \geq (y+2)^2 - y^2$$

$$= 4y + 4 \quad [\because y \geq 3 \text{ as } y \text{ is an odd prime number}]$$

$$\geq 16 \qquad \ldots\ldots (ii)$$

(i) and (ii) are contradictory to each other.

Hence, there is no primitive Pythagorean triple x, y, z such that all of x, y, z are prime numbers.

15.2.8. There are primitive Pythagorean triples in which two of x, y, z are prime.

For example, $\quad$ 3, 4, 5

11, 60, 61

19, 180, 181

It is not known whether there exist infinitely many such triples.

15.2.9. Theorem :

If $ab = c^n$ where $\gcd(a, b) = 1$, then a and b are n^{th} powers, *i.e.* there exist positive integers a_1, b_1 for which $a = a_1^n$ and $b = b_1^n$.

Proof : If any of a or b is 1, then the result is obvious.

Suppose that $a > 1$ and $b > 1$.

$$\left.\begin{array}{l} a = p_1^{k_1} p_2^{k_2} \ldots p_r^{k_r} \\ b = q_1^{j_i} q_2^{j_2} \ldots q_s^{j_s} \end{array}\right\} \quad \text{(prime factorisations of } a, b)$$

$$\gcd(a, b) = 1$$

Hence, $p_m \neq q_n$ for any $m, n \quad 1 \leq m \leq r, \quad 1 \leq n \leq s$

Hence, prime factorisation of ab is given by

$$ab = p_1^{k_1} \ldots p_r^{k_r} \cdot q_1^{j_1} \ldots q_s^{j_s}$$

Suppose that $c = u_1^{l_1} u_2^{l_2} \ldots u_t^{l_t}$ is the prime factorisation of c.

Then, $c^n = u_1^{l_1 n} u_2^{l_2 n} \ldots u_1^{l_t n}$

As $ab = c^n$

or, $p_1^{k_1} \ldots p_r^{k_r} \cdot q_1^{j_1} \ldots q_s^{j_s} = u_1^{nl_t} \ldots u_t^{nl_t}$

Thus, primes $u_1, \ldots, u_t$ are $p_1, \ldots, p_r, q_1, \ldots, q_s$ in some order.
Also $nl_1, \ldots, nl_t$ are corresponding exponents $k_1, \ldots, k_r, j_1, \ldots, j_s$.
Thus, each of the integers $k_1, \ldots, k_r, j_1, \ldots, j_s$ must be divisible by *n*.

Now, let $a_1 = p_1^{k_1/n} p_2^{k_2/n} \ldots p_r^{k_r/n}$

and $b_1 = q_1^{j_1/n} q_2^{j_2/n} \ldots q_s^{j_s/n}$

Hence, $a_1^n = a$

$b_1^n = b$ as desired

15.2.10. Theorem :

For a primitive Pythagorean triple *x*, *y*, *z*, each pair of the integers *x*, *y* and *z* is relatively prime.

Proof : Suppose that $\gcd(x, y) = d > 1$.

Then there exists a prime *p* such that $p \mid d$.

As $d \mid x$ and $d \mid y$, $p \mid x$ and $p \mid y$.

But then $p \mid (x^2 + y^2)$

or, $p \mid z^2$

∴ $p \mid z$

So, $\gcd(x, y, z) \geq p > 1$

But this is a contradiction because $\gcd(x, y, z) = 1$ as *x*, *y*, *z* is a primitive Pythagorean triple.
Thus, our assumption that $d > 1$ is incorrect.
Hence, *x* and *y* are relatively prime.
We can prove in a similar manner that $\gcd(y, z) = \gcd(x, z) = 1$.
Thus, each pair of the integers *x*, *y* and *z* is relatively prime.

15.2.11. Theorem :

All the solutions of the Pythagorean equation $x^2 + y^2 = z^2$ satisfying the conditions $\gcd(x, y, z) = 1$, $2 \mid x, x > 0$, $y > 0$, $z > 0$ are given by the formulas $x = 2st$, $y = s^2 - t^2$, $z = s^2 + t^2$ for integers $s > t > 0$ such that $\gcd(s, t) = 1$ and $s \not\equiv t$ (mod 2).

Proof : Let *x*, *y*, *z* be a primitive Pythagorean triple.

$$x^2 + y^2 = z^2$$

Let's assume that x is even.

Then from theorem at para 15.2.5 it follows that y and z are both odd.

Hence, $(z - y)$ and $(z + y)$ are both even.

Suppose that $z - y = 2u$ and $z + y = 2v$

$$x^2 + y^2 = z^2$$

or, $$x^2 = z^2 - y^2$$

or, $$x^2 = (z - y)(z + y)$$

or, $$\frac{x^2}{4} = \frac{(z - y)(z + y)}{4}$$

or, $$\left(\frac{x}{2}\right)^2 = \left(\frac{z - y}{2}\right)\left(\frac{z + y}{2}\right)$$

or, $$\left(\frac{x}{2}\right)^2 = uv$$

Let $$d = \gcd(u, v)$$

$$d \mid u,\ d \mid v$$

Hence, $d \mid (u - v)$ and $d \mid (u + v)$

$\therefore$ $$d \mid y \text{ and } d \mid z$$

$\therefore$ $$\gcd(y, z) \geq d$$

From theorem at para 15.2.10, it follows that $d = 1$.

[$\because$ x, y, z is a primitive Pythagorean triple.]

Hence u and v are relatively prime.

Now, $$\left(\frac{x}{2}\right)^2 = uv$$

Hence, it follows from the theorem at para 15.2.9 above that u and v are each perfect squares.

Let $$u = t^2$$

$$v = s^2$$

where s and t are positive integers.

Now, $$z = v + u = s^2 + t^2$$

$$y = v - u = s^2 - t^2$$

$$x^2 = 4vu = 4s^2t^2$$

$\therefore$ $$x = 2st$$

Let $$d = \gcd(s, t)$$

$$d \mid s \text{ and } d \mid t$$

Hence, $d \mid z$ and $d \mid y$

or, $d \mid \gcd(y, z)$

But $\gcd(y, z) = 1$

Hence, $d = 1$

or, $\gcd(s, t) = 1$

If s and t both are even or odd, then y and z both would be even which is not possible.

Hence, exactly one of s, t is even and the other is odd.

Hence, $s \not\equiv t \pmod 2$.

Conversely, let s and t be two integers such that

$$s > t > 0$$

$$\gcd(s, t) = 1$$

and $$s \not\equiv t \pmod 2$$

For $x = 2st$, $y = s^2 - t^2$ and $z = s^2 + t^2$

$$x^2 + y^2 = (2st)^2 + (s^2 - t^2)^2$$
$$= (s^2 + t^2)^2 = z^2$$

Let $\gcd(x, y, z) = d$.

Suppose that $d > 1$.

Let p be any prime divisor of d.

As exactly one of s, t is even and the other is odd, z is odd. (It follows from $s \not\equiv t \pmod 2$.)

Now, $p \mid d$ and $d \mid z$.

Hence, $p \mid z$

Hence, $p \neq 2$ as z is odd.

Now, $p \mid x$, $p \mid y$ and $p \mid z$.

Hence, $p \mid z + y$ and $p \mid z - y$.

$\therefore$ $p \mid 2s^2$ and $p \mid 2t^2$

$\therefore$ $p \mid s$ and $p \mid t$

$\therefore$ $\gcd(s, t) \geq p > 1$

But this is a contradiction as $\gcd(s, t) = 1$

Hence, by contradiction, it is established that our original assumption $d > 1$ is incorrect.

Accordingly, $d = 1$ and thus, x, y, z constitute a primitive Pythagorean triple.

15.2.12. Preceding theorem at para 15.2.11 gives us a mechanism to constitute "primitive Pythagorean triples".

The same are given as

$$x = 2st,\ y = s^2 - t^2,\ z = s^2 + t^2$$

where, $s > t > 0$, $\gcd(s, t) = 1$ and exactly one of s, t is even while the other is odd.

Let's take $t = 1, s = 2.$

So, $x = 4,\ y = 3,\ z = 5$

For $t = 2, s = 3$

$x = 12,\ y = 5,\ z = 13$

For $t = 2, s = 5$

$x = 20,\ y = 21,\ z = 29$

15.3 Ramanujan number

15.3.1. Before we discuss another interesting number called "Ramanujan number" let's ponder over following question.

"Can we classify every natural number as 'interesting' or 'uninteresting'?"

Which natural numbers are 'interesting'?

Which natural numbers are 'uninteresting'?

The attempt to classify every natural number as 'interesting' or 'uninteresting' leads to a paradox called the interesting numbers paradox.

Suppose that there exists a non-empty set S of uninteresting natural numbers.

Then S has a least element, say k. But then k is an interesting number because k is the smallest uninteresting number. This is a contradiction.

This reasoning leads to what we call the interesting numbers paradox.

Isn't it funny?

15.3.2. $9 = 1^3 + 2^3$

Can we express 9 as the sum of two cubes in any other way?

It is easy to see that 9 cannot be expressed as the sum of cubes of two positive integers in any other way. With little efforts we can also see that 9 cannot be expressed as the sum of two cubes in any other way even if negative cubes (cube of a negative integer) are allowed.

15.3.3. The smallest positive integer which can be expressed as the sum of two cubes (positive or negative) in two different ways is 91.

$$91 = 216 - 125 = 6^3 + (-5)^3$$
$$= 64 + 27 = 4^3 + 3^3$$

15.3.4. The smallest positive integer which can be expressed as the sum of two cubes (positive cubes) in two different ways is 1729.

$$1729 = 1 + 1728 = 1^2 + 12^3$$
$$= 729 + 1000 = 9^3 + 10^3$$

1729 is known as the Ramanujan number.

It is also known as the Taxicab number or Ramanujan–Hardy number.

15.3.5. There is an interesting story related to Ramanujan number. British mathematician G. H. Hardy had gone to visit S. Ramanujan in a hospital. Mr. Hardy said that he came in a taxi with the number "1729" which seemed a fairly ordinary number. Ramanujan said that it was not an ordinary number. He pointed out that 1729 was the smallest number which can be expressed as the sum of two cubes in two different ways.

15.3.6. Who was this genius ***S. Ramanujan***?

S. Ramanujan (1887-1920) was born in town *'Erode'*, near *Chennai* in the state of Tamilnadu. His father was a book keeper in a cloth merchant's shop.

Every year, December 22, birthday of Ramanujan, is celebrated as the 'National Mathematics Day' in India in the honour of this mathematician.

"The Man Who Knew Infinity" is a book authored by Robert Kanigel in 1991.

This book is about S. Ramanujan. Based on this book, a movie of the same name was released in 2015.

Have you watched this movie?

15.3.7. Ramanujan numbers are the positive integers that can be expressed as the sum of cubes of two positive integers in *n* ways.

Ramanujan's 1-way solution : Integers that can be expressed as the sum of two cubes in at least one way. For example,

$$2 = 1^3 + 1^3$$
$$9 = 2^3 + 1^3$$
$$16 = 2^3 + 2^3$$

Ramanujan's 2-way solution : Integers that can be expressed as the sum of two cubes in at least two ways. For example,

$$1729 = 12^3 + 1^3 = 10^3 + 9^3$$
$$4104 = 16^3 + 2^3 = 15^3 + 9^3$$
$$13832 = 24^3 + 2^3 = 20^3 + 18^3$$
$$20683 = 27^3 + 10^3 = 24^3 + 19^3$$

Ramanujan's 3-way solution : Integers that can be expressed as the sum of two cubes in at least three ways. For example,

$$87539319 = 167^3 + 436^3 = 228^3 + 423^3 = 255^3 + 414^3$$

15.3.8. A specific number is a positive integer that is the product of three distinct prime numbers.

For example, $$30 = 2 \times 3 \times 5$$

Hence, 30 is a specific number.

$$1729 = 7 \times 13 \times 19$$

Hence, 1729 is also a specific number.

15.3.9. 1729 is a very interesting number. This number is also related to elliptic curves and $k3$ surfaces. These concepts are useful in string theory and quantum physics.

The concept of $k3$ surface was used by mathematician Andrew Wiles for solving Fermat's last theorem. (Fermat's last theorem states that the equation $x^n + y^n = z^n$ has no integral solutions in x, y, z for $n > 2$.)

This statement called Fermat's last therem was articulated by French mathematician Pierre de Fermat in 1637. The proof of this statement was not known until 1990s when mathematician Andrew Wiles proved it.

15.4 Narcissistic Number

15.4.1. Do you know that the number 153 has a very interesting property?

153 has 3 digits.

Now raise each digit of 153 to power 3 and obtain their sum.

What do we get?

$$1^3 = 1$$

$$5^3 = 125$$

$$3^3 = 27$$

$$\therefore \quad 1^3 + 5^3 + 3^3 = 153$$

Some other 3-digit numbers have same property.

For example, $$370 = 3^3 + 7^3 + 0^3$$

$$371 = 3^3 + 7^3 + 1^3$$

$$407 = 4^3 + 0^3 + 7^3$$

Such numbers are called narcissistic numbers or Armstrong numbers or plus perfect numbers or pluperfect digital invariant (PPDI).

In general, for a k-digit natural number $n = d_k d_{k-1} \ldots d_2 d_1$ ($d_1, d_2, \ldots, d_k$ are digits of n), n is called a narcissistic number if

$$n = d_k^k + d_{k-1}^k + \ldots + d_2^k + d_1^k$$

In other words, a k-digit number n is a narcissistic number if the sum of its digits raised to power k is equal to n.

15.4.2. How do we obtain narcissistic numbers?

For 1-digit numbers :

$0^1 = 0$	$5^1 = 5$
$1^1 = 1$	$6^1 = 6$
$2^1 = 2$	$7^1 = 7$
$3^1 = 3$	$8^1 = 8$
$4^1 = 4$	$9^1 = 9$

Hence, all 1–digit numbers are narcissistic numbers.

For 2-digit numbers :

Let $N = ab$ (a and b are digits of N.)

$$= 10a + b$$

If N is a narcissistic number,

$$a^2 + b^2 = 10a + b$$

or, $a^2 - 10a + b^2 - b = 0$

For, $a = 1$, we get $b^2 - b - 9 = 0$

or, $\left(b - \dfrac{1}{2}\right)^2 - \dfrac{37}{4} = 0$

Thus, b has no integral solution.

For, $a = 2$, $b^2 - b - 16 = 0$ For, $a = 3$, $b^2 - b - 21 = 0$

For, $a = 4$, $b^2 - b - 24 = 0$ For, $a = 5$, $b^2 - b - 25 = 0$

For, $a = 6$, $b^2 - b - 24 = 0$ For, $a = 7$, $b^2 - b - 21 = 0$

For, $a = 8$, $b^2 - b - 16 = 0$ For, $a = 9$, $b^2 - b - 9 = 0$

None of these equations have any integral solution.

Hence, we can conclude that there are no 2-digit narcissistic numbers.

For 3–digit numbers :

Let $N = abc$ (a, b and c are digits of N.)

$$= 100a + 10b + c$$

If N is a narcissistic number,

$$a^3 + b^3 + c^3 = 100a + 10b + c$$

If we take $a = 1$,

$$1 + b^3 + c^3 = 100 + 10b + c$$

or, $b^3 + c^3 = 10b + c + 99$

Thus, $b^3 + c^3$ is the sum of two 2-digit numbers, i.e. 99 and $10b + c$.

$\therefore$ $$99 \le b^3 + c^3 \le 198$$

Given this condition, only following combinations of b and c are possible:

b	***c***	***b***	***c***
0	5	5	0
1	5	5	1
2	5	5	2
3	5	5	3
4	5	5	4
4	4		

After verifying for these possible combinations of b and c, we find that 153 is the only 3-digit narcissistic number with 1 as the 1st digit.

Similarly, we can find out other 3-digit narcissistic numbers.

15.4.3. Thus, we see that all 1-digit numbers are narcissistic numbers.

There are no 2-digit narcissistic numbers.

There are only four 3-digit narcissistic numbers 153, 370, 371 and 407.

15.4.4. How many narcissistic numbers are there?

It is easy to see that the number of narcissistic numbers is limited.

Let $N = d_n d_{n-1} \ldots d_2 d_1$ be an n-digit number with $d_1, d_2, \ldots, d_n$ as its digits.

Then, $$d_1^n + d_2^n + \ldots + d_n^n \le 9^n + 9^n + \ldots + 9^n = n9^n$$

Also, $$N = d_n 10^{n-1} + d_{(n-1)} 10^{n-2} + \ldots + d_2 10 + d_1 \ge 10^{n-1}$$

$$10^{(n-1)} > n9^n \text{ for } n > 60$$

Thus, a narcissistic number cannot have more than 60 digits.

Therefore, evidently the number of narcissistic numbers is limited.

15.4.5. There exist only 88 narcissistic numbers. The largest of the narcissistic numbers consists of 39 digits.

15.4.6. So far we have discussed narcissistic numbers in decimal system i.e. base 10. The concept of narcissistic numbers can be generalised to any base.

For example, 5 can be written in base 3 as 12, a 2-digit number.

$$12 = 1 \times 3^1 + 2 \times 3^0 = 3 + 2 = 5$$

Now, $$1^2 + 2^2 = 1 + 4 = 5$$

Thus, 5 is a narcissistic number in base 3.

15.5 Happy Number

15.5.1. $4^2 = 16$

Sum of squares of digits of $16 = 1^2 + 6^2 = 37$

Sum of squares of digits of $37 = 3^2 + 7^2 = 58$

Repeat the process

$$5^2 + 8^2 = 89$$

$$8^2 + 9^2 = 145$$

$$1^2 + 4^2 + 5^2 = 42$$

$$4^2 + 2^2 = 20$$

$$2^2 + 0^2 = 4$$

We get the number 4 *i.e.*, the number we started with.

Please note that this process terminates if and only if we get 1 at some step.

Otherwise, this process continues in an infinite cycle without ever reaching 1.

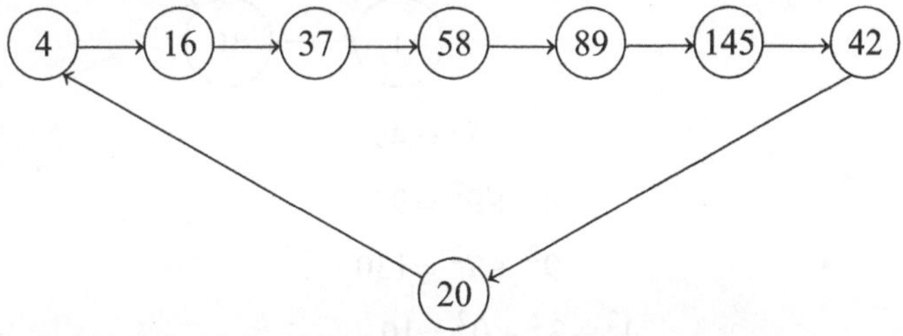

Such numbers are called sad or unhappy numbers.

Now consider the number 13.

Repeat the process as above for 13.

$$1^2 + 3^2 = 10$$

$$1^2 + 0^2 = 1$$

Thus, the process ends in a finite number of steps, leading to 1.

Such numbers are called happy numbers.

15.5.2. This process may lead to many types of loops. For example, consider the number 116.

You can verify that doing the process as above for 116 (i.e. replacing the number with the sum of the squares of its digits) leads to the following loop.

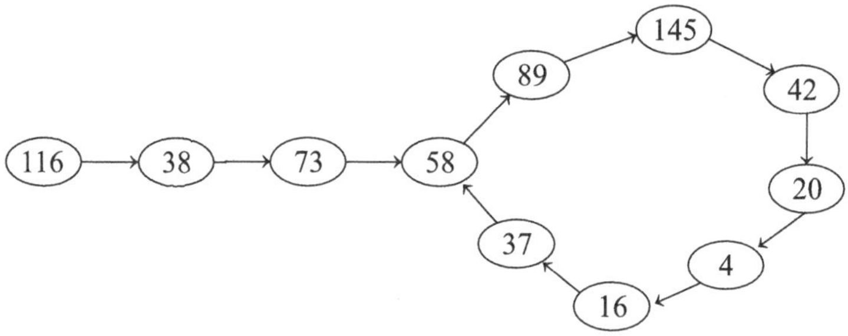

15.5.3. A happy number is a number which eventually reaches 1 when replaced by the sum of squares of its digits. For example, 7, 13 and 94 are happy numbers.

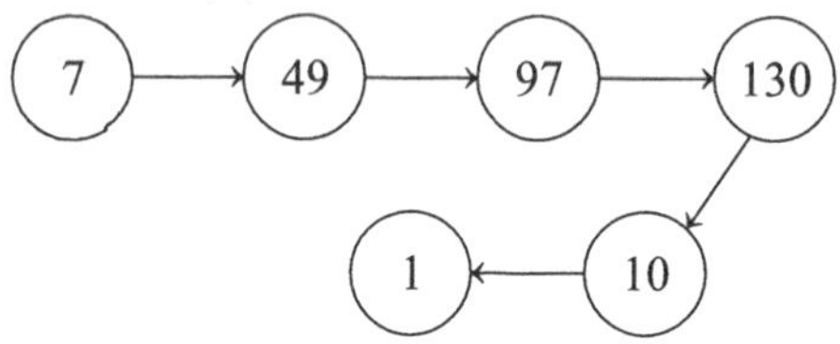

$$7^2 = 49$$
$$4^2 + 9^2 = 97$$
$$9^2 + 7^2 = 130$$
$$1^2 + 3^2 + 0^2 = 10$$
$$1^2 + 0^2 = 1$$

Similarly, you can verify for other numbers.

4 and 116 are examples of unhappy or sad numbers.

15.5.4. First few happy numbers are 1, 7, 10, 13, 19, 23, 28, 31, 32, 44, 49 etc.

15.5.5. Is there any number n such that consecutive numbers n and $(n+1)$ are both happy numbers?

For 31, $3^2 + 1^2 = 10$

$1^2 + 0^2 = 1$

For 32, $3^2 + 2^2 = 13$

$1^2 + 3^2 = 10$

$1^2 + 0^2 = 1$

Thus, 31 and 32 are consecutive happy numbers.

(129, 130), (192, 193), (262, 263) and (301, 302) are few other examples of consecutive happy numbers.

15.5.6. Are there any happy prime numbers (i.e. the numbers which are both happy and prime)?

7, 13, 19, 23, 31 etc. are few examples of happy primes.

15.6 Repunit

15.6.1. Consider following numbers.

1
11
111
1111
11111
111111

These numbers consist of only digit 1's.

Such positive integers consisting of only digit 1 are called repunits.

The terms "repunit" comes from the words "repeated" and "unit".

15.6.2. Repunits can be written as under :

$$1 = 1$$
$$11 = 1 + 10$$
$$111 = 1 + 10 + 100$$
$$1111 = 1 + 10 + 100 + 1000$$
$$11111 = 1 + 10 + 100 + 1000 + 10000$$

Thus, in general, for a repunit consisting of n 1's,

$$\underbrace{11...11}_{n\ 1\text{'s}} = 1 + 10 + 100 + \ldots + 10^{n-1}$$

$$= \frac{10^n - 1}{10 - 1} = \frac{10^n - 1}{9}$$

We use the symbol R_n to denote the repunit consisting of n consecutive 1's.

15.6.3. The square of repunits exhibit an interesting pattern.

$$1^2 = 1$$
$$11^2 = 121$$
$$111^2 = 12321$$
$$1111^2 = 1234321$$
$$11111^2 = 123454321$$

15.6.4. Now see the following pattern.

$$2+3^2=11$$
$$22+33^2=1111$$
$$222+333^2=111111$$
$$2222+3333^2=11111111$$
$$22222+33333^2=1111111111$$

Can you prove it?

Generalising this result, we get

$$\underbrace{22.....2}_{n\text{ times}}+\left(\underbrace{33.....3}_{n\text{ times}}\right)^2=\underbrace{11......1}_{2n\text{ times}}$$

Left Hand Side (LHS) $=2R_n+(3R_n)^2=2R_n+9R_n^2$

$$=2\frac{(10^n-1)}{9}+9\frac{(10^n-1)^2}{9^2}=\frac{10^n-1}{9}[2+10^n-1]$$

$$=\frac{(10^n-1)(10^n+1)}{9}=\frac{10^{2n}-1}{9}=R_{2n}=\underbrace{11......1}_{2n\text{ times}}$$

= Right Hand Side (RHS)

15.6.5. A repunit that is a prime number is also known as a repunit prime.

For example, $R_2=11$ is a repunit prime.

15.6.6. If n is a composite number, R_n is also composite.

Proof : As n is composite, $n=pq$ for some p, q with $1<p, q<n$

$$R_n=\frac{10^n-1}{9}=\frac{10^{pq}-1}{9}$$

$$10^{pq}-1=(10^p-1)(10^{(q-1)p}+10^{(q-2)p}+\ldots+10^p+1)$$

$$\therefore \quad \frac{10^{pq}-1}{9}=\left(\frac{10^p-1}{9}\right)(10^{(q-1)p}+10^{(q-2)p}+\ldots+10^p+1)$$

Thus, $R_n=R_pk$ for some integer $k>1$

Also, $R_p>1$ as $p>1$

Thus, $R_p \mid R_n$ and $1<R_p<R_n$

Therefore, R_n is a composite number.

15.6.7. If n is composite, R_n is necessarily a composite number.

However, if n is a prime number, R_n is not necessarily a prime.

For example, $R_5=11111=41\times 271$

$R_7=1111111=239\times 4649$

15.6.8. There is scarcity of prime numbers among repunits. Upto 2007, only following repunit primes have been identified.

$R_2, R_{19}, R_{23}, R_{317}, R_{1031}, R_{49081}, R_{86453}, R_{109297}, R_{270343}$

15.7 Triangular Numbers

15.7.1. ***Numbers of dots***

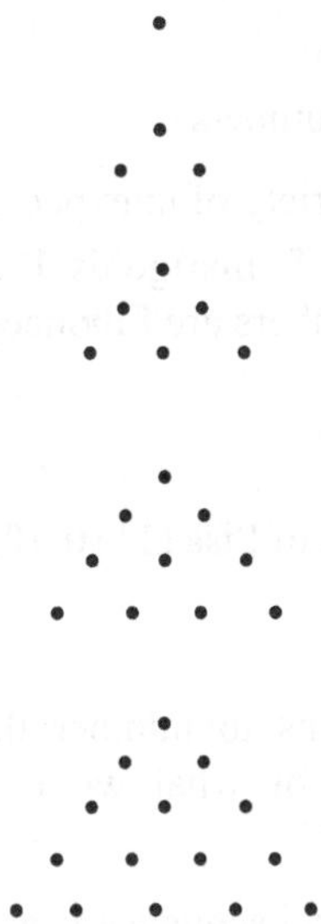

1

3

6

10

15

Each of these numbers 1, 3, 6, 10, 15, … represents the number of dots that can be arranged evenly in an equilateral triangle.

These numbers are called triangular numbers.

$$1 = 1$$
$$3 = 1 + 2$$
$$6 = 1 + 2 + 3$$
$$10 = 1 + 2 + 3 + 4$$
$$15 = 1 + 2 + 3 + 4 + 5$$

Thus, a triangular number is the sum of consecutive numbers beginning with 1.

15.8 Fibonacci Numbers

15.8.1. Consider following sequence of numbers:

1, 1, 2, 3, 5, 8, 13, 21, 34, 55, ……

Can you see the pattern here?

For the sake of notation, let's denote n^{th} term of the sequence by u_n.

Then, $u_1 = 1$

$u_2 = 1$

$$u_3 = 2\ (= 1 + 1 = u_2 + u_1)$$
$$u_4 = 3\ (= 2 + 1 = u_3 + u_2)$$
$$u_5 = 5\ (= 3 + 2 = u_4 + u_3)$$
$$u_6 = 8\ (= 5 + 3 = u_5 + u_4)$$
$$u_7 = 13\ (= 8 + 5 = u_6 + u_5)$$

Thus, each term in this sequence (after 2nd term) is the sum of two preceding terms.

This sequence is called the Fibonacci sequence.

Terms of this sequence are called Fibonacci numbers.

15.8.2. Fibonacci numbers occur in nature in a variety of unexpected ways.

For example, lilies have 3 petals, buttercups 5, marigolds 13, asters 21. Most daisies have 34, 55 or 89 petals. All these numbers are Fibonacci numbers.

Isn't it interesting?

15.8.3. Who (or what) is Fibonacci?

One of the greatest mathematicians - Leonardo of Pisa (1180-1250) - wrote under the name of Fibonacci.

Fibonacci was born in Pisa, Italy.

Fibonacci made many important contributions to number theory. Ironically, however, he is remembered today mainly for what we just discussed *i.e.*, ''Fibonacci sequence and Fibonacci numbers.''

15.8.4. The general rule of formulation of Fibonacci sequence is as under:

$$u_1 = 1$$
$$u_2 = 1$$
$$u_n = u_{n-1} + u_{n-2} \qquad \text{for } n \geq 3$$

15.8.5. Theorem :

For the Fibonacci sequence, $\gcd(u_n, u_{n+1}) = 1$ for every $n \geq 1$.

Proof : Suppose that $d \mid u_n$ and $d \mid u_{n+1}$.

Let us assume that $d > 1$.

Now, $\quad u_{n+1} - u_n = u_{n-1}$

As $\quad d \mid u_n$ and $d \mid u_{n+1}$, $\quad d \mid u_{n-1}$

Similarly, $\quad d \mid u_{n-2} \qquad [\because u_{n-2} = u_n - u_{n-1}]$

Continuing backwards, ultimately we get $d \mid u_1$.

But $\quad u_1 = 1$

Thus, $d \mid 1$ and $d > 1$.

But this is absurd.

Hence, no $d (> 1)$ divides u_n and u_{n+1}.

$\therefore \quad \gcd(u_n, u_{n+1}) = 1$ for every $n \geq 1$

15.8.6. Are there any prime numbers among Fibonacci numbers?

$$u_3 = 2$$
$$u_5 = 5$$
$$u_7 = 13$$
$$u_{11} = 89$$

These are all prime numbers.

Do you notice that all n here (subscript of u_n) are also prime, 3, 5, 7, 11?

So, can we say that u_n is prime whenever n is a prime?

No, this is not true.

For $n = 19$, $u_{19} = 4181 = 37 \times 113$

How many prime Fibonacci numbers are there?

It is not known whether the number of prime Fibonacci numbers is infinite.

Before we discuss few other interesting numbers, let's discuss few properties related to the "sum and number of divisors".

15.9 The Sum and Number of Divisors

15.9.1. What are the divisors of 18?

1, 2, 3, 6, 9 and 18 are the positive divisors of 18.

Thus, number of divisors = 6

Sum of divisors = 39

In general, for a positive integer n, $\tau(n)$ denotes the number of positive divisors of n and $\sigma(n)$ denotes the sum of these divisors.

15.9.2. You can verify the following

$\tau(1) = 1, \quad \sigma(1) = 1$

$\tau(2) = 2, \ \sigma(2) = 3$

$\tau(3) = 2, \ \sigma(3) = 4$

$\tau(4) = 3, \ \sigma(4) = 7$

$\tau(5) = 2, \quad \sigma(5) = 6$

15.9.3. $\tau(n) = 2$ if and only if n is a prime number.

Proof : If n is a prime number, only 1 and n are its divisors.

Hence, $$\tau(n) = 2$$

On the other hand, if $\tau(n) = 2$, then it has only two divisors.

Obviously, 1 and n are divisors of n.

Therefore, n has only 1 and n as its divisors.

Thus, n is a prime number.

15.9.4. $\sigma(n) = n+1$ if and only if n is a prime number.

Proof : If n is a prime number, it has only 1 and n as its divisors.

Hence, $$\sigma(n) = n+1$$

On the other hand, if $\sigma(n) = n+1$, it implies that n has only two divisors n and 1. Thus, n is a prime number.

15.9.5. Theorem:

If $n = p_1^{k_1}\ p_2^{k_2} \ldots p_r^{k_r}$ is the prime factorisation of $n > 1$, then the possible divisors of n are precisely these integers d of the form

$$d = p_1^{a_1}\ p_2^{a_2}\ \ldots\ p_r^{a_r}$$

where $0 \le a_i \le k_i \quad (i = 1, 2, 3, \ldots, r)$

Proof : If $a_1 = a_2 = \ldots = a_r = 0,\ d = 1$

and if $a_1 = k_1, a_2 = k_2, \ldots.\ a_r = k_r, d = n$

Now suppose that d is a divisor of n different from 1 and n.

So $n = dd'$ where $1 < d\ , d' < n$

Let's write both d and d' as a product of primes (not necessarily distinct).

$$d = q_1\ q_2 \cdots q_s$$

$$d' = t_1\ \ t_2 \ldots t_u \qquad (q_i, t_j \text{ are primes})$$

Now, $$p_1^{k_1}\, p_2^{k_2} \ldots p_r^{k_r} = (q_1\ q_2 \ldots q_s)\,(t_1 t_2 \ldots t_u)$$

We know that prime factorisation of any positive integer is unique.

Hence, each q_i must be one of the p_j

Hence, $$d = q_1\ q_2 \cdots q_s$$
$$= p_1^{a_1}\ p_2^{a_2} \ldots p_r^{a_r}$$

where $0 \le a_i \le k_i$

Conversely, every $d = p_1^{a_1}\, p_2^{a_2} \ldots p_r^{a_r}\ (0 \le a_i \le k_i)$ is a divisor of n because we can write $n = p_1^{k_1}\, p_2^{k_2} \ldots p_r^{k_r}$

$$= (p_1^{a_1}\, p_2^{a_2} \ldots p_r^{a_r})\,(p_1^{k_1 - a_1}\ \ p_2^{k_2 - a_2}\ \ldots\ p_r^{k_r - a_r}) = dd'$$

15.9.6. Consider positive integer 12.

$$12 = 4 \times 3 = 2^2 \times 3^1$$

How do we obtain a divisor of 12?

As per para 15.9.5 above, any divisor is of the form $2^{a_1} \times 3^{a_2}$ where $0 \le a_1 \le 2$, $0 \le a_2 \le 1$,

We need to choose a power of 2 out of three possible options—$2^0, 2^1, 2^2$.

Similarly, we need to choose a power of 3 out of two possible options—$3^0, 3^1$.

Hence, number of divisors of 12

$$=3\times2=6$$

Please note that each term in the expansion of $(1+2+2^2)(1+3)$ is a divisor of 12.

$1, 2, 2^2, 1\times3, 2\times3, 2^2\times3$ are all divisors of 12.

Also, these are the only divisors of 12.

Hence, sum of divisors of 12

$$=(1+2+2^2)(1+3)$$

$$=\frac{(2^3-1)(3^2-1)}{(2-1)(3-1)}$$

$$=\frac{7}{1}\times\frac{8}{2}=28$$

We can generalise this result to obtain expressions for the number and the sum of divisors of any positive integer.

15.9.7. Theorem :

If $n=p_1^{k_1}p_2^{k_2}\dots p_r^{k_r}$ is the prime factorisation of $n>1$, then

(a) $\tau(n)=(k_1+1)(k_2+1)\dots(k_r+1)$ and

(b) $\sigma(n)=\left(\frac{p_1^{k_1+1}-1}{p_1-1}\right)\left(\frac{p_2^{k_2+1}-1}{p_2-1}\right)\dots\left(\frac{p_r^{k_r+1}-1}{p_r-1}\right)$

Proof : According to the theorem at para 15.9.5 above, the positive divisors of n are precisely following integers:

$$d=p_1^{a_1}p_2^{a_2}\dots p_r^{a_r}$$

where $0\le a_i\le k_i$

Thus, there are k_1+1 choices for exponent a_1, k_2+1 choices for exponent a_2, ..., and k_r+1 choices for a_r.

Hence, number of divisors *i.e.*, $\tau(n)=(k_1+1)(k_2+1)\dots(k_r+1)$

Now consider the following product

$$(1+p_1+p_1^2+\dots+p_1^{k_1})(1+p_2+p_2^2+\dots+p_2^{k_2})\dots(1+p_r+p_r^2+\dots+p_r^{k_r})$$

Please note that each divisor of n appears exactly once as a term in the expansion of this product.

Hence, sum of divisors *i.e.*, $\sigma(n)$

$$=(1+p_1+p_1^2+\dots+p_1^{k_1})(1+p_2+p_2^2+\dots+p_2^{k_2})\dots(1+p_r+p_r^2+\dots+p_r^{k_r})$$

$$=\left(\frac{p_1^{k_1+1}-1}{p_1-1}\right)\left(\frac{p_2^{k_2+1}-1}{p_2-1}\right)\dots\left(\frac{p_r^{k_r+1}-1}{p_r-1}\right)$$

15.9.8. Find the number and sum of divisors of 180.

Sol. $180 = 4 \times 9 \times 5 = 2^2 \times 3^2 \times 5$

Number of divisors $= \tau(180) = (2+1)(2+1)(1+1) = 18$

Sum of divisors $= \sigma(180)$

$$= \left(\frac{2^3-1}{2-1}\right)\left(\frac{3^3-1}{3-1}\right)\left(\frac{5^2-1}{5-1}\right)$$

$$= 7 \times 13 \times 6 = 546$$

15.9.9. Consider the function $f : N \to N$, $f(n) = n$ where N is the set of positive integers.

So,
$$f(1) = 1$$
$$f(2) = 2$$
$$f(3) = 3$$

and so on.

Such functions are called number-theoretic or arithmetic functions.

Any function whose domain of definition is the set of positive integers is said to be a number-theoretic or arithmetic function.

Now, by definition in this case, $f(mn) = mn = f(m)\,f(n)$

A number-theoretic function f is said to be multiplicative if

$$f(mn) = f(m)\,f(n) \quad \text{whenever} \quad \gcd(m, n) = 1$$

15.9.10. Theorem :

The functions τ and σ are both multiplicative functions.

Proof : If either m or n is equal to 1, then obviously

$$\tau(mn) = \tau(m)\,\tau(n) \text{ and } \sigma(mn) = \sigma(m)\,\sigma(n)$$

Now, let's assume that $m > 1$, $n > 1$ and $\gcd(m, n) = 1$.

Suppose that $m = p_1^{k_1} p_2^{k_2} \dots p_r^{k_r}$ and $n = q_1^{j_1} q_2^{j_2} \dots q_s^{j_s}$ are the prime factorisations of m and n respectively.

$$\gcd(m, n) = 1$$

Hence, no p_i can occur among the q_t.

Thus, prime factorisation of the product mn is given by

$$mn = p_1^{k_1} p_2^{k_2} \dots p_r^{k_r}\, q_1^{j_1} q_2^{j_2} \dots q_s^{j_s}$$

Hence, by theorem at para 15.9.7 above,

$$\tau(mn) = [(k_1+1)\dots(k_r+1)][(j_1+1)\dots(j_s+1)] = \tau(m)\,\tau(n)$$

Similarly,
$$\sigma(mn) = \left[\frac{p_1^{k_1+1}-1}{p_1-1} \dots \frac{p_r^{k_r+1}-1}{p_r-1}\right]\left[\frac{q_1^{j_1+1}-1}{q_1-1} \dots \frac{q_s^{j_s+1}-1}{q_s-1}\right]$$

$$= \sigma(m)\,\sigma(n)$$

Thus, τ and σ are multiplicative functions.

15.10 Perfect Numbers

15.10.1. Consider number 12.

1, 2, 3, 4, 6 and 12 are divisors of 12.

Excluding 12, 1, 2, 3, 4 and 6 are proper divisors of 12.

$$1+2+3+4+6=16>12$$

Hence, 12 is called an abundant number.

If the sum of proper divisors of a number is greater than the given number, the number is called an abundant number.

15.10.2. Now, consider number 8.

1, 2, 4 and 8 are divisors of 8.

Excluding 8, 1, 2 and 4 are proper divisors of 8.

$$1+2+4=7<8$$

Hence, 8 is called a deficient number.

If the sum of proper divisors of a number is less than the given number, the number is called a deficient number.

15.10.3. Now, consider number 6.

1, 2, 3 and 6 are divisors of 6.

Excluding 6, 1, 2 and 3 are proper divisors of 6.

$$1+2+3=6$$

Hence, 6 is called a perfect number.

If the sum of proper divisors of a number is equal to the given number, the number is called a perfect number.

15.10.4. Suppose that n is a perfect number.

By definition, $\sigma(n)-n=n$

Hence, $\sigma(n)=2n$

For example, $\sigma(6)=1+2+3+6=12=2\times 6$

15.10.5. Are there perfect numbers other than 6?

Consider the number 28.

1, 2, 4, 7, 14 and 28 are divisors of 28.

$$\sigma(28)=1+2+4+7+14+28$$
$$=56=2\times 28$$

Hence, 28 is a perfect number.

6, 28, 496, 8128 and 33550336 are first five perfect numbers.

Thus, it is apparent that the perfect numbers are rare.

15.10.6. How many perfect numbers are there?

It is not yet known whether there are finitely many or infinitely many perfect numbers.

15.10.7. Now, let's consider an interesting property of perfect numbers.

$$6 = 2 \times 3 = 2(1+2) = 2(2^2 - 1)$$

$$28 = 4 \times 7 = 2^2(1+2+2^2) = 2^2(2^3 - 1)$$

$$496 = 16 \times 31 = 2^4(1+2+2^2+2^3+2^4) = 2^4(2^5 - 1)$$

We can see that all these even perfect numbers are of the form $2^{(k-1)}(2^k - 1)$ where $2^k - 1$ is a prime number.

Is it true in general?

15.10.8. Theorem :

If $2^k - 1$ is a prime ($k > 1$), then $n = 2^{(k-1)}(2^k - 1)$ is perfect and every even perfect number is of this form.

Proof : Suppose that $2^k - 1 = p$ is a prime number.

Now, consider the integer $n = 2^{(k-1)} p$

Suppose that d is a common divisor of both $2^k - 1$ and p.

$$d \mid 2^{k-1}$$

$$d \mid p$$

$\therefore$ $$d \mid (2 \times 2^{k-1} - p)$$

$\therefore$ $$d \mid 1$$

Hence, $$d = 1$$

Thus, $$\gcd(2^{k-1}, p) = 1$$

From theorem at para 15.9.10 above, it follows that

$$\sigma(n) = \sigma(2^{k-1} p)$$

$$= \sigma(2^{k-1})\sigma(p) \quad (\because \sigma \text{ is a multiplicative function})$$

$$= (2^k - 1)(p+1)$$

$$= (2^k - 1)2^k$$

$$= 2[2^{k-1}(2^k - 1)] = 2n$$

Hence, n is a perfect number.

Now, let's assume that n is an even perfect number.

So, we can write n as $n = 2^{k-1} m$.

where m is an odd integer and $k \geq 2$,

Obviously, $\gcd(2^{k-1}, m) = 1$

$\therefore$ $\sigma(n) = \sigma(2^{k-1} m) = \sigma(2^{k-1})\,\sigma(m)$

$= (2^k - 1)\,\sigma(m)$

As n is a perfect number, $\sigma(n) = 2n = 2^k m$

Hence, $(2^k - 1)\,\sigma(m) = 2^k m$ ...(i)

$\therefore$ $(2^k - 1) \mid 2^k m$

But $2^k - 1$ and 2^k are relatively prime.

Hence, $2^k - 1 \mid m$

$\therefore$ $m = (2^k - 1)M$

On substituting this result into equation (1) we get

$$(2^k - 1)\sigma(m) = 2^k (2^k - 1)M$$

or, $\sigma(m) = 2^k M$

Please note that both m and M are divisors of m with $M < m$.

Hence, $2^k M = \sigma(m) \geq m + M = 2^k M$

Hence, $\sigma(m) = m + M$

It means that m has only two divisors m and M.

This is possible if and only if m is prime and $M = 1$.

Thus, $n = 2^{k-1}(2^k - 1)$ with $2^k - 1$ being a prime number.

Thus, every even perfect number is of this form only.

15.10.9. From the preceding theorem, it follows that if we find a prime number of the form $2^k - 1$ we have found an even perfect number i.e. $2^{k-1}(2^k - 1)$.

Thus, the problem of finding even perfect numbers reduces to the search for primes of the form $2^k - 1$.

15.10.10. Which of the following is prime?

$2^2 - 1 = 3$	is a prime
$2^3 - 1 = 7$	is a prime
$2^4 - 1 = 15$	is not a prime
$2^5 - 1 = 31$	is a prime
$2^6 - 1 = 63$	is not a prime

and so on.

Can you note the pattern?

$2^k - 1$ is prime only if k is prime.

Now verify which of the following is prime.

$2^3 - 1 = 7$ is a prime

$3^3 - 1 = 26$ is not a prime

$4^3 - 1 = 63$ is not a prime

$5^3 - 1 = 124$ is not a prime

Do you notice the pattern?

$a^k - 1$ is a prime only if $a = 2$.

This pattern leads us to the following theorem.

15.10.11. Theorem :

If $a^k - 1$ is a prime ($a > 0$, $k \geq 2$), then $a = 2$ and k is also prime.

Proof : We know that

$$a^k - 1 = (a-1)(a^{k-1} + a^{k-2} + \ldots + a + 1)$$

$$a^{k-1} + a^{k-2} + \ldots + a + 1 \geq a + 1 > 1$$

As $a^k - 1$ is prime, $a - 1$ must be equal to 1.

i.e., $a - 1 = 1$

or, $a = 2$

Now, suppose that k is composite.

Let $k = rs$ $r > 1, s > 1$

Now, $a^k - 1 = a^{rs} - 1 = (a^r)^s - 1$

$$= (a^r - 1)(a^{r(s-1)} + a^{r(s-2)} + \ldots + a^r + 1)$$

Now, both factors on the right are greater than 1.

But this is not possible because $a^k - 1$ is prime.

This contradiction leads to the conclusion that k must be prime.

15.10.12.

$$2^2 - 1 = 3$$

$$2^3 - 1 = 7$$

$$2^5 - 1 = 31$$

$$2^7 - 1 = 127$$

3, 7, 31 and 127 are primes.

Thus $2^p - 1$ is prime for $p = 2, 3, 5, 7$.

Hence, we obtain following perfect numbers.

$$2(2^2-1)=6$$
$$2^2(2^3-1)=28$$
$$2^4(2^5-1)=496$$
$$2^6(2^7-1)=8128$$

For next prime number $p=11, 2^p-1$ is not a prime number.

15.10.13. Are there infinitely many primes of the form 2^p-1 where p is a prime number? The answer to this question is not known.

15.11 Mersenne Primes

15.11.1. All numbers M_n of the form $M_n=2^n-1$, $(n\geq 1)$ are called Mersenne numbers.

Thus,
$$M_1=2^1-1=1$$
$$M_2=2^2-1=3$$
$$M_3=2^3-1=7$$
$$M_4=2^4-1=15$$

15.11.2. The Mersenne numbers that happen to be prime are called Mersenne primes.

For example,
$$M_2=3$$
$$M_3=7$$
$$M_5=31$$
$$M_7=127$$

There are all Mersenne primes.

15.12 Amicable Numbers

15.12.1. Consider numbers 220 and 284.

220 has following proper divisors :

1, 2, 4, 5, 10, 11, 20, 22, 44, 55 and 110

284 has following proper divisors :

1, 2, 4, 71 and 142

Sum of proper divisors of 220

$$=1+2+4+5+10+11+20+22+44+55+110=284$$

Sum of proper divisors of 284 $=1+2+4+71+142=220$

Thus, each of these two numbers is equal to the sum of all the positive proper divisors of the other number.

Such pairs of numbers are called amicable or friendly numbers.

15.12.2. Let m and n be amicable numbers.

Then, by definition,

$$\sigma(m) - m = n$$

and
$$\sigma(n) - n = m$$

or,
$$\sigma(m) = \sigma(n) = m + n$$

15.13 Fermat Numbers

15.13.1. All numbers F_n of the form $F_n = 2^{2^n} + 1, n \geq 0$ are called Fermat numbers.

$$F_0 = 2^{2^0} + 1 = 2^1 + 1 = 3$$

$$F_1 = 2^{2^1} + 1 = 4 + 1 = 5$$

$$F_2 = 2^{2^2} + 1 = 2^4 + 1 = 17$$

$$F_3 = 2^{2^3} + 1 = 2^8 + 1 = 257$$

F_0, F_1, F_2, F_3 are all primes.

If F_n is prime, it is said to be a Fermat prime.

Thus, F_0, F_1, F_2, F_3 are Fermat primes.

15.13.2. It turns out that F_0, F_1, F_2, F_3 and F_4 are primes.

Is F_5 a prime?

Solved Examples

1. Give examples of five Pythagorean triple.

Sol. Pythagorean triples are given by the following formulas:

$x = 2st \qquad y = s^2 - t^2 \qquad z = s^2 + t^2$

where $s, t > 0, s > t$

So, we can obtain following five Pythagorean triples for various values of s and t.

s	t	x	y	z
2	1	4	3	5
3	1	6	8	10
3	2	12	5	13
4	1	8	15	17
4	2	16	12	20

You can verify that $x^2 + y^2 = z^2$ for all these triples.

(i) $x = 4,\ y = 3,\ z = 5$ $\quad x^2 + y^2 = 4^2 + 3^2 = 16 + 9 = 25 = 5^2 = z^2$

(ii) $x = 6,\ y = 8,\ z = 10$ $\quad x^2 + y^2 = 6^2 + 8^2 = 36 + 64 = 100 = 10^2 = z^2$

(iii) $x = 12,\ y = 5,\ z = 13$ $\quad x^2 + y^2 = 12^2 + 5^2 = 144 + 25 = 169 = 13^2 = z^2$

(iv) $x = 8,\ y = 15,\ z = 17$ $\quad x^2 + y^2 = 8^2 + 15^2 = 64 + 225 = 289 = 17^2 = z^2$

(v) $x = 16,\ y = 12,\ z = 20$ $\quad x^2 + y^2 = 16^2 + 12^2 = 256 + 144 = 400 = 20^2 = z^2$

Please note that all of these Pythagorean triples are not primitive Pythagorean triples.

For example, $\gcd(6, 8, 10) = 2$

$\gcd(16, 12, 20) = 4$

Hence, (6, 8, 10) and (16, 12, 20) are not primitive Pythagorean triples.

2. Give examples of three primitive Pythagorean triples.

Sol. Primitive Pythagorean triples are given by the following formulas:

$$x = 2st \quad y = s^2 - t^2 \quad z = s^2 + t^2$$

where $s, t > 0$, $s > t$, $\gcd(s, t) = 1$ and $s \not\equiv t \pmod 2$

Let's take $s = 2, 3, 5$ and choose t in such a way that t is less than s, relatively prime to s and exactly one of s and t is even and the other is odd.

So, we can obtain following three primitive Pythagorean triples.

s	t	x	y	z
2	1	4	3	5
3	2	12	5	13
5	2	20	21	29

You can verify that $x^2 + y^2 = z^2$ for all these triples.

3. If x, y, z is a primitive Pythagorean triple then exactly one of the integers x or y is divisible by 3. Prove.

Sol. Primitive Pythagorean triples are given by the formulas:

$$x = 2st \quad y = s^2 - t^2 \quad z = s^2 + t^2$$

where $s, t > 0$, $s > t$, $\gcd(s, t) = 1$ and $s \not\equiv t \pmod 2$

If either $3 \mid s$ or $3 \mid t$, then evidently $3 \mid x$

Also $3 \nmid y$ because 3 divides exactly one of s and t. $\quad [\because \gcd(s, t) = 1]$

Thus, the given claim is true in this case.

Now, suppose that $3 \nmid s$ and $3 \nmid t$.

By Fermat's theorem, $s^2 \equiv 1 \pmod 3$

$t^2 \equiv 1 \pmod 3$

$\therefore$ $s^2 - t^2 \equiv 0 \pmod 3$

Hence, $3 \mid y$

Also, $3 \nmid x$ in this case.

Hence, 3 divides exactly one of x and y.

Thus, the given claim is established.

4. A Pythagorean triangle is defined to be a right triangle whose sides are of integral length. Prove that the radius of the inscribed circle of a Pythagorean triangle is always an integer.

Sol. The centre of the inscribed circle of any triangle lies at the point of concurrence of all the angular bisectors of the triangle.

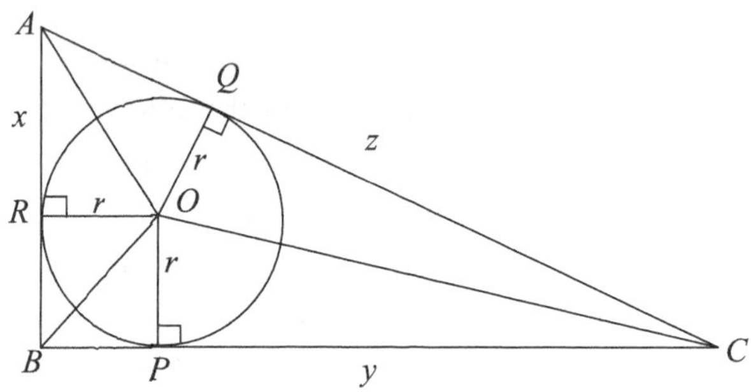

OA, OB and OC are angular bisectors of angles $\angle A$, $\angle B$ and $\angle C$ respectively.

Let r be the radius of inscribed circle.

So $OP = OQ = OR = r$

Also $AB = x, BC = y, CA = z$

Area of triangle ABC = Sum of areas of triangles OAB, OBC and OCA

Hence, $\frac{1}{2} \times BC \times AB = \frac{1}{2} \times AB \times OR + \frac{1}{2} BC \times OP + \frac{1}{2} \times CA \times OQ$

or, $\frac{1}{2} xy = \frac{1}{2} rx + \frac{1}{2} ry + \frac{1}{2} rz$

or, $xy = r(x + y + z)$ ...(i)

As ABC is a right triangle, it follows from Pythagoras theorem that $x^2 + y^2 = z^2$.

We know that the positive integral solutions of the equation $x^2 + y^2 = z^2$ are given by

$$x = 2kst \qquad y = k(s^2 - t^2) \qquad z = k(s^2 + t^2)$$

where k, s, t are positive integers.

$$s > t, \gcd(s, t) = 1 \text{ and } s \not\equiv t \pmod 2$$

Replacing x, y, z in equation (i) by these values we get,

$$(2kst)\, k(s^2 - t^2) = r[2kst + k(s^2 - t^2) + k(s^2 + t^2)]$$

or, $$2kst(s^2 - t^2) = r(2st + 2s^2)$$

or, $$2kt(s^2 - t^2) = 2r(s + t)$$

or, $$kt(s - t) = r$$

$\therefore$ $$r = kt(s - t)$$

which is an integer.

Thus, radius r is an integer.

5. If x, y, z is a primitive Pythagorean triple, then $x + y$ and $x - y$ are congruent modulo 8 to either 1 or 7. Prove.

Sol. Primitive Pythagorean triples are given by the following formulas:

$$x = 2st \qquad y = s^2 - t^2 \qquad z = s^2 + t^2$$

where $s, t > 0$, $s > t$ $\gcd(s, t) = 1$ and $s \not\equiv t \pmod 2$

Now, $$x + y = 2st + s^2 - t^2 = (s + t)^2 - 2t^2$$

Exactly one of s and t is even and the other is odd. $[\because s \not\equiv t \pmod 2]$

Hence, $s + t$ is always odd. Odd integers are of one of the forms $8k + 1$, $8k + 3$, $8k + 5$ or $8k + 7$.

$\therefore$ $$(s + t)^2 \equiv 1 \pmod 8$$

If t is even, it has one of the forms $8k$, $8k + 2$, $8k + 4$ or $8k + 6$.

$\therefore$ $$t^2 \equiv 0, 4 \pmod 8$$

$\therefore$ $$2t^2 \equiv 0 \pmod 8$$

Hence, $$(s + t)^2 - 2t^2 \equiv 1 \pmod 8$$

If t is odd, $$t^2 \equiv 1 \pmod 8$$

$\therefore$ $$2t^2 \equiv 2 \pmod 8$$

$\therefore$ $$(s + t)^2 - 2t^2 \equiv 1 - 2 \pmod 8$$

or, $$(s + t)^2 - 2t^2 \equiv 7 \pmod 8$$

Hence, $$x + y \equiv 1 \text{ or } 7 \pmod 8$$

Similarly, it can be proved that $x - y \equiv 1$ or $7 \pmod 8$

6. For a primitive Pythagorean triple x, y, z, the product xy is divisible by 12 and xyz is divisible by 60. Prove.

Sol. Primitive Pythagorean triples are given by the following formulas:

$$x = 2st \qquad y = s^2 - t^2 \qquad z = s^2 + t^2$$

where $s, t > 0, s > t \quad \gcd(s, t) = 1$ and $s \not\equiv t \pmod 2$

Thus, one of s, t is always even and the other is odd.

$\therefore \quad 4 \mid 2st$

or, $\quad 4 \mid x$

From problem (3) above, we know that 3 divides one of x and y.

Hence, $\quad 12 \mid xy \quad \ldots$(i)

Now, we claim that 5 divides one of x, y, z.

If $5 \mid s$ or t, then $5 \mid x$.

So, let's assume that $5 \nmid s$ and $5 \nmid t$.

Then, s^2 and t^2 have one of the forms $5k+1$ and $5k+4$.

If both s^2 and t^2 are of the same form $5k+1$ or $5k+4$, then $s^2 - t^2$ *i.e.*, y is divisible by 5.

If one of s^2 and t^2 is of the form $5k+1$ and the other is of the form $5k+4$, then $s^2 + t^2$ i.e. z is divisible by 5.

Thus, one of x, y, z is always divisible by 5. ....(ii)

From (i) and (ii), it follows that $60 \mid xyz$.

7. Which of the following is not a Ramanujan number?

1729, 4104, 13832, 20683

Sol.

$$1729 = 12^3 + 1^3 = 10^3 + 9^3$$

$$4104 = 16^3 + 2^3 = 15^3 + 9^3$$

$$13832 = 24^3 + 2^3 = 20^3 + 18^3$$

$$20683 = 27^3 + 10^3 = 24^3 + 19^3$$

All these numbers can be expressed as the sum of cubes of two positive integers in two different ways.

Thus, all these numbers are Ramanujan numbers.

8. Is 1634 a narcissistic number?

Sol. 1634 is a 4-digit number.

$$1^4 = 1$$

$$6^4 = 1296$$

$$3^4 = 81$$

$$4^4 = 256$$

$$1^4 + 6^4 + 3^4 + 4^4 = 1 + 1296 + 81 + 256$$
$$= 1634$$

Since the sum of 4th powers of the digits of 4-digit number 1634 is equal to 1634 itself, it is a narcissistic number.

9. Is 44 a happy number?

Sol. 44

$$4^2 + 4^2 = 16 + 16 = 32$$

$$3^2 + 2^2 = 9 + 4 = 13$$

$$1^2 + 3^2 = 1 + 9 = 10$$

$$1^2 + 0^2 = 1$$

Replacing the numbers with the sum of the squares of its digits leads to the following loop :

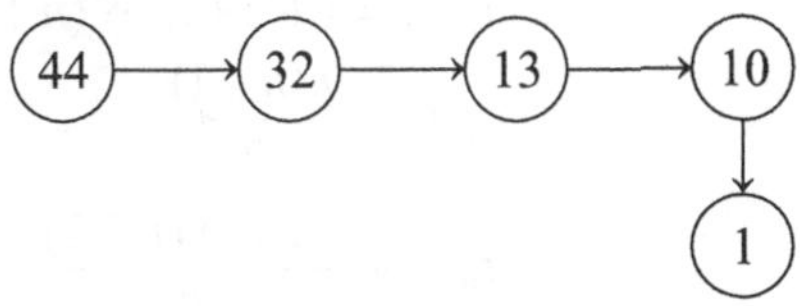

Since the loop terminates in 1, 44 is a happy number.

10. Let R_m and R_n be repunits. If $m|n$, then $R_m | R_n$. Prove.

Sol. Let $n = km$ $[\because m | n]$

We know that $x^n - 1 = (x^m - 1)(x^{(k-1)m} + x^{(k-2)m} + \ldots + x^m + 1)$

Let's substitute $x = 10$.

So, we get $10^n - 1 = (10^m - 1)(10^{(k-1)m} + 10^{(k-2)m} + \ldots + 10^m + 1)$

or, $\dfrac{10^n - 1}{9} = \dfrac{(10^m - 1)}{9}(10^{(k-1)m} + 10^{(k-2)m} + \ldots + 10^m + 1)$

or, $R_n = R_m l$ where $l = (10^{(k-1)m} + 10^{(k-2)m} + \ldots + 10^m + 1)$ is a non-zero integer.

Thus, $R_m | R_n$

11. A number is triangular if and only if it is of the form $\dfrac{n(n+1)}{2}$ for some $n \geq 1$. Prove.

Sol. Suppose that a number N is triangular.

So, by definition, N is the sum of consecutive integers beginning with 1.

Suppose $N = 1 + 2 + n + \ldots + n = \dfrac{n(n+1)}{2}$

Thus, N is of the form $\dfrac{n(n+1)}{2}$.

Conversely, suppose that N is a number of the form $\frac{n(n+1)}{2}$, $n \geq 1$.

$$N = \frac{n(n+1)}{2} = 1 + 2 + \ldots + n$$

Thus, N is the sum of consecutive numbers beginning with 1.

Hence, N is a triangular number.

12. The sum of any two consecutive triangular numbers is a perfect square. Prove.

Proof : Let t_n and t_{n+1} be two consecutive triangular numbers where

$$t_n = 1 + 2 + \ldots + n$$

and
$$t_{n+1} = 1 + 2 + \ldots + (n+1)$$

Hence,
$$t_n = \frac{n(n+1)}{2}$$

$$t_{n+1} = \frac{(n+1)(n+2)}{2}$$

Now,
$$t_n + t_{n+1} = \frac{n(n+1)}{2} + \frac{(n+1)(n+2)}{2}$$

$$= \frac{(n+1)}{2}(n + n + 2)$$

$$= \frac{(n+1)\,2(n+1)}{2} = (n+1)^2$$

which is a perfect square.

13. The difference between the squares of two consecutive triangular numbers is always a cube. Prove.

Proof : Let t_n and t_{n+1} be two consecutive triangular numbers.

$$t_n = 1 + 2 + \ldots + n = \frac{n(n+1)}{2}$$

$$t_{n+1} = 1 + 2 + \ldots + (n+1) = \frac{(n+1)(n+2)}{2}$$

Now,
$$t_{n+1}^2 - t_n^2 = \left[\frac{(n+1)(n+2)}{2}\right]^2 - \left[\frac{n(n+1)}{2}\right]^2$$

$$= \frac{(n+1)^2}{4}[(n+2)^2 - n^2]$$

$$= \frac{(n+1)^2}{4}(n^2 + 4n + 4 - n^2)$$

$$= \frac{(n+1)^2}{4} 4(n+1) = (n+1)^3$$

which is a cube.

14. Find gcd of Fibonacci numbers u_5 and u_6.

Sol. By definition,

$$u_1 = 1$$
$$u_2 = 1$$
$$u_3 = u_1 + u_2 = 2$$
$$u_4 = u_2 + u_3 = 3$$
$$u_5 = u_3 + u_4 = 5$$
$$u_6 = u_4 + u_5 = 8$$

Now, we can find $\gcd(u_5, u_6)$ using Euclidean Algorithm.

$$8 = 1 \times 5 + 3$$
$$5 = 1 \times 3 + 2$$
$$3 = 1 \times 2 + 1$$
$$2 = 2 \times 1 + 0$$

Thus, $\gcd(u_5, u_6) = 1$

Please note that the gcd of any two consecutive Fibonacci numbers is 1.

15. If $2 \mid u_n$ then $4 \mid (u_{n+1}^2 - u_{n-1}^2)$. Prove. ($u_n$ denotes n^{th} Fibonacci number.)

Sol. By definition,

$$u_{n+1} = u_n + u_{n-1}$$

or, $u_n = (u_{n+1} - u_{n-1})$

$$2 \mid u_n$$

Hence, both of u_{n+1} and u_{n-1} are either even or odd.

And in that case, $u_{n+1} + u_{n-1}$ is also even.

Thus, $2 \mid (u_{n+1} - u_{n-1})$

and $2 \mid (u_{n+1} + u_{n-1})$

$\therefore$ $4 \mid (u_{n+1} + u_{n-1})(u_{n+1} - u_{n-1})$

or, $4 \mid (u_{n+1}^2 - u_{n-1}^2)$

16. Find the number and sum of divisors of 116.

Sol. $116 = 2^2 \times 29$

This is the prime factorization of 116.

Hence, number of divisors of 116 *i.e.*, τ (116)

$$= (2+1)(1+1) = 3 \times 2 = 6$$

Sum of divisors of 116 *i.e.*, $\sigma(116)$

$$= \left(\frac{2^3 - 1}{2 - 1}\right)\left(\frac{29^2 - 1}{29 - 1}\right) = 7 \times 30 = 210$$

17. For any integer $n \geq 1$, number of divisors $\tau(n) \leq 2\sqrt{n}$. Prove.

Sol. Let d be a divisor of n.

So, $$n = d\left(\frac{n}{d}\right)$$

One of d and $\frac{n}{d}$ has to be less than or equal to $\sqrt{n}$.

Otherwise, if both d and $\frac{n}{d}$ are greater than $\sqrt{n}$, then, $d\left(\frac{n}{d}\right)$

$$> \sqrt{n} \times \sqrt{n} = n$$

which is not possible.

Now, let $d_1, d_2, ..., d_{\tau(n)}$ be the divisors of n.

Therefore, $$n = d_1\left(\frac{n}{d_1}\right)$$

$$= d_2\left(\frac{n}{d_2}\right)$$

....

....

$$= d_k\left(\frac{n}{d_k}\right) \quad \text{for some } k$$

where $d_i \leq \sqrt{n}$ for $1 \leq i \leq k$

As one of the factors in the representation above has to be less than or equal to $\sqrt{n}$, it is possible to write n in the above form where 1st factor is always less than or equal to $\sqrt{n}$.

As all divisors get represented in the above form, total number of divisors

i.e., $$\tau(n) = 2k \leq 2\sqrt{n}$$

18. Find the number of divisors of 16 and 25.

Sol. $$16 = 2^4$$

$$\tau(16) = 4 + 1 = 5$$

$$25 = 5^2$$

$$\tau(25) = 2 + 1 = 3$$

The number of divisors is odd in both cases.

19. $\tau(n)$ is an odd integer if and only if n is a perfect square. Prove. ($\tau(n)$ denotes the number of divisors of n.)

Sol. Let $n = p_1^{k_1} p_2^{k_2} \ldots p_r^{k_r}$ be the prime factorization of n.

$$\tau(n) = (k_1 + 1)(k_2 + 1)\ldots(k_r + 1)$$

Suppose that $\tau(n)$ is odd.

Then, each of $k_i + 1$ has to be odd.

So, each of k_i has to be even.

Let $$k_i = 2s_i$$

Then $$n = p_1^{k_1} p_2^{k_2} \ldots p_r^{k_r}$$

$$= p_1^{2s_1} p_2^{2s_2} \ldots p_r^{2s_r}$$

$$= (p_1^{s_1} p_2^{s_2} \ldots p_r^{s_r})^2$$

Thus, n is a perfect square.

Now suppose that n is a perfect square.

So prime factorization of n has to be of the form:

$$n = (p_1^{s_1} p_2^{s_2} \ldots p_r^{s_r})^2$$

$$= p_1^{2s_1} p_2^{2s_2} \ldots p_r^{2s_r}$$

Now, $$\tau(n) = (2s_1 + 1)(2s_2 + 1)\ldots(2s_r + 1)$$

which is an odd integer.

20. No power of a prime can be a perfect number. Prove.

Sol. Let $N = p^r$ where p is a prime number. $r \geq 1$

Now $$\sigma(N) = \sigma(p^r) = \frac{p^{r+1} - 1}{p - 1}$$

Suppose that N is a perfect number.

So, $$\sigma(N) = 2N$$

or, $$\frac{p^{r+1} - 1}{p - 1} = 2p^r$$

or, $$p^{r+1} - 1 = 2p^{r+1} - 2p^r$$

or, $$2p^r - p^{r+1} = 1$$

$\therefore$ $$p \mid 1$$

But this is not possible.

This contradiction leads to the conclusion that no powers of a prime can be a perfect number.

21. Every even perfect number is a triangular number. Prove.

Sol. Every even perfect number n is of the form $2^{k-1}(2^k - 1)$.

Let
$$n = 2^{k-1}(2^k - 1)$$
$$= \frac{2^k(2^k - 1)}{2}$$
$$= \frac{N(N+1)}{2} \quad \text{where } N = 2^k - 1$$

We know that any number of the form $\frac{N(N+1)}{2}$ is a triangular number.

22. Unit digit of every even perfect number is either 6 or 8. Prove.

Sol. Let n be an even perfect number.

Then n is of the form $2^{k-1}(2^k - 1)$ where $2^k - 1$ is a prime.

As $2^k - 1$ is a prime, k has to be prime.

If $k = 2$,
$$n = 2^{k-1}(2^k - 1)$$
$$= 2(2^2 - 1) = 6$$

Thus, the result holds true for $k = 2$.

Now let's assume that $k > 2$.

As k is a prime number, it has one of the forms $4m + 1$ or $4m + 3$.

If k is of the form $4m + 1$,
$$n = 2^{k-1}(2^k - 1)$$
$$= 2^{4m}(2^{4m+1} - 1)$$
$$= 2^{8m+1} - 2^{4m}$$
$$= 2 \times 16^{2m} - 16^m$$

If k is of the form $4m + 3$,
$$n = 2^{k-1}(2^k - 1)$$
$$= 2^{4m+2}(2^{4m+3} - 1)$$
$$= 2^{8m+5} - 2^{4m+2}$$
$$= 2 \times 16^{2m+1} - 4 \times 16^m$$

Now, please note that any power of 16 has unit digit 6.

i.e., $16^t \equiv 6 \pmod{10}$ for any positive integer t.

It can be easily proved by induction on t.

Now using this result,

If k is of the form $4m+1$, $n = 2\times 16^{2m} - 16^{m}$

$$\equiv 2\times 6 - 6 \pmod{10}$$

$$\equiv 6 \pmod{10}$$

If k is of the form $4m+3$,

$$n = 2\times 16^{2m+1} - 4\times 16^{m}$$

$$\equiv 2\times 6 - 4\times 6 \pmod{10}$$

$$\equiv -12 \pmod{10}$$

$$\equiv 8 \pmod{10}$$

Thus, an even perfect number always has 6 or 8 as its unit digit.

23. Please verify whether 17 is a Mersenne prime and Fermat prime.

Sol. Mersenne numbers are of the form

$$M_n = 2^n - 1, n \geq 1$$

For, $n=4$, $M_4 = 15$

For, $n=5$, $M_5 = 31$

Thus, 17 is not a Mersenne number.

Fermat numbers are given by

$$F_n = 2^{2^n} + 1, n \geq 0$$

For, $n=2$,

$$F_2 = 2^{2^2} + 1 = 2^4 + 1 = 17$$

Also, 17 is a prime number.

Thus, 17 is a Fermat prime but not a Mersenne prime.

24. If m and n are amicable numbers ($m \neq n$) then none of m and n are perfect numbers. Prove.

Sol. By definition of amicable numbers,

$$\sigma(m) - m = n \text{ and } \sigma(n) - n = m$$

$$\therefore \quad \sigma(m) = \sigma(n) = m + n$$

Suppose that m is a perfect number.

Then $\sigma(m) = 2m$ (By definition of perfect number)

$$\therefore \quad 2m = m + n$$

or, $m = n$

But pair of amicable numbers consists of different numbers.

This contradiction proves the required result.

25. Fermat numbers are of the form.

$$F_n = 2^{2^n} + 1, n \geq 0$$

$$F_0 = 3, F_1 = 5, F_2 = 17, F_3 = 257, F_4 = 65537$$

All these numbers are prime. Prove that Fermat number F_5 is composite.

Sol. Let $a = 2^7$ and $b = 5$

$$1 + ab = 1 + 2^7 \times 5 = 641$$

$$1 + ab - b^4 = 1 + (a - b^3)b$$

$$= 1 + 3b = 16 = 2^4$$

Now,

$$F_5 = 2^{2^5} + 1 = 2^{32} + 1$$

$$= 2^4 2^{28} + 1 = 2^4 a^4 + 1$$

$$= (1 + ab - b^4)a^4 + 1$$

$$= (1 + ab)a^4 + (1 - a^4 b^4)$$

$$= (1 + ab)a^4 + (1 - ab)(1 + ab)(1 + a^2 b^2)$$

$$= (1 + ab)[a^4 + (1 - ab)(1 + a^2 b^2)]$$

Thus, F_5 is composite,

$$1 + ab = 641$$

Hence, $641 | F_5$

Exercise

1. Obtain all primitive Pythagorean triples x, y, z in which one of x, y, z is 12.

2. 3, 4, 5 is a primitive Pythagorean triple involving consecutive positive integers. Find all such primitive Pythagorean triples.

3. There exist infinitely many Pythagoreans triples x, y, z whose even member x is a perfect square. Prove.

4. 4104 is a Ramanujan number. Verify.

5. 370 is a narcissistic number. Verify.

6. Find all 3-digit narcissistic numbers.

7. Number of narcissistic numbers is finite. Prove.

8. Verify whether 18 is a happy number or not.

9. Let R_n denote repunit courting of n consecutive 1's. If $d \mid R_m$ and $d \mid R_n$, then $d \mid R_{m+n}$. Prove.

10. If $\gcd(m, n) = 1$, then $\gcd(R_m, R_n) = 1$. Prove.

11. If n is a triangular number, then $9n + 1$, $25n + 3$ and $49n + 6$ are all triangular numbers. Prove.

12. Let t_n denote n^{th} triangular number. Then $t_1 + t_2 + \ldots + t_n = \dfrac{n(n+1)(n+2)}{6}$, $n \geq 1$. Prove.

13. Prove that the square of any odd multiple of 3 is the difference of two triangular numbers.

14. Find two triangular numbers whose sum and difference are also triangular numbers.

15. If triangular number t_n is a perfect square, then $t_{4n(n+1)}$ is also a square. Prove.

16. For $n = 1, 2, 3, 4, 5$, verify that $5u_n^2 + 4(-1)^n$ is a perfect square. u_n is the nth Fibonacci number. Verify.

17. If $3 \mid u_n$, then $9 \mid (u_{n+1}^3 - u_{n-1}^3)$. u_n is the nth Fibonacci number. Prove.

18. $u_{n+3} \equiv u_n \pmod 2$. Prove.

And thus establish that u_3, u_6, u_9, ... are all even integers. u_n is the nth Fibonacci number.

19. $u_{n+5} \equiv 3u_n \pmod 5$. Prove.

And thus establish that u_5, u_{10}, u_{15}, ... are all divisible by 5. u_n is the nth Fibonacci number.

20. Sum of squares of first n Fibonacci numbers is given by $u_1^2 + u_2^2 + \ldots + u_n^2 = u_n u_{n+1}$. Prove. u_n is the nth Fibonacci number.

21. $\sigma(n)$ (Sum of divisors of n) is an odd integer if and only if n is a perfect square or twice a perfect square. Prove.

22. If n is a square-free integer, then $\tau(n) = 2^r$, where r is the number of prime divisors of n. Prove.

23. If $n > 1$ is a composite number, then $\sigma(n) > n + \sqrt{n}$. Prove.

24. A perfect square cannot be a perfect number. Prove.

25. The product of two odd primes is never a perfect number. Prove.

26. An even perfect number always ends in the digits 6 or 28. Prove.

27. If n $(n > 6)$ is an even perfect number, then the sum of the digits of n is congruent to 1 modulo 9. Prove.

28. If n is a perfect number, then $\sum_{d|n} \frac{1}{d} = 2$. Prove.

29. Prove that no proper divisors of a perfect number can be perfect.

30. There are infinitely many deficient numbers. Prove.

31. There are infinitely many abundant numbers. Prove.

32. $17296 = 2^4 \times 23 \times 47$

$18416 = 2^4 \times 1151$

Verify that 17296 and 18416 are amicable numbers.

33. A prime number cannot be one of an amicable pair. Prove.

34. If m and n are an amicable pair with $m > n$, then m is a deficient number. Prove.

35. If m and n are an amicable pair with m even and n odd, then n is a perfect square. Prove.

36. Mersenne number M_{29} is composite. Prove.

37. For $n \geq 2$, the last digit of the Fermat number $F_n = 2^{2^n} + 1$ is 7. Prove.

38. The Fermat number F_n is never a perfect square. Prove.

39. For $n > 0$, the Fermat number F_n is never a triangular number. Prove.

40. For any Fermat number $F_n = 2^{2^n} + 1$, $n > 0$, prove that $F_n \equiv 5$ or $8 \pmod 9$ according as n is odd or even.

Answers

1. Two such primitive Pythagorean triple— (5, 12, 13) and (12, 35, 37).

2. 3, 4, 5 is the only such primitive Pythagorean triple

6. 153, 370, 371 and 407

8. 18 is not a happy number.

14. 15 and 21 are two such triangular numbers. There are many such pairs of triangular numbers.

16

Key Concepts and Results of Number Theory

1. **The Division Algorithm :** a and b are integers, with $b > 0$. Then there exist unique integers d and r satisfying,

$$a = db + r \qquad 0 \leq r < b$$

d is called quotient and r is called remainder in the division of a by b.

2. **Well-ordering Principle :** Every non-empty set S of non-negative integers contains a least element.
3. If $a \mid b$ and $c \mid d$, then $ac \mid bd$ where, a, b, c, d are integers and $a \neq 0$, $c \neq 0$.
4. If $a \mid b$ and $b \mid c$, then $a \mid c$ where, a, b, c are integers and $a \neq 0$, $b \neq 0$.
5. $a \mid b$ and $b \mid a$ if and only if $a = \pm b$ where a, b are integers.
6. If $a \mid b$ and $b \neq 0$ then $|a| \leq |b|$ where a, b are integers.
7. If $a \mid b$ and $a \mid c$, then $a \mid (bx + cy)$ for arbitrary integers x and y. a, b, c are integers.
8. An integer is divisible by 2 if and only if its unit digit is divisible by 2.
9. An integer is divisible by 4 if and only if the number formed by the last two digits of the integer is divisible by 4.
10. An integer is divisible by 8 if and only if the number formed by the last three digits of the integer is divisible by 8.
11. An integer is divisible by 16 if and only if the number formed by the last four digits of the integer is divisible by 16.
12. An integer is divisible by 5 if and only if its unit digit is divisible by 5 *i.e.*, the unit digit is 0 or 5.

13. An integer is divisible by 3 if and only if the sum of digits of the integer is divisible by 3.
14. An integer is divisible by 9 if and only if the sum of digits of the integer is divisible by 9.
15. An integer is divisible by 11 if and only if the difference of sums of alternate digits of the integer is divisible by 11.
16. Any integer can be written in the form or $2k$ of $2k+1$.
17. Any integer is of one of the forms $3k$, $3k+1$ or $3k+2$.
18. The square of an integer always of the form $3k$ or $3k+1$.
19. The square of an integer is always of the form $4k$ or $4k+1$.
20. The square of an integer always has one of the forms $8k$, $8k+1$ or $8k+4$.
21. $4 \nmid n^2+2$ for any integer n.
22. If n is an odd integer, n^2-1 is divisible by 8.
23. The product of any three consecutive integers is divisible by 6.
24. The product of any four consecutive integers is divisible by 24.
25. If integers p and q are odd, then p^2+q^2 is even but not divisible by 4.
26. For any integer a, one of the integers a, $a+2$, $a+4$ is divisible by 3.
27. The sum of the squares of two odd integers cannot be a perfect square.
28. The sum of squares of three consecutive integers cannot be a perfect square.
29. For integer $n>3$, n, $n+2$ and $n+4$ cannot be all prime.
30. The sum of squares of five consecutive integers is not a square.
31. Any integer has an even number of factors except when it is a perfect square.
32. a and b are integers, not both zero. For a positive integer d, $d=\gcd(a, b)$ if and only if

    (a) $d \mid a$ and $d \mid b$, and

    (b) whenever $c \mid a$ and $c \mid b$, then $c \mid d$

    (gcd (a, b) denotes the greatest common divisor of a and b.)
33. If $a=qb+r$, then gcd $(a, b)=$ gcd (b, r). a, b, q, r are integers. $b \neq 0$.
34. If $n>0$, then gcd $(na, nb)=n$ [gcd (a, b)].
35. Given integers a and b (both a and b are not zero), there exist integers x and y such that gcd $(a, b)=ax+by$.
36. If a and b are given integers (a and b are not both zero), then the set $T=\{ax+by \mid x, y$ are integers$\}$ is precisely the set of all multiples of $d=$ gcd (a, b).

37. a and b are integers (a and b are not both zero). Then a and b are relatively prime if and only if there exist integers x and y such that $ax + by = 1$.

38. If gcd $(a, b) = d$, then gcd $\left(\frac{a}{d}, \frac{b}{d}\right) = 1$.

39. If $a \mid c$ and $b \mid c$ with gcd $(a, b) = 1$, then $ab \mid c$.

40. **Euclid's lemma :** If $a \mid bc$ with gcd $(a, b) = 1$, then $a \mid c$.

41. For positive integers a and b, [gcd (a, b)] [lcm (a, b)] $= ab$.

42. For positive integers a and b, lcm $(a, b) = ab$ if and only if gcd $(a, b) = 1$.

43. For any integer $N = 10X + Y$, N is divisible by 7 if and only if $X + 5Y$ is divisible by 7.

44. The cube of any integer has one of the forms $9n$, $9n + 1$ or $9n + 8$.

45. gcd $(a, a+1) = 1$ for any integer a.

46. gcd $(a, b) = 1$ and gcd $(a, c) = 1$ for integers a, b, c. Then gcd $(a, bc) = 1$.

47. For integers a, b if gcd $(a, b) = 1$, then gcd $(a^2, b^2) = 1$.

48. Given integers, $a, b, k, k > 0$, $lcm(ka, kb) = k\,[lcm(a, b)]$.

49. For a prime number p and integer a, if $p \mid a^2$, then $p^2 \mid a^2$.

50. An equation in one or more unknown that is to be solved in the integers is called Diophantine equation. $ax + by = c$ is a linear Diophantine equation in unknowns x and y. a, b, c are given integers and a, b are not both zero. The given equation has a solution if and only if $d \mid c$ where $d =$ gcd (a, b). If x_0, y_0 is any particular solution of this equation then all other solutions are given by

$$x = x_0 + \left(\frac{b}{d}\right) t$$

$$y = y_0 - \left(\frac{a}{d}\right) t$$

where t is an arbitrary integer.

51. Let a, b, c be positive integers. There is no solution of $ax + by = c$ in positive integers if $a + b > c$.

52. a and b are relatively prime positive integers. Then, the Diophantine equation $ax - by = c$ has infinitely many positive solutions.

53. If p is a prime and $p \mid a_1 a_2 \ldots a_n$ then $p \mid a_k$ for some k, where $1 \le k \le n$.

54. If $p, q_1, q_2, \ldots, q_n$ are all prime and $p \mid q_1, q_2, \ldots, q_n$, then $p = q_k$ for some k, where $1 \le k \le n$.

55. **Fundamental Theorem of Arithmetic :** Every positive integer $n > 1$ is either a prime or a product of primes. If we ignore the sequence in which the factors occur, the representation as a product of primes is unique.
56. For testing primality of a given positive integer $a > 1$, it is sufficient to verify divisibility of a by all primes not exceeding $\sqrt{a}$.
57. Consider integers 11, 111, 1111, 11111, ... These integers, written as strings of 1's, are called repunit.
58. Any prime number (> 3) is always of the form $6n + 1$ or $6n + 5$. Thus, any prime number (> 3) is always of the form $6n + 1$ or $6n - 1$.
59. Each integer of the form $3n + 2$ has a prime factor of this form.
60. If $p > 3$ is a prime number then $p^2 + 2$ is composite.
61. p is a prime. $p | a^n$. Then $p^n | a^n$.
62. There is an infinite number of primes.
63. Let $P^{\#}$ be the product of all primes less than or equal to prime number p. Then the number of the form $p^{\#} + 1$ is called Euclidean number.
64. Arbitrarily large gap occurs between consecutive primes.
65. A pair of odd integers p and $p + 2$ that are both primes is called twin primes.
66. There is an infinite number of primes of then form $4n + 3$.
67. If all the n ($n > 2$) terms of the Arithmetic progression $p, p + d, p + 2d, \ldots,$ $p + (n - 1)d$ are prime numbers, then the common difference d is divisible by every prime $q < n$.
68. If p and $p^2 + 2$ are primes, then $p^3 + 2$ is also a prime.
69. If $n > 4$ is composite, then n divides $(n - 1)!$.
70. Every integer of the form $n^4 + 4$ with $n > 1$, is composite.
71. Every integer $n > 11$ can be written as the sum of two composite numbers.
72. Let $N = p_1^{n_1} p_2^{n_2} \ldots P_r^{n_r}$, where $p_1, p_2, .., p_r$ are distinct prime numbers and $n_1, n_2, \ldots, n_r > 1$. N is a square if and only if all $n_1, n_2, \ldots, n_r$ are even integers.
73. An integer is said to be square-free if it is not divisible by the square of any integer greater than 1. An integer $n > 1$ is square-free if and only if n can be factored into a product of distinct primes. Further, every integer $n > 1$ is the product of a square-free integer and a perfect square.
74. If gcd $(a, b) = c$ then gcd $(a^2, b^2) = c^2$.
75. a and b are positive integers. gcd $(a, b) = 1$ and ab is a perfect square. Then, a and b are perfect squares.

76. An odd integer $n > 1$ is a prime if and only if it is not expressible as a sum of three or more consecutive positive integers.

77. Given that $p | n$ for all primes $p \leq \sqrt[3]{n}$, then $n > 1$ is either a prime or the product of two primes.

78. $\sqrt{p}$ is irrational for any prime p.

79. If $n > 2$ then there exists a prime p satisfying $n < p < n!$.

80. For $n > 1$, every prime divisor of $n! + 1$ is an odd integer that is greater than n.

81. Repunit R_n denotes a string of n 1's. For repunits R_n, the following results are true. (m, n are positive integers.)
   (i) If $n | m$, then $R_n | R_m$
   (ii) If $q | R_n$ and $q | R_m$ then $q | R_{n+m}$
   (iii) If gcd $(n, m) = 1$, then gcd $(R_n, R_m) = 1$

82. For $n > 1$, $n!$ is never a perfect square.

83. Given a positive integer n, two integers a and b are said to be congruent modulo n, if n divides $a - b$ (i.e., $a - b = kn$ for some integer k).

84. Suppose $n > 1$ is a fixed integer. a, b and c are arbitrary integers. The following properties hold true.
   (i) $a \equiv a \pmod{n}$.
   (ii) If $a \equiv b \pmod{n}$, then $b \equiv a \pmod{n}$.
   (iii) If $a \equiv b \pmod{n}$ and $b \equiv c \pmod{n}$ then $a \equiv c \pmod{n}$.
   (iv) If $a \equiv b \pmod{n}$ and $c \equiv d \pmod{n}$ then $a + c \equiv b + d \pmod{n}$.
   (v) If $a \equiv b \pmod{n}$ and $c \equiv d \pmod{n}$ then $ac \equiv bd \pmod{n}$.
   (vi) If $a \equiv b \pmod{n}$ then $a + c \equiv b + c \pmod{n}$.
   (vii) If $a \equiv b \pmod{n}$ then $ac \equiv bc \pmod{n}$.
   (viii) If $a \equiv b \pmod{n}$ then $a^x \equiv b^x \pmod{n}$ for any positive integer x.

85. In general, a collection of n integers $a_1, a_2, \ldots, a_n$ is said to from a complete set of residues or a complete system of residues modulo n if $a_1, a_2, \ldots, a_n$ are congruent to $0, 1, 2, \ldots, n-1$ modulo n in some order.

86. For arbitrary integers a and b, $a \equiv b \pmod{n}$ if and only if a and b leave same non-negative remainder when divided by n.

87. If $ca \equiv cb \pmod{n}$, then $a \equiv b\left(\bmod \frac{n}{d}\right)$, where $d = \gcd(c, n)$.

88. If $ca \equiv cb \pmod{p}$ and $p \nmid c$, where p is a prime number, then $a \equiv b \pmod{p}$.

89. An equation of the form $ax \equiv b \pmod{n}$ is called a linear congruence. If for some integer x_0, $ax_0 \equiv b \pmod{n}$, then x_0 is a solution of the given linear congruence.

90. The linear congruence $ax \equiv b \pmod{n}$ has a solution if and only if $d \mid b$, where $d = \gcd(a, n)$. If $d \mid b$, then it has d mutually incongruent solutions modulo n.
91. If $\gcd(a, n) = 1$, then the linear congruence $ax \equiv b \pmod{n}$ has a unique solution modulo n. This solution is called the (multiplicative) inverse of a modulo n.
92. If a is an odd integer, then $a^2 \equiv 1 \pmod{8}$.
93. For any integer a, $a^4 = 0$ or $1 \pmod{5}$.
94. If the integer a is not divisible by 2 or 3, then $a^2 \equiv 1 \pmod{24}$.
95. If $a_1, a_2, .., a_n$ is a complete set of residues modulo n and $\gcd(a, n) = 1$, then $aa_1, aa_2, .., aa_n$ is also a complete set of residues modulo n.
96. Any n consecutive integers form a complete set of residues modulo n.
97. The product of any set of n consecutive integers is divisible by n.
98. $a \equiv b \pmod{n_1}$ and $a \equiv b \pmod{n_2}$. Then $a \equiv b \pmod{n}$ where $n = lcm(n_1, n_2)$.
99. The unit digit of any perfect square is 0, 1, 4, 5, 6 or 9.
100. The unit digit of a^4 for any integer a is 0, 1, 5 or 6.
101. For a given integer N, let M be the integer formed by reversing the order of the digits of N. Then $N - M$ is divisible by 9.
102. 19 is not a divisor of $n^2 + 1$ for any integer n.
103. $\frac{n^5}{5} + \frac{n^2}{3} + \frac{7}{15}n$ is an integer for every integer n.
104. Any one of the integers 0, 1, 2, 3, 4, 5, 6, 7, 8, 9 can occur as the unit digit of a^3 (for integer a).
105. 2^n divides an integer N if and only if 2^n divides the number made up of the last n digits of N.
106. R_n denotes the repunit consisting of n consecutive 1's. $9 \mid R_n$ if and only if $9 \mid n$.
107. $11 \mid R_n$ if and only if n is even.
108. **Fermat's Theorem :** Let p be a prime. Suppose that $p \nmid a$. Then $a^{p-1} \equiv 1 \pmod{p}$. for any integer a.
109. If p is a prime, then $a^p \equiv a \pmod{p}$ for any integer a.
110. If p and q are distinct primes with $a^p \equiv a \pmod{q}$ and $a^q \equiv a \pmod{p}$, then $a^{pq} \equiv a \pmod{pq}$
111. A composite integer n is called pseudoprime if $n \mid (2^n - 2)$. 341 is the smallest pseudoprime. In general, a composite integer n for which $a^n \equiv a \pmod{n}$ is called a pseudoprime to the base a. When $a = 2$, n is simply said to be a pseudoprime. There are infinitely many pseudoprimes to any given base. The

composite numbers that are pseudoprimes to every base a, that is, $a^n \equiv a \pmod{n}$, are called absolute "pseudoprimes" or "Carmichael numbers".

112. If n is an odd pseudoprime, then $M_n = 2^n - 1$ is also a pseudoprime.

113. **Wilson's theorem :** If p is a prime, then $(p-1)! \equiv -1 \pmod{p}$.

114. Converse of Wilson's Theorem is also true. If $(n-1)! \equiv -1 \pmod{n}$, then n is a prime number.

115. A congruence of the form $ax^2 + bx + c = 0 \pmod{n}$, with $a \neq 0 \pmod{n}$ is called a quadratic congruence.

116. The quadratic congruence $x^2 + 1 \equiv 0 \pmod{p}$, where p is an odd prime, has a solution if and only if $p \equiv 1 \pmod{4}$.

117. $(p-1)! + 1$ is divisible by p (By Wilson's theorem). Hence, $(p-1)! + 1$ is a composite number. As there are infinitely many primes, there are infinitely many composite numbers of the form $n! + 1$.

118. **Euler's Phi-function :** For $n \geq 1$, $\phi(n)$ denotes the numbers of positive integers not exceeding n that are relatively prime to n.

119. For $n > 1$, $\phi(n) = n - 1$ if and only if n is prime.

120. If p is a prime and $n > 0$, then $\phi(p^n) = p^n - p^{n-1} = p^n\left(1 - \frac{1}{p}\right)$.

121. Given integers a, b, c, gcd $(a, bc) = 1$ if and only if gcd $(a, b) = 1$ and gcd $(a, c) = 1$

122. The function ϕ is a multiplication function.

123. If the integer $n > 1$ has the prime factorization $n = p_1^{k_1} p_2^{k_2} \ldots p_r^{k_r}$, then

$$\phi(n) = (p_1^{k_1} - p_1^{k_1-1})(p_2^{k_2} - p_2^{k_2-1})\ldots(p_r^{k_r} - p_r^{k_r-1})$$
$$= n\left(1 - \frac{1}{p_1}\right)\left(1 - \frac{1}{p_2}\right)\ldots\left(1 - \frac{1}{p_r}\right)$$

124. For $n > 2$, $\phi(n)$ is an even integer.

125. Let $n > 1$ and gcd $(a, n) = 1$. If $a_1, a_2, \ldots, a_{\phi(n)}$ are the positive integers less than n and relatively prime to n, then $aa_1, aa_2, \ldots, aa_{\phi(n)}$ are congruent modulo n to $a_1, a_2, \ldots, a_{\phi(n)}$ is some order.

126. **Euler's Theorem :** If $n \geq 1$ and gcd $(a, n) = 1$ then $a^{\phi(n)} \equiv 1 \pmod{n}$.

127. For any integer a, a^5 and a have the same unit digit.

128. $7 \mid a$. Then either $a^3 + 1$ or $a^3 - 1$ is divisible by 7.

129. Let p be a prime and gcd $(a, p) = 1$. Then $n \equiv a^{p-2} b \pmod{p}$ is a solution of the linear congruence $ax = b \pmod{p}$.

130. a and b are integers not divisible by the prime p. If $a^p \equiv b^p$ (mod p), then $a \equiv b$ (mod p).
131. If p is an odd prime, then $1^p + 2^p + 3^p + .. + (p-1)^p \equiv 0 \pmod p$
132. Let p and q be distinct odd primes such that $(p-1) \mid (q-1)$. If gcd $(a, pq) = 1$, then $a^{q-1} \equiv 1 \pmod{pq}$.
133. Let $M_p = 2^p - 1$ where p is a prime. If M_p is composite, then M_p is a pseudoprime.
134. If n is an odd integer, then $\phi(2n) = \phi(n)$.
135. If n is an even integer, then $\phi(2n) = 2\phi(n)$.
136. $\phi(3n) = 3\phi(n)$ if and only if $3 \mid n$.
137. The equation $\phi(n) = \phi(n+2)$ is satisfied by $n = 2(2p-1)$ whenever p and $2p-1$ are both odd primes.
138. There are infinitely many integers n for which $\phi(n)$ is a perfect square.
139. For any prime p, if $a^p \equiv b^p$ (mod p), then $a^p \equiv b^p$ (mod p^2).
140. $\frac{1}{2}\sqrt{n} \le \phi(n) \le n$ for all $n \ge 1$.
141. For a given integer n, the equation $\phi(x) = n$ has only a finite number of solutions.
142. Let $n = 2p$ where p is an odd prime. Then $a^{n-1} \equiv a$ (mod n) for any a.
143. An absolute pseudoprime or Carmichael number is square-free.
144. Let n be a composite square-free integer. Suppose $n = p_1\ p_2 \ldots p_r$, where the p_i's are distinct primes. If $p_i - 1 \mid n-1$ for $i = 1, 2, .., r$, then n is an absolute psedoprime or Carmichael number.
145. If p is an odd prime, then $1^{p-1} + 2^{p-1} + 3^{p-1} + \ldots + (p-1)^{p-1} \equiv -1 \pmod p$.
146. If p and q are distinct primes, then $p^{q-1} + q^{p-1} \equiv 1 \pmod{pq}$.
147. An integer $n > 1$ is prime if and only if $(n-2)! = 1$ (mod n).
148. Given a prime number p, $(p-1)! \equiv p-1 \pmod{1+2+3+\ldots+(p-1)}$.
149. $\phi(3n) = 2\phi(n)$ if and only if $3 \nmid n$.
150. $\phi(n) = \frac{n}{2}$ if and only if $n = 2^k$ for some $k \ge 1$.
151. If n has r distinct prime divisors, then $\phi(n) \ge \frac{n}{2^r}$.
152. If n has r distinct odd prime divisors, then $\phi(n)$ is divisible by 2^r.
153. If p is prime, then $\phi(n) = 2p$ has a solution if and only if $2p+1$ is prime.

154. If $n > 1$ is a composite number, then $\phi(n) \leq n - \sqrt{n}$.
155. If n and $n+2$ are a pair of twin primes, then $\phi(n+2) = \phi(n) + 2$
156. If $\phi(n) \mid n-1$, then n is a square-free integer.
157. $m \mid n$. Then $\phi(m) \mid \phi(n)$.
158. There is no integer n for which $\phi(n) = \frac{n}{4}$.
159. m and n are relatively prime positive integers. Then $m^{\phi(mn)} + n^{\phi(mn)} \equiv 1$ (mod mn).
160. Let $f(n)$ = sum of the positive integers less then n and relatively prime to n. Then $f(m) = f(n)$ implies that $m = n$.
161. An absolute pseudo prime or Carmichael number is necessarily odd.
162. **Last two digits of a perfect square :**

Last digit of a perfect square	Corresponding last two digits
0	00
1	01, 21, 41, 61, 81
4	04, 24, 44, 64, 84
5	25
6	16, 36, 56, 76, 96
9	09, 29, 49, 69, 89

163. There is no perfect square between any two consecutive perfect squares.
164. **Properties of Cubes :** For any positive integer a.

    (i) $a^3 \equiv 0, 1, 6 \pmod 7$

    (ii) $a^3 \equiv 0, 1, 8 \pmod 9$

165. M = Sum of two squares, say $M = p^2 + q^2$

    N = Sum of two squares, say $N = x^2 + y^2$

    Then, MN can also be expressed as a sum of two squares.
166. Product of two consecutive natural numbers cannot be a perfect square.
167. Product of three consecutive natural numbers cannot be a perfect square.
168. Product of four consecutive natural numbers cannot be a perfect square.
169. The sum of digits of a perfect square cannot be 15.
170. For any perfect square number n, the number of its tail zeros (i.e. the digit 0's on its right end) must be even.

171. An odd perfect square greater than 9 must have an even tens digit (second last digit).

172. Any positive integer $n \geq 10$ cannot be a perfect square number if it is formed by the same digit.

173. Every natural number can be expressed as the sum of squares of four integers. This is called Lagrange's four-square theorem.

174. For any integer k, the numbers of the forms $3k+2$, $4k+2$, $4k+3$, $5k+2$, $5k+3$, $8k \pm 2$, $8k \pm 3$, $8k \pm 7$ cannot be perfect squares.

175. The sum of 1 and the product of any four consecutive integers is a perfect square.

176. The technique of proof by mathematical induction consists of two parts.

For any statement S, we need to prove that

(a) S is true for some integer $n = k_0$.

(b) If S is true for $n = k$, it is true for $n = k+1$.

(a) is called the basis for the induction and (b) is called the induction step.

Please note that for proving any statement, we need to prove both (a) and (b).

If either of the conditions (a) or (b) fail, then the result is not established.

177. **Archimedean property :** If a and b are any positive integers, then there exists a positive integer n such that $na \geq b$.

178. Many times, we use a variant of the induction principle, known as the second principle of finite induction.

Second principle of finite induction : Let S be a set of positive integers with the following properties :

(a) The integer m belongs to S.

(b) If n is a positive integer such that 1, 2, ..., n belong to S, then $n+1$ must also be in S.

Then S is the set of all positive integers $\geq m$.

179. The pigeonhole principle is stated as under.

When $m+1$ pigeons enter m pigeonholes, there must be at least one hole having more than 1 pigeon. (m is a positive integer.)

We can also state it as under.

When $m+1$ pigeons enter n pigeonholes, there must be one hole having at least $\left[\frac{m}{n}\right]+1$ pigeons.

180. For any positive integer n and any integer k satisfying $0 \leq k \leq n$, binomial coefficient $\binom{n}{k}$ is defined as $\binom{n}{k} = \frac{n!}{k!(n-k)!}$

181. The expansion of $(a+b)^n$ can be written as

$$(a+b)^n = \binom{n}{0} a^n + \binom{n}{1} a^{n-1}b + \binom{n}{2} a^{n-2}b^2 + \ldots + \binom{n}{n-1} ab^{n-1} + \binom{n}{n} b^n$$

or, $$(a+b)^n = \sum_{k=0}^{n} \binom{n}{k} a^{n-k} b^k$$

This is known as the binomial theorem.

182. The coefficients in the expansion of $(a+b)^n$ are $\binom{n}{0}, \binom{n}{1}, \binom{n}{2}, \ldots, \binom{n}{n}$ in order.

183. $\binom{n}{k} + \binom{n}{k-1} = \binom{n+1}{k} \qquad (1 \le k \le n)$

184. For a real number x, $[x]$ denotes the largest integer less than or equal to x. $[x]$ is the unique integer that satisfies following condition.

$$x-1 < [x] \le x$$

185. Every real number x can be written in the form $x = [x] + \{x\}$ where $[x]$ is the greatest integer function and $0 \le \{x\} < 1$. $\{x\}$ is called fractional part of x.

186. If n is a positive integer and p is a prime, then the exponent of the highest power of p that divides $n!$ is

$$\sum_{K=1}^{\infty} \left[\frac{n}{p^k}\right]$$

187. $[a+b] \ge [a] + [b]$ where a and b are arbitrary real numbers.

188. n and r are positive integers. $1 \le r \le n$. The binomial coefficient $\binom{n}{r} = \dfrac{n!}{r!(n-r)!}$ is an integer.

189. For real number x and integer n, $[x+n] = [x] + n$.

190. For any real number x, $[x] + [-x] = \begin{cases} 0, & \text{if } x \text{ is an integer} \\ -1, & \text{if } x \text{ is not an integer} \end{cases}$

191. For positive real numbers x and y, $[x][y] \le [xy]$.

192. For an integer $n \ge 0$, $\left[\frac{n}{2}\right] - \left[-\frac{n}{2}\right] = n$.

193. $\dfrac{(2n)!}{(n!)^2}$ is an even integer for any positive integer n.

194. Let n be a natural number. Then $\left[\frac{n}{1}\right] + \left[\frac{n}{2}\right] + \left[\frac{n}{3}\right] + \ldots \left[\frac{n}{n}\right] + [\sqrt{n}]$ is even.

195. $\{x\} + \{y\} = 1$ if and only if x and y both are non-integers and $x+y$ is an integer.

196. For any real number x and any positive integer n,

$$[x]+\left[x+\frac{1}{n}\right]+\ldots+\left[x+\frac{n-1}{n}\right]=[nx]$$

197. Any rational number can be represented as $\frac{p}{q}$ where p and q are integers and $q \neq 0$. We can represent this number in the form of terminating decimal or non-terminating decimal by repetitive division. If we obtain 0 after certain numbers of divisions, we get a terminating decimal. Division by q can lead to 0 remainder only if q is of the form $2^m 5^n$ where m, n are integers and $m, n \geq 0$.

The decimal form of a rational number is always a terminating decimal or non-terminating recurring decimal. In other words, a terminating decimal and non-terminating recurring decimal represent rational numbers.

198. Every number on number line represents either a rational number or an irrational number. Any number has three possible representations in decimal form.

(a) Terminating decimal

(b) Non-terminating recurring decimal

(c) Non-terminating non-recurring decimal

Terminating decimal and non-terminating recurring decimal represent a rational number whereas non-terminating non-recurring decimal represents an irrational number.

199. For rational numbers a and b, $\frac{a+b}{2}$ is a rational number between a and b.

200. a $(a \neq 0)$ is rational number whereas b is an irrational number. Then $a + b$ and ab are irrational numbers.

201. For a positive integer n, there does not exist any integer p such that $p^2 = n$. Then $\sqrt{n}$ is an irrational number.

202. Let a, b, n be integers such that $n = ab$. If $\sqrt{n} = \sqrt{ab}$ is an irrational number, then, $\sqrt{a} + \sqrt{b}$ is also irrational.

203. $x^2 + y^2 = z^2$

The set of integers satisfying this equation is called a Pythagorean triple. The triple is said to be a primitive pythagorean triple if $\gcd(x, y, z) = 1$.

204. If x, y, z is a primitive Pythagorean triple, then one of the integers x or y is even, while the other is odd.

205. There is no primitive Pythagorean triple x, y, z such that all of x, y, z are prime numbers.

206. There are primitive Pythagorean triple in which two of x, y, z are prime.

207. If $ab = c^n$ where gcd(a, b) = 1, the a and b are n^{th} powers. i.e. there exist positive integers a_1, b_1 for which $a = a_1^n$ and $b = b_1^n$.

208. For a primitive Pythagorean triple x, y, z, each pair of the integers x, y and z is relatively prime.

209. All the solutions of the Pythagorean equation $x^2 + y^2 = z^2$ satisfying the conditions gcd $(x, y, z) = 1$, $2 \mid x, x > 0, y > 0, z > 0$ are given by the formulas $x = 2st$, $y = s^2 - t^2$, $z = s^2 + t^2$ for integers $s > t > 0$ such that gcd(s, t) = 1 and $s \not\equiv t \pmod 2$.

210. Ramanujan numbers are the positive integers that can be expressed as a sum of cubes of two positive integers in two different ways. 1729 is the smallest Ramanujan number.

211. A specific number is a positive integer that is the product of three distinct prime numbers.

212. For a k-digit natural number $n = d_k\ d_{k-1} \ldots d_2 d_1$ ($d_1\ d_2, \ldots d_k$ are digits of n), n is called a narcissistic number if

$$n = d_k^k + d_{k-1}^k + .. + d_2^k + d_1^k$$

In other words, a k-digit number n is a narcissistic number if the sum of its digits raised to power k is equal to n.

213. All 1-digit numbers are narcissistic numbers. There are no 2-digit narcissistic numbers. There are only four 3-digit narcissistic numbers, 153, 370, 371 and 407.

214. A narcissistic number cannot have more than 60 digits. Thus, the number of narcissistic numbers is limited.

215. There exist only 88 narcissistic numbers. The largest of the narcissistic numbers consists of 39 digits.

216. A happy number is a number which eventually reaches 1 when replaced by the sum of the squares of its digits. First few happy numbers are 1, 7, 10, 13, 19, 23, 28, 31, 32, 44, 49 etc.

217. A triangular number is the sum of consecutive numbers beginning with 1.

218. The general rule of formulation of Fibonacci sequence is as under ;

$$u_1 = 1,\ u_2 = 1$$

$$u_n = u_{n-1} + u_{n-2} \qquad \text{for } n \geq 3$$

219. For the Fibonacci sequence, gcd $(u_n, u_{n+1}) = 1$ for every $n \geq 1$.

220. In general, for a positive integer n, $\tau(n)$ denotes the number of positive divisors of n and $\sigma(n)$ denotes the sum of these divisors.

221. $\tau(n) = 2$ if and only if n is a prime number.

222. $\sigma(n) = n + 1$ if and only if n is a prime number.

223. If $n = p_1^{k_1}\ p_2^{k_2} \ldots p_r^{k_r}$ is the prime factorization of $n > 1$, then the possible divisors of n are precisely these integers d of the form

$$d = p_1^{a_1}\ p_2^{a_2} \ldots p_r^{a_r} \text{ where } 0 \le a_i \le k_i \qquad (i = 1, 2, .., r)$$

224. If $n = p_1^{k_1}\ p_2^{k_2} \ldots p_r^{k_r}$ is the prime factorization of $n > 1$, then

(a) $\tau(n) = (k_1 + 1)\,(k_2 + 1)..(k_r + 1)$ and

(b) $\sigma(n) = \left(\dfrac{p_1^{k_1+1} - 1}{p_1 - 1}\right)\left(\dfrac{p_2^{k_2+1} - 1}{p_2 - 1}\right)\cdots\left(\dfrac{p_r^{k_r+1} - 1}{p_r - 1}\right)$

225. The functions τ and σ are both multiplicative functions.

226. If the sum of proper divisors of a number is greater than the given number, the number is called an abundant number.

227. If the sum of proper divisors of a number is less than the given number, the number is called a deficient number.

228. If the sum of proper divisors of a number is equal to the given number, the number is called a perfect number.

229. Suppose that n is a perfect number. By definition, $\sigma(n) - n = n$. Hence, $\sigma(n) = 2n$.

230. 6, 28, 496, 8128 and 33550336 are first five perfect numbers.

231. If $2^k - 1$ is a prime $(k > 1)$, then $n = 2^{(k-1)}\ (2^k - 1)$ is perfect and every even perfect number is of this form.

232. If $a^k - 1$ is a prime $(a > 0,\ k \ge 2)$, then $a = 2$ and k is also prime.

233. All numbers M_n of the form $M_n = 2^n - 1\ (n \ge 1)$ are called Mersenne numbers. The Mersenne numbers that happen to be prime are called mersenne primes.

234. For given two positive integers m and n, each integer is equal to the sum of all positive proper divisors of the other. Such pairs of integers are called amicable or friendly numbers.

235. Let m and n be amicable numbers. Then, by definition,

$$\sigma(m) - m = n$$

and

$$\sigma(n) - n = m$$

or,

$$\sigma(m) = \sigma(n) = m + n$$

236. All numbers F_n of the form $F_n = 2^{2^n} + 1,\ n \ge 0$ are called Fermat numbers.

237. If $x,\ y,\ z$ is a primitive Pythagorean triple then exactly one of the integers x or y is divisible by 3.

238. A Pythagorean triangle is defined to be a right triangle whose sides are of integral length. The radius of the inscribed circle of a Pythagorean triangle is always an integer.

239. A number is triangular if and only if it is of the form $\frac{n(n+1)}{2}$ for some integer $n \geq 1$.

240. The sum of any two consecutive triangular numbers is a perfect square.

241. The difference between the squares of two consecutive triangular numbers is always a cube.

242. No power of a prime can be a perfect number.

243. Every even perfect number is a triangular number.

244. Unit digit of every even perfect number is either 6 or 8.

245. If m and n are amicable numbers $(m \neq n)$ then none of m and n are perfect numbers.

246. There exist infinitely many Pythagoreans triples x, y, z whose even member x is a perfect square.

247. $\sigma(n)$ (Sum of divisors of n) is an odd integer if and only if n is a perfect square or twice a perfect square.

248. A perfect square cannot be a perfect number.

249. The product of two odd primes is never a perfect number.

250. No proper divisors of a perfect number can be perfect.

251. There are infinitely many deficient numbers.

252. There are infinitely many abundant numbers.

253. A prime number cannot be one of an amicable pair.

254. If m and n are an amicable pair with $m > n$, then m is a deficient number.

255. If m and n are an amicable pair with m even and n odd, then n is a perfect square.

256. The Fermat number F_n is never a perfect square.

257. For $n > 0$, the Fermat number F_n is never a triangular number.

258. Consider the equation $x^n + y^n = z^n$ where x, y, z and n are positive integers. This equation has no solution for $n > 2$. This is called Fermat's last theorem.

17
Olympaid Problems

1. Show that the equation $a^3 + (a+1)^3 + (a+2)^3 + (a+3)^3 + (a+4)^3 + (a+5)^3 + (a+6)^3 = b^4 + (b+1)^4$ has no solutions in integers a, b. **[RMO 2017]**

Sol. Since $a, a+1, a+2, \ldots, a+6$ are seven consecutive integers, they are congruent to 0, 1, 2, 3, 4, 5, 6 modulo 7 in some order.

Hence, $a^3 + (a+1)^3 + (a+2)^3 + (a+3)^3 + (a+4)^3 + (a+5)^3 + (a+6)^3$

$$\equiv 0^3 + 1^3 + 2^3 + \ldots + 6^3 \pmod 7$$

$$\equiv 0 + 1 + 1 + 6 + 1 + 6 + 6 \pmod 7$$

$$\equiv 0 \pmod 7$$

Thus, LHS is divisible by 7.

$$b^4 + (b+1)^4$$

$$b \equiv 0, 1, 2, 3, 4, 5 \text{ or } 6 \pmod 7$$

$$\therefore \quad b^2 \equiv 0, 1, 2, 4 \pmod 7$$

$$\therefore \quad b^4 \equiv 0, 1, 2, 4 \pmod 7$$

$$\therefore \quad (b+1)^4 \equiv 0, 1, 2, 4 \pmod 7$$

b and $b+1$ together cannot be congruent to 0 modulo 7.

$$\therefore \quad b^4 + (b+1)^4 \not\equiv 0 \pmod 7$$

Thus, RHS is not divisible by 7.

Therefore, LHS is divisible by 7 whereas RHS is not divisible by 7.

Hence, the given equation has no solution in integers.

2. Show that there is a positive integer n such that $n!$ when written in decimal notation ends with exactly 1993 zeros. **[INMO 1993]**

Sol. For any prime k and positive integer n, the highest power of k which divides n is equal to

$$\left[\frac{n}{k}\right]+\left[\frac{n}{k^2}\right]+\left[\frac{n}{k^3}\right]+\ldots$$

Therefore, the number of zeros with which n ends when written in decimal representation equals the highest power of 5 which divides n.

Hence, we have to find n such that the highest power of 5 that divides n is equal to 1993.

For n, the highest power of 5 that divides n

$$=\left[\frac{n}{5}\right]+\left[\frac{n}{5^2}\right]+\ldots$$

$$\leq \frac{n}{5}+\frac{n}{5^2}+\ldots$$

$$=\frac{n}{5}\times\frac{5}{4}=\frac{n}{4}$$

We have $\frac{n}{4}\geq 1993$

$\therefore \quad n\geq 7972$

The highest power of 5 that divides $7975! = 1991$

$\therefore$ The highest power of 5 that divides $7985! = 1993$

Hence, 7985 is one of the solutions.

Please note that 7986, 7987, 7988 and 7989 are also solutions.

3. Find the number of zeros at the end of

(i) $\left(\frac{10^3-1}{9}\right)!$ (ii) $(5^{20}-1)!$

(iii) $\sum_{n=1}^{20}(5n)!$ (iv) Product of 1, 2, 3, …, 1994

[RMO 1994 Delhi]

Sol. (i) $\left(\frac{10^3-1}{9}\right)! = 111!$

$\therefore$ Number of zeroes at the end of 111 !

$$=\left[\frac{111}{5}\right]+\left[\frac{111}{5^2}\right]$$

$$=22+4=26$$

(ii) $(5^{20}-1)!$

$\therefore$ Number of zeroes at the end

$$=\left[\frac{5^{20}-1}{5}\right]+\left[\frac{5^{20}-1}{5^2}\right]+\ldots+\left[\frac{5^{20}-1}{5^{19}}\right]$$

$$=(5^{19}-1)+(5^{18}-1)+\ldots+(5-1)$$

$$=5\left(\frac{5^{19}-1}{5-1}\right)-19=\frac{5^{20}-5}{4}-19$$

(iii) $\sum_{n=1}^{20}(5n)!$

For $(5r)!$

$$1\le r\le 20$$

Highest power of 5 that divides $(5r)!$

$$=\left[\frac{5r}{5}\right]+\left[\frac{5r}{5^2}\right]=r+\left[\frac{r}{5}\right]$$

$$=\begin{cases} r, & 1\le r<5 \\ r+1, & 5\le r<10 \\ r+2, & 10\le r<15 \\ r+3, & 15\le r<20 \\ r+4, & r=20 \end{cases}$$

Hence, number of zeroes at the end of $\sum_{n=1}^{20}(5n)!$

$$=\sum_{r=1}^{4}r+\sum_{r=5}^{9}(r+1)+\sum_{r=10}^{14}(r+2)+\sum_{r=15}^{19}(r+3)+\sum_{r=20}^{20}(r+4)$$

$$=\sum_{r=1}^{20}r+5+2\times 5+3\times 5+4$$

$$=\frac{20\times 21}{2}+34$$

$$=210+34=244$$

(iv) Number of zeroes at the end of 1994!

$$=\left[\frac{1994}{5}\right]+\left[\frac{1994}{5^2}\right]+\left[\frac{1994}{5^3}\right]+\left[\frac{1994}{5^4}\right]$$

$$=398+79+15+3=495$$

4. Consider an $n \times n$ array of numbers

$$\begin{pmatrix} a_{11} & a_{12} & a_{13} & \cdots & a_{1n} \\ a_{21} & a_{22} & a_{23} & \cdots & a_{2n} \\ \vdots & & & & \vdots \\ a_{n1} & a_{n2} & a_{n3} & \cdots & a_{nn} \end{pmatrix}$$

Suppose each row consists of the n numbers 1, 2, 3, …, n in some order and $a_{ij} = a_{ji}$ for $i = 1, 2, \ldots, n$ and $j = 1, 2, \ldots, n$. If n is odd, prove that the numbers $a_{11}, a_{22}, a_{33}, \ldots, a_{nn}$ are 1, 2, 3, …, n in some order. **[RMO 2001]**

Sol. Each row consists of the n numbers 1, 2, 3, …, n in some order.

For any integer k $(1 \le k \le n)$, k occurs once in each row.

Thus, it occurs n times in the matrix.

Let's deliberate the number of occurrences of k off the diagonal.

As $a_{ij} = a_{ji}$, for each occurrence of k above the diagonal, there is a corresponding occurrence below it. Thus, k appears even number of times off the diagonal. However, as k appears n times in the matrix and n is odd, k must appear at least once on the diagonal. This is true for each $k, 1 \le k \le n$. As total number of integers on the diagonal is n, each k appears exactly once on the diagonal.

This implies that $a_{11}, a_{22}, a_{33}, \ldots, a_{nn}$ is a permutation of 1, 2, 3, …, n.

5. Prove that the product of the first 200 positive even integers differs from the product of the first 200 positive odd integers by a multiple of 401. **[RMO 2001]**

Sol.

$$2 \equiv -399 \pmod{401}$$
$$4 \equiv -397 \pmod{401}$$
$$6 \equiv -395 \pmod{401}$$
$$\vdots$$
$$400 \equiv -1 \pmod{401}$$

$\therefore\ 2 \times 4 \times 6 \times \ldots \times 400 \equiv (-1) \times (-3) \times \ldots \times (-399) \pmod{401}$

or, $2 \times 4 \times 6 \times \ldots \times 400 \equiv 1 \times 3 \times \ldots \times 399 \pmod{401}$

$\therefore (2 \times 4 \times 6 \times \ldots \times 400) - (1 \times 3 \times \ldots \times 399)$ is divisible by 401.

6. Consider the set $X = \{1, 2, 3, \ldots, 9, 10\}$. Find two disjoint non-empty subsets A and B of X such that

(a) $A \cup B = X$;

(b) prod (A) is divisible by prod (B), where for any finite set of numbers C, prod (C) denotes the product of all numbers in C ;

(c) The quotient $\dfrac{\text{prod}(A)}{\text{prod}(B)}$ is as small as possible.

[RMO 2003]

Sol. The prime factors of the numbers in set $\{1, 2, 3, \ldots, 9, 10\}$ are 2, 3, 5 and 7. Also, only $7 \in X$ has the prime factor 7.

Hence, it cannot appear in B. Otherwise, 7 in the denominator would not get cancelled. Thus $7 \in A$.

It also implies that $\dfrac{\text{prod }(A)}{\text{prod }(B)} \geq 7.$

The numbers having prime factor 3 are 3, 6, 9. So, 3 and 6 should belong to one of A and B, and 9 belong to the other.

Let's take $3, 6 \in A, 9 \in B$

Also 5 divides 5 and 10.

Let's take $5 \in A, 10 \in B$

Further, let's take $1, 2, 4 \in A, 8 \in B$.

Thus, $A = \{1, 2, 3, 4, 5, 6, 7\}, B = \{8, 9, 10\}$

Now, $$\frac{\text{prod }(A)}{\text{prod }(B)} = \frac{1 \times 2 \times 3 \times 4 \times 5 \times 6 \times 7}{8 \times 9 \times 10} = 7$$

Thus, 7 is the minimum value of $\dfrac{\text{prod }(A)}{\text{prod }(B)}$.

There are other possibilities as well for A and B.

For example, 1 may belong to either A and B. We may also take

$$A = \{3, 5, 6, 7, 8\}, B = \{1, 2, 4, 9, 10\}$$

7. Positive integers are written on all the faces of a cube, one on each. At each corner (vertex) of the cube, the product of the numbers on the faces that meet at the corner is written. The sum of the numbers written at all the corners is 2004. If T denotes the sum of the numbers on all the faces, find all the possible values of T. **[RMO 2004]**

Sol. Let $ABCDPQRS$ be a cube, and the numbers a, b, c, d, e, f be written on the faces $ABCD$, $BQRC$, $PQRS$, $APSD$, $ABQP$, $CRSD$ respectively.

Then, the products written at the corners A, B, C, D, P, Q, R, S are respectively $ade, abe, abf, adf, cde, bce, bcf, cdf$.ss

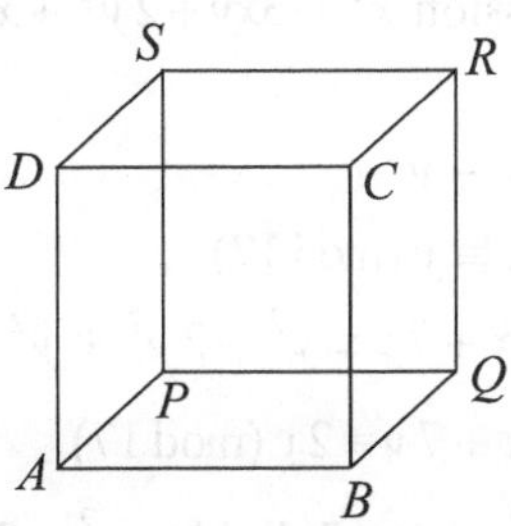

$$\begin{aligned} ade + abe + abf + adf + cde + bce + bcf + cdf \\ &= ae(d+b) + af(b+d) + ce(d+b) + cf(b+d) \\ &= (b+d)(ae + af + ce + cf) \\ &= (b+d)[a(e+f) + c(e+f)] \\ &= (b+d)(e+f)(a+c) \\ &= 2004 \end{aligned}$$

$$2004 = 2^2 \times 3 \times 167$$

167 is a prime number.

As positive integers are written on the faces of the cube,

$$b+d, e+f, a+c \geq 2$$

Hence, following possibilities are there

Possibilities	$b+d$	$e+f$	$a+c$
1	2	6	167
2	2	3	334
3	4	3	167
4	2	2	501

Please note that these are the only possibilities as far as different possible values of T are concerned.

Hence, the possible values of $T = a+b+c+d+e+f$ are $2+6+167 = 175$, $2+3+334 = 339$, $4+3+167 = 174$ and $2+2+501 = 505$.

Thus, there are four possible values of T — 174, 175, 339 and 505.

8. If x, y are integers and 17 divides both the expressions $x^2 - 2xy + y^2 - 5x + 7y$ and $x^2 - 3xy + 2y^2 + x - y$, then prove that 17 divides $xy - 12x + 15y$.

[RMO 2005]

Sol. Please note that

$$x^2 - 3xy + 2y^2 + x - y = (x-y)(x-2y+1)$$

As 17 divides the expression $x^2 - 3xy + 2y^2 + x - y$, it divides either $x - y$ or $x - 2y + 1$.

Suppose that 17 divides $x - y$.

$$\therefore \quad x \equiv y \pmod{17}$$

Hence, $x^2 - 2xy + y^2 - 5x + 7y \equiv y^2 - 2y^2 + y^2 - 5y + 7y \pmod{17}$

or, $\quad x^2 - 2xy + y^2 - 5x + 7y \equiv 2y \pmod{17}$

Thus, the given condition that 17 divides $x^2 - 2xy + y^2 - 5x + 7y$ implies that 17 also divides $2y$ and hence y itself.

But then $x \equiv y \pmod{17}$ implies that 17 divides x also.
Hence, in this case 17 divides $xy - 12x + 15y$.
Suppose, on the other hand, 17 divides $x - 2y + 1$.
Thus, $x \equiv 2y - 1 \pmod{17}$ and hence, $x^2 - 2xy + y^2 - 5x + 7y \equiv y^2 - 5y + 6 \pmod{17}$.
Thus, 17 divides $y^2 - 5y + 6$.
But $x \equiv 2y - 1 \pmod{17}$ also implies that $xy - 12x + 15y \equiv 2(y^2 - 5y + 6) \pmod{17}$
Since, 17 divides $y^2 - 5y + 6$, it follows that 17 divides $xy - 12x + 15y$.

9. Prove that there are infinitely many positive integers n such that $n(n+1)$ can be expressed as a sum of two positive squares in at least two different ways. (Here $a^2 + b^2$ and $b^2 + a^2$ are considered as the same representation.) **[RMO 2006]**

Sol. Let $Q = n(n+1)$

Suppose we choose $n = m^2$.

Now, $$Q = m^2(m^2+1) = (m^2)^2 + m^2$$

If m^2 itself is a sum of two squares, say $m^2 = p^2 + q^2$, then

$$Q = (p^2 + q^2)(m^2 + 1) = (pm + q)^2 + (p - qm)^2$$

Please note that the two representations for Q are distinct.
It is possible to choose n in this manner.
Let's take $m = 5k$, $p = 3k$, $q = 4k$ where k is a positive integer.

Then, $$m^2 = p^2 + q^2$$

As k can be chosen in an infinite number of ways, there are infinitely many such positive integers n.

10. Find the least possible value of $a + b$, where a, b are positive integers such that 11 divides $a + 13b$ and 13 divides $a + 11b$. **[RMO 2006]**

Sol. $11 \mid (a + 13b)$

$\therefore$ $11 \mid (a + 2b)$

$\therefore$ $11 \mid (6a + 12b)$

Hence, $11 \mid (6a + b)$ ...(i)

Also, $13 \mid (a + 11b)$

$\therefore$ $13 \mid (a - 2b)$

$\therefore$ $13 \mid 6a - 12b$

Hence, $13 \mid (6a + b)$ ...(ii)

As gcd $(11, 13) = 1$, it follows from Eqs. (i) and (ii) that

$$143 \mid (6a + b) \qquad (\because\ 11 \times 13 = 143)$$

$\therefore 6a + b = 143k$ for some natural number k.

Now, $\quad 6a + 6b = 143k + 5b = 144k + 6b - (k + b)$

$\therefore \quad 6 \mid (k + b)$

Hence, $\quad k + b \geq 6$

Now

$$\begin{aligned} 6a + 6b &= 143k + 5b \\ &= 138k + 5(k + b) \\ &\geq 138 + 5 \times 6 = 168 \end{aligned}$$

$$\therefore \quad a + b \geq 28$$

$$11 \mid (a + 2b)$$

$$13 \mid (a - 2b)$$

If we take $a = 23$ and $b = 5$, all these conditions are satisfied.

Thus, the minimum value of $a + b$ is 28.

11. In a book with page numbers from 1 to 100, some pages are torn off. The sum of the numbers on the remaining pages is 4949. How many pages are torn off?

[RMO 2009]

Sol. Suppose r pages of the book are torn off.

Please note that the page numbers on both the sides of a page are consecutive numbers i.e., of the form $2k - 1$ and $2k$.

Thus, their sum is of the form $4k - 1$.

Thus, the sum of the numbers on the torn pages must be of the form

$$(4k_1 - 1) + (4k_2 - 1) + \ldots + (4k_r - 1) = 4(k_1 + k_2 + \ldots + k_r) - r$$

The sum of the numbers of all the pages in the untorn book is

$$1 + 2 + 3 + \ldots + 100 = 5050$$

Hence, the sum of the numbers on the torn page is $5050 - 4949 = 101$.

We therefore have

$$4(k_1 + k_2 + \ldots + k_r) - r = 101 \qquad \ldots\text{(i)}$$

Taking congruence modulo 4 on both sides, we have

$$0 - r \equiv 1 \pmod 4$$

$$\therefore \quad r \equiv -1 \pmod 4$$

or, $\quad r \equiv 3 \pmod 4$

Thus, $r = 4l + 3$ for some $l \geq 0$.

Suppose $r \geq 7$ and $k_1 < k_2 < k_3 < \ldots < k_r$

Then, $4(k_1 + k_2 + \ldots + k_r) - r = 4(k_1 + k_2 + \ldots + k_7) - 7$

$$+ 4(k_8 + \ldots + k_r) - (r - 7)$$

$$\geq 4(k_1 + k_2 + \ldots + k_7) - 7$$

$$\geq 4(1 + 2 + \ldots + 7) - 7$$

$$= 4 \times 28 - 7 = 105 > 101$$

Since, the sum of numbers on the torn pages is 101, this is not possible.

Hence, $r < 7$

Also, r is of the form $4l + 3$.

Thus, only possible value of r is 3.

Hence, $r = 3$.

From Eq. (1) it follows that $k_1 + k_2 + k_3 = 26$

Distinct positive integers k_1, k_2, k_3 can be chosen in several ways.

12. Show that $3^{2008} + 4^{2009}$ can be written as product of two positive integers each of which is larger than 2009^{182}. **[RMO 2009]**

Sol. We use the following factorisation:

$$x^4 + 4y^4 = (x^2 + 2xy + 2y^2)(x^2 - 2xy + 2y^2)$$

Please note that for any integers x, y,

$$\left.\begin{aligned} x^2 + 2xy + 2y^2 &= (x + y)^2 + y^2 \geq y^2 \\ x^2 - 2xy + 2y^2 &= (x - y)^2 + y^2 \geq y^2 \end{aligned}\right\} \quad \ldots\text{(i)}$$

Now, $$3^{2008} + 4^{2009} = 3^{2008} + 4(4^{2008})$$

$$= (3^{502})^4 + 4(4^{502})^4$$

Taking $x = 3^{502}$ and $y = 4^{502}$,

$$3^{2008} + 4^{2009} = ab \quad \ldots\text{(ii)}$$

where $a = x^2 + 2xy + 2y^2$,

$b = x^2 - 2xy + 2y^2$

From Eq. (i) it follows that $a \geq (4^{502})^2$, $b \geq (4^{502})^2$

Also, $$(4^{502})^2 = 2^{2008} > 2^{2002}$$

$$= (2^{11})^{182} > (2009)^{182} \quad (\because 2^{11} = 2048 > 2009)$$

$\therefore$ $$a, b > 2009^{182} \quad \ldots\text{(iii)}$$

Thus, by Eqs. (ii) and (iii), we get the desired result.

13. Find the number of positive integers n less than 1991 for which $6 \mid n^2 + 3n + 2$.

[INMO 1991]

Sol. $n^2 + 3n + 2 = (n+1)(n+2)$ and $6 = 2 \times 3$

If 6 is a divisor of $n^2 + 3n + 2$, then the following possibilities are there:

(a) 6 is a divisor of $n+1$.

(b) 6 is a divisor of $n+2$.

(c) 3 is a divisor of $n+1$ and 2 is a divisor of $n+2$.

(d) 2 is a divisor of $n+1$ and 3 is a divisor of $n+2$.

Please also note that all these possibilities are mutually exclusive.

Let's discuss these possibilities one-by-one.

(a) If 6 is a divisor of $n+1$,

$$n + 1 = 6k$$

or, $$n = 6k - 1$$

$$n < 1991$$

$\therefore$ $$6k - 1 < 1991$$

$\therefore$ $$k < 332 \qquad \text{(Also } k \geq 1\text{)}$$

Thus, there are 331 possible values of n in this case.

(b) If 6 is a divisor of $n+2$,

$$n + 2 = 6k$$

or, $$n = 6k - 2$$

$$n < 1991$$

$\therefore$ $$6k - 2 < 1991$$

$\therefore$ $$k \leq 332 \qquad \text{(Also } k \geq 1\text{)}$$

Thus, there are 332 possible values of n in this case.

(c) If 3 is a divisor of $n+1$ and 2 is a divisor of $n+2$, among 6 possible forms of n ($6k$, $6k+1$, $6k+2$, $6k+3$, $6k+4$ and $6k+5$) $6k+2$ form is the only possibility.

Thus, $$6k + 2 < 1991$$

$\therefore$ $$k \leq 331 \qquad \text{(Also } k \geq 0\text{)}$$

Thus, there are 332 possible values of n in this case.

(d) If 2 is a divisor of $n+1$ and 3 is a divisor of $n+2$, among 6 possible forms of n ($6k$, $6k+1$, $6k+2$, $6k+3$, $6k+4$ and $6k+5$) $6k+1$ form is the only possibility.

Thus, $$6k + 1 < 1991$$

$\therefore$ $$k \leq 331 \qquad \text{(Also } k \geq 0\text{)}$$

Thus, there are 332 possible values of n in this case.

Thus, there are $331 + 332 + 332 + 332 = 1327$ possible values of n.

14. Given any nine integers show that it is possible to choose, from among them, four integers a, b, c, d such that $a + b - c - d$ is divisible by 20. Further show that such a selection is not possible, if we start with eight integers instead of nine.

[INMO 2001]

Sol. Following possibilities are there:

(i) Suppose that in the given set of 9 integers, there are four integers a, b, c, d such that each of them is congruent to the same integer r modulo 20.

Then, obviously $a + b \equiv c + d \pmod{20}$

(ii) Suppose that there are two pairs of integers (a, c) and (b, d) in the given set such that

$$a \equiv c \pmod{20}$$
$$b \equiv d \pmod{20}$$

Then, $$a + b \equiv c + d \pmod{20}$$

Please note that for the given set of nine integers if number of distinct remainders modulo 20 is less than or equal to 6, possibilities (i) or (ii) will always be applicable.

If the number of distinct reminders is greater than 6, possibilities (iii) or (iv) below will be applicable.

(iii) If possibilities (i) and (ii) are not applicable, suppose that three integers out of nine given integers are congruent to the same integer modulo 20. Then, there are total 7 different remainders modulo 20.

Possible number of pairs of remainders $= {}^7C_2 = 21$

Possible number of remainders when divided by $20 = 20$

Hence, by pigeonhole principle, there are at least two pairs (say a, b and c, d) with same remainders.

Thus, $$a + b \equiv c + d \pmod{20}$$

(iv) If (i), (ii) and (iii) above are not applicable, there are eight or nine possible remainders. Hence, number of pairs of remainders

$$= {}^8C_2 \text{ or } {}^9C_2$$
$$= 28 \text{ or } 36 \text{ which is greater than } 20.$$

Hence, by pigeonhole principle, there are at least two pairs (say *a*, *b* and *c*, *d*) with same remainders.

Thus, $$a + b \equiv c + d \pmod{20}$$

Please note that the desired result does not hold good for possibility (iii) above if we have a set of eight integers (instead of nine integers) *i.e.*, if three integers out of eight given integers are congruent to the same integer modulo 20, then there are total 6 different remainders and ${}^6C_2 = 15$ possible number of pairs of remainders.

Thus, we cannot apply pigeonhole principle.

15. Determine the least positive value taken by the expression $a^3 + b^3 + c^3 - 3abc$ as *a*, *b*, *c* vary over all positive integers. Find also all triples (*a*, *b*, *c*) for which this least value is attained. **[INMO 2002]**

Sol. We observe that

$$Q = a^3 + b^3 + c^3 - 3abc$$
$$= \frac{1}{2}(a + b + c)[(a - b)^2 + (b - c)^2 + (c - a)^2]$$

Since we are looking for the least positive value taken by Q, it follows that *a*, *b*, *c* are not all equal.

Thus, $a + b + c \geq 1 + 1 + 2 = 4$ and $(a - b)^2 + (b - c)^2 + (c - a)^2 \geq 1 + 1 + 0 = 2$

Thus, we see that $Q \geq 4$

Taking $a = 1$, $b = 1$ and $c = 2$,

we get $Q = 4$.

Therefore, the least value of Q is 4 and this is achieved only by $a + b + c = 4$ and $(a - b)^2 + (b - c)^2 + (c - a)^2 = 2$.

The triples for which $Q = 4$ are therefore given by (*a*, *b*, *c*) = (1, 1, 2), (1, 2, 1), (2, 1, 1).

16. Let x_1 be a given positive integer. A sequence $(x_n)_{n=1}^{\infty} = (x_1, x_2, x_3, \ldots)$ of positive integers is such that x_n, for $n \geq 2$, is obtained from x_{n-1} by adding some non-zero digit of x_{n-1}. Prove that

(a) the sequence has an even number.

(b) the sequence has infinitely many even numbers. **[INMO 2005]**

Sol. (a) Let us assume that there are no even numbers in the sequence. This means that x_{n+1} is obtained from x_n, by adding a non-zero even digit of x_n to x_n, for each $n \geq 1$.

Let E be the left most even digit in x_1 which may be taken in the form $x_1 = O_1O_2...O_kED_1D_2...D_l$ where $O_1, O_2, ..., O_k$ are odd digits ($k \geq 0$), D_1, D_2, ..., D_{l-1} are even or odd, and D_l is odd, $l \geq 1$.

Since, each time we are adding at least 2 to a term of the sequence to get the next term, at some stage, we will have a term of the form

$$x_r = O_1O_2...O_kE999..9F \text{ where } F = 3, 5, 7 \text{ or } 9.$$

Now we are forced to add E to x_r to get x_{r+1}, as it is the only even digit available. After at most four steps of addition, we see that some next term is of the form $x_s = O_1O_2...O_kG000...M$ where G replaces E of x_r, $G = E + 1$, $M = 1$, 3, 5 or 7. But x_s has no non-zero even digit. Thus, the sequence terminates at this stage. This is a contradiction as the given sequence has infinitely many terms.

Hence, the sequence has some even number as its term.

(b) If there are only finitely many even terms and x_t is the last even term, then the sequence $(x_n)_{n=t+1}^{\infty} = (x_{t+1}, x_{t+2}, ...)$ is obtained in a similar manner and hence must have an even term by (a). This is a contradiction. Thus, $(x_n)_{n=1}^{\infty}$, has infinitely many even terms.

17. It is known that 2726, 4472, 5054, 6412 have the same remainder when they are divided by some two-digit natural number *m*. Find the value of *m*.

Sol. For excluding the effect of the unknown remainder, the three differences by the four given numbers can be used to replace the original four numbers.

Then,
$$m \mid (4472 - 2726) \Rightarrow m \mid 1746$$
$$1746 = 2 \times 3^2 \times 97$$
$$m \mid (5054 - 4472) \Rightarrow m \mid 582$$
$$582 = 2 \times 3 \times 97$$
$$m \mid (6412 - 5054) \Rightarrow m \mid 1358$$
$$1358 = 2 \times 7 \times 97$$

97 is the unique two-digit common divisor of the differences.

Hence, $m = 97$

18. Prove that the number $\underbrace{11......11}_{1997 \text{ times}}\ \underbrace{22......22}_{1998 \text{ times}}5$ is a perfect square.

[Yugoslavia 1998]

Sol. $N = \underbrace{11......11}_{1997 \text{ times}} \times 10^{1999} + \underbrace{22......22}_{1998 \text{ times}} \times 10 + 5$

$$= \frac{1}{9}(10^{1997} - 1)10^{1999} + \frac{2}{9}(10^{1998} - 1)10 + 5$$

$$= \frac{1}{9}(10^{3996} + 2 \times 5 \times 10^{1998} + 25)$$

$$= \left[\frac{1}{3}(10^{1998} + 5)\right]^2$$

$$= \left(\frac{1\overbrace{00\ldots\ldots00}^{1997\text{ times}}5}{3}\right)^2$$

$$= (\underbrace{33\ldots\ldots33}_{1997\text{ times}}5)^2$$

19. Find the greatest common divisor of the numbers $A_n = 2^{3n} + 3^{6n+2} + 5^{6n+2}$ when $n = 0, 1, \ldots, 1999$. **[Romania 1999]**

Sol. We have $A_0 = 1 + 9 + 25 = 35 = 5 \times 7$

Using congruence mod 5, it follows that

$$A_n \equiv 2^{3n} + 3^{6n+2} \equiv 2^{3n} + 9^{3n+1}$$
$$\equiv 2^{3n} + (-1)^{3n+1} \pmod 5$$

For $n = 1$, $A_1 \equiv 9 \not\equiv 0 \pmod 5$

Hence, 5 is not a common divisor.

On the other hand,

$$A_n = 8^n + 9 \times 9^{3n} + 25 \times 25^{3n}$$
$$\equiv 1 + 2 \times 2^{3n} + 4 \times 4^{3n}$$
$$\equiv 1 + 2 \times 8^n + 4 \times 64^n$$
$$\equiv 1 + 2 \times 1^n + 4 \times 1^n \equiv 7 \equiv 0 \pmod 7)$$

Therefore 7 divides A_n, for all integers $n \geq 0$.

Consequently, the greatest common divisor of the numbers $A_0, A_1, \ldots, A_{1999}$ is 7.

20. Find all the positive integers a, b, c such that $a^3 + b^3 + c^3 = 2001$.

[Romania 2001]

Sol. We can assume without loss of generality that $a \leq b \leq c$.

It is obvious that $1^3 + 10^3 + 10^3 = 2001$.

We prove that (1, 10, 10) is the only solution of the equation, except for its permutations.

First, we prove following lemma.

Suppose n is an integer. The remainder of n^3 when divided by 9 is 0, 1 or –1.

$$n \equiv 0, 1, 2, 3, 4, 5, 6, 7 \text{ or } 8 \pmod 9$$

$\therefore$ $$n^3 \equiv 0, 1, 8, 27, 64, 125, 216, 343 \text{ or } 512 \pmod 9$$

$\therefore$ $$n^3 \equiv 0, 1, -1, 0, 1, -1, 0, 1 \text{ or } -1 \pmod 9$$

or, $$n^3 \equiv 0, 1 \text{ or } -1 \pmod 9$$

Now, 2001 is of the form $9k+3$.

As a^3, b^3, c^3 are of the forms $9k, 9k \pm 1$, only possibility is that all of a^3, b^3 and c^3 are of the form $9k+1$.

Hence, all of a, b, c are of the form $3k+1$.

Thus, a, b, c belong to the set $\{1, 4, 7, 10, 13, \ldots\}$.

If $c \geq 13$, $a^3 + b^3 + c^3 > c^3 = 2197$

If $c \leq 7$, $a^3 + b^3 + c^3 \leq 3 \times 7^3 = 1029$

Hence, only possible value of c is 10.

$\therefore$ $$a^3 + b^3 = 1001$$

If $b < c = 10$, $a^3 + b^3 \leq 2 \times 7^3 = 686$

Hence, $$b = 10$$

Thus, $b = c = 10$ and $a = 1$ is the only possible solution.

If we consider all possible permutations, $(a, b, c) \in \{(1, 10, 10), (10, 1, 10), (10, 10, 1)\}$.

21. Let n be a non-negative integer. Find all the non-negative integers a, b, c, d such that $a^2 + b^2 + c^2 + d^2 = 7 \times 4^n$. **[Buzau 2001]**

Sol. For $n = 0$ we have the solutions (2, 1, 1, 1), (1, 2, 1, 1), (1, 1, 2, 1) and (1, 1, 1, 2).

Suppose $n \geq 1$.

Please not that $a^2 + b^2 + c^2 + d^2 \equiv 0 \pmod 4$

Square of an integer is of the form $4k$ or $4k+1$.

Therefore, all four squares must be of the form either $4k$ or $4k+1$.

(i) If a, b, c, d are odd numbers, set $a = 2x+1, b = 2y+1, c = 2z+1, d = 2t+1$. The given equation reduces to

$$4x(x+1) + 4y(y+1) + 4z(z+1) + 4t(t+1) = 4(7 \times 4^{n-1} - 1)$$

Since $n(n+1)$ is a multiple of 2, the left-hand side is divisible by 8. Hence $7 \times 4^{n-1} - 1$ must be even.

Consequently, $n = 1$ and the equation $a^2 + b^2 + c^2 + d^2 = 28$ has the solution (3, 3, 3, 1), (1, 1, 1, 5), and all their permutations.

(ii) If a, b, c, d are even numbers, then setting $a=2x, b=2y, c=2z, d=2t$ leads to

$$x^2+y^2+z^2+t^2=7\times 4^{n-1}$$

This is of the same form as original equation. Therefore, all of x, y, z, t must be either even or odd. If the process recursively yields only even numbers (till we get 1), we get $(2^{n+1}, 2^n, 2^n, 2^n)$ as the solution. If we get odd numbers after certain steps, by (i), (3, 3, 3, 1) and (1, 1, 1, 5) are the only possible solution. Hence, we get $(3\times 2^{n-1}, 3\times 2^{n-1}, 3\times 2^{n-1}, 2^{n-1})$, $(2^{n-1}, 2^{n-1}, 2^{n-1}, 5\times 2^{n-1})$ as the solution.

Thus, we obtain the solutions

$(2^{n+1}, 2^n, 2^n, 2^n)$, $(3\times 2^{n-1}, 3\times 2^{n-1}, 3\times 2^{n-1}, 2^{n-1})$,
$(2^{n-1}, 2^{n-1}, 2^{n-1}, 5\times 2^{n-1})$ and all their permutations.

22. Find the smallest value for n for which there exist the positive integers $x_1, \dots, x_n$ with $x_1^4+x_2^4+\dots+x_n^4=1998$. **[Iasi 1998]**

Sol. Observe that for any integer x, x^4 is always of the form $16k$ or $16k+1$.

$$1998=16\times 124+14$$

Hence, it follows that $n\ge 14$.

If $n=14$, all the numbers $x_1, x_2, \dots, x_{14}$ must be odd.

Let $\qquad x_k^4=16a_k+1$

Then $\qquad a_k=\dfrac{x_k^4-1}{16}$

Hence, $a_k\in\{0, 5, 39, 150\dots\}$ and $a_1+a_2+\dots+a_{14}=124$.

It follows that $a_k\in\{0, 5, 39\}$ for all $k, 1\le k\le 14$.

$$124=5\times 24+4$$

The number of the terms a_k equal to 39 is 1 or 6 for the sum of a_i's to attain the form $5k+4$.

If $a_k=39$ for one term, sum of remaining terms $=124-39=85$ which is not possible as $\Sigma a_i\le 5\times 13=65$ for the remaining terms.

Also $a_k=39$ for six terms is not possible as $39\times 6=234>124$.

Hence, $n\ge 15$.

It is easy to verify that following equalities hold true.

$$1998=5^4+5^4+3^4+3^4+3^4+3^4+3^4+3^4+3^4+3^4+3^4+2^4+1^4+1^4+1^4$$

$$=5^4+5^4+4^4+3^4+3^4+3^4+3^4+3^4+3^4+1^4+1^4+1^4+1^4+1^4+1^4$$

Hence, $n=15$.

23. Can one find 16 three-digit numbers, using only 3 digits, without having two of them with the same remainder when divided by 16? **[Bulgaria 1998]**

Sol. Assume that there are 16 numbers having distinct remainders when divided by 16.

Thus, all 16 numbers yield different remainders –0, 1, 2, …, 15, when divided by 16.

Thus, 8 numbers are odd and 8 numbers are even.

Hence, all 3 digits cannot be all even or odd.

Let's assume that two of them are even (*a* and *b*) and one is odd (*c*).

There are 9 odd three digit numbers that can be formed with these digits:

$$\overline{aac}, \overline{abc}, \overline{acc}, \overline{bac}, \overline{bbc}, \overline{bcc}, \overline{cac}, \overline{cbc}, \overline{ccc}$$

Let $a_1, a_2, \ldots, a_9$ be the two-digit numbers obtained by erasing the last digit (*c*) from the above sequence.

For any two of the given 16 numbers where n_1, n_2, n_3 and n_1', n_2', n_3' are digits of the given two numbers,

$100n_1 + 10n_2 + n_3 \not\equiv 100n_1' + 10n_2' + n_3' \pmod{16}$

For the above set of 9 odd numbers, $n_3 = n_3' = c$

Hence, $\quad 100n_1 + 10n_2 \not\equiv 100n_1' + 10n_2' \pmod{16}$

or, $\quad 10n_1 + n_2 \not\equiv 10n_1' + n_2' \pmod{8}$

Thus, no two of the given nine integers $a_1, a_2, \ldots, a_9$ yield same remainders when divided by 8.

However, there are only eight possible remainders when divided by 8.

Hence, two of the given nine integers will definitely yield same remainder when divided by 8.

This is a contradiction.

The same conclusion follows when two digits are odd and only one is even.

Hence, it is not possible to find 16 three-digit numbers, using only 3 digits, without having two of them with the same remainder when divided by 16.

24. Find all the positive integers *n*, $n \geq 1$, such that $n^2 + 3^n$ is a perfect square. **[Bulgaria 1998]**

Sol. Let *m* be a positive integer such that $m^2 = n^2 + 3^n$

$\therefore \quad (m-n)(m+n) = 3^n$

Thus, there exists integer $k \geq 0$ such that $m - n = 3^k$ and $m + n = 3^{n-k}$.

Obviously, $\quad m - n < m + n$

$\therefore \quad 3^k < 3^{n-k}$

Thus, $\quad k < n - k$

$\therefore \quad n-2k>0$

$\therefore \quad n-2k \geq 1$

If $n-2k=1$, then $2n=(m+n)-(m-n)=3^{n-k}-3^{k}$

$$=3^{k}(3^{n-2k}-1)$$

$$=3^{k}(3^{1}-1) \quad (\because n-2k=1)$$

$$=2\times 3^{k}$$

So, $\quad n=3^{k}=2k+1$

It can be established by the method of mathematical induction that $3^{k}>2k+1$ for $k\geq 2$.

Hence, $k=0$ or 1 are the only possibilities.

For $k=0$ and $k=1$, the given condition is satisfied.

Therefore, $n=1$ or $n=3$.

If $n-2k>1$, then $n-2k\geq 2$ and $k\leq n-k-2$.

It follows that $3^{k}\leq 3^{n-k-2}$, and consequently

$$2n=3^{n-k}-3^{k}$$

$$\geq 3^{n-k}-3^{n-k-2}$$

$$=3^{n-k-2}(3^{2}-1)$$

$$=8\times 3^{n-k-2}$$

$$\geq 8[1+2(n-k-2)] \quad [\because 3^{m}=(1+2)^{m}\geq 1+2m]$$

$$=16n-16k-24$$

which implies $8k+12\geq 7n$

On the other hand, $n\geq 2k+2$

Hence, $7n\geq 14k+14$

This is a contradiction.

Thus, the only possible values for n are 1 and 3.

25. Find all the integers x and y so that

$$(x+1)(x+2)(x+3)+x(x+2)(x+3)+x(x+1)(x+3)+x(x+1)(x+2)=y^{2x}$$ **[Iasi 1998]**

Sol. (i) If $x\geq 1$, then y^{2x} is a square.

The numbers $x, x+1, x+2, x+3$ are of the forms $4k$, $4k+1$, $4k+2$, $4k+3$ not necessarily in this order.

Therefore, one of the four terms, $x, x+1, x+2, x+3$ is definitely of the form $4k$.

Hence, three summands of the left-hand side are divisible by 4 and the fourth is of the form $4k + 2$.

Thus, the sum on the left-hand side is of the form $4k + 2$.

However, a perfect square cannot be of the form $4k + 2$.

This is a contradiction.

Thus, we conclude that $x \leq 0$.

(ii) If $x \leq -4$, all of $x, x+1, x+2, x+3$ are negative integers.

Therefore, the left-hand side is a negative number.

However, the right-hand side is a positive number.

This is a contradiction.

Thus, we conclude that $x \geq -3$.

Now, we need to verify only for $x = -3, -2, -1, 0$.

For $x = -3$, we get

$$-6 = y^{-6}$$

or, $$y^6 = \frac{-1}{6}$$

It has no integral solution.

For $x = -2$, we get

$$2 = y^{-4}$$

or, $$y^4 = \frac{1}{2}$$

It has no integral solution.

For $x = -1$, we get

$$-2 = y^{-2}$$

or, $$y^2 = -\frac{1}{2}$$

It has no integral solution.

For $x = 0$, we get

$$6 = y^0$$

This is not possible.

Hence, there are no integral solutions for x and y.

26. Find the number of five-digit perfect squares having the last two digits equal.

[Iasi 1999]

Sol. Let $n = abcdd$ be the desired 5-digit perfect square where a, b, c, d are digits of n.

Therefore, $$n = 100abc + 11d \quad \text{...(i)}$$

We know that 0, 1, 4, 5, 6, 9 are only possible unit digits of a perfect square. ... (ii)

From (i) it also follows that

$$n \equiv 3d \pmod 4 \quad \text{...(iii)}$$

For $d = 1, 5, 6, 9$

$$n \equiv 3, 3, 2, 3 \pmod 4 \quad \text{(by (iii))}$$

But we know that a perfect square cannot be congruent to 2 or 3 modulo 4.

Hence, $d = 0, 4$ are the only possibilities.

(i) If $d = 0$, $n = 100abc$

Hence, n can be a perfect square if and only if abc is a perfect square.

Thus, abc belongs to the following set of 3-digit perfect squares.

$$\{10^2, 11^2, ..., 31^2\}$$

Thus, there are 22 possible solutions.

(ii) If $d = 4$, $n = 100abc + 44$,

Let $n = p^2$

As n is even, p is even.

Let $$p = 2k$$

$\therefore$ $$4k^2 = 100abc + 44$$

or, $$abc = \frac{k^2 - 11}{25}$$

If k is of the form $5t$,

$$abc = \frac{k^2 - 11}{25} = \frac{25t^2 - 11}{25}$$

which is not an integer for any integral value of t.

If k is of the form $5t + 1$,

$$abc = \frac{k^2 - 11}{25} = \frac{25t^2 + 10t - 10}{25} = t^2 + \frac{2(t-1)}{5}$$

If t is of the form $5m + 1$, it is an integer.

Hence, possible values of $t = 11, 16, 21, 26, 31$.

Thus, there are five possible solutions.

If k is of the form $5t+2$,

$$abc=\frac{k^2-11}{25}=\frac{25t^2+20t-7}{25}=t^2+\frac{(20t-7)}{25}$$

which cannot be an integer for any value of t.

If k is of the form $5t+3$,

$$abc=\frac{k^2-11}{25}=\frac{25t^2+30t-2}{25}=t^2+\frac{(30t-2)}{25}$$

which cannot be an integer for any value of t.

If k is of the form $5t+4$

$$abc=\frac{k^2-11}{25}=\frac{25t^2+40t+5}{25}=t^2+\frac{(8t+1)}{5}$$

If t is of the form $5m+3$, this is an integer.

Hence, possible values of t are 13, 18, 23, 28.

Thus, there are four different solutions.

Therefore, there are 31 five-digit perfect squares having the last two digits equal.

27. Find all the integers n so that the number $\sqrt{\frac{4n-2}{n+5}}$ is rational.

[Mures 2001]

Sol. Suppose $\frac{4n-2}{n+5}=\frac{a^2}{b^2}$, where a and b are coprime integers.

We obtain,
$$n=\frac{2b^2+5a^2}{4b^2-a^2}=-5+\frac{22b^2}{4b^2-a^2},$$

$$4b^2-a^2\neq 0$$

As a and b are coprime, a^2 and b^2 are also coprime.

Therefore, b^2 and $4b^2-a^2$ are also coprime.

It follows that $4b^2-a^2$ divides 22.

Therefore, $4b^2-a^2\in\{-22,-11,-1,1,11,22\}$

Please note that $4b^2-a^2$ is of the form $4t$ or $4t+3$.

Hence, $4b^2-a^2=-1$ or $4b^2-a^2=11$.

If $4b^2-a^2=-1$, then $(2b-a)(2b+a)=-1$ and consequently,

$$\begin{cases}2b-a=-1\\2b+a=1\end{cases}\text{ or }\begin{cases}2b-a=1\\2b+a=-1\end{cases}$$

We obtain $b=0$.

However, this is not possible.

If $4b^2 - a^2 = 11$, then $\begin{cases} 2b - a = 1 \\ 2b + a = 11 \end{cases}$ or $\begin{cases} 2b - a = 11 \\ 2b + a = 1 \end{cases}$

We obtain $a = 5$, $b = 3$ or $a = -5$, $b = 3$ and $n = 13$.

Thus, $n = 13$ is the only possible solution.

28. Let n be an even positive integer and let a, b be positive coprime integers. Find a and b if $a + b$ divide $a^n + b^n$. **[Bucharest 2002]**

Sol. $a + b$ divides $a^n + b^n$.

As n is even, we have

$a^n - b^n = (a^2 - b^2)(x^{t-1} + x^{t-2}y + \ldots + y^{t-1})$ where $t = \frac{n}{2}$, $x = a^2$, $y = b^2$

Since, $a + b$ is a divisor of $a^2 - b^2$, it follows that $a + b$ is a divisor of $a^n - b^n$.

Thus, $a + b$ divides $2a^n = (a^n + b^n) + (a^n - b^n)$, and $2b^n = (a^n + b^n) - (a^n - b^n)$.

But a and b are coprime numbers, and so $gcd\,(2a^n, 2b^n) = 2$.

Therefore $a + b$ is a divisor of 2.

Hence $a = b = 1$.

29. The last four digits of a perfect square are equal. Prove that they are all zero. **[Bucharest 2002]**

Sol. Let n be the desired perfect square.

Suppose that digit a appears in the last four places.

Thus, $n \equiv a \times 1111 \pmod{10^4}$

$\therefore$ $n \equiv a \times 1111 \pmod{16}$

We know that 0, 1, 4, 5, 6, 9 are the possible values for unit digit of a perfect square.

Hence, $a = 0, 1, 4, 5, 6$ or 9

(i) If $a = 0$, we have got the desired result.

(ii) If $a = 1$, $n \equiv 1111 \pmod{16}$

$\equiv 7 \pmod{16}$

If $a = 4$, $n \equiv 4444 \pmod{16} \equiv 12 \pmod{16}$

If $a = 5$, $n \equiv 5555 \pmod{16} \equiv 3 \pmod{16}$

If $a = 6$, $n \equiv 6666 \pmod{16} \equiv 10 \pmod{16}$

If $a=9$, $n \equiv 9999 \pmod{16} \equiv 15 \pmod{16}$

For any integer k,

$$k \equiv 0, 1, 2, 3, 4, 5, 6, 7, 8, 9, 10, 11, 12, 13, 14, 15 \pmod{16}$$

$\therefore\ k^2 \equiv 0, 1, 4, 9 \pmod{16}$

Thus, a perfect square cannot be congruent to 7, 12, 3, 10 or 15 modulo 16.

Hence, a cannot have any value other than 0.

30. Let $m, n > 1$ be integers. Solve in positive integers the equation $x^n + y^n = 2^m$.

[Bucharest 2002]

Sol. Let $d = gcd(x, y)$ and $x = da$, $y = db$, where $\gcd(a, b) = 1$.

$$x^n + y^n = 2^m$$

$$\therefore \quad d^n (a^n + b^n) = 2^m$$

Hence, $a^n + b^n = 2^k$, for some integer k.

Please note that a and b both have to be even or odd as $a^n + b^n$ is even.

However, they both cannot be even as $\gcd(a, b) = 1$.

Hence, both a and b are odd.

$$\therefore \quad a^2 \equiv 1 \pmod 8$$

$$\text{And} \quad b^2 \equiv 1 \pmod 8$$

Therefore, if n is even,

$$a^n + b^n = (a^2)^{n/2} + (b^2)^{n/2}$$

$$\equiv 1 + 1 \pmod 8$$

$$\equiv 2 \pmod 8$$

$$\therefore \quad 2^k \equiv 2 \pmod 8$$

$$\therefore \quad k = 1$$

This implies that $a = b = 1$.

Hence, $\quad d^n = 2^{m-1}$

Thus, $d = 2^r$, for some integer r.

Hence, $m - 1 = nr$ is the desired solution.

If n is odd,

$$a^n + b^n = (a+b)(a^{n-1} - a^{n-2}b + \ldots + b^{n-1})$$

2nd term on the right side has odd numbers of terms (n) with each term being odd.

Hence, it is odd.

We have $$a^n + b^n = 2^k$$

$\therefore$ $$a + b = 2^k$$

and $$a^{n-1} - a^{n-2}b + \ldots + b^{n-1} = 1$$

This is possible only if $a = b = 1$ and $k = 1$.

Now, we can solve in the same way as we solved for the possibility of n being even.

Thus, we get $m - 1 = nr$.

Hence, desired solution is $x = y = 2^{\frac{m-1}{n}}$.

31. Find all the positive integers a, b for which $a^4 + 4b^4$ is a prime number.

[Ohrid 2000]

Sol. Please note that

$$\begin{aligned} a^4 + 4b^4 &= a^4 + 4b^4 + 4a^2b^2 - 4a^2b^2 \\ &= (a^2 + 2b^2)^2 - 4a^2b^2 \\ &= (a^2 + 2b^2 + 2ab)(a^2 + 2b^2 - 2ab) \\ &= [(a+b)^2 + b^2][(a-b)^2 + b^2] \end{aligned}$$

As $(a+b)^2 + b^2 > 1$, $a^4 + 4b^4$ can be a prime number only if $(a-b)^2 + b^2 = 1$.

For $a = b = 1$, $(a-b)^2 + b^2 = 1$ and $a^4 + 4b^4 = 5$ are prime.

If any of a or b is greater than 1, $(a-b)^2 + b^2$ is greater than 1.

Thus, $a^4 + 4b^4$ cannot be a prime number.

Hence, $a = b = 1$ is the only possible value of a and b for which $a^4 + 4b^4$ is a prime number.

32. For any natural number n, expressed in base 10, let $S(n)$ denotes the sum of all digits of n. Find all natural numbers n such that $n^3 = 8(S(n))^3 + 6nS(n) + 1$.

[RMO 2016]

Sol. $n^3 = 8(S(n))^3 + 6nS(n) + 1$

$\therefore$ $$n^3 - 8(S(n))^3 - 1 = 6nS(n)$$

or, $$(n)^3 + (-2S(n))^3 + (-1)^3 = 3 \times n \times (-2S(n))(-1)$$

We know that

$$a^3 + b^3 + c^3 - 3abc = (a+b+c)(a^2 + b^2 + c^2 - ab - bc - ca)$$

$\therefore a^3 + b^3 + c^3 - 3abc = 0$ if and only if $a + b + c = 0$ or $a = b = c$

$$a = b = c$$

$\Rightarrow$ $$n = -2S(n) = -1$$

But n is a natural number.
Hence, this possibility is ruled out.
So, the only possible option is

$$a+b+c=0$$

$\therefore$ $$n-2S(n)-1=0$$

or, $$n-S(n)=S(n)+1 \quad \ldots(i)$$

For a k-digit number n,

$$S(n) \le 9k$$

$\therefore$ $$n = 2S(n)+1 \le 18k+1$$

Also $$n \ge 10^{k-1}$$

For $k>2$, $$10^{k-1} > 18k+1$$

(This result can be proved easily using the principle of mathematical induction.)
Hence, n can be either a 1-digit or 2-digit number. ...(ii)
Please note that any integer n can be written as

$$n = a_k a_{k-1} \ldots a_1 a_0$$

where $a_0, a_1, \ldots a_{k-1}, a_k$ are digits of n

$\therefore$ $$n = a_k 10^k + a_{k-1}10^{k-1} + \ldots + 10a_1 + a_0$$

$\therefore$ $$n - S_n = (a_k 10^k - a_k) + (a_{k-1}10^{k-1} - a_{k-1}) + \ldots + 9a_1$$

$10^l - 1$ is always divisible by 9 for all $l \ge 0$.

$\therefore n - S_n$ is always divisible by 9. ...(iii)

From (ii), it follows that $S(n)$ can only take values lying between 1 and 18.
As $n - S(n) = S(n)+1$ and $n - S(n)$ is divisible by 9, only possible values of $S(n)$ are 8 and 17.
For $S(n)=8$, $n=17$
For $S(n)=17$, $n=35$ which is not possible as $S(n) \ne 17$ for $n=35$.
Hence, $n=17$ is the only solution.

33. Let a, b, c be positive integers such that a divides b^2, b divides c^2 and c divides a^2. Prove that abc divides $(a+b+c)^7$. **[RMO 2002]**

Sol. $a \mid b^2, b \mid c^2, c \mid a^2$

Each term in the expansion of $(a+b+c)^7$ is of the form

$P_{ijk}\, a^i b^j c^k$ where $0 \le i, j, k \le 7$ and $i+j+k=7$

If $i, j, k \ge 1$ obviously $a^i b^j c^k$ is divisible by abc.

So, let's consider those cases where one or two of i, j, k are 0.

Suppose that $i = j = 0$

Now, $c^7 = c \times c^2 \times c^4$

$b \mid c^2$

$a \mid b^2$ and $b \mid c^2$

$\therefore$ $b^2 = ax$ and $c^2 = by$ (for some integers x and y)

$\therefore$ $c^4 = b^2 y^2 = axy^2$

$\therefore$ $a \mid c^4$ ...(i)

Thus, $abc \mid c^7$

Similarly, it can be proved that $abc \mid a^7$ and $abc \mid b^7$.

Now, let's consider those cases where one of i, j, k is 0.

Suppose $i = 0$

So, we have $b^j c^k$ where $j + k = 7$, $j, k \geq 1$.

Now, following possibilities are there-

$$bc^6, b^2c^5, b^3c^4, b^4c^3, b^5c^2, b^6c$$

$$bc^6 = bc \times c^5$$

$$b^2c^5 = b^2c \times c^4$$

By (i), $a \mid c^4$

Hence, $abc \mid bc^6$ and $abc \mid b^2c^5$

$$b^3c^4 = b^2 \times bc^4$$

$$b^4c^3 = b^2 \times b^2c^3$$

$$b^5c^2 = b^2 \times b^3c^2$$

$$b^6c = b^2 \times b^4c$$

As $a \mid b^2$, abc divides each of these terms.

In the similar manner, we can establish divisibility by abc when $j = 0$ or $k = 0$.

Thus, it is established that each term in the expansion of $(a + b + c)^7$ is divisible by abc.

Hence, $abc \mid (a + b + c)^7$.

34. Let a, b, c be three natural numbers such that $a< b< c$ and gcd $(c-a, c-b)=1$. Suppose there exists an integer d such that $a+d, b+d, c+d$ form the sides of a right-angled triangle. Prove that there exist integers l, m such that $c+d=l^2+m^2$. **[RMO 2007]**

Sol. As $a+d, b+d, c+d$ form the sides of a right-angled triangle and $a< b< c$,

$$(c+d)^2=(a+d)^2+(b+d)^2$$

This reduces to $d^2+2d\,(a+b-c)+a^2+b^2-c^2=0$

Solving the quadratic equation for d, we obtain

$$d=-(a+b-c)\pm\sqrt{(a+b-c)^2-(a^2+b^2-c^2)}$$
$$=-(a+b-c)\pm\sqrt{2\,(c-a)\,(c-b)}$$

As $a+d, b+d, c+d$ form the sides of a right-angled triangle,

$$a+d+b+d>c+d$$

$\therefore$ $$a+b+d-c>0$$

Hence, only possible solution for d is

$$d=-(a+b-c)+\sqrt{2\,(c-a)\,(c-b)}$$

Since d is an integer, $2\,(c-a)\,(c-b)$ must be a perfect square.

$\therefore 2\,(c-a)\,(c-b)=x^2$ for some integer x

But gcd $(c-a, c-b)=1$

Hence, we have $\quad c-a=2u^2, c-b=v^2$

or, $\quad c-a=u^2, c-b=2v^2$

where $u>0$, $v>0$ and gcd $(u, v)=1$

In either of the cases $\quad d=-(a+b-c)+2uv$

In the first case,

$$c+d=2c-a-b+2uv$$
$$=(c-a)+(c-b)+2uv$$
$$=2u^2+v^2+2uv$$
$$=(u+v)^2+u^2$$

Thus, we have established that $c+d$ is the sum of two non-zero squares.

Similarly, in the second case we get $c+d=v^2+(u+v)^2$.

Thus, $c+d$ is the sum of two squares.

35. Do there exist three distinct positive real numbers a, b, c such that the numbers a, b, c, $b+c-a$, $c+a-b$, $a+b-c$ and $a+b+c$ form a 7-term arithmetic progression in some order? **[INMO 2002]**

Sol. Let a, b, c be three distinct positive real numbers such that $a, b, c, b+c-a$, $c+a-b, a+b-c$ and $a+b+c$ form a 7-term arithmetic progression in some order.

We may assume that $a< b< c$.

Then, there are only two cases:

(I) $a+b-c< a< c+a-b< b< c< b+c-a< a+b+c$ and

(II) $a+b-c< a< b< c+a-b< c< b+c-a< a+b+c$

Case I $a+b-c< a< c+a-b< c< b+c-a< a+b+c$

Let d be the common difference.

Thus, we see that $c=a+b+c-2d,\ b=a+b+c-3d,\ a=a+b+c-5d$

Adding these, we see that $a+b+c=5d$.

But then $a=0$. However, it is given that a is a positive real number. Therefore, this possibility is not applicable.

Case-II $a+b-c< a< b< c+a-b< c< b+c-a< a+b+c$

Again, we see that $c=a+b+c-2d,\ b=a+b+c-4d,\ a=a+b+c-5d$

We thus obtain $a+b+c=\left(\frac{11}{2}\right)d.$

This gives $a=\frac{1}{2}d,\ b=\frac{3}{2}d,\ c=\frac{7}{2}d$

Please note that $\quad a+b-c=a+b+c-6d=-\left(\frac{1}{2}\right)d$

However, we also get

$$a+b-c=\left[\left(\frac{1}{2}\right)+\left(\frac{3}{2}\right)-\left(\frac{7}{2}\right)\right]d=-\left(\frac{3}{2}\right)d$$

It follows that $3d=d$ giving $d=0$. But this is impossible.

Thus, there are no three distinct positive real numbers a, b, c such that a, b, c, $b+c-a, c+a-b, a+b-c$ and $a+b+c$ form a 7-term arithmetic progression in some order.

36. Find all primes p and q, and even numbers $n>2$, satisfying the equation

$p^n+p^{n-1}+\ldots+p+1=q^2+q+1$ **[INMO 2003]**

Sol. Obviously $p\neq q$.

The given equation can be written in the following form

$$p\,(p^{n-1}+p^{n-2}+\ldots+1)=q\,(q+1)$$

If $q \leq p^{\frac{n}{2}} - 1$, then $q < p^{\frac{n}{2}}$ and hence, $q^2 < p^n$

Thus, we obtain $q^2 + q < p^n + p^{\frac{n}{2}} < p^n + p^{n-1} + \ldots + p$ $(\because n > 2)$

Thus, there are no solutions for p and q in this case.

Now suppose that $q \geq p^{\frac{n}{2}}$

Since, $n > 2$ and is an even number, $\frac{n}{2}$ is a natural number larger than 1. This implies that $q \neq p^{\frac{n}{2}}$ by the given condition that q is a prime.

Therefore, $q \geq p^{\frac{n}{2}} + 1$

We may also write the given equation in the following form

$$p(p^n - 1) = (p-1)\,q(q+1)$$

This shows that q divides $(p^{\frac{n}{2}} - 1)\,(p^{\frac{n}{2}} + 1)$.

But $q \geq p^{\frac{n}{2}} + 1$ and q is a prime.

Hence, the only possibility is $q = p^{\frac{n}{2}} + 1$.

This gives $p\,(p^{\frac{n}{2}} - 1) = (p-1)\,(q+1) = (p-1)\,(p^{\frac{n}{2}} + 2)$

Simplification leads to $3p = p^{\frac{n}{2}} + 2$

This shows that p divides 2.

Thus, $p = 2$.

Substituting $p = 2$ and $q = p^{\frac{n}{2}} + 1$ in the original equation we get

$2^n = 4 + 3 \times 2^{\frac{n}{2}}$

Thus, $2^{\frac{n}{2}} | 4$

$\therefore \frac{n}{2} \leq 2$

or, $n \leq 4$

Hence, $p = 2$, $q = 5$, $n = 4$ is the only possible solution.

It is easy to verify that these values of p, q, n indeed satisfy the given equation.

37. Let S denote the set of all 6-tuples (a, b, c, d, e, f) of positive integers such that $a^2+b^2+c^2+d^2+e^2=f^2$.

Consider the set $T=\{abcdef:(a, b, c, d, e, f)\in S\}$. Find the greatest common divisor of all the members of T. **[INMO 2004]**

Sol. If we take $a=b=c=1, d=2, e=3, f=4$

We get $a^2+b^2+c^2+d^2+e^2=f^2$

Here, $abcdef=24$

Hence, gcd (members of T) ≤ 24 ...(i)

Now, let's consider various possible forms of a, b, c, d, e, f - $3k, 3k+1, 3k+2$, as under :

Possibilities	Number of terms of the forms $3k$ among a, b, c, d, e	Number of terms of the forms $3k+1$ or $3k+2$ among a, b, c, d, e	Consequent form of f^2	Remarks
1	5	0	$3k$	$abcdef$ is divisible by 3.
2	4	1	$3k+1$	$abcdef$ is divisible by 3.
3	3	2	$3k+2$	This is not possible because square (f^2) cannot be of the form $3k+2$
4	2	3	$3k$	$abcdef$ is divisible by 3.
5	1	4	$3k+1$	$abcdef$ is divisible by 3.
6	0	5	$3k+2$	This is not possible because square (f^2) cannot be of the form $3k+2$

Thus, $abcdef$ is always divisible by 3. ...(ii)

Now, let's consider various possible forms of a, b, c, d, e, f - $8k, 8k+1, 8k+2, 8k+3, 8k+4, 8k+5, 8k+6, 8k+7$ as under :

Possibilities	**Number of terms of the forms $8k$, $8k+2$, $8k+4$, $8k+6$ among a, b, c, d, e**	**Number of terms of the forms $8k+1$, $8k+3$, $8k+5$, $8k+7$ among a, b, c, d, e**	**Form of f^2**	**Remarks**
1	5	0	$8k$ or $8k+4$	*abcdef* is divisible by 8.
2	4	1	$8k+1$ or $8k+5$	$8k+5$ form of f^2 is not possible because square cannot be of this form. Otherwise *abcdef* is divisible by 8.
3	3	2	$8k+2$ or $8k+6$	This is not possible because square (f^2) cannot be of these forms.
4	2	3	$8k+3$ or $8k+7$	This is not possible because square (f^2) cannot be of these forms.
5	1	4	$8k$ or $8k+4$	*abcdef* is divisible by 8.
6	0	5	$8k+5$	This is not possible because square (f^2) cannot be of these forms.

Thus, *abcdef* is always divisible by 8. ...(iii)

$$\gcd(3, 8) = 1$$

Therefore, from (ii) and (iii) it follows that $24 \mid abcdef$.

Thus, 24 divides all members of T. ...(iv)

From (i) and (iv) it follows that gcd of members of T equals 24.

38. Let a and b be positive integers. When $(a^2 + b^2)$ is divided by $(a + b)$, the quotient is q, the reminder r. Find all pairs (a, b), such that $q^2 + r = 1977$.

[IMO 1977]

Sol. $q^2 + r = 1977$ ...(i)

From the division algorithm, it follows that

$$a^2 + b^2 = (a + b)\, q + r, \text{ where } 0 \le r < a + b \quad \text{...(ii)}$$

and so
$$q + \frac{r}{a+b} = \frac{a^2 + b^2}{a+b}$$

$$r < a + b$$

$\therefore$
$$\frac{r}{a+b} < 1$$

Hence,
$$\frac{a^2 + b^2}{a+b} = q + \frac{r}{a+b} < q + 1$$

Also, by A.M. – G.M. (Arithmetic Mean – Geometric Mean) inequality,

$$\frac{a^2 + b^2}{2} \ge ab$$

$\therefore$
$$a^2 + b^2 \ge 2ab$$

or,
$$2a^2 + 2b^2 \ge a^2 + b^2 + 2ab$$

$\therefore$
$$2\,(a^2 + b^2) \ge (a + b)^2$$

or,
$$\frac{a^2 + b^2}{a+b} \ge \frac{a+b}{2}$$

$\therefore$
$$q + 1 > \frac{a^2 + b^2}{a+b} \ge \frac{a+b}{2}$$

or,
$$2\,(q + 1) > a + b \quad \text{...(iii)}$$

$$q^2 + r = 1977$$

$\therefore$
$$q^2 \le 1977$$

Thus,
$$q \le 44$$

By (iii),
$$r < a + b < 2 \times 45 = 90$$

On the other hand, using (i) we get,

$$q^2 = 1977 - r > 1977 - 90 = 1887$$

i.e.,
$$1887 < q^2 \le 1977$$

$$43^2 = 1849$$

$$44^2 = 1936$$

$$45^2 = 2025$$

Thus, $44^2 = 1936$ is the only perfect square lying between 1887 and 1977.

Hence, $q = 44$ and accordingly $r = 1977 - q^2 = 1977 - 1936 = 41$.

Substituting to (ii), we get

$$a^2 + b^2 = 44\,(a + b) + 41$$

or,
$$(a - 22)^2 + (b - 22)^2 = 1009$$

One of the squares on the L.H.S. must be greater than the half of 1009. Therefore, one square lies between 505 and 1009. The squares lying between 505 and 1009 are as under.

529, 576, 625, 676, 729, 784, 841, 900, 961

Among given possible options only, $1009 - 784 = 225$ is a perfect square.

Hence, $$|a - 22| = 28 \qquad (\because 28^2 = 784)$$

and $$|b - 22| = 15 \qquad (\because 15^2 = 225)$$

Hence, $a = 50$, $b = 7, 37$

Hence, the possible (a, b) pairs are

(7, 50), (37, 50), (50, 7), (50, 37)

39. Is it possible to choose 1983 distinct positive integers, all less than or equal to 10^5, no three of which are consecutive terms of an arithmetic progression?

[IMO 1983]

Sol. Let us choose the set consisting of all positive integers whose base 3 representations contain only the digits 0 and 1 (i.e. no 2's).

$$3^{10} < 10^5 < 3^{11}$$

Hence, these numbers have at most 11 digits; the largest one among them is

$$11\ 111\ 111\ 111_3 = 88573_{10}$$

The number of such numbers is $2^{11} - 1 = 2047$ (0 is not among them).

Suppose, x, y and z are three elements of the chosen set of numbers (in base 3) in arithmetic progression.

Then $$x + z = 2y$$

The number $2y$ contains only digits 0 and 2. Hence x and z must match digit-by-digit.

Thus $x = z$, which is impossible.

Hence, the chosen 2047 numbers contain no arithmetic progression of length 3.

Thus, the desired selection is possible.

40. Find one pair of positive integers, a, b, such that $ab\,(a + b)$ is not divisible by 7 and $(a+b)^7 - a^7 - b^7$ is divisible by 7^7. **[IMO 1984]**

Sol. $ab\,(a + b)$ is not divisible by 7. ...(i)

$(a+b)^7 - a^7 - b^7$ is divisible by 7^7. ...(ii)

Using the binomial theorem we get,

$$(a+b)^7 - a^7 - b^7 = 7ab\,(a+b)\,(a^2 + ab + b^2)^2 \quad \text{...(iii)}$$

Since, $ab\,(a + b)$ is not divisible by 7, we must choose a and b such that 7^6 divides $(a^2 + ab + b^2)^2$ or equivalently, $a^2 + ab + b^2$ is divisible by $7^3 = 343$.

We try to choose a pair a, b such that $b = 1$, and for some integer k

$$a^2 + a + 1 = 343k, \text{ i.e. } a^2 + a + (1 - 343k) = 0 \quad \text{...(iv)}$$

This happens exactly if the discriminant of this equation of degree 2 in a is a perfect square, which means that

$$1 - 4\,(1 - 343k) = 1372k - 3$$

is a perfect square. This is true for $k = 1$, as $1369 = 37^2$.

Hence, (iv) becomes

$$a^2 + a - 342 = 0$$

$$\therefore \qquad a = 18,\ b = 1$$

7 does not divide $18 \times 1 \times 19$.

Thus, the pair $(a, b) = (18, 1)$ satisfies the given conditions.

41. Given a set M of 1985 distinct positive integers, none of which has a prime divisor greater than 26. Prove that M contains a subset of 4 elements whose product is the 4th power of an integer. **[IMO 1985]**

Sol. The possible prime divisors of the elements of M are

$$2, 3, 5, 7, 11, 13, 17, 19, 23$$

These are 9 distinct primes.

Any element of M can be written in the form

$$2^{p_1} \times 3^{p_2} \times 5^{p_3} \times \ldots \times 23^{p_9}$$

Let's assign 9-tuple $(p_1, p_2, ..., p_9)$ to every element where

$$p_i = \begin{cases} 1 & \text{if } p_i \text{ is odd} \\ 0 & \text{if } p_i \text{ is even} \end{cases}$$

Total number of possible 9-tuples

$$= 2^9 = 512$$

As there are only 512 possible tuples, any set of more than 512 tuples is bound to have repetition of tuples.

M has 1985 members.

For any given member M_1, we can find another member M'_1 in M such that M_1 and M'_1 correspond to the same tuple.

Hence, $M_1 M'_1$ is a perfect square and thus $\sqrt{M_1 M'_1}$ is an integer.

Now, consider following set of integers

$$\sqrt{M_1 M'_1}, \sqrt{M_2 M'_2}, ..., \sqrt{M_{512} M'_{512}}, \sqrt{M_{513} M'_{513}}$$

where $M_1, M'_1, M_2, M'_2, ..., M_{512}, M'_{512}, M_{513}, M'_{513}$ are all different members of M.

Again, these integers have the same set of prime divisors as members of M.

Hence, among the given set of 513 integers, there is bound to be two members corresponding to the same tuple.

Thus, $$\sqrt{M_i M_i'}\sqrt{M_j M_j'} = n^2$$

for some integers i, j, n

Hence, $$M_i M_i' M_j M_j' = n^4$$

42. Let d be any positive integer not equal to 2, 5 or 13. Show that one can find distinct a, b in the set $\{2, 5, 13, d\}$ such that $ab - 1$ is not a perfect square.

[IMO 1986]

Sol. If a and b are among the first three numbers of the set, then the values of $(ab - 1)$ are 9, 25, 64 which are perfect squares.

Only possible other numbers of the form $ab - 1$ are $2d - 1, 5d - 1, 13d - 1$.

Suppose that all these numbers are perfect squares.

$$2d - 1 = p^2 \quad ...(i)$$

$$5d - 1 = q^2 \quad ...(ii)$$

$$13d - 1 = r^2 \quad ...(iii)$$

From (i), it follows that p is odd.

Hence, p^2 is of the form $8k+1$.

$\therefore \qquad 2d-1=8k+1$

or, $\qquad d=4k+1$

Hence, d is odd.

Thus, q and r are even.

Let $q=2q'$, $r=2r'$

Subtracting, (iii) from (ii), we get

$$8d=r^2-q^2=(r-q)(r+q)$$
$$=4(r'-q')(r'+q')$$

or, $\qquad 2d=(r'-q')(r'+q')$

As L.H.S. is even, R.H.S. must also be even.

Also $r'-q'$ and $r'+q'$ are both either even or odd. In either case, we get a contradiction because L.H.S. is divisible by 2 but not by 4 ($\because d$ is odd).

Hence, all possible values of $ab-1$ can not be a perfect square.

43. Prove that for each positive integer n there exist n consecutive positive integers none of which is a prime or a prime power. **[IMO 1989]**

Sol. For a given n we are looking for that value of M for which none of the n consecutive numbers

$$2+M, 3+M, \ldots, (n+1)+M \qquad \ldots(i)$$

is a prime number or a prime power.

An integer k is not a prime or the power of a prime if it has two coprime divisors both less than k.

Let $i+M$ be a term in (i).

If i divides M then $M=im_i$ for some positive integer m_i

$\therefore \qquad i+M=i(1+m_i)$

Suppose that i also divides m_i then M is a multiple of i^2.

Please also note that in this case i and $1+m_i$ have no common factors.

Thus, i and $1+m_i$ are coprime factors of $i+M$ as required.

$M=((n+1)!)^2$ is a number of the given property as i^2 divides $((n+1)!)^2$ for all i less than or equal to $n+1$.

Thus, $2+((n+1)!)^2, 3+((n+1)!)^2, \ldots, (n+1)+((n+1)!)^2$ is the desired set of n consecutive positive integers none of which is a prime or a prime power.

44. Show that there exists a set A of positive integers with the property that for any infinite set of primes (S), there exist two positive integers m in A and n not in A, each of which is a product of k distinct elements of S for some $k \geq 2$.

[IMO 1994]

Sol. Define the set A as follows:

A consists of those positive integers whose prime factorisation satisfies that

(a) The index of any prime factor is 1.

(b) The number of prime factors is not less than the smallest prime divisor of the given number.

Let $S = \{p_1, p_2, \ldots\}$ where $p_1 < p_2 < p_3 <..<$ is an arbitrary infinite set of primes.

Set k to be equal to p_1 ($p_1 \geq 2$).

Let $m = p_1 p_2 \ldots p_{p_1}$ and $n = p_2 p_3 \ldots p_{p_1+1}$

Both these numbers are products of p_1 prime numbers and their factors are all from S. By the definition of A, the first number, m is in A. On the other hand, $n \notin A$ because n has only p_1 prime factors and $p_1 < p_2$. Thus, the set A as defined above satisfies the requirements.

45. Let p be a prime number. Prove that there exists a prime number q such that for any integer n, the number $n^p - p$ is not divisible by q.

[IMO 2003]

Sol. Let $S = \dfrac{p^p - 1}{p-1} = 1 + p + p^2 + \ldots + p^{p-1}$

$$\equiv 1 + p \pmod{p^2} \quad \ldots\text{(i)}$$

Let $S = q_1^{r_1} q_2^{r_2} \ldots q_k^{r_k}$ be the prime factorization of S.

If $\quad q_i \equiv 1 \pmod{p^2}$ for each i, $1 \leq i \leq k$

Then, $\quad S \equiv 1 \pmod{p^2}$

Hence, $\quad p \equiv 0 \pmod{p^2}$ [by (i)]

or, $\quad p^2 \mid p$

But this is not possible.

Hence, S has a prime factor q such that $q \not\equiv 1 \pmod{p^2}$ ...(ii)

We claim that q is the desired prime number.

Now, suppose that $n^p - p$ is divisible by q for some integer n.

$$n^p \equiv p \pmod{q} \quad \ldots\text{(iii)}$$

$$\therefore \quad (n^p)^p \equiv p^p \pmod{q}$$

or, $n^{p^2} \equiv p^p \pmod{q}$

q is a prime factor of S.

Hence, by (i), $q \mid p^p - 1$

Hence, $n^{p^2} \equiv 1 \pmod{q}$ ...(iv)

Also, $n^{q-1} \equiv 1 \pmod{q}$ (by Fermat's little theorem) ...(v)

(Please note that $q \nmid n$ because if $q \mid n$, $q \mid 1$ by (iv))

As $p^2 \nmid (q-1)$, gcd $(p^2, q-1) \mid p$ [refer (ii)]

Let gcd $(p^2, q-1) = d$ and $p = ds$

Then, there exist integers x and y such that $d = p^2x + (q-1)\,y$.

Hence, $n^p = n^{ds}$

$= n^{p^2xs} n^{(q-1)\,ys}$

$\equiv 1 \pmod{q}$ [by (iv) and (v)]

Also, $n^p \equiv p \pmod{q}$ [by assumption in (iii)]

Hence, $p \equiv 1 \pmod{q}$

$\therefore$ $S = 1 + p + \ldots + p^{p-1}$

$\equiv p \pmod{q}$

$\Rightarrow$ $q \mid p$ ($\because$ $q \mid S$)

Hence, $q = p$ ($\because$ q and p both are prime numbers.)

As $S \equiv 1 + p \pmod{p^2}$, $q \mid S$ and $q = p$ imply that $p \mid 1$. [by (i)]

This is a contradiction.

Hence, our assumption that $n^p \equiv p \pmod{q}$ for some integer n is incorrect.

Thus, there exists a prime number q such that for any integer n, the number $n^p - p$ is not divisible by q.

46. For m and n positive integers, $n > m > 1$, the last three decimal digits of 1978^n is the same as the last three decimal digits of 1978^m. Find m and n such that $m + n$ has the least possible value. **[IMO 1978]**

Sol. 1978^n and 1978^m has the same last three digits if and only if 1000 divides their difference.

$$1978^n - 1978^m = 1978^m(1978^{n-m} - 1) \qquad \text{...(i)}$$

As $1000 = 8 \times 125$, we have to examine divisibility by 8 and 125.

The second factor [in (i)] is odd and only the first power of 2 divides 1978.

Hence, m has to be at least 3, i. e., $m \geq 3$. ...(ii)

Only the factor $1978^{n-m} - 1$ can be divisible by 125.

The last digits of the powers of 1978 are 8, 4, 2, 6, 8, 4, ...

Thus, the pattern gets repeated at an interval of four.

Obviously, 5 divides $1978^{n-m} - 1$ only if the last digit is 6.

i. e. if $n - m = 4k$ ...(iii)

Since, $1978 \equiv -22 \pmod{125}$

$$(1978)^4 \equiv (-22)^4 \pmod{125}$$

$$(-22)^4 \equiv 6 \pmod{125}$$

$\therefore$ $(1978)^4 \equiv 6 \pmod{125}$

125 divides $1978^{4k} - 1$ if and only if 125 divides $6^k - 1 = (1+5)^k - 1$

Applying the binomial theorem,

$$(1+5)^k - 1 = 5k + 5^2 \frac{k(k-1)}{2} + \ldots$$

Except for first two terms in the expansion, the other terms are divisible by $5^3 = 125$.

Hence, we need to examine $5k + 25\frac{k(k-1)}{2} = \frac{5k}{2}(5k-3)$ for divisibility by 125.

$5k - 3$ is relatively prime to 125 and $5k$ is divisible by 125 if 25 divides k.

Therefore, k is at least 25.

Thus, $n - m = 4k \geq 100$ [refer (iii)]

$m \geq 3$ [by (ii)]

Now, $n + m = n - m + 2m \geq 106$

Thus, the minimal value of $n + m$ is 106.

Corresponding values of m, n are $m = 3$, $n = 103$.

47. Let $S = \{1, 2, 3, \ldots, 280\}$. Find the smallest integer n such that each n-element subset of S contains five numbers which are pairwise relatively prime.

[IMO 1991]

Sol. First, we show that a 216-element subset of S which does not contain five pairwise relatively prime numbers.

Pick the multiples of 2, 3, 5 and 7 from S and denote the subset thus obtained by N. Denote also by N_i the multiples of i in S and its cardinality by usual $|N_i|$.

Clearly, $|N_2| = 140, |N_3| = 93, |N_5| = 56, |N_7| = 40$

$|N_2 \cap N_3|$, for example, is the number of the common multiples of 2 and 3, i.e. the multiples of 6.

By the principle of inclusion and exclusion, we know that

$$|N_2 \cup N_3 \cup N_5 \cup N_7| = \sum|N_i| - \sum|N_i \cap N_j| + \sum|N_i \cap N_j \cap N_k| - |N_2 \cap N_3 \cap N_5 \cap N_7|$$

Now, let us compute values of these terms.

$$|N_2 \cap N_3| = 46, |N_2 \cap N_5| = 28,$$
$$|N_2 \cap N_7| = 20, |N_3 \cap N_5| = 18,$$
$$|N_5 \cap N_7| = 8, |N_3 \cap N_7| = 13$$
$$|N_2 \cap N_3 \cap N_5| = 9,$$
$$|N_2 \cap N_3 \cap N_7| = 6,$$
$$|N_2 \cap N_5 \cap N_7| = 4,$$
$$|N_3 \cap N_5 \cap N_7| = 2,$$
$$|N_2 \cap N_3 \cap N_5 \cap N_7| = 1$$

Thus, $|N| = (140 + 93 + 56 + 40) - (46 + 28 + 20 + 18 + 8 + 13) + (9 + 6 + 4 + 2) - 1 = 216$

Choosing now any five elements of N at least one of the four subsets N_2, N_3, N_5 and N_7 will be represented twice and these two numbers are not relatively prime.

Next, we prove that no matter how do we select 217 numbers from S there are 5 pairwise relatively prime ones among the selected numbers; the smallest value of n we are looking for is hence 217.

There are 59 primes among the first 280 positive integers. Adjoining also 1 to these 59 numbers we get a 60-element set, denote it by P. Now there are 220 composite numbers in S; they form the set T.

We now list 8 disjoint subsets of T, each comprising five pairwise relatively prime elements

$$M_1 = \{2 \times 23, 3 \times 19, 5 \times 17, 7 \times 13, 11^2\},$$
$$M_2 = \{2 \times 29, 3 \times 23, 5 \times 19, 7 \times 17, 11 \times 13\},$$
$$M_3 = \{2 \times 31, 3 \times 29, 5 \times 23, 7 \times 19, 11 \times 17\},$$
$$M_4 = \{2 \times 37, 3 \times 31, 5 \times 29, 7 \times 23, 11 \times 19\},$$
$$M_5 = \{2 \times 41, 3 \times 37, 5 \times 31, 7 \times 29, 11 \times 23\},$$
$$M_6 = \{2 \times 43, 3 \times 41, 5 \times 37, 7 \times 31, 13 \times 17\},$$
$$M_7 = \{2 \times 47, 3 \times 43, 5 \times 41, 7 \times 37, 13 \times 19\},$$
$$M_8 = \{2^2, 3^2, 5^2, 7^2, 13^2\}$$

Consider now an arbitrary 217-element subset H of S. If H and P have at least 5 common elements then we are done. These 5 numbers are pairwise coprime.

We may hence assume that there are at most 4 elements of P in H and thus its further 213 elements are all composite. This means that there are at most 7 missing from the altogether 220 composite numbers in S and thus one of the sets M_i is contained in H. This M_i comprises the 5 numbers as desired.

Thus, the desired smallest integer n is 217.

48. Find all integers a, b, c satisfying $1 < a < b < c$ such that $(a-1)(b-1)(c-1)$ is a divisor of $abc-1$. **[IMO 1992]**

Sol. Let
$$Q = \frac{abc-1}{(a-1)(b-1)(c-1)} \quad \text{...(i)}$$

We have to find those integral values of a, b, c for which Q is an integer.

Clearly,
$$Q = \frac{abc}{(a-1)(b-1)(c-1)} - \frac{1}{(a-1)(b-1)(c-1)} \quad \text{...(ii)}$$
$$= \left(1+\frac{1}{a-1}\right)\left(1+\frac{1}{b-1}\right)\left(1+\frac{1}{c-1}\right) - \frac{1}{(a-1)(b-1)(c-1)}$$
$$> \left[1+\frac{1}{(a-1)(b-1)(c-1)}\right] \quad \text{...(iii)}$$

Also
$$Q < \left(1+\frac{1}{a-1}\right)\left(1+\frac{1}{b-1}\right)\left(1+\frac{1}{c-1}\right) \quad \text{...(iv)}$$

If any of a, b, c is even, abc is even and thus, $abc-1$, i.e. numerator of Q, is odd. Thus, all of a, b, c must be even in this case, as all terms of denominator, $a-1$, $b-1$, $c-1$, must be odd.

If all of a, b, c are odd, then $abc-1$ is even and so is denominator.

Thus, for Q to be an integer, all of a, b, c should be either even or odd. ...(v)

Now, let us consider various possibilities.

(i) Suppose $a \geq 4$

From (v) it follows that $b \geq 6$ and $c \geq 8$.

From (iv) it follows that
$$Q < \left(1+\frac{1}{4-1}\right)\left(1+\frac{1}{6-1}\right)\left(1+\frac{1}{8-1}\right) = \frac{192}{105}$$

By (iii), $Q > 1$

Thus, $1 < Q < 2$

There are no integers between 1 and 2.

Hence, the only possible values of a are 2 and 3.

(ii) If $a = 2$, then both b and c are even. [by (v)]

Thus, $b \geq 4$ and $c \geq 6$

From (iv) it follows that

$$Q < \left(1+\frac{1}{2-1}\right)\left(1+\frac{1}{4-1}\right)\left(1+\frac{1}{6-1}\right) = \frac{16}{5}$$

Also, by (iii), $Q > 1$

Thus, $Q = 2$ or 3

As a, b, c are all even, Q is odd.

Thus, $Q = 3$

Putting $a = 2$ and $Q = 3$ in (i), we get

$$2bc - 1 = 3\,(b-1)\,(c-1)$$

or, $(b-3)\,(c-3) = 5 = 1 \times 5$

Thus, $b = 4$ and $c = 8$.

The triplet (2, 4, 8) is a solution.

(iii) If $a = 3$, then both b and c are odd. [by (v)]

Thus, $b \geq 5$ and $c \geq 7$

From (iv) it follows that

$$Q < \left(1+\frac{1}{3-1}\right)\left(1+\frac{1}{5-1}\right)\left(1+\frac{1}{7-1}\right) = \frac{35}{16}$$

Also, by (iii), $Q > 1$

Thus, $Q = 2$

Putting $a = 3$ and $Q = 2$ in (i), we get

$$2 = \frac{3cb-1}{2\,(b-1)\,(c-1)}$$

or, $(b-4)\,(c-4) = 11 = 1 \times 11$

Thus, $b = 5$ and $c = 15$.

The triplet (3, 5, 15) is the other solution.

49. The positive integers a and b are such that $15a + 16b$ and $16a - 15b$ are both squares of positive integers. What is the least possible value that can be taken by the smaller of these two squares? **[IMO 1996]**

Sol. If $15a + 16b = r^2$ and $16a - 15b = s^2$ for some whole numbers r and s then

$$r^4 + s^4 = 225\,(a^2 + b^2) + 256\,(a^2 + b^2) + 2 \times 15a \times 16b - 2 \times 16a \times 15b$$

$$= 481\,(a^2 + b^2) = 13 \times 37\,(a^2 + b^2)$$

gcd $(13, 37) = 1$

Therefore, $r^4 + s^4$ is divisible by both 13 and 37. ...(i)

Let p be a prime number of the form $4k + 1$.

Let $$p = 4k + 1$$

Please note that both 13 and 37 are primes of the form $4k + 1$ with k being odd.

Suppose that $x^4 + y^4 \equiv 0 \pmod{p}$

If $x^4 \equiv 0 \pmod{p}$ then obviously, $y^4 \equiv 0 \pmod{p}$.

Now, suppose that $x^4 \not\equiv 0 \pmod{p}$ and $y^4 \not\equiv 0 \pmod{p}$ but $x^4 + y^4 \equiv 0 \pmod{p}$.

By Fermat's little theorem, in this case,

$$x^{p-1} \equiv 1 \pmod{p}$$

and $$y^{p-1} \equiv 1 \pmod{p}$$

$\therefore$ $$x^{4k} \equiv 1 \pmod{p}$$

and $$y^{4k} \equiv 1 \pmod{p}$$

$\therefore$ $$x^{4k} \equiv y^{4k} \pmod{p} \qquad \text{...(ii)}$$

Also $$x^4 + y^4 \equiv 0 \pmod{p}$$

or, $$x^4 \equiv -y^4 \pmod{p}$$

$\therefore$ $$x^{4k} \equiv -y^{4k} \pmod{p} \qquad \text{(if } k \text{ is odd) ...(iii)}$$

Thus, by (ii) and (iii), we get

$$1 \equiv -1 \pmod{p}$$

$\therefore$ $$p = 2$$

This is a contradiction because p is a prime number of the form $4k + 1$.

Hence, if $x^4 + y^4 \equiv 0 \pmod{p}$, then $x^4 \equiv 0 \pmod{p}$ and $y^4 \equiv 0 \pmod{p}$ where p is a prime number of the form $4k + 1$, k being odd. ...(iv)

By (i), $r^4 + s^4$ is divisible by both 13 and 37.

Both 13 and 37 are prime numbers of the form $4k + 1$, k being odd.

Hence, it follows from (iv) that both r and s are multiples of both 13 and 37 i.e., 481.

Thus, $$r \geq 481, \quad s \geq 481$$

If we take $r = s = 481$, we get

$$15a + 16b = 481^2$$

$$16a - 15b = 481^2$$

These equations lead to the following solution.

$$a = 481 \times 31 = 14911, \ b = 481$$

Hence, the least positive value of the smaller one of the two squares is

$$481^2 = 231361$$

50. Determine all pairs (a, b) of positive integers, such that $(ab^2 + b + 7)$ divides $(a^2b + a + b)$. **[IMO 1998]**

Sol. Let $A = a^2b + a + b$ and $B = ab^2 + b + 7$

If B divides A, then it also divides $bA - aB$.

$$bA - aB = b^2 - 7a$$

Since $a \geq 1$ we have $b^2 \leq ab^2$

Therefore, $$b^2 - 7a < ab^2 + b + 7 = B$$

Let $$b^2 - 7a \geq 0$$

Then B is dividing a non-negative integer smaller than B itself which is not possible.

Thus, $b^2 - 7a$ is equal to zero.

Then $b^2 - 7a$ and thus b, as a multiple of 7, can be written as $b = 7c$.

Hence $49c^2 - 7a = 0$ and $a = 7c^2$ (c is a positive integer). These pairs $(a, b) = (7c^2, 7c)$ already satisfy the conditions since

$$A = 49c^4 7c + 7c^2 + 7c = 7c\,(49c^4 + c + 1)$$

$$B = 7c^2 49c^2 + 7c + 7 = 7\,(49c^4 + c + 1)$$

i.e., $$A = cB$$

Assuming now that $b^2 - 7a < 0$; its opposite, the positive integer $7a - b^2 < 7a$ is divisible by B. Note that b now cannot exceed 2, otherwise $B = ab^2 + b + 7 \geq 9a + 10$ and thus B cannot divide a positive number less than $7a$.

Hence, $b = 1$ or $b = 2$.

(a) if $b = 1$ then $7a - b^2 = 7a - 1$. If this is a multiple of $B = a + 8$ then writing $7a - 1 = 7\,(a + 8) - 57$ shows that B has to divide 57. The positive divisors of 57 are: 57, 19, 3, 1, and thus $a + 8$ is 19 or 57 *i.e.*, $a = 11$ or $a = 49$.

Thus, $A = 133 = 7 \times 19$, $B = 19$ and $A = 2451 = 43 \times 57$, $B = 57$

(b) if $b = 2$ then $7a - b^2 = 7a - 4$ and $B = 4a + 9$. The division $4\,(7a - 4) = 7\,(4a + 9) - 79$ yields that B is now dividing 79. Since this prime number has no divisor of the form $4a + 9$, we get no solution for $b = 2$.

Thus, the solutions for (a, b) are $(7c^2, 7c)$ where c is an arbitrary positive integer and also (11, 1) and (49, 1).

EXERCISE

1. Show that $n^2 + 17$ is divisible by 18 for infinitely many n.
2. If p is a prime greater than 3, prove that $24 \mid (p^2 - 1)$.
3. Prove that no integer in the sequence 11, 111, 1111, 11111, ..., is the square of an integer.
4. Given any three integers show that one can always select two (say a and b) such that $a^3 b - b^3 a$ is a multiple of 30.
5. Given any three integers one can always select two such that $a^3 b - b^3 a$ is a multiple of 24. Prove.
6. Prove that any integer $n > 11$ is sum of two positive composite numbers.
7. Prove that there are infinitely many integers n such that $4n^2 + 1$ is divisible by both 13 and 5.
8. If n is greater than 1, show that n cannot divide $2^n - 1$.
9. If $a, b, n > 1$ then $(a^n - b^n)$ cannot be a factor of $(a^n + b^n)$. Prove.
10. If m is a natural number, then $(2^m - 1)$ and $(2^m + 1)$ are co-prime. Prove.
11. $(1 + a)^n \geq 1 + na$ for $a \geq 1$. Prove.
12. If a is odd, show that $a^{(2^n)} - 1$ is divisible by 2^{n+2} but not by 2^{n+3}.
13. Determine the digit 'a' so that the 101-digit number 888........ 8a9999 ....9 [50 times 8 & 50 times 9] is divisible by 7.
14. Let a be co-prime to m. Show that there exists a number b such that $ab = 1 \pmod{m}$.
15. If n is divisible by an odd prime and $n > 3$, prove that $2^n + 1$ has at least two distinct prime divisors.
16. If $ab = 1 \pmod{m}$ where a and b are positive integers, show that both a and b are co-prime to m.
17. Show that for any natural numbers n the number $\underbrace{11\ldots1}_{2n\ 1's} - \underbrace{22\ldots2}_{n\ 2's}$ is the square of an integer.

18. Prove that every number in the sequence 49, 4489, 444889, ..., $\underbrace{44\ldots4}_{n\ 4\text{'s}}\ \underbrace{88\ldots8}_{(n-1)\ 8\text{'s}}9$ is the square of an integer.

19. If n is an even natural number, then $13^n + 6$ is always divisible by 7. Prove.

20. Prove that the number $2222^{5555} + 5555^{2222}$ is divisible by 7.

21. Prove that the product of four consecutive natural numbers is never a square.

22. Given n numbers x_1, x_2, ..., x_n each of which is ±1, such that $x_1x_2 + x_2x_3 + \ldots x_nx_1 = 0$. Prove that n is a multiple of 4.

23. Prove that from any 100 integers it is always possible to choose a set of numbers whose sum is divisible by 100.

24. Prove that from any set of 52 integers it is always possible to choose two whose sum, or else whose difference, is divisible by 100.

25. If p is prime and a and b are any two integers, then $(a+b)^p \equiv a^p + b^p \pmod{p}$. Prove.

26. Prove that the sum $\frac{1}{3} + \frac{1}{5} + \frac{1}{7} + \ldots + \frac{1}{2n+1}$ is never an integer.

27. Given 17 positive integers all having prime factors less than 10, prove that there are two integers whose product is a perfect square.

28. Let $p_1, p_2, \ldots, p_n$ be the first n primes. Prove that $P_n = p_1 p_2 \cdots p_n + 1$ is never a perfect square.

29. Let $a < b$ be any two natural numbers. Show that from any set of b consecutive natural numbers, we can always select two numbers whose product is a multiple of ab.

30. Let $a_1, a_2, \ldots, a_n$ be any combination of numbers from 1 to n. If n is odd, prove that the product $(a_1 - 1)(a_2 - 2)\ldots(a_n - n)$ must be even.

31. Find the last three digits of $3 \times 7 \times 11 \times \ldots \times 2003$.

32. Prove that there is no positive number n such that $2n^2 + 1, 3n^2 + 1$ and $6n^2 + 1$ are all perfect squares.

33. Find the last four digits of $1 \times 3 \times 5 \times 7 \times \ldots \times 2017$.

34. Find the number of positive integral solutions of $xyz = 360$.

35. Find all values of n such that $4n+9$ and $9n+4$ are both perfect squares.

36. Find all positive integral solutions for the equation $x^2 - y! = 2001$.

37. Find all integers n, such that $(n-3)$ divides $n^2 - 3$.

38. Prove that $n^3 + 2n$ is the multiple of 3 for all n.

39. Find all primes p such that $\frac{2^{p-1} - 1}{p}$ is a perfect square.

40. A decimal number N is written in base r. What will be the number of digits in base r.

41. Show that there is no integer that satisfies the equation $(n-3)^3 + n^3 = (n+3)^3$.

42. Find the remainder when $12^{34^{56^{78}}}$ is divided by 90.

43. Prove that for any pair of positive integers m and n, $4mn - (m+n)$ cannot be a perfect square.

44. Show that for any natural number n, $2^n + 3^n + 5^n + 6^n$ cannot be a perfect cube.

45. Prove that $16^n + 10n - 1$ is a multiple of 25 for all n. n is a positive integer.

46. Prove that $25^n + 12^n - 1$ is a multiple of 36 for all n. n is a positive integer.

47. Prove that $(300^{3000} - 1)$ is divisible by 1001.

48. If the square of three whole numbers is in arithmetic progression then their common difference must be a multiple of 24. Prove.

49. Find the last two digits of $((((2016)^{2017})^{2018})^{2019})^{2020}$.

50. Find a prime p which divides successive integers of the form $n^2 + 3$.

51. If two consecutive integers of the from $n^3 + 5$ are divisible by a prime p, what are the possible values of p?

52. Given any five integers, show that one can always select three such that their sum is divisible by 3.

53. n prime numbers are in arithmetic progression show that their common difference must be divisible by all primes that are less than n.

54. Prove that 3^k+1 is divisible by 2 but not divisible by 4 if k is even.

55. Prove that n^k+1 is not divisible by $(n+1)$ if k is even, for $n>2$.

56. Prove that no number of the form x^2+1 where x is an integer can have a factor of the from $4k+3$.

57. If p is prime then prove that all prime factors of 2^p-1 are greater than p.

58. Positive integers a and b are such that $a+b=\frac{a}{b}+\frac{b}{a}$. What is the value of a^2+b^2?

59. Let $E(n)$ denotes the sum of even digits of n. What is the value of $E(1)+E(2)+\ldots+E(100)$?

60. How many two-digit positive integers N has the property that the sum $N+N'$ (where N' is the number obtained by reversing the digits) is a perfect square?

61. If $3^x+2^y=985$ and $3^x-2^y=473$, what is the value of xy?

62. A subset B of the set of first 100 positive integers has the property that no two elements of B sum to 125. What is the maximum possible number of elements in B?

63. Digits of a positive integer n are four consecutive integers in decreasing order when read from left to right. What is the sum of possible remainders when n is divided by 37?

64. Find the number of ordered pairs (x, y) for which LCM $(x, y)=600$. x, y are positive integers.

65. p is a prime number. Prove that $7p+3^p-4$ cannot be a perfect square.

66. Prove that for no non-negative integer n, both $(n+2)$ and (n^2+n+1) are perfect cubes.

67. a, b, c, d are integers. $d\equiv 0 \pmod 5$ and there is a number m ($m\not\equiv 0 \pmod 5$) such that $am^3+bm^2+cm+d\equiv 0 \pmod{25}$. Prove that there exists a number n such that $a+bn+cn^2+dn^3\equiv 0 \pmod 5$.

68. Given n is odd, prove that $1^n+2^n+\ldots+k^n$ is divisible by $\sum_{i=1}^{k} i$.

69. If p is an odd prime and $n\neq k(p-1)$ then $p\mid\sum_{r=1}^{p-1} r^n$.

70. m and n are two positive integers. Prove that $3^m + 3^n + 1$ cannot be a perfect square.

71. gcd $(a, b) = 1$ and c is any natural number. Then, there exists an integer $k < a$ such that $a \mid (c + kb)$. Prove.

72. Product of ten consecutive numbers cannot be a perfect square. Prove.

73. Let $p > 3$ be a prime. Prove that $1 \times 2 + 2 \times 3 + \ldots [(p-2) \times (p-1)] \equiv 0 \bmod p$.

74. a and b are co-prime. Prove that there exists a number $k < b$ such that $a^k \equiv 1 \pmod b$.

75. Let $n + 1$ be a multiple of 24. Show that the sum of all factors of n is a multiple of 24.

76. Prove that $11^n + 15n - 1$ is a multiple of 25 for all n. n is a positive integer.

77. Prove that $13^n + 36n - 1$ is a multiple of 48 for all n. n is a positive integer.

78. If p is prime, show that all factors of $2^p - 1$ are of the from $2kp + 1$ where k is an integer.

79. What is the remainder when $1 \times 2 \times 3 + 2 \times 3 \times 4 + \ldots + 98 \times 99 \times 100$ is divided by 101.

80. Consider n^2 unit squares in the xy-plane centred at point (i, j) with integer coordinates, $1 \le i \le n, 1 \le j \le n$. It is required to colour each unit square in such a way that whenever $1 \le i < j \le n$ and $1 \le k < l \le n$, the three squares with centres at (i, k), (j, k), (j, l) have distinct colours. What is the least possible number of colours needed? **[RMO 2017]**

81. Suppose x is a nonzero real number such that both x^5 and $20x + \frac{19}{x}$ are rational numbers. Prove that x is a rational number. **[RMO 2019]**

82. Suppose 91 distinct positive integers greater than 1 are given such that there are at least 456 pairs among them which are relatively prime.
Show that one can find four integers a, b, c, d among them such that gcd $(a, b) =$ gcd $(b, c) =$ gcd $(c, d) =$ gcd $(d, a) = 1$. **[RMO 2019]**

83. Show that there are infinitely many 4-tuples (a, b, c, d) of natural numbers such that $a^3 + b^4 + c^5 = d^7$.

Answers

13. $a=5$ **31.** 875 **33.** 0625 **34.** 180 **35.** $n=0, 28$

36. $x=45,\ y=4$ **37.** $-3, 0, 1, 2, 4, 5, 6, 9$ **39.** 3, 7

40. $[\log_r N]+1$ **42.** 36 **49.** 16 **50.** 13

51. 167 **58.** 2 **59.** 400 **60.** 16 **61.** 48

62. 62 **63.** 217 **64.** 105 **79.** 0 **80.** $2n-1$